Routes and Roots

Routes and Roots

Navigating Caribbean and Pacific Island Literatures

Elizabeth M. DeLoughrey

 UNIVERSITY OF HAWAI'I PRESS
Honolulu

This book has been published with the aid
of a subvention from the Hull Memorial
Publication Fund of Cornell University.

The author's royalties will be contributed to the
Oceania Centre for Arts and Culture, Suva, Fiji.

Library of Congress Cataloging-in-Publication Data

DeLoughrey, Elizabeth M.
    Routes and roots : navigating Caribbean and Pacific island
literatures / Elizabeth M. DeLoughrey.
        p. cm.
    Includes bibliographical references and index.
    ISBN 978-0-8248-3122-6 (hardcover : alk. paper)
    ISBN 978-0-8248-3472-2 (pbk : alk. paper)
    1. Caribbean literature—20th century—History and criticism.
2. Pacific Island literature—20th century—History and criticism.
I. Title.
    PN849.C3D45 2007
    860.9'9729—dc22

                                            2006035364

University of Hawai'i Press books are printed on acid-free paper
and meet the guidelines for permanence and durability of the Council
on Library Resources.

Designed by University of Hawai'i Press production staff
Printed by The Maple-Vail Book Manufacturing Group

For
Lizzy Murphy and Duke
DeLoughrey

Contents

Preface

Genealogies of Place

The comparative literary geographies mapped in this book are unique and this has generated some interest in the origins of this project and my own particular relationship, as a white woman from Boston, to the Caribbean and the Pacific Islands. On the one hand, it is gratifying that the structures of western academic thought provide for a prefacing acknowledgment in which one may outline an ancestral and academic genealogy, a narrative whakapapa in accordance with many of the indigenous epistemologies engaged in this book. On the other hand, this surprise about my own investment in this project and my accountability to these contexts may also signal assumptions about these literatures' lack of translatability, their profound localness, and, most worryingly, their lack of significance to global discourse that is, presumably, concerned only with the literatures produced by northern metropoles and continents. Here I would like to outline my own genealogical connections to these texts and contexts, particularly as they have contributed to my own shifting understanding of space and place.

My initial encounters with Caribbean literatures came through the aegis of anglophone postcolonial, feminist, and African-American studies, and it was the signs of orality in these texts, such as the broad language registers of the creole continuum, the self-deprecating humor, the naming practices, the nonstandard English, the trickster stories, and the sinews that connect language, ethnicity, and class that seemed immediate and familiar to my own upbringing. Although the racial and historical geographies explored here are radically different from my own, I recognized these tropes of orality and the historical silences they often stood for in my own extended family. My readings in Pacific Island literatures broadened these links between language and power and also helped me understand, on a more global and comparative scale, the ways in which geography was so vitally important to history and by extension, its literary representations. As a shore dweller from the North Atlantic, a product of an altogether different history of island diaspora, I came to recognize the seascapes of both regions' literatures and, over time, my own historical and spatial connection to these antipodean archipelagoes. I grew up with a distinct sense of regional and white ethnicity inherited from the working class Irish and Scottish Catholic sides of my family; both were late nineteenth-century migrants to New England and carried their own histories of dispersal and settlement through Nova Scotia, Prince Edward Island, and the greater Boston area. These legacies are necessarily in fragments, but my work on the British empire and its global reaches has helped me to understand why these genealogical narratives were substituted by an emphasis on the present and the silences produced by the process of emigration and assimilation. Through the lens of postcolonial scholarship, I have been able to frame the incomplete and perhaps wishful narratives of these legacies of dispersal; rumors of a deported Irish ancestor for union agitation, reputed involvement in the Easter 1916 rebellion, and insinuating connections to the IRA. On the Scottish side, with roots in the Canadian Maritimes, there are remnants of songs, a bard reputedly filmed by Smithsonian anthropologists, memories of Gaelic language speakers. I am less concerned with the accuracy of these fragments than the ways in which a concentration on the legacies of diaspora and settlement in other parts of the world illuminated my own understanding of my regional home and place in global history. New England, a place I was raised to believe in as a locus of intense resistance to British colonization, was also, as I learned in adulthood, an active participant in the Atlantic/Caribbean slave trade and in the colonization of the Pacific Islands. It is this recognition of the white settlement of the U.S. in its postcolonial complexity—as simultaneous colony and colonizer—that allowed me to shift my own disciplinary boundaries from the British legacies of colonialism to the ongoing and pervasive expansion of the U.S. in this book. Traveling to Aotearoa/New Zealand to pursue studies in Maori literature and language as a graduate student also helped me to understand the British colonial trajectories that led Scots and Irish to the Pacific rather than the transatlantic trajectory of my ancestors. This is to say that while I examine the trajectories of black and indigenous diasporas throughout this book, I came to see the ways in which both histories were constitutive and constituted by the British diaspora—the largest human migration of its time. This is a book deeply invested in deconstructing the "worlding" mechanism of empire (Spivak 1985) and concerned with destabilizing the notion of a transparent universal (read: European) subject. This move is crucial because it allows me to reposition my own genealogy in the complex intersection of multiple colonial histories and to "unlearn my privilege" as "loss" (Spivak 1990, 10). I had already commenced this unlearning process in my early attempts to reconcile my family's ambiguity about class mobility, intellectualism, and being labeled "lace-curtain Irish." As I discovered, the "unlearning" needs to be bridged to a reconstructive effort to remap these histories in ways that highlight what Édouard Glissant calls the "complicity of relation."

I explore Glissant's model of relation to the land in detail in this book so in this preface I want simply to foreground a relation to place that accounts for both long-term and short-term settlement, an understanding of space that does not simply conflate territory with ancestry. Although it is utilized for the diasporic model of the Caribbean, I want to emphasize that the history and discourse of diaspora is not engaged here to deflect from indigenous genealogies and articulations, as Teresia Teaiwa warns about the process of drawing facile analogies between disparate regions (2005, 2006). Diaspora in Glissant's use does not preclude prior and ongoing indigenous presence; his concept uses the platform of shared commitment to place in order to stage a dialogue between the two. As a model of rooting the histories of routed peoples, Glissant's notion of a "complicity of relation" also demands accountability, a method of reading power relations through narratives of place and displacement. It is a model that is flexible enough to bring together places linked by history and geography, one that we might find in texts such as Derek Walcott's *Omeros*, in which *genealogies of place* provide the model of rendering history that is at once rooted in local memory and yet can accommodate the diverse and often opposing new settlements. It is a necessary model diversity that does not romanticize indigeneity nor pathologize diaspora. This is the tidalectic model of roots and routes that is traced throughout this book, a vital whakapapa of place that works against the rigid claims of ethnic nationalism.

Geologically speaking, the global south is a space constituted by far more water than land and thus an apt place to consider the ways in which maritime histories and the transoceanic imaginary have been constituted in relation to landfall and settlement. So while this book focuses on the ethnic models of African and European diaspora in relation to indigenous peoples of the Caribbean and Pacific, this model of tidalectics does not preclude the sustained engagement with other diasporas, particularly from South and East Asia. In fact, writers of South Asian descent in both the Caribbean and the Pacific Islands have written extensively about the process of crossing kala pani, or dark waters, to the distant islands of plantation indenture. The model of a "complicity of relation" necessarily includes these other layerings of settlement and while space limitations prevent me from taking this up in this particular book, I insist on their vitality to this model of tidalectics in both regions.

The novels and works explored here extend the complicity of relation in time and space, a model of political engagement that was already familiar to me through my own extended family, a legacy provided by my grandparents that continues to sustain. My academic privileges have been clarifying and alienating at the same time from the very roots that sustain this project. Nevertheless I want to foreground the contributions of my paternal grandparents, to whom this book is dedicated, whose material circumstances were deeply circumscribed yet this never impeded the geographies of their imagination or their hospitality, humor, or the generosity of their spirit. My maternal grandmother has also been a tremendous teacher about local engagement and a worldliness discovered through reading. This has been a legacy embedded in me through my parents, Tom and Judy DeLoughrey, whose own critical thinking and teasing humor have kept me grounded and helped me negotiate the broad geographies I was fortunate to travel through the research and writing of this book.

Routes and Roots was written on various shores of the Atlantic and Pacific oceans and came into being through the generous efforts of many friends, family, and colleagues. From the beginning, Chris Harbrant, Peter Hulme, Radhika Mohanram, and Sangeeta Ray were careful and patient readers of these chapters. Without their support across multiple seas, completing this project would not have been possible. The book's title is drawn from James Clifford's work, whose body of scholarship made an impact on my research well before we had the chance to meet in person at the University of California, Santa Cruz, where I completed the manuscript draft. My thanks to him and my hosts in the Center for Cultural Studies for the opportunity to live in an oceanic setting while I wrote of fluidity and routes. I would also like to thank Catherine Rice for stewarding the manuscript when she was editor at Cornell University Press, and my current editor, Masako Ikeda, for transcending the rigid marketing formulas for book series and for supporting a project that seeks to complicate geographic and disciplinary boundaries. My interaction with academic presses about this project was instructive and taught me a great deal about the need for publishing stewardship in postcolonial studies as well as the marginalization of Caribbean and Pacific Island literatures that generated this project to begin with. I thank the Hull Memorial Publication Fund of Cornell University for providing subvention support to offset publication costs.

My colleagues from Cornell's Society for the Humanities Diaspora

Fellowship (2001–2002), especially Dominick LaCapra, supplied vital feedback on my first chapter, while Shivaun Hearne patiently answered my questions about her father's work and influences. My work on the Pacific benefited from the "Re-Imagining Indigenous Cultures" seminar at the 2003 NEH Summer Institute at the East-West Center and the University of Hawai'i at Manoa. I thank my hosts and colleagues for their friendship and stimulating discussions that summer. Mahalo nui loa to the Protect Kaho'olawe 'Ohana for the July 2003 huaka'i and for allowing me to witness firsthand the devastation and the fragile regeneration of the island of Kanaloa and the navigators. This was an immersion that continues to inspire. My sincere thanks to Lingikoni Vaka'uta for allowing me to reproduce his stunning rendition of Hina in his painting *No'o 'Anga* (Tied shark).

I was born in a U. S. Naval hospital and while this has probably contributed to my desire to decolonize the trajectories of U. S. militarization across the seas, it has done nothing for my sea legs. My own terrors of deep-water navigation were expanded and confirmed on a Sea Education Association (SEA) trip that helped me understand the bodily rigors and nautical grammar of working on a ship and why one drinks like a sailor upon disembarking. My thanks to Brian Hopewell for providing me with the opportunity to learn the ropes working on the 134-foot steel brigantine, *SSV Robert C. Seamans*, across a stormy Kaua'i channel and beyond.

The second part of this book, on roots, grew from graduate study in Aotearoa/New Zealand. I would like to thank Fulbright for supporting this research, Margareta Gee at the Alexander Turnbull Library for her generous supply of June Mitchell's archival documents, Briar Wood and Maureen Lander for their insights on flax symbologies, and Ken Arvidson for his support and active engagement with the ideas in this portion of the book. Merle Collins has been patient with her time and feedback during the revisions to the final chapter, and April Shemak has been a tremendous friend and resource for this and many other projects. I would also like to thank Chad Allen, Jon Battista, Martin Bernal, LeGrace Benson, Murray Chapman, Chris Connery, Ralph Crane, Carole Boyce Davies, Vince Diaz, June Ellis, Esther Figueroa, Renée Gossen, George Handley, Wilson Harris, Paget Henry, J. Kehaulani Kauanui, A. Keala Kelly, Susan Najita, Vilsoni Hereniko, Zita Nunes, Marcus Rediker, Te Ahukaramu Charles Royal, Elaine Savory, Paul Sharrad, Katerina Teaiwa, Teresia Teaiwa, Larry Thomas, Rob Wilson, Houston Wood, as well as members of the Caribbean Studies List, the Postcolonial List, and the Oceanic Anthropology

Discussion Group for their engagement and insights on the different epistemologies I trace out in this book.

At Cornell, I thank my undergraduate students for traveling to so many
places with these texts, the dedicated students of my "Transoceanic Diasporas" class, Michelle Elleray and Jolisa Gracewood for establishing and
sustaining the Pacific Island Reading Group, my colleagues Laura Brown
and Nicole Waligora-Davis for their support, and Krupa Shandilya for her
work on the index. Warm thanks to Catherine Burwell, Amy DeLoughrey,
Arianne Gaetano, Sarah Mattaliano, and Geoffrey Schramm for their love
and humor over the course of this voyage. Finally, I am indebted to Christopher Harbrant, who has been my co-pilot in these transoceanic travels
from the Caribbean to the rough shores of Ngarunui. This work would
never have been completed without the daily guidance of my navigating
star and grounding earth, my own routes and roots, Chris and Grendel.

Note on the Text

This book's comparative focus on native and diaspora literatures aims to uphold these histories and continuing struggles; to avoid privileging any one group over another I have chosen not to capitalize terms associated with ethnicity or place, including the term "native." At times "native" is used interchangeably with "indigenous." This interchangeability does not mean that the terms are static; the use varies greatly according to place, history, and political agenda. Where applicable, I try to use specific terms such as "Kanaka Maoli," which I use synonymously with "Hawaiian." Like the word "native," the terms "Hawaiian" and "Tahitian" refer to indigenous peoples rather than later settlers. When possible, I have used the cognate terms "Maori," "Kanaka Maoli," and "Ma'ohi" over terms such as "native" and "indigenous" to highlight local terminology and, following the lead of Noenoe Silva, to foreground the cultural connections between these diverse points of the region. In keeping with Pacific publishing protocol, I have not italicized words in Polynesian languages such as Maori, Hawaiian, and Samoan. Due to my own limited knowledge of the languages, and to maintain some consistency with my sources, I have not employed macrons or double vowels for emphasis.

Tidalectics

Navigating Repeating Islands

> I am the supple rhythm of the seas;
> I recreate the world on islands.
> —Eric Roach, "The World of Islands"

In the poem from which this epigraph is drawn, Tobagonian writer Eric Roach inscribes "a shoal of sea-beleaguered lands" bequeathed to the contemporary Caribbean subject. They are "difficult . . . to inherit" due to their violent history of colonization and their complex layering of native and diaspora populations. For Roach, the islands are a space where "indigenous blood still stains the grass," signifying the corporal residue of history, its localization and merger with natural space, and the landscape's propensity to absorb and reflect human history. "Those whom bondage bit to bone" are legible for historical recuperation because their artistic abilities transform this "flowering rock" of an island into song, prayer, dance, and music. The speaker quoted in the epigraph emerges in the last few lines; she represents the region as a dancer whose castanet is the moon, a "phoenix Eve" who feminizes the Adamic myth of island origins. She speaks of the Caribbean's creolization of cultures in fluid and intoxicating terms, as "the mingled wine of the world's grapes" and, by extension, the product of breakage and reassembly. After establishing this Mediterranean connection, the poem concludes with the lines of the epigraph, a testimony to the natural rhythm of the sea, the cycle of regeneration after unspeakable violence, the oceanic origins of islands and their metonymic worldliness. Roach's dense layering of geology and human history is cyclical; the tidal rhythm of the sea generates islands, just as the flows of maritime trade and transoceanic diaspora "recreate the world on islands." In turn, "the world on islands" suggests that each isle might be read metonymically as the globe. Building on the title, we might conclude that this poem reflects "The world of islands" as much as it represents the *worldliness* of islands (Roach 1992, 147).

I have chosen Roach's poem to open this book on comparative island literatures because it synthesizes the complex relationship between geography and history, the insular and the global, and routes and roots. The poem foregrounds our own location on a terraqueous globe, a watery planet that renders all landmasses into islands surrounded by the sea. Nevertheless, we maintain a cartographic hierarchy of space; our cognitive maps do not chart a shared islandness across the globe. Assumptions about size, location, history, and political importance seem to determine how island spaces are mapped so that we are more likely to perceive the islandness of Jamaica than, say, Iceland. Although islands are scattered all over the globe, the spaces that signify as islands are generally the small landmasses close to the equator, lands associated with tropical fertility, former colonies and outposts of empire that are deemed remote, exotic, and isolated by their continental visitors. By recognizing this often arbitrary division between islands and continents, we can pinpoint how geography has been used to uphold a series of cultural and political assumptions. This book seeks to complicate the ways in which certain island spaces have been deemed ahistorical and isolated by foregrounding how the process of colonization has relegated these spaces into museums or laboratories for tourism, anthropological inquiry, or sociological praxis. One of the central but unacknowledged ways in which European colonialism has constructed the trope of the isolated island is by mystifying the importance of the sea and the migrations across its expanse. In order to recuperate the centrality of the ocean in island discourse, I turn to Kamau Brathwaite's theory of "tidalectics," a methodological tool that foregrounds how a dynamic model of geography can elucidate island history and cultural production, providing the framework for exploring the complex and shifting entanglement between sea and land, diaspora and indigeneity, and routes and roots.

What is to be gained from a comparative literature project that highlights the intersections between space and time, place and history? Tidalectics engage what Brathwaite calls an "alter/native" historiography to linear models of colonial progress. This "tidal dialectic" resists the synthesizing telos of Hegel's dialectic by drawing from a cyclical model, invoking the continual movement and rhythm of the ocean. Tidalectics also foreground alter/native epistemologies to western colonialism and its linear and materialist biases.[1] As a geopoetic model of history, Brathwaite images the ongoing and palpable heritage of "submerged mothers" who cross the seas, "coming from one continent/continuum, touching another, and then receding . . . from the island(s) into the perhaps creative chaos of the(ir) future" (1999, 34). I build upon this feminized vision of history to destabilize the myth of island isolation and to engage the island as a world as well as the worldliness of islands. I interpret tidalectics as a dynamic and shifting relationship between land and sea that allows island literatures to be engaged in their spatial and historical complexity.

The title of this book, *Routes and Roots*, employs these homonyms in relation to the tidalectic between sea and land. The subtitle employs the term "navigation" to emphasize the role of islander agency in terms of "charting" and "steering" a course and to highlight the role of nonwestern epistemologies of time-space. In fact, Brathwaite's vision of fluid time-space has much in common with the Pacific wayfinding system of moving islands, termed "etak" in the Caroline Islands of Micronesia. As scholars such as David Lewis and Vicente Diaz have explained, Pacific models of ocean navigation differ from western paradigms because they do not flatten and stabilize space through the bird's eye view of nautical charts. Instead, Pacific navigators have developed a complex system of charting a vessel's movement through space where the voyaging canoe is perceived as stable while the islands and cosmos move towards the traveler. "Etak is a polydimensional system that involves both direction and time, and therefore movement. The etak conception of moving islands is an essentially dynamic one" (Lewis 1994, 184). This concept of moving islands has provided an innovative model of approaching the intersections of indigenous and cultural studies (see Diaz and Kauanui 2001). In contradistinction to western models of passive and empty space such as *terra* and *aqua nullius*, which were used to justify territorial expansion, the interlinked concepts of tidalectics and moving islands foreground alter/native models of reckoning space and time that require an active and participatory engagement with the island seascape. An emphasis on maritime vessels foregrounds their contributions to the formation of island history. Postcolonial seafaring is invoked here as a practice and as a metaphor for navigating a course that is not overdetermined by the trajectories of western colonization. Attention to movement offers a paradigm of rooted routes, of a mobile, flexible, and voyaging subject who is not physically or culturally circumscribed by the terrestrial boundaries of island space.

In an effort to position island cultures in the world historical process, I examine how these methodologies of charting transoceanic migration and landfall help elucidate the ways in which theories and peoples travel on a global scale. The rationale for this mode of inter-island comparison is to move beyond restrictive national, colonial, and regional frameworks and to foreground shared histories, particularly as they are shaped by geography. Both etak and tidalectics offer an interdisciplinary approach that places contemporary islands in a dialogue with each other as well as their continental counterparts. In fact, as I will explain, these tropical island cultures have helped constitute the very metropoles that have deemed them peripheral to modernity.

As the first comparative study of Caribbean and Pacific Island literatures in English, this book takes geography as a starting point to argue that the land/sea relationship has been conducive to complex patterns of migration and settlement, creating literatures of diaspora and indigeneity that complicate the colonial vision of isolated tropical isles. Like Brathwaite, Édouard Glissant reminds us that the "island embodies openness. The dialectic between inside and outside is reflected in the relationship of land and sea" (1989, 139).[2] This "openness" reflects a tidalectic between routes and roots, a methodology of reading island literatures that structures this book. Thus the first section examines the literature of maritime routes and what I term the "transoceanic imaginary,"[3] exploring Derek Walcott's maxim that the "the sea is history." The second section turns to the land in order to excavate native roots in nation-building literatures. Both sections are particularly attentive to the ways in which the metaphors of routes and roots are gendered, offering a critique of how masculine travelers are naturalized in their voyages across feminized lands and seas. Overall, the comparative frame of *Routes and Roots* navigates uncharted spaces in postcolonial studies, a field that has not adequately addressed the ways in which indigenous discourses of landfall have mitigated and contested productions of transoceanic diaspora.

Most comparative literature projects demarcate their epistemological boundaries through the concept of national difference; this enables scholars to speak of shared history, language, religion, and cultural mores that are bounded by the modern nation state. As a postcolonial study of two regions that cannot be contained by the organizing parameters of one shared language, one colonial history, or one dominant nation-state (or even postcolonial status), *Routes and Roots* shifts the discourse to the concept of the island region and, by extension, problematizes national frameworks. As such, it is a project informed by the contemporary trajectories of migration and globalization. While the focus here is generally anglophone, the complexity of the migration of peoples and texts to and from diverse English-speaking metropoles has necessarily demanded a new paradigm to justify the comparison of such large regions. Diaspora studies has provided a vital and innovative framework for transnational comparison and has been a central influence on this work, but its tendency to focus on a particular ethnic group of (male) travelers limits its applicability. In fact, here I want to complicate diaspora theory's substitution of a national framework by an ethnic or racial one.

One of the larger objectives of this book is to examine the ways in which regionalism and diaspora studies, while they seem to offer the potential to dismantle the gendered, ethnic, and class hierarchies of the state, often inscribe remarkably analogous structures. Scholars have pointed out the ways in which privileged masculine subjects imagine citizenship by invoking feminized metaphors of the nation that preclude women's active participation, yet there is a strikingly similar gendering of diaspora. Like the operative metaphors of national belonging that encode a semantic collapse between women and (mother)land, diasporic discourses often position masculine subjects as normative travelers who rely upon a feminized sea in order to imaginatively regenerate across time and space. This is why, in the language of diaspora and globalization, masculinized trajectories of nomadic subjects and capital attain their motility by invoking feminized flows, fluidity, and circulation, while the feminine (as an organizing concept) and women (as subjects) are profoundly localized. To be localized in this case does not operate with the ideological potential of the dictum "think globally, act locally," but rather registers as symbolic and physical stasis. We have only to turn to Michel Foucault's gloss on Gilles Deleuze and Félix Guattari's *Anti-Oedipus* to recognize the pervasiveness of these gendered celebrations of travel. He writes, "Prefer what is positive and multiple, difference over uniformity, flows over unities, mobile arrangements over systems. *Believe that what is productive is not sedentary but nomadic*" (1972, my emphasis xiii). In a remarkable appropriation of the very terms with which women's bodies are associated and theorized—difference, multiplicity, production, and flows—the masculine nomad achieves mobility precisely through the erasure of women's corporeal, ontological, and economic capacity for (re)production. Since the model of (masculine) diaspora has increasingly become a stand-in for the postcolonial predicament, it is all the more important to insist on tracing its points of erasure, particularly its neglect of indigenous studies, which has an entirely different relationship to the history of land, nation-building, and the nation-state. This tension between (feminized) histories of diaspora and indigeneity is explored through the tidalectics of routes and roots.

The broad comparative nature of this book demands an engagement with multiple disciplines, and while it is deeply informed by postcolonial studies, the breadth of the project means that it cannot be categorized easily under a postcolonial rubric. The Caribbean and Pacific Islands do not fit neatly into a postcolonial paradigm because they do not share simultane ous colonial histories even though they have been (and still are) occupied at different points by Christian, Spanish, French, British, and American capitalist empires. In fact the continuity of indigenous presence in the Pacific when contrasted with the decimation of native cultures in the Caribbean is a testament to the radical historical differences of colonialism in each region. Indigenous activists in the Pacific have pointed towards the epistemic erasures implicit in the linear definitions of the "post" of postcolonialism as they struggle with the ongoing inequities in white-settler states. And while the political methodologies of native sovereignty movements may not suit the Caribbean's celebration of creolized and composite cultures, the transnational thrust of diaspora theory often poses a profound epistemological challenge to the localizing focus of indigeneity. These challenges to any homogenizing framework of comparison point to the need for a dynamic methodology that engages the intersections of time-space without fixing or freezing either. Thus tidalectics foreground three key ideas: how both regions share a complex history of migration patterns before and after colonization; how the island topos entails an exchange between land and sea that translates into the discourse of "ex-isles" and settlement; and finally, how these vital links between geography, history, and cultural production facilitate a reading of island literatures. This emphasis on geography is not environmentally determinist because it encodes an active, participatory ecology. As the etak or moving-islands model demonstrates, the landscape participates in the historical process, resisting the synthesizing narrative of conquest. It is by insisting on the tidalectics between land and sea and by remapping the Caribbean and Pacific alongside each other that particular discourses of diaspora, indigeneity, and sovereignty can be examined in ways that challenge and complement each other, foregrounding the need for simultaneous attention to maritime routes and native roots.

Navigating Repeating Islands

To understand the contemporary literary production of the Caribbean and Pacific, one must engage with the long colonial history of mapping island spaces. Although it has not attracted much attention in postcolonial studies, the desire for islands—"nesomania" in James Michener's words (quoted in Day 1987, 1)—was a trademark of European maritime empires. Countless explorers directed their efforts towards the discovery of the "Antilles"; utopian counter-lands or ante-islands that, in my reading, offer a deeper historical model for what Antonio Benítez-Rojo refers to as the "repeating island" (1992). Benítez-Rojo has famously employed chaos theory to imagine the fractal expansion of the culture of the Caribbean across the globe, transported by contemporary migrants. As helpful as his theory of repeating islands is for a positive and creative vision of diaspora and resettlement, I want to place it in juxtaposition to older and more pernicious models of colonial island expansion.

By turning to the "root" or originary island of what would become a global anglophone island empire, we see that England's claim to islandness, a suppression of Wales and Scotland, derives from the political establishment of the United Kingdom and its subsequent colonial expansion overseas. England constituted itself as an island by its expansion into the territory of its immediate neighbors and, as many have demonstrated, constructed its earliest formulations of racial difference through the colonization of its first island colony, Ireland. Consequent to a long history of colonial practice, the cultural topography once associated with imperial England (its isolation from continental Europe) then becomes projected onto *other* island spaces that are reformulated as remote and isolated only in relation to the geographies of industrialized Great Britain.[4] This enabled the argument that England's limited terrestrial space justified its need for island colonies, visible in nineteenth-century British Colonial Secretary C. S. Adderley's assertion that "this little island wants not energy, but only territory and basis to extend itself; its sea-girt home would then become the citadel of one of the greatest of the empires" (quoted in Hyam 1993, 2). Here Britain is articulated as an expanding isle as it extends its insular geography through global empire-building. The tension between the contained English isle and its propensity to expand outwards by maritime rule draws attention to how conceptions of limited island space were vital to "spawning" an Anglo-Saxon diaspora into colonial territories. Although the population of England (and the rest of Europe) did greatly expand due to the availability of food crops and labor resources from the colonies, the *limitations* of island space were not the problem so much as the inequitable distribution of territory, the result of an emergent capitalism that turned the terrestrial commons into private property. Thus, England's "island story," a narrative of invasion and settlement, is transformed from a space of received colonists (early Anglo-Saxon invaders) to a bounded sovereign entity that refuses migrants while propelling its people outwards to people its island colonies.[5] Over the centuries Great Britain is discursively refashioned as a repeating island throughout its colonies in the Caribbean and Pacific, as suggested by the toponyms New Albion, New Britain, New Hebrides, New Ireland, and "Little England," or Barbados.

The notion of the isolated island has material and metaphorical mean-ings derived from a complex history of European expansion into contained spaces. This repeating-island story arose from early experiments in defor-estation, colonization, enslavement, and plantation monoculture, which were first tested in the eastern Atlantic islands. Demonstrating how island space functioned as a laboratory, Alfred Crosby concludes that European experiments in the Canaries and Madeira taught colonists that they must seek lands that were: (1) remote enough to discourage the epidemiological susceptibility of Europeans; (2) distant enough to minimize the islanders' defense against western diseases; (3) isolated from large mammals such as horses to ensure colonial military advantage; and finally, (4) lands uninhab-ited by maritime peoples (1986, 102). In the grammar of empire, *remoteness* and *isolation* function as synonyms for island space and were considered vital to successful colonization. Although all islands are isolated by etymo-logical definition, their remoteness has been greatly exaggerated by trans-oceanic visitors. The myth of the remote isle derives from an amplification of the nautical technologies of the arrivant and an erasure of islanders' maritime histories. As Greg Dening reminds us, "Every living thing on an island has been a traveller. Every species of tree, plant, and animal on an island has crossed the beach" (1980, 31).

European experiments in the eastern Atlantic archipelagoes coupled with ancient European narratives of mythic islands contributed greatly to the later (re)construction and settlement of the Caribbean and Pacific Islands and a discursive refashioning of their isolation. This model of isola-tion has led to some strange observations about island space and cultures. For instance, French philosopher Charles de Montesquieu, writing at the height of European expansion, determined that "the inhabitants of islands have a higher relish for liberty than those of the continent . . . the sea sepa-rates them from great empires" (1748, Book XVIII). Although the French Navy was by then developing a global empire of overseas colonies from the Caribbean to the Indian Ocean and would soon be claiming territories in the Pacific, Montesquieu argued that "conquerors are stopped by the sea" (Book XVIII). In fact, islands were especially sought for colonization by all of the major maritime powers because their strategic positioning was vital to the flow of maritime traffic, their long coastlines provided multiple access points for trade and defense, they provided necessary stopover points for the refitting and the restocking of ships, and their contained spaces facili-tated greater control of colonized and enslaved populations who, without access to maritime vessels, were less likely to escape (see Grove 1995, 63). The fact that islands and their inhabitants are positioned as remote and isolated belies their centrality to world trade and their consistent visitation by colonials, missionaries, shipwreck, anthropology, and tourism. In effect, the narrative of island isolation is dependent upon these visitors. Popular U.S. television shows and films such as *Survivor*, *Lost*, and *The Beach* continue to capitalize upon the myth of the isolated tropical island, as does the tourist industry. Not surprisingly, there are few if any historical testimonies from Pacific or Caribbean Islanders bemoaning their distance from Europe.

Paradoxically, the island of colonial discourse is simultaneously positioned as isolated yet deeply susceptible to migration and settlement. The construction of isolated island space is an implicit consequence of European colonialism and has a tremendously complex history. The island has functioned in various historical eras as a new Eden, a sociopolitical utopia, a refreshment stop for long maritime journeys, and the contained space where shipwrecked men (or boys) may reconstruct their metropolitan homes. The archipelagoes of the Canary and Madeira islands were the first laboratories for European maritime imperialism and the first sugar plantations of the Atlantic. This experiment in island colonization, deforestation, plantocracy, and slavery was then repeated throughout the Caribbean. The use of one archipelago as an ideological and social template for the next reveals the ways in which the colonial discourse of islands repeated itself, rhizomatically, along a westward trajectory. For example, the eastern Atlantic islands were not only the first laboratories of empire, but also an important cartographic point that caused Christopher Columbus to situate his "discovery" of the West Indies as "off the Canary Islands" (1992, 16). This cognitive mapping is rendered materially visible when we remember that Columbus picked up sugar cane there and transplanted it to the Caribbean.

Tropical islands have not only functioned as colonial or sociopolitical laboratories of experiment, but they have facilitated tremendous ecological, anthropological, and biological theories. As Richard Grove has documented, islands provided the material bases for the establishment of the natural sciences, and the first scientific academies and botanical gardens of Europeans were founded in island colonies. Moreover, European deforestation of the Canary and Caribbean islands positioned these spaces as laboratories for the study of global climate and ecology; the colonial devastation of natural resources created the first environmental conservation laws of Spain, Britain, and France (1995, 6). The European colonization of archipelagoes across the planet was crucial to facilitating Alfred Wallace and Charles Darwin's separate voyages around the world. Their independent observations of island flora and fauna enabled both men to establish the theory of species origins, adaptation, and evolution. Building upon the long narrative tradition of depicting islands as social and ecological utopias, Jean-Jacques Rousseau turned to the Atlantic, Indian Ocean, and Pacific Islands to construct his vision of the *homme naturale*.[6] The island cultures of the Caribbean (and later the Pacific) were some of the earliest sites of western ethnography. Both island regions provided European observers with a space to theorize racial purity and difference, as they do to this day; contemporary theories of creolization derive from the contained spaces of the Caribbean just as ideas about indigeneity continue to be developed and contested in the Pacific. Alfred Wegener's theory of continental drift was made possible by the study of island flora and fauna (Nunn 1994, 22). Island topographies, labor, and resources have not only materially benefited Europe (such as the sugar plantations), but have provided the botanical, anthropological, biological, environmental, and ideological space for European laboratories, experiment, and development. The trope of island refreshment, fecundity, and exoticism would be repeated throughout Pacific Island visitation, and finds its contemporary manifestation in tourism discourse.[7] In fact, the colonial era provided the ideological template for contemporary tourist consumption of island resources. Both forces overlap in their mutual construction of these spaces as remote and isolated, mystifying the islands' contributions to modernity. As Marshall Sahlins explains, "The heretofore obscure histories of remote islands deserve a place alongside the self-contemplation of the European past—or the history of 'civilizations' for their own remarkable contributions to an historical understanding" (1985, 72).

I have given this broad sketch of colonial island representation to suggest that those spaces deemed the most external to the march of world history may be its sources of production. This offers us a deeper understanding about the almost compulsive nature of the repeating-island story, its Mediterranean roots, and how, to draw from Peter Hulme, one "ideological discourse comes into existence through a process of tactical adaptation of earlier discourses" (1981, 56). For example, just after Columbus's return from his first voyage, an eighth-century legend reemerged in Europe that detailed the exodus of seven bishops from Lisbon to an uncharted Atlantic island where they erected a Christian utopia. Significantly, this island was called "Antillia," the counter-island, and frequently appeared on pre-Columbian maps. Antillia signifies the circulation of island myths across Europe and suggest a discursive construction of predetermined islands that were literally mapped before they were found. This island myth was well known to Columbus; before he departed on his first transatlantic voyage, the astronomer Paolo dal Pozzo Toscanelli recommended Antillia as a stopover on the way to Cathay. This represents a slippage between the nonspace of "utopia" to an idealistic space of expectation—"eutopia"—that would be incorporated into Medieval and Renaissance cartography. This "Columbian hermeneutics of discovery" (Zamora 1993, 136) is articulated in Brathwaite's poem "The Emigrants." The Caribbean speaker observes: "Columbus from his after-/deck watched heights he hoped for/rocks he dreamed, rise solid from my simple water." The speaker asks:

> What did this journey mean, this
> new world mean: dis-
> covery? Or a return to terrors
> he had sailed from, known before? (1973, 52)

In this dream vision of rocks that emerge from the ocean, Brathwaite, like Roach, invokes a cyclical notion of time and a dynamic model of generative space. The tautological nature of his "dis-/covery" is rhetorically articulated through the consonance of the navigator's "return to terror." Historians have argued that to Columbus, discovery meant finding what was "known before"; this cyclical conception of time might be connected to the legends circulating amidst Europeans that anticipated island landfall on the westward passage to "the Indies."[8] Since Marco Polo's narrative had already described great archipelagoes in Asia, Columbus's arrival to the Caribbean seemed to have been predestined in a collapse of time-space between Antillian and Asian islands. This is evident in cartographic representations that erase the Americas so that the Atlantic Ocean merges with the Pacific. This conflation of time and space is strikingly apparent in Columbus's dual name for the Caribbean as the "West Indies" (Pacific) and the "Antilles" (Atlantic). Although it was less geographic confusion than an ideological one, Daniel Defoe's conflation of a Pacific island (Juan Fernandez) with a Caribbean one (Tobago) led to a confused geographical setting for *Robinson Crusoe* (see Grove 1995, 227). Of course, neither could have known that geologically speaking, the Caribbean region did arise out of the Pacific, the world's originary ocean. These moving and repeating islands then "emerged" in the toponyms of empire: thus we have the Virgin Islands (from the European legend of St. Ursula), Brazil (an Irish island legend), and Tahiti's reformulation as the island of Aphrodite, or Nouvelle Cythére.[9]

In contrast to the notion that islands represent fixed, static spaces, these repeating-island stories highlight how island constructions traveled with

European migration and voyaging. While St. Ursula's islands and Antillia became cartographically fixed by Columbus in the Caribbean, other imagined islands like the Antipodes (Terra Australis Incognita) moved westward, out of the Atlantic region into the Pacific. Walcott describes this masculine quest for the utopian island as a "near-delirium" for a Nouvelle Cythére, nesomania for what was always "far and feverish"—a feminized utopia that "dilate(d) on the horizon" (1986, 481). Hundreds of explorers, including James Cook, were sent to the Pacific to obtain this illusory counter-island to the northern hemisphere. Of course, these imagined island topographies were never homogenously defined. Within their own time period they represented a system of ante-islands; heterotopias that were alternately idyllic or inhabited by ruthless cannibals. This is apparent in the colonial polarization of islanders into what Bernard Smith (1985) describes as "hard" and "soft" primitives, and in the naming of the Caribbean as the realm of cannibals, a contrast to a presumably more peaceful "Pacific."[10]

Like orientalism, a system of "islandism" was constructed less through contact with others than through the textual exchange between Europeans. This is visible in the ideological construction of anticipated island landfall and the vast array of artistic and literary depictions of island topoi, shipwrecks, and contact with "Indians" that dominated the colonial imagination. Considering the multiple waves of European voyagers, cartographers, botanists, beachcombers, traders, slavers, missionaries, and colonial officials to every single island in the Pacific and Caribbean, and the resulting eradication of many island inhabitants, the perpetuation of this image of island isolation can best be described as a European myth that seeks to erase the colonial intentionality of the past.

The desire for depopulated islands in which European men could refashion themselves helps to explain why, between 1788 and 1910, over 500 desert-island stories were published in England alone (Carpenter 1984, 8) and why *Robinson Crusoe* underwent six reprintings in its first year of publication (1719). The Robinsonades, or island solitude and adventure stories so popular in western Europe in the eighteenth and nineteenth centuries, may have been inspired by *Robinson Crusoe*, but Defoe's sources indicate that the genre's origins extend across space and time to the east.[11] While the desert-island genre did not originate in Europe, it certainly found its most receptive audience there. Widely read in the British colonies, the novel was one of the first secular texts to be translated into Maori (1852). In the Caribbean, *Robinson Crusoe* is described by Walcott as "our first book, our profane Genesis" (1986, 92). In "Crusoe's Journal" he observes, "Posing as naturalists,/drunks, castaways, beachcombers, all of us/yearn for those fantasies of innocence" (94). But this innocence, Walcott remarks elsewhere, can be likened to the "hallucination of imperial romance," a narrative in which the spaces of the most brutal forms of human subjugation, the slave islands, are labeled in sweet utopian terms, as "Fortunate Isles" and "Sugar Islands." This begs Walcott's question: "When they named these [islands] . . . was it nostalgia or irony?" (306).

Since the colonial expansion of Europe, its literature has increasingly inscribed the island as a reflection of various political, sociological, and colonial practices; in texts from Thomas More's *Utopia* to Shakespeare's *The Tempest*, the island is a material and discursive site for experiments in governance, racial mixing, imprisonment, and enslavement. Broadly speaking, European inscriptions of island topoi have often upheld imperial logic and must be recognized as ideological tools that helped make colonial expansion possible. Diana Loxley has shown that the island-adventure genre was central to the indoctrination of British boys into the emerging ideologies of muscular Christianity, British nationalism, and empire. It is not only that the resources and labor of island spaces were vital to the expansion of Europe and its subsequent industrialization; inscribing these islands as isolated suppressed their relationship to the colonial metropole and minimized knowledge of their contributions to the production of British literature. This is apparent in the incredibly popular narratives of *accidental* arrival to island shores through shipwreck which have a direct—albeit mystifying—relationship to the height of colonial expansion.

The self-made male who accidentally colonizes a desert isle has been a powerful and repeated trope of empire building and of British literature of the eighteenth and nineteenth centuries. In fact, these Robinsonades have been described as a literary "frenzy" (J. Ballantyne 1994, 267). From these nineteenth-century island-adventure novels—which include Robert Louis Stevenson's *Treasure Island* and R. M. Ballantyne's *The Coral Island*—we might outline the following general patterns or narrative tropes. First, the accidental arrival, via shipwreck, of a Christian, European male (often a boy) to island shores. The island is deserted, constructed as *terra nullius* (empty land), tropical, and extremely fertile. (Indeed, there are few Arctic island-adventure stories.) As Loxley has shown, the island's lack of inhabitants provides a *tabula rasa* for colonialism and the birth of a new social order. Third, the new landscape is submitted to European rule through domestication and cultivation; the protagonist develops new skills as a result. In fact, the island is often represented as a female body; as Loxley remarks, "an unrelenting feature of island discourse is that the adventurer-hero of this free environment should not be constrained by the hegemonising power of the feminine" (1990, 56). The landscape is then subjected to empirical observation and experiment, which leads to rational control of unknown natural forces. Fifth, the protagonist fears the arrival of indigenous islanders whom he assumes are cannibals; in a reversal of power relations, he believes the islanders desire to consume him. Paradoxically, this presumption is not derived from empirical science but learned through the oral traditions of sailors' yarns and travelers' tales, which are invoked for dramatic affect and as a validation of the expanding colonial textuality of island space.

In the sixth step of the successful Robinsonade, the colonist's experience on the island leads to philosophical reflections on biological, religious, social, and/or political origins. These reflections are vital to counter the fear of regression due to the protagonist's lack of European books, a language community, woolen clothing, and Christian social mores. If the protagonist is isolated on the island, his fears are realized through trope number eight: the arrival of a non-European, non-Christian subject. This reverses colonial relations by positioning the islander as intrusive arrivant and the European colonist as the natural inhabitant. By bringing together the work of Mary Louise Pratt (1992) and Greg Dening, we recognize their "contact zone" on the beach, a space of "beginnings and endings . . . the frontiers and boundaries of islands" (1980, 32). Since this is a traveling or "restless native," one of the most feared icons of the colonial archive, this arrival is often associated with violence to the European in the form of kidnapping, infanticide, cannibalism, or murder. This in turn justifies a European moral imperative to respond with technological violence (firearms). After the display of force, trope number ten becomes possible: the assimilation of the islander into European social mores through indoctrination into European language, Christianity, labor, and dress. Through this process "the native" is renamed and becomes the primary source of labor. After a period of the accumulation of wealth and knowledge, the supremacy of European technology is reiterated by the arrival of a large ship, a "floating island" that transports its human and material resources to the metropole. Since the European has conquered his island, he departs to narrate the tale from the northern metropole, usually abandoning his island slaves, servants, mistress, wife, or children. In fact, the pairing of the desert-island-adventure narrative with its first-person inscription from the safety and familiarity of the colonial center is an integral and final trope of the Robinsonade; it assures the reading public of the ability to adapt and even rule in distant overseas territories with the guarantee of return and an uncomplicated assimilation back into the metropole. As Loxley has demonstrated, the island sanitizes and dehistoricizes the violence of the colonial process, providing "a laboratory for the propagation and nurturing of a perfect masculinity" (1990, 117).

These colonial narratives of island adventure were integral to normalizing the crossing of great expanses of space and in naturalizing the British diaspora to its island colonies. By imagining the ship as a nation and the island as a mere extension of the ship (which was already interpellated as a "floating island"), the migration of voluntary colonists was depicted in attractive terms that emphasized the bounded and controlled nature of island space. The great achievement of these hundreds upon hundreds of Robinsonades is that they also imparted a new spatial logic to the British reading public in which time and space were compressed; the presumed primitivism of the island colony was contrasted to the progressive modernity of the metropole, without recognition of the ways in which the uneven exchange of resources, labor, information, and even the Robinsonades themselves made these temporal and economic divisions possible. Over time, metropolitans came to identify the island as a remote, tropical, and geographical ideal divorced from the industrial temperate north, which of course was created *by* exploitation of the islands of the global south. Robinson Crusoe, we must remember, was a plantation owner on the way to obtain African slaves when his ship wrecked in the Caribbean. The spatial disconnection between a consuming reading public and the island-adventure genre suggests that the timeless and remote island can only signify as such when it is constructed in binary opposition to the history and geography of its continental visitors.

We may very well ask whether the representation of, to draw from one famous American television series, an idyllic "Fantasy Island" is necessarily a cause for alarm. The problem with perpetuating images of island isolation is that they relegate islanders to a remote and primitive past, denying them entrance into the modernity of their colonial "motherlands." Although these formulaic motifs were vital to the production of two centuries' worth of Robinsonades, they also appear in the representation of islands by some anthropologists, and they have been used to justify both military and tourist occupation of tropical island spaces. Like the presumably static "native" visited by the traditional anthropologist, islanders are often depicted in western discourse as symbols of the evolutionary past. Scholars have demonstrated that the indigenous association with place (especially in the wake of his/her colonial *dis*placement) is often interpreted as natural confinement. According to Arjun Appadurai, this derives from the "quintessentially mobile" white male anthropologist, who visits indigenous people in their "natural environment" (1996, 39). James Clifford (1988) and Johannes Fabian (1983) have pointed out that Enlightenment ideology and European anthropological praxis often position native peoples in a homogenous, prepositional time antecedent to the western narrative of linear progress. It is in this way that island societies are dehistoricized and represented as an undeveloped and premature moment in the trajectory of biological and cultural evolution.

The ideological apparatus associated with the Robinsonades may also be traced to anthropological uses of the term "culture island," which signifies "an isolated group or area; especially: *an isolated ethnological group*" (my emphasis). Here *Webster's Dictionary* highlights an implicit connection between bounded space and culture, a conflation that has been vital to evolutionary anthropological models. As always, the construction of the island as remote is contingent upon the cultural and geographic center that employs it. For example, Patrick Kirch explains that island societies have been "fertile intellectual terrain for anthropology . . . [and] have long provided inspirational material for the advance of anthropological method and theory" (1986, 1). Historian Oskar Spate referred to the "insular" Pacific Islands as "'so splendidly splittable into Ph.D. topics'" (quoted in Kirch 1986, 2). Kirch cites a number of important anthropological theories that derived from island topography, including structuralism and functionalism. As in other discursive fields, island boundedness is confused with closure to uphold the myth of the hermetically sealed laboratory. Significantly, Kirch points out that anthropologists were so entrenched in island boundedness, isolation, and atemporality ("shallow time depth") that archeological inquiries were hardly made until recently; interpretations of heavily scrutinized islands such as Tikopia were so focused on "internal processes of change" that "regional [transoceanic] exchange networks" were overlooked (1986, 4). The refusal to recognize the maritime technologies of non-European peoples has prevented the larger scientific community from recognizing the intentional settlement of the Americas by sea rather than by the Bering Strait thesis, which posits herds of animals as the real agents of migration and therefore history.

In fact, the cartographic and ethnic partition of the Pacific into Melanesia, Polynesia, and Micronesia highlights the ways in which ocean voyaging and exchange between the islands were threatening to the continental arrivants. Likewise, spurious cultural divisions were also made between the "peaceful Arawaks" of the Caribbean and the supposedly anthropophagous Caribs.[12] Recent scholarship demonstrates that, like Oceania, the region had been interconnected by maritime trade routes for centuries before

European arrival. This reminds us that most areas interpellated as remote and isolated isles are in fact *archipelagoes* with long maritime histories of interconnection. This ideological division of archipelagoes into isolated islands traveled westward with the colonists, rerouting their classical Mediterranean roots in the Caribbean and the Pacific.

Geologist Patrick Nunn, remarking on the "the continuation of the islands under the sea," explains that most islands "are no more than the tips . . . of huge ocean-floor volcanoes: to pretend that their formation can be diagnosed solely from looking at those parts above sea level is ludicrous" (1994, 112). In a similar vein, Robert Sullivan's poem "Ocean Birth" inscribes the emergence of the islands from the sea and imagines their human residents on "the skin of the ocean" (2005, 37). Geologically and symbolically speaking, the earth's surface cannot represent its deep history; the island poet must plumb the subterranean and the subaquatic layers of human and planetary change. These depths reflect shared experience across time and space in Kamau Brathwaite's assertion that "the unity is submarine" (1974, 64), positioning the islands as autonomous and geologically, historically, and culturally connected to their neighbors. Glissant builds upon Brathwaite's vision when he adopts "submarine roots" as a model of regional history. He writes, "[s]ubmarine roots: that is floating free, not fixed in one position in some primordial spot, but extending in all directions in our world through its networks and branches" (1989, 67). It is this fundamental connection between geography and history that allows Glissant to draw insightful parallels between French neocolonialism in Martinique and Micronesia. He upholds "the reality of archipelagoes in the Caribbean or the Pacific provides a natural illustration of the thought of Relation," a model for a tidal dialectic that engages multiple temporalities, complex and dynamic space, multilingualism, and orally transmitted knowledges (1997, 34–35).

We must question the perpetuation of the isolated isle because it depopulates the islands of those who contributed significantly to the world's financial, scientific, and ideological development. C. L. R. James and Sidney Mintz have pointed out the error in relegating the Caribbean to an archaic periphery when in fact the earliest machines of industrial slavery were created in their sugar plantations.[13] This is not merely an issue of erasing the past because it can be traced to current imperial expansion. For instance, the U.S. military was able to carry on its 1946 nuclear testing in Bikini (Micronesia) based on the island's supposed remoteness and insignificant population. Yet Micronesia's remoteness did not deter President Harry Truman from deciding to create a strategic trust territory that same year in order to militarize the Marshall, Caroline, and Mariana islands and place them under the governorship of the U.S. Navy. Years later, when Micronesians lobbied for demilitarization and self-governance, Secretary of State Henry Kissinger retorted: "There are only 90,000 people out there. Who gives a damn?"[14] Yet under the People's Revolutionary Government, Grenada's population was similar in size and ideals of sovereignty, and the United States certainly did "give a damn."

In fact, the Bikini Atoll was not *remote enough* to prevent the neighboring Rongelap Islanders from suffering the deadly effects of nuclear fallout carried by the wind. It was not remote enough to prevent nuclear contamination of the Pacific and its spread to Africa, Antarctica, and Europe. It was not remote enough to prevent its detailed photographic documentation by the U.S. military to ensure that tens of thousands of nuclear test images were distributed worldwide as a testament to their apocalyptic power in the Cold War. This troubling legacy of U.S. imperialism is not only unknown by most Americans, it has been shown by Teresia Teaiwa (2000) to have been eroticized by the two-piece bathing suit that was named after these devastating experiments. In a disturbing full circle from colonial to tourist occupation and consumption, Bikini Atoll has been designated one of the best tourist spots for scuba diving in the military wreckage. One company calls the Bikini trip an "island adventure" and, while admitting the region's extensive militarization, entices tourists to visit to "get a real sense as to how Robinson Crusoe must have felt."[15]

Island colonization, land alienation, and indigenous displacement are connected to contemporary tourism in Donald Kalpokas's 1974 poem, "Who am I?" Writing as a student in Fiji about his home in the dually colonized New Hebrides, Kalpokas was a vital part of the independence movement and ultimately became Vanuatu's prime minister. His polemic poem explains how his land "was alienated through fraud" and the "Protocols of 1914," which divided his home between England and France.

> I travel abroad with my identity card
> For I am stateless and have no right. . . .
> Who am I, lost in this ocean of confusion?
> . . . I am that third citizen of my country,
> The only condominium in the world. (quoted in Subramani 1992, 50)

Kalpokas's poem raises compelling questions about the connections between colonial and tourist models of the repeating island and how they restructure landscape to mimic other island colonies. Although Pacific voyagers settled Vanuatu over four thousand years ago, the Portuguese explorer Pedro Fernández de Quirós assumed he had discovered Antillia, the great southern ante-island, so he named the largest island of the group Australia del Espiritu Santo. A century later, the French explorer Antoine de Bougainville interpellated the same islands as Les Grandes Cyclades, naming them after the Greek isles in the Aegean Sea. Less than a decade later, they were renamed the New Hebrides after Scottish islands by James Cook. Although there were important historical differences between colonial powers, this repeating-island story is striking because it highlights an ideological *contraction* of island space and time between the Atlantic and Pacific as a product of European *expansion*. Moreover, the British and French used their Caribbean Island colonies as models for the remapping and restructuring of Vanuatu. As such, this became an all-too-familiar colonial island story about plantation monoculture, illegal recruitment and kidnapping of island labor (blackbirding), and native alienation from land, culture, and resources.[16]

The 1914 protocols that open the first lines of Kalpokas's poem reflect the dual system of Anglo-French governance called "the condominium," a historical contract that alienated the region's indigenous occupants and a reference to the new architectures of tourism, which also relegates ni-Vanuatu to "third citizenship." His poem demonstrates that native land alienation has been exacerbated by tourism and U.S. militarization, reflecting multiple colonial demands upon the economy and resources. The speaker has no sovereign ship of state in this "ocean of confusion." He concedes that "at least" he "is still able to swim," but parodies the Robinsonade in his fear that he may be "washed ashore/On the desert of a French Pacific Republic." Given the long and complex history of Pacific Island voyaging, Kalpokas's depiction of an indigenous speaker as flotsam at sea, without a vessel of sovereignty or directionality in navigating a course towards landfall suggests a troubling tidalectic between transoceanic migration and a loss of sovereignty. Moreover, the speaker's displacement from the land renders him a castaway in his own ancestral ocean. It also makes him a captive of the Robinsonade narrative, in which he fears the depopulation of his own island home, a "desert" space, unoccupied and devoid of sustaining water. Ironically, his island is not represented through indigenous topography but rather is mapped by the dry colonial name, "French Pacific Republic." Given the metaphorical relationship between the ship and the state, we can interpret Kalpokas's speaker as deprived of his own vessel of sovereignty due to the dual appropriation of a "French Pacific" Ocean and a Platonic ship of the "Republic."

Writing in Fiji about the decolonization process at home, Kalpokas's poem gives us an opportunity to think through the ways in which island literature has been deeply informed by the transoceanic imaginary. Reflecting back to the Eric Roach poem that opened this chapter, we can see that Kalpokas is similarly concerned with the worldliness of island geography and history, and inscribes a tidalectic imagination in which the loss of land is interpreted from the perspective of the sea. His depiction of an "ocean of confusion," in which rights and citizenship are in flux for the island subject, reflects a maritime imagery of globalization, a grammar of fluidity and flow that is directly connected to the territorial scramble for the seas.

The Transoceanic Imaginary

> You want to hear my history? Ask the sea.
> —Derek Walcott, "The Sea is History"

I have emphasized the close relationship between British maritime expansion and the discursive construction of tropical island space to provide a new model for understanding anglophone literary genealogies. A tidalectic engagement with the formulation of British literature demonstrates the ways in which the chronotope (time-space) of the island—from *The Tempest* to *Robinson Crusoe*—is as vital to this literary canon as the sea. While postcolonial studies has revealed the ways in which empire-building was a constitutive element of British literature, we are only just beginning to understand that it was the desert-island *and* nautical-adventure genres that were vital to imagining this transoceanic empire. Where the desert-isle genre emphasizes the boundedness of islands, tidalectics engage with their watery surroundings, foregrounding the routes of the oceanic imaginary. In fact, writers of the Pacific and Caribbean have turned to narratives of transoceanic migration to undermine the myth of the confined islander, an ontological contrast to the mobile European male who produces world history by traversing space. Turning to the sea, we destabilize the myth of island isolation and open up new possibilities for engaging a dynamic history of time-space.

Half of the world's population lives within a few miles of the sea, and when we include its staggering depths, 95 percent of the earth's biosphere is ocean. The sea is often described in cosmologies as the space of human origins, a narrative upheld by the biological sciences. Marine biologist Sylvia Earle explains that "our origins are there, reflected in the briny solution coursing through our veins and in the underlying chemistry that links us to all other life" (1995, 15). The ocean supports our lives on this planet through its hydrologic cycles and is often described as the earth's lungs, responsible for the "planetary respiratory rhythm"; Earle asserts that "every breath we take is linked to the sea" (1995, xiv). Despite our complete dependence on this dynamic originary space, it remains one of radical alterity. The sea, to Roland Barthes, is a "non-signifying field." He exclaims: "Here I am, before the sea; it is true that it bears no message. But on the beach, what material for semiology!" (1972, 112). Barthes's terrestrial bias may be questioned when we consider how the subject *internalizes* this alterity by rendering the sea in the blood. For example, Jacques Cousteau observes that "our flesh is composed of myriads of cells, each one of which contains a miniature ocean . . . comprising all the salts of the sea, probably the built-in heritage of our distant ancestry, when some mutating fish turned into reptiles" (1976, 13). According to Elisabeth Mann Borgese, humans may have swum before they walked. Just as the vastness of the sea challenges our limited concepts of space, so the ocean is at once our origin and "our liquid future" (1975, 17), destabilizing our notions of linear human time. Borgese explains, "Every drop of water that existed on the earth or around it billions of years ago is still there, whether in solid form or liquid or gaseous . . . every drop is still there" (18).

The sea is conceptually linked to human origins and exploring these fluid histories offers an alternative to the rigid ethnic genealogies of colonialism and nationalism. In other words, the ocean's perpetual movement is radically decentering; it resists attempts to fix a locus of history. Focusing on seascape rather than landscape as the fluid space of historical production allows us to complicate the nation-state, which encodes a rigid hierarchy of race, class, gender, religion, and ethnicity for its representative subjects. Because the surface of the ocean is unmarked by its human history and thus cannot be monumentalized in the tradition of colonial landscapes, a turn to the seas as history can produce an equalizing effect, allowing us to recognize the long maritime histories of island peoples prior to the arrival of Europeans. In fact, Caribbean and Pacific Islanders were noted for their massive voyaging canoes, and their ability to navigate thousands of maritime miles during an era when Europeans had not determined longitude and were consistently wrecking their ships. As a chronotope of the moving island and a unifying symbol of routes and roots, I foreground the trace of the word "canoe," a term introduced to the English language as a transliteration of the Taíno (Arawak) term "canoas." The Pacific Islands have a significant parallel in the term "vaka." As *vessels of history*, canoes and vaka are vital to the historical genealogy of both regions, a point explored in the first section of this book.

The Pacific and Caribbean islands were first settled about 4,000 BCE by multiple seafaring arrivals from the continental lands to their respective west. Both areas were marked by complex processes of interculturation, trade, and migration, which challenge attempts to determine an originary home for the early island migrants. The process of arrival and adaptation highlights the ways in which land and sea are territorialized by migrant populations, and offers a complex alter/native historiography to European colonial models of the past. This tidalectic approach marks a significant break from colonial maps that depict land and sea as unmarked, atemporal, and feminized voids, *terra nullius* and *aqua nullius*, unless traversed and/or occupied by (male) European agents of history.

Placing these island regions in a dialogue with each other allows us to see the complex historical relationships to the waters that surround them. Like the island, the ocean has functioned as a space of human origins; thus the sea and voyaging motifs are prevalent in cosmogenesis narratives of each region. For example, Walcott's meditation on "Origins" positions his human speaker as "foetus of plankton" (1986, 11).[17] The sea is history in Walcott's poem "Names," which begins: "My race began as the sea began/ with no nouns, and with no horizon . . . with a different fix on the stars" (305). Drawing attention to how the production of space also produces race—and its naming and therefore its conceptual confinement—Walcott's poem highlights the aporia between language and its object, mapping and space. The ocean's incomprehensibility is mirrored cosmologically in deep space (the stars), producing a metaphor of origins that also undermines the structures of language used to represent it. The human employment of language and maps is precisely how, Walcott explains, "the mind was halved by a horizon" (305). In this poem, dedicated to Kamau Brathwaite, "the stick to trace our names on the sand" is merely provisional. Ultimately our creator, the sea, will "erase" all human inscriptions such as language and cartography (306).

Inscribing the sea as origin, while a provisional human effort at historiography, is also an enduring characteristic of island literature. Walcott's speaker becomes a namable subject only after sharing island space with other artisan-migrants such as a "goldsmith from Benares," a "stonecutter from Canton," and a "bronzesmith from Benin" (306). The poem questions how to refashion Old World art forms for newly creolized societies after the dehumanizing wake of slavery and indenture. Ultimately, the shared history of transoceanic migration to the islands provides an inexhaustible spatial imaginary for reflections on origins. Caribbean writers have inscribed the Atlantic as an originary space for the peoples of the African diaspora, in a tidalectic engagement between continents. To Walcott's characters in *Omeros*, "*Mer* was both mother and sea" (1990, 231) while in Grace Nichols's poetry, the structures of time-space collapse in the traumatic birth through the "middle passage womb" (1983, 5). By tracing a connection to the past through ancestry and genealogy, a characteristic trope of postcolonial writing in that it destabilizes the universalizing (and dehumanizing) narrative of colonial history, these writers make a familial claim to space that naturalizes the process of diaspora.

Since all arrivants to islands before the twentieth century came by water, the sea is often positioned as an origin for the diverse peoples of the Caribbean and the Pacific. Writing from Fiji, Pacific theorist Epeli Hau'ofa has explained, "all of us in Oceania today, whether indigenous or otherwise, can truly assert that the sea is our common heritage" (1997, 142). Jamaican novelist Patricia Powell (1998) has inscribed the nineteenth-century voyages from China to the Caribbean in ways that situate the sea as origin and liken the experience of indenture ships to the brutalities of the middle passage. Trinidadian writer Ramabai Espinet inscribes crossing kala pani or the dark waters between India and the Caribbean in similarly traumatic terms, as "a passage into death and sickness and unending labour, and into a light that was the present" (2003, 284). Fijian writer Subramani opens his novella "Gone Bush" with the words: "In the beginning was the sea . . . everything came out of the sea . . . from it came the goddess of life" (1988, 77). Although the Indian protagonist "seemed . . . [like] someone from a landlocked culture whose people were riders of horses" (77), like Walcott's narrator, the process of migration to the islands has realigned this character's relationship towards the sea.[18]

By employing a tidalectic framework, we can highlight the transoceanic trajectories of diaspora to the Caribbean and Pacific islands, underlining their shared similarities in geo-pelagic relation rather than the limiting model of national frameworks. As long as it does not bracket off the referents of history, as Joan Dayan (1996) aptly warns of some theories of the black Atlantic, the transoceanic imaginary can be a powerful metaphor to signal the cultural transition to new island landscapes, complicating the notion of static roots and offering a fluid paradigm of migratory routes.[19] As a constitutive element of tidalectics, the transoceanic imaginary foregrounds the fluid connection between the Pacific and Caribbean islands and the role of geography—and oceanography—in shaping cultural production. The focus on island migration as a vital narrative trope of these regions is helpful because it can accommodate any number of arrivals and highlights the process of human sedimentation. Importantly, migration is not valorized as a facile metaphor for masculine agency in history. The cultural and historical production of those who cannot and do not travel, particularly women, must be considered as a constitutive element in the framework of the routing of diaspora. Moreover, a focus on the production of local roots needs to problematize the gendered conflation of women with land and, by extension, the land with national belonging. Engaging a tidalectic model of routes and roots as a comparative frame to connect two different island regions foregrounds the conceptual similarities of geography and history, such as the association of women with space and men with time. This comparative tidalectic also allows for the emergence of historical and social contrast, such as the tension between diaspora and indigeneity, which highlights the distinctiveness between and within the regions' literary production. This book seeks to highlight the ways in which the process of migration and settlement produces diasporic and indigenous subjects in an active relationship with the land and sea.

The transoceanic imagination, produced by "peoples of the sea," is vital to postcolonial writing of the past two decades and is particularly visible in Pacific and (black) Atlantic studies. Building upon the work of James Clifford (1988 and 1992) and Marcus Rediker (1987), Paul Gilroy has famously rendered the "shape of the Atlantic as a system of cultural exchanges" where "the movements of black people—not only as commodities but engaged in various struggles towards emancipation, autonomy, and citizenship—provides a means to reexamine the problems of nationality, location, identity and historical memory" (1993, 16). Although the ocean is a primary space to imagine the histories of diaspora, it is also a vital space for the production of the indigenous Pacific. This is particularly evident in the work of Hau'ofa, a Pacific anthropologist and director of the Oceania Centre for Arts and Culture, who provides an essential theoretical framework to destabilize the myth of island isolation. He asserts, "There is a gulf between viewing the Pacific as 'islands in a far sea' and as 'a sea of islands.' The first emphasizes dry surfaces in a vast ocean far from the centers of power, exaggerating their smallness and remoteness, whereas the latter places islands "in the totality of their relationships" (1993b, 7). He explains:

> The idea that (Oceania) is too small, too poor and too isolated . . . overlooks culture history, and the contemporary process of what

might be called "world enlargement" carried out by tens of thousands
of ordinary Pacific Islanders . . . making nonsense of all national and
economic boundaries, borders that have been defined only recently,
criss-crossing an ocean that had been boundless for ages before Captain Cook's apotheosis. (6)

Drawing from the western conceit that masculine movement across space
produces history, Hauʻofa destabilizes the conflation of the indigenous
islander with static land by drawing upon the transoceanic imagination.
His theory of a "sea of islands" reorients land and territory-based analysis
towards the complex processes of interculturation generated by ancient and
contemporary transoceanic movement. Inspired by the dynamic expansion
of the volcanic island of Hawaiʻi, and quoting Walcott's aphorism that "the
sea is history," Hauʻofa determines that "our roots, our origins are embedded in the sea," which is "our pathway to each other" (1997, 147, 148).
Hauʻofa's early anthropological work was conducted in Trinidad and he
has maintained an important conceptual connection between both island
regions. His theory of island history is remarkably like Glissant's model
of "submarine roots" (1989, 67) and Brathwaite's postulation that island
"unity is submarine" (1974, 64).[20] A view of the archipelagoes as a submarine rhizome is shared by these theorists whose works permeate various
linguistic, cultural, and geographic borders.

The transoceanic imagination is a hallmark of island theorists and
diaspora discourse. Like Hauʻofa and Glissant, Benítez-Rojo's work on the
repeating island employs aquatic metaphors to focus on the waters of the
Caribbean, asserting that the region is a "meta-archipelago" with "neither
a boundary nor a centre" (1992, 4). He highlights the diaspora of Caribbean peoples in an effort to destabilize ethnic essentialism and configures
the region as being as much in flux as the waters that surround it. By visu-
alizing the archipelago as an island that repeats itself into varying fractal
spaces, Benítez-Rojo concludes: "the culture of the Caribbean . . . is not
terrestrial but aquatic . . . [it] is the natural and indispensable realm of
marine currents, of waves, of folds and double folds, of fluidity and sinu-
osity" (11). Water appeals because of its lack of fixity and rootedness; as
Gaston Bachelard explains, it is a "transitory element. It is the essential
ontological metamorphosis between heaven and earth. A being dedicated
to water is a being in flux" (1983, 6). Since migration and creolization are
so characteristic of island cultural formations, watery trajectories provide an
apt metaphor for ethnicities "in flux." To foreground transoceanic migrations that brought African, Asian, European, and indigenous settlers to

the islands destabilizes rigid genealogical roots and offers a fluid meta-phor for dynamic routes. For example, Samoan writer Albert Wendt refers to himself as "a pelagic fish on permanent migration" (1995b, 13). Wal-cott refers to the Caribbean as "the liquid Antilles" (1986, 44) and charts an "iconography of the sea" (240). This provides an aquatic space that is materially unmarked by European monuments and an alter/native imag-inary for postcolonial island history. These "webbed networks" (Gilroy 1993, 29) suggest that bodies of water unite black Atlantic, Caribbean, and Pacific peoples and have the potential to dissolve the artificial boundaries of nation-states.

As helpful as these models are for rethinking the ethnic origins and boundaries of the nation, the recent tendency to configure the sea as a space beyond territorialism also can exaggerate the agency of migrants and minimize their experiences of border policing. In other words, these maritime theories often valorize transoceanic diaspora without adequately questioning the historical and economic *roots* for migrant *routes*. For exam-ple, Benítez-Rojo's *The Repeating Island* uses marine currents as its trope for superseding social and political hegemonies where the "peoples of the sea" travel across the globe, and "certain dynamics of their culture also repeat and sail through the seas of time" (1992, 16), seemingly without linguistic or national boundaries. Remarkably, these theorists turn to the borderlessness of the ocean only to imagine a body of migrants who are bounded by the limits of race and gender. This formulation of transoceanic male agents of history has ample historical precedence in British imperial-ism. Thus while we embrace these new formulations of fluid transoceanic movement, we must be cautious about the ways in which they recirculate discarded paradigms of nationalism and regionalism. Secondly, we must also pay close attention to the ways in which the conceptual move to claim ocean space may derive from neocolonial expansion and a radical new ter-ritorialism of the seas. Pinpointing its mechanism is particularly difficult when theorizing the ocean as a space of history. The ocean, as Glissant reminds us of the Caribbean Sea, tends to deflect and refract meaning. As Christopher Connery has demonstrated, the ocean has "long functioned as capital's myth element" (1996, 289), creating a lacuna precisely where we should be able to trace the expansion of both capital and empire.

Diaspora studies privilege space, so I would like to shift from these spatial theories of transoceanic migration to examine how they have trav-elled across time. For it is by historicizing these "peoples of the sea" that one finds a surprising—and disturbing—congruence. In the nineteenth century, English travel historian James Anthony Froude had written extensively of whom he had called the "children of the sea," but he was referring to British settlers and their fleets in his travel narrative *Oceana, or, England and Her Colonies* (1886). In fact, this valorization of transoceanic migration was a crucial component of British empire building. Froude exclaims that "the sea is the natural home of Englishmen; the Norse blood is in us, and we rove over the waters, for business or pleasure, as eagerly as our ancestors" (1886, 18). In his later and more infamous work, *The English in the West Indies* (1888), Froude proudly recites the maritime destiny that allowed the English to claim the Caribbean Sea from the Spanish and French. Although Froude is considered an anathema to Caribbean scholars, his words are clearly reminiscent of Benítez-Rojo when the latter explains, "The Antilleans' insularity does not impel them toward isolation, but on the contrary toward travel, toward exploration, toward the search for fluvial and marine routes" (1992, 25). Froude's sense that "the sea is the easiest of highways" (1886, 11–12) is echoed in Hau'ofa's assertion that "the sea is our pathway to each other, and to everyone else" (1997, 148). Once the British girded the globe with submarine telegraph cables and standardized sea travel with steam ships in the late nineteenth century, the ocean became an increasingly accessible conduit for imperial technology and travel. Thus Froude's interpellation of the ocean was merely attempting to *naturalize* the ways in which British maritime imperialism had achieved their network of submarine cables, shipping lines, and fleets to rule the waves. Froude's American contemporary, Capt. Alfred Thayer Mahan, in *The Influence of Sea Power upon History* (1894), had argued that "the sea presents itself . . . [as] a great highway; or better, perhaps, of a wide common, [marked by] lines of travel called trade routes [that] reflect the history of the world" (1957, 25). In making what became an influential argument for the rise of the U.S. maritime empire, Mahan invoked those English ancestors of the Americans to argue that "an inborn love of the sea, the pulse of that English blood which still beat[s] in their veins, keep[s] alive all those tendencies and pursuits upon which a healthy sea power depends" (1957, 38–39). Like Froude, Mahan merges the fluidity of the sea with the racialized blood of Anglo-Saxon diaspora to naturalize colonial and military expansion.

In these particular cases, the transoceanic imaginary entails a valorization of international travel, an unmarked male and elite class, and a suppression of the experiences of women, indentured laborers, slaves, refugees, and many other *forced* migrations that represent the majority of nineteenth-century and contemporary diasporas. By naturalizing the "peoples of the sea," these theories depoliticize and dehistoricize trajectories of migration. Claiming marine travel as cultural or genealogical essence or, in Gilroy's terms, "cross-cultural fluidity," these writers may overlook colonial and neocolonial motives for transnational migrancy. It certainly cannot be a coincidence that theories valorizing transnational migrants emerge during the highest peaks of migration in the nineteenth century and in our contemporary globalized moment. As poetic as it may seem, most migrants do not choose to permanently leave their homes because their saline blood flows like the oceans or because they inherited a maritime sensibility through their ancestors. In fact, while this may be an era of the greatest movements of people in global history, it seems that the only migrants who relocate by sea are the elite on luxury vessels, whose wealth exceeds the constraints of the nation, or the ultradispossessed on makeshift watercraft, whose poverty prevents their navigation of a vehicle of national sovereignty. While clearly my work is aligned with diaspora theory to foreground migrant agency, I suggest that it is problematic to claim "fluvial and marine routes" for peoples that do not have the backing of a military fleet and the type of imperial power that undergirds Froude's celebration of the late nineteenth-century "Caucasian tsunami" (Crosby 1986, 300).

I want to emphasize what is generally invisible to diaspora studies and racialize the dominant discourse of the "Caucasian tsunami" in order to interrogate its imperial metaphors of migration and regionalism. My invocations of Froude's geographic imagination are intended to historicize transatlantic discourse and to highlight how the process of migration is integral to regionalist metaphors. In fact, one cannot envision a united region like the Caribbean or Pacific if there are no migrants linking the islands together. Hauʻofa's (1993b) vision of Oceania, for instance, was facilitated by his travel to Hawaiʻi, just as George Lamming's (1984) primary identification of the Caribbean as a region occurred on a transatlantic voyage with other West Indians. Yet regional and diasporic paradigms, while they may seem to exceed the limitations of the nation, often reflect their imperial roots and routes. If I may extend this analysis further back into the history of British imperialism, we see that Froude had a political precursor in this quest to unify diverse islands into a federated archipelago. James Harrington's *The Commonwealth of Oceana* (1656) is Froude's primary inspiration. Harrington has the following to say about the recently consolidated (read: colonized) British archipelago: "The situation of these countries, being islands . . . seems to have been designed by God for a commonwealth . . . . The sea gives the law to the growth of Venice, but the growth of Oceana gives the law to the sea" (Harrington quoted in Froude 1886, 2–3). Interestingly, Harrington evokes Pliny the Elder's model of imperial space which positions Rome at the center of the Mediterranean

Sea, a space "chosen by...providence...to unite scattered empires, to make manners gentle, to draw together...the uncouth tongues of so many nations" (Pliny quoted in Leed 1991, 136). Likewise, Harrington's divine commonwealth attempted to homogenize the unequal political and social relations between Ireland, Scotland, England, and Wales. His theory of a divinely designed archipelago was then appropriated by Froude, who applied this to the islands of the Pacific and then later to the British colonies of the Caribbean. Like current diaspora theories that focus on transoceanic migration, Froude argued that the British empire was primarily connected through maritime routes. "Oceana" he surmised, "would be a single commonwealth embraced in the arms of Neptune" (1886, 2). Froude remarks that Harrington would be "incredulous" to know that two centuries after his treatise

> More than fifty-million Anglo-Saxons would be spread over the vast continent of North America, carrying with them their religion, their laws, their language, and their manners; that the globe would be circled with their fleets; that in the Southern Hemisphere they would be in possession of territories larger than Europe, and more fertile than the richest parts of it; that wherever they went they would carry with them the genius of English freedom. (1886, 2)

Although all of these theories celebrate migrancy, Froude clearly draws upon the rhetoric of divine destiny, where the Anglo-Saxons are positioned, not in the centralizing metaphors of Pliny's Roman empire, but as diasporic Israelites, who "settled" and "multiplied" (1886, 2). Their "portmanteau biota," as Crosby would have it, is ignored in Froude's emphasis on culture rather than pathogens, democracy rather than enslavement and dispossession. Froude's vision of white diaspora excludes the material circumstances of British and Asian indentured laborers, African slaves, and the peoples who occupied these lands before the "genius of English freedom" was forced upon them.[21] This freedom, of course, was constituted by these experiments in enslavement and colonial rule.

By juxtaposing these imperial narratives of Anglo-Saxon diaspora alongside contemporary formulations of maritime migration in the black Atlantic and Pacific I do not mean that they are equivalent.[22] But their similar imaginaries suggest that we as scholars need to be attentive to the ways in which metaphors of spatial mobility, or routes, are adapted over time and may have colonial roots. Of course, my position as an American, residing in the belly of the beast, so to speak, means that this book is implicated in

30

its own critique. As we know from Edward Said (1983) and James Clifford (1992), theories travel and change across space and time; the naturalizing discourse of territorial belonging evidenced in diaspora theory demonstrates its effectiveness for diverse populations of different historical eras. The use of aquatic metaphors, a maritime grammar of the "peoples of the sea," helps us to recognize the importance of the ocean in the transnational imaginary and in diaspora theory in general. Moreover, historicizing the grammar of diaspora demonstrates how the sea is historically and imaginatively territorialized and cannot function as a facile *aqua nullius* or a blank template for transoceanic migration.

Our Common Heritage: The Blue Revolution

Why has there been such recent growth in the field of transoceanic diaspora studies, in viewing social, historical, and political relationships in terms of Atlantic, Pacific, and Indian Ocean studies? Why, when our relationship to the ocean is more estranged and distant than in any other period of human history, are academics suddenly concerned with the history of the sea? To give this an ecological frame, we might say that this heightened interest in the sea derives from our participation in its environmental pollution, similar to the ways in which colonists of the past deforested islands and then mystified this through romanticized ecology and conservation discourse. As Carolyn Merchant (1983) has shown, colonial powers fetishize what they have effectively destroyed. In juxtaposing oceanic discourse at the end of the nineteenth century with its contemporary counterparts, I also want to suggest that the rise in naturalized images of transoceanic diaspora derives from increased maritime territorialism. The modern tendency to incorporate and internalize fluid transnational spaces (as the sea in the blood) may suggest less about an attempt to transcend the boundaries of the ethnic nation-state than the desire to imaginatively integrate the nation's new maritime territory. Tracing the link between literature and empire, we see that this has historical precedence. For example, scholars have demonstrated that the rise of British maritime imperialism in the eighteenth century was reflected and sustained by its nautical literature. The United States, which wrested maritime dominance from the British in the nineteenth century, also naturalized its expanding naval fleets through the maritime novel. I suggest that just as these literary texts reflected military expansion into the seas, our current efforts to rethink the sea as history arise from a new era of global ocean governance and militarization. This is visible in Hau'ofa's seminal theory of a sea of islands, where the language that he employs to articulate "our common inheritance" (1997, 124), is derived from an unprecedented remapping of global sovereignty and common space: the 1982 U. N. Convention on the Law of the Sea (UNCLOS). While postcolonial studies has been concerned with mapping and territorialism, the field has not been attentive to the radical shifts in governance of 71 percent of the world's surface. Atlas, we might remember, was a god of the sea, linking the cartographic production of space with human understandings of the ocean. As I explain in the first chapter, the imperial measurement or rule of the ocean produced latitude and longitude and our modern understanding of universal time. By extension, the process of mapping the Atlantic with the passages of slave ships was crucial to rendering global Euclidean space and to our apprehensions of modernity.

To contextualize the significance of the U. N. Convention on the Law of the Sea we have to place it in the broader historical frame of European expansion and the rise of maritime empires. The first voyage of Columbus resulted in the Treaty of Tordesillas (1493–1494), which halved the world between the Spanish and Portuguese Christian empires by placing a vertical border through the Atlantic Ocean. This act catalyzed European debates about ocean space as property in which Renaissance writers such as Hugo Grotius reinvigorated ancient Roman laws about the nature of *mare clausem* and *mare liberum* (closed and open seas) as they were being redrawn in the Dutch East India territories (Anand 1993). With the rise of the colonial powers, a doctrine of "freedom of the seas" prevailed, defined and controlled by naval military forces. By World War II, ocean space was being rapidly armed, claimed, and mapped by the major maritime empires. The Pacific Ocean was particularly susceptible to American allegations that threats to their national security justified the appropriation of the seas for defense and the testing of missiles and nuclear weapons (Anand 1993, 75–77). By 1945, the first year of the Cold War, President Truman violated the freedom of the seas doctrine with his proclamation that the fisheries and maritime mineral resources contiguous to the U.S. coasts were national territory, greatly extending the littoral (coastal) state to 200 miles out to sea. Two years later Truman violated international law by annexing Micronesia, a "sea of islands" as large as the north Atlantic Ocean, an acquisition that more than doubled U.S. territory. When we factor in the 3.9 billion acres of submarine land and resources, 1.7 times the size of onshore territory, Truman actually *tripled* the size of the United States (National Academy of Sciences 1989, 1). Truman's proclamation had grown out of wartime oceanographic technologies that had revealed tremendous oil and manganese reserves on the ocean floor, subsoil, and beds; combined with the postwar interest in establishing submarine atomic weapons and the disposal of nuclear waste, the proclamation catalyzed a new territorialism of the oceans, an international struggle over ocean sovereignty that is ongoing today. In fact, at no other time in history are so many transnational oil companies prospecting and drilling for petroleum and hydrocarbons on the seabed floors.

UNCLOS was created by these contestations over ocean governance, and its charter was forged out of complex relations between the emergent postcolonial states and the dominant western powers. Because the number of sovereign territories doubled after World War II, developing states that had comparatively little in the way of economic leverage were able to gain a new majority lobbying power in the United Nations (Anand 1993, 79). The first U. N. Conference on the Law of the Sea was held in 1958; by the late 1960s, a vital "Third World coalition" became very active, revealing a "surprising cohesion" in terms of lobbying for material access to ocean resources that were dominated by the major maritime powers (Seyom Brown et al. 1977, 25–27). In 1967, Malta Representative Arvid Pardo made a historic address to the U. N. General Assembly. Using his position as a representative from a recently postcolonial island, he called for a resolution that would configure the ocean and its resources as the common heritage of mankind, shared equally among all nations—landlocked and coastal, industrialized and postcolonial. Likening the military scramble for the oceans to the carving up of Africa, Pardo called to replace the freedom of the seas doctrine with one of common heritage, based on the premise of peaceful purpose (Pardo 1975, ii). Pointing out the great economic inequities in the former colonies of Europe, the 1982 Convention legalized a provision that the General Assembly had recognized in 1967: the realm of the "high seas" was the "common heritage" of all nations, and revenue generated from seabed mining, exploration, and fishing must be evenly distributed across the globe, with particular recognition of the needs of the poorer nations (Anand 1993, 82; Allott 1993, 65–66). Because it ratified the interconnectedness of ecosystems and peoples, the 1982 Convention was heralded as the "first comprehensive, binding, enforceable, international environmental law," which, by establishing the notion of a common heritage, planted "the seed of a new economic order, of a new economic philosophy, and of a new relationship among people and between people and nature" (Borgese 1993, 33).

Importantly for the island writers I have mentioned, the Convention also sanctioned the concept of archipelagic waters, crucial to island nations in that it invested them with greater jurisdiction to protect and manage seaborne traffic, fish harvesting, and pollution (Van Dyke 1993a, 13). This was a literal and cartographic remapping of presumably isolated isles into a "sea of islands." The most powerful resistance to the treaty came from the United States, which accused the 1982 Convention of "communism" because it demarcates deep ocean space as a global commons, transforming *mare clausem* into *mare nostrum*. As Borgese points out, these allegations elide the point that the 1982 Convention refuses any territorialization of deep ocean space and thus circumvents future monopolies on maritime resources (1998, 59). Therefore *mare nostrum*, "our sea," represents a transnational agreement of mutual participation, conservation, and obligation (Allott 1993, 59). In many ways, the 1982 Convention legitimated indigenous philosophemes of environmental guardianship, particularly those drawn from the Pacific Islands (see Moana Jackson 1993a, 1993b).

It is difficult to image the extent to which the entire globe was remapped because of the ocean's alterity to continental humans and because the land bias of metropolitan centers often considers deep ocean space to be out of sight and out of mind. Yet in this radical territorial shift, the most important remapping of the globe in recent history, the 1982 Convention expanded the sovereignty of coastal nations to 12 nautical miles, their contiguous zones to 24 nautical miles, and established an Exclusive Economic Zone (EEZ) of 200 nautical miles. All in all, this translates to roughly 38 million square nautical miles of newly territorialized ocean space. The 1982 Convention enabled all coastal states to extend their territories into the ocean and claim seabed resources such as oil and minerals as well as pelagic fish as national assets.[23] (See Figures 1–3.) Of course, many states do not have 200 nautical miles between them and their neighbors, which has caused considerable difficulties in establishing the borders of the new ocean territories. In fact, these maritime boundaries are so heavily contested that it was a significant challenge to obtain maps for reproduction in this volume, particularly ones that represent ocean space to scale. Figure 1, a map of maritime claims and the worldwide EEZ, illustrates the dramatic ways in which all nation-states have expanded into the ocean in the past twenty-five years. Figure 2, reflecting the EEZ of the United States and its Pacific Island territories, demonstrates the vast and strategic stretches of Oceania controlled by the U.S. Navy. Figure 3, of the EEZ in the Pacific Islands, provides an excellent visual representation of the ways in which a "sea of islands" may literally expand its terrestrial borders, remapping what otherwise might be dismissed as insignificant "dots" on the globe or, as Charles de Gaulle described the Caribbean, "specks of dust" (quoted in Glissant, 1989, n.p.). While on the one hand legislators were forced to recognize the

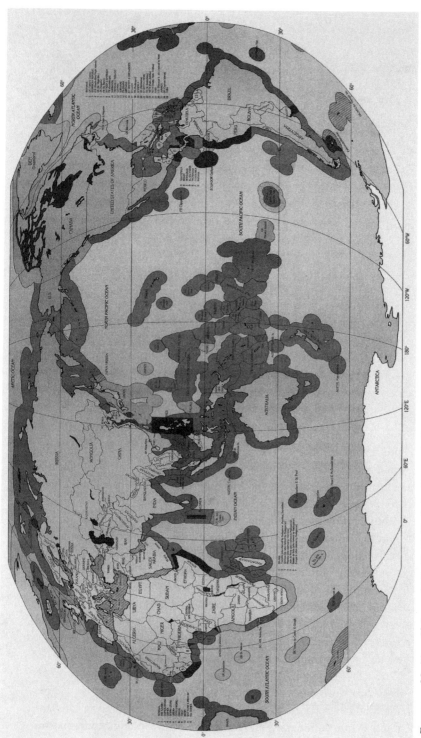

FIGURE 1. Maritime Claims and Worldwide Exclusive Economic Zones. Courtesy of Judith Fenwick.

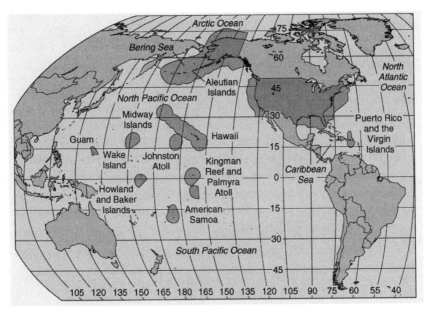

Figure 2. U.S. Exclusive Economic Zones.

fluidity of the earth's only ocean and abandon the myth of seven seas, on the other hand the scramble for the oceans fixed this fluid dynamic space to suit a new era of maritime territorialism.

Pardo's vision for a shared global commons—an international governance that would ensure that 71 percent of the world's surface would not be polluted, exploited, armed with nuclear weapons, and pillaged of its biotic and mineral resources by industrialized nations—has certainly not been realized. The vast oceanic stretches of Micronesia, those areas even well beyond nuclearized Bikini and Enewetak, have been dumping grounds for U.S. toxic chemicals such as Agent Orange, dioxins, and nuclear radiation (Van Dyke 1993b, 221), a poignant reminder that the Latin for *vastus* signifies the ocean as well as waste. At least twenty-three naval nuclear reactors rest on the ocean floor, mainly from nuclear-powered submarines, while an additional fifty nuclear weapons have been reported lost at sea (Handler 1993, 420).

This is a dire time for our terraqueous globe, but the island writers discussed in this book have derived some hopeful models from ocean governance. First, in just the most material of terms, this radical remapping of the globe has greatly increased the political and economic viability of

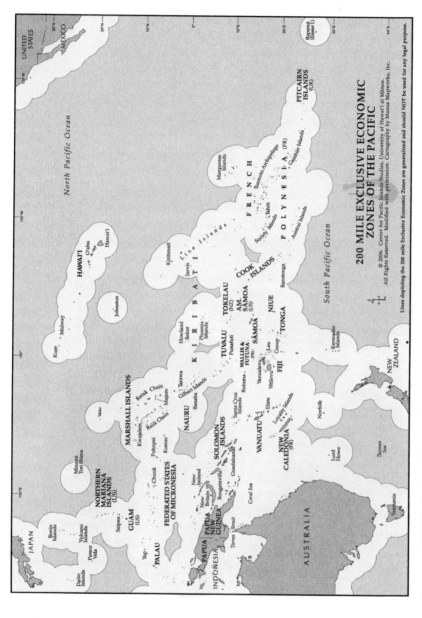

FIGURE 3. 200 Mile Exclusive Economic Zones of the Pacific. Courtesy of Center for Pacific Island Studies, University of Hawai'i, Manoa Mapworks.

many small island nations, not to mention their literal presence on the world map. Second, island writers have provided new ways to destabilize national and ethnic boundaries by drawing upon a transoceanic imaginary that reflects the origins of island cultures as well as their imbrication in the fluid trajectories of globalization. Reminding us of the irony that the Law of the Sea encouraged a territorialism over those marine areas where none existed before, Hau'ofa turns to those other interpellations of the sea in which it is "an open and ever flowing reality," envisioning the ocean, like Pardo, as "our waterway to each other" and a "route to the rest of the world" (1997, 143–144).

As a "Blue Revolution" (Borgese 1998, 14), this model of the ocean as common heritage reflects a new territorialism of the globe as well as a vision of its deterritorialism, making a vital yet unacknowledged contribution to the spatial configuration of diaspora, indigenous, and postcolonial studies. One of the primary ways the ocean can be deterritorialized is through the tidalectic imagination of island literatures. Jamaican author Andrew Salkey is one of the few writers to take up the nuclearization of the seas in his hilarious short story collection, *Anancy, Traveller* (1992). His trickster spider-hero decides to solve this problem of "dread technology" (134) by confronting the ruling powers of the United States, the "Land of the Super-I," a space of surveillance and hyperindividualism. To do so, Anancy "tief every scrap of *tonium*" held by the "Holocaust" office in "Washing Town" and in "all the other nukes countries" (19). Then he concocts a "ganja and mushroom tea" to get his military and political opponents "dreamy and nice, like them on the verge o' making poem" (134). This allows him to "tief way the powers power" (129) from "them that don't consider island people as real people, no how" (130). He hides these items in a bag at the bottom of an "ocean that see plenty, know plenty and hold secret tight as magnet" (11). Since "is only fish (he) can trust" (21), Anancy and his pelagic companions are the only ones to "know how sea bottom going save the world!" (21). Salkey's text is a "Blue Revolution" of sorts, a reversal of the rendering of sea as waste that establishes a creative deterritorialism of the oceans through a localizing creole sensibility. He also marshals a different kind of submarine unity between islanders and their nonhuman allies in the seas. Of course, what Anancy and sea bottom do with all of this poisonous "tonium" remains outside the boundaries of the text—suitably, Salkey leaves the seabed unfathomed.

Other Caribbean allegories have not been so hopeful about the new territorialism of the seas and have questioned who benefits from the "Blue Revolution." I would like to conclude this section by turning briefly to

Ana Lydia Vega's short story, "Cloud Cover Caribbean" ("Encancara-nublado") to demonstrate its engagement with these new models of oceanic territorialism, particularly the ways in which the United States has asserted maritime dominance in the region. This Puerto Rican text pinpoints U.S. imperialism as one of the obstacles to Caribbean regionalism and highlights the ways in which the lack of *national* sovereignty over the seas prevents *regional* belonging. Moreover, Vega parodies the construction of a masculine Caribbean regional identity through the objectification of women. Her work exemplifies some of the more troubling aspects of the new maritime territorialism and the way in which women's bodies function as aquatic metaphors while being excluded from regional participation. The publication of her collection in the same year as the 1982 Convention and her depiction of these "Stories of shipwreck" suggest a direct engagement with the colonial castaways of the past and the fate of contemporary "boat people" or *balseros* in the wake of contemporary models of ocean governance.

Vega opens her allegorical story with the protagonist Antenor escaping his home on a "makeshift vessel" on a "wretched sea adventure" that seems like a "pleasure cruise" compared to his experience of poverty, famine, and terror from the *tonton macoutes* in Haiti (1989, 106–107). In addition to its Trojan roots, Antenor's name is playfully drawn from the nineteenth-century Haitian anthropologist, diplomat, and pan-Caribbeanist, Joseph-Anténor Firmin, who had argued presciently for the equality of the races in an era of biological determinism and called for an Antillean Federation half a century before it was attempted in the British West Indies. Antenor then rescues two separate victims of shipwreck, a Dominican and a Cuban, whose disdain for their black Haitian host and competitive behavior suggest the impossibility of a pan-Caribbean union. The failed allegory of Caribbean regionalism is placed in the context of colonial shipwreck narratives, in which Antenor plays "the discoverer while secretly wondering if the world really is round," who fears that he may plunge off the edge "into the fabled chasms of the monsters" (106). Antenor is unsurprised by the appearance of the "shipwrecked" Dominican, Diogenes, named after the Greek cynic thought to be a founder of cosmopolitanism. After having "established an international brotherhood of hunger, a solidarity of dreams," the two men are annoyed but unsurprised by the appearance of the Cuban Carmelo, who appears "beside the proverbial plank of the shipwrecked sailor" (107). Although the omniscient narrator switches between the linguistic and cultural registers of their nations, the three men spend much of their time fighting over food, rum, and women, indicating that even Vega's narrative framework cannot contain the complexities of Caribbean (male) identity.

Vega places her story in the long colonial tradition of shipwreck and castaway narratives that mystified the process of European maritime expansion. Antenor's lack of knowledge about the contours of the earth and his fear of monsters aligns him with the founding navigator of the region, Columbus, who is invoked when Antenor determines that "Miami was as far off as China" (110). Yet the author undermines this patriarch's legacy by juxtaposing these fantastic fears alongside the more pressing terrors of famine and violence by the *macoutes*. This calls into question the models of ethnic diaspora upheld by Froudian "people of the sea" by demonstrating the inability for contemporary "boat people" to effectively navigate or chart their own journeys on land or at sea. Far from being *aqua nullius*, the sea in Vega's story represents a trickster character, often rocking the boat and upsetting human relations. The sea is also described as an "ugly thing" and a "muscled arm," a metaphor that becomes clear when the men start fighting, capsize the boat, and are intercepted by an American ship. "The captain, an Aryan, Apollo-like seadog," has the men pulled on board and barks: "'Get those niggers down there and let the spiks take care of them'" (110). The refugees are led "to the ship's hold" (110). The Mediterranean grammar that Vega employs to categorize this seascape, such as Antenor, Diogenes, Apollo, and the confused cartographies of Columbus, evokes the ways in which the Aegean was used as a template for the mapping of the Caribbean, a space historian W. Adolphe Roberts once described as a "potent womb, our sea of destiny, the Mediterranean of the West" (1940, 19).

Fifty years after Roberts, Benítez-Rojo would also imagine the flows of the region in feminized terms, critiquing the capitalist project as "inseminating the Caribbean womb with the blood of Africa" (1992, 5). In Vega's "ship's hold," a clear reference to the middle passage and a new space for the Caribbean's primary export, human labor, the men encounter an altogether different mapping of the transoceanic imaginary. The Mediterranean model for naming the figures in this story (Diogenes was "a neoclassical baptismal flourish" 107) is juxtaposed to the men's interpellation into the colonial hierarchies of race ("niggers") and language ("spiks"). In the hold, the Dominican and Cuban men have the initial "pleasure of hearing their mother tongue spoken," which even the Haitian "welcomed" (110). But Vega dismantles regional identification based on language and critiques her own omnipotence as narrator when a "Puerto Rican voice growled through the gloom: 'If you want to feed your bellies here you're going to have to work, and I mean work. A gringo don't give nothing away. Not to his own mother'" (111). The "growling" aligns this anonymous vernacular voice with the Aryan "sea-dog" and homogenizes these diverse Caribbean migrants under the rubric of exploited labor. The denial of maternal identification (to motherland or mother tongue) is the price paid to the gatekeeper of the hold, the cost of their assimilation into the U.S. nation-state, metonymically represented by the Aryan ship. Read tidalectically, we can see that the gendering of the land/sea relationship is articulated in terms of a feminized motherland and a fluid Caribbean "womb." In fact, the only moment the three bickering men had found common "ground" on the boat is when they spoke of the "internationally famous backsides of the island's famous beauties" (109). As sexualized or maternal objects, women are invoked as the necessary symbolic background to the larger male theatre of national and regional identification. This gendered split between the regional/national is much like the rendering of the global/local, which positions "women and femininity as rooted, traditional, and charged with maintaining domestic continuity in the face of flux and instability caused by global movements that, explicitly or not, embody a quality of masculinity" (Freeman 2001, 1017). Like the concept of a woman in every port, this relation between roots and routes literalizes the sexual tidalectic between a cruder set of homonyms: "land, ho" and "seamen." [24]

Benítez-Rojo's ideal that "the Peoples of the Sea (are) traveling together toward the infinite" (1992, 16) is complicated when we consider the limitations imposed on refugees and transoceanic voyagers. Had Antenor been without his Dominican and Cuban companions, his fate may have been radically different. Thanks to an interdiction agreement signed in 1981 between Ronald Reagan and Jean-Claude Duvalier, the United States agreed to intercept Haitian refugees coming by boat and forcibly return them to Haiti, an agreement that violated international law and the refugee interception provisions established by the Law of the Sea. [25] In the face of this history, Vega's short story brilliantly adopts and then discards all the possible sites of identification for Caribbean "peoples of the sea": from geopolitical status to masculinity, from linguistic affiliation to the coerced production of global capitalism. In 1962 C. L. R. James declared: "The Caribbean is now an American sea. Puerto Rico is its show piece" (1993, 308). Writing a year after the Reagan proclamation claimed 4 million square miles of the marine space of the continental United States and its island colonies (including Puerto Rico), Vega's story highlights the ways in which the policies of colonial nation-states engage tidalectically with the fate of those adrift at sea.

As a "Blue Revolution," the Law of the Sea continues to challenge our notions of time and space, in a continuing and necessary dialogue on ocean governance. As Hau'ofa demonstrates, it is a model for an "oceanic identity [that] transcend[s] insularity," but it cannot be interpreted without addressing territorial claims from the land. The "sea is our pathway to each other and to everyone else," but utilizing metaphors of feminine fluidity often suppresses the violence of the crossing and erases the continual military surveillance of ocean space. It is only by addressing the violence alongside the ocean's hopeful potentials that we might determine that "the sea is our most powerful metaphor, the ocean is in us" (Hau'ofa 1997, 148).

Routes and Roots

In engaging the tidalectic relationship between the homonyms "routes" and "roots," this study builds upon a body of cultural studies scholarship in an attempt to explore the nexus of time-space in postcolonial island literatures. Because this work destabilizes the national, ethnic, and even regional frameworks generally employed for literary study, it cannot take any of these parameters for granted. As such, it is a work concerned with metaphors of origins and belonging as well as their current political negotiations and even mystifications. My first chapter, "Middle Passages: Modernity and Creolization," explores how the ocean functions as a metonymic history for the millions of Africans who were transported across the Atlantic. I outline a history of the ways in which British maritime expansion sought to render the vastness of ocean *space* into temporalized *place* through a system of cognitive and literal maps that ranged from nautical literature to the charting of longitude. Building upon the work of Atlantic historians and diaspora theorists, I turn to the chronotope of the transatlantic ship, exploring how the multiethnically constituted slave ships that crossed the Atlantic suggest a type of time-space compression prior to industrial modernity. I focus on John Hearne's novel *The Sure Salvation* (1981), a fictionalization of the middle passage that suggests that if "space is a practiced place" (de Certeau 1984, 117), one may read a narrative "practice" of the Atlantic Ocean. In his revision of Herman Melville's *Benito Cereno*, Hearne inscribes an illegal English slave ship in 1860, decades after abolition, symbolizing the failures of linear chronologies of progress. Moreover, his depiction of the ship's stasis, its immobility and timelessness amidst a literal waste of feces, blood, vomit, and sperm that envelops the ship and the middle passage experience, immobilizes the telos of movement across space needed to render the progress of history. Consequently, *The Sure Salvation* renders the sea as history through the metaphor of the sea as waste. The corporeality of the ship, its workers, and its slaves emphasizes an embodied history and the ways in which the bourgeois racialization of dirt and pollution was constituted in the oceanic "waste" of Atlantic modernity.

In this exploration of the sea as a dynamic space of cultural, ontological, and historical origins, I build upon Glissant's assertion that "the abyss is a tautology" in which the ocean signifies a "vast beginning . . . whose time is marked by these balls and chains gone green" (1997, 6). This beginning is linked to the creation of modern time through the Atlantic slave trade and the construction of longitude, which harnessed the fluidity of the ocean to homogenize the globe into universal time. In this chapter, the ocean is figuratively sounded as a space of black diaspora origins, a gesture that Caribbean writers share with Walcott to "harvest ancestral voices from [the] surf" (1986, 16) and to chart what the "historian cannot hear: the howls/of all the races that crossed the water" (285).

Chapter 2, "Vessels of the Pacific: An Ocean in the Blood," examines how Pacific Island writers have mobilized precolonial seafaring routes as the historical roots to globalizing fluidity and flows. Inspired by Caribbean writers such as Walcott, and by the fact that the islands are literally growing through geological activity, scholars like Hauʻofa have conceptualized the region as a dynamic "sea of islands," connected by ancient and modern travelers. Because the transoceanic imagination employs the ship or voyaging canoe as a vessel that sustains regionalism, this chapter traces out a genealogy of Pacific vehicles of sovereignty, the Vaka Pasifika. To recover the voyaging canoe as a vessel of history, I begin with a discussion of how the region has become synonymous with the economic entity, Asia Pacific, and trace how the U.S. military fostered the myth of island isolation as part of its nuclearization and "scramble for the oceans" during the Cold War. Military-funded projects from Pacific anthropology to Thor Heyerdahl's celebrated *Kon-Tiki* journey were able to justify these ideas of island isolation only by dismissing the histories of Polynesian seafaring that led to the settlement of every island in the largest ocean on the globe, and by replacing these historic routes with trajectories of Aryan migration.

After exploring the close relationship between the militarization of the Pacific and its epistemic by-products in anthropology and area studies, I turn to the revitalization of indigenous seafaring histories, evident in the 1976 voyage of the Hawaiian canoe *Hokuleʻa* to Tahiti and visible in contemporary Pacific literatures. I explore how the concept of the vessel shifts from its interpellation as empty basin to a corporeal metaphor of a people's genealogy, history, and sovereignty. In my exploration of Vincent Eri's novel *The Crocodile* and Tom Davis's *Vaka*, I demonstrate that like the grammar of diaspora, canoe metaphysics draw from fluid metaphors of kinship and blood. This chapter argues that narratives of Pacific voyaging reflect a complex discourse of indigenous diaspora or native routes that likens the fluidity of the maritime region to ethnic kinship, positioning the Pacific vaka as a vehicle of ancestral and global history and inscribing the "ocean in the blood." The concept of the vessel renders tidalectics visible—it is the principal way in which roots are connected to routes, and islands connected to the sea. Whether imagined as a voyaging canoe, a naval ship, a raft, or as ethnic blood, the vessel is integral to claims to sovereignty in the region.

In an era of globalization, travel remains a seductive concept that is positively coded along the lines of progress and innovation. It still remains questionable to what extent the shift from national to diasporic literary studies over the past two decades entails a self-reflexive and critical recognition of the contemporary economic, military, and material manifestations of global capitalism. Moreover, the ways in which these theories of travel and diaspora are racialized and gendered have not been fully explored. Although scholars have done much to deepen our understanding of migrancy, nomadology, and diaspora, many have overlooked the ways in which stability and rootedness are often conflated with stagnancy, indigeneity, and women. Mary Gordon has noted that literature in the Americas "connects females with stasis and death; males with movement and life" (1991, 17). Given the fact that the etymological root of diaspora is spore and sperm (Helmreich 1992, 243), it is not surprising that western literary narratives, as Eric Leed demonstrates, produce history through a masculine telos of the "spermatic journey." Building upon their insights, Janet Wolff has cogently argued that "just as practices and ideologies of *actual* travel operate to exclude or pathologize women, so the use of that vocabulary as metaphor necessarily produces androcentric tendencies in theory" (1992, 224). As Carole Boyce Davies points out, "It is not an accident that it happens to be men who are asserting the right to theory and travel" (1992, 45). Thus the first section of *Routes and Roots* is particularly attentive to the ways in which masculine travelers are positioned on a ship that is likened to the world, a homosocial rendering of the domestic realm without women. What are the consequences of valorizing a masculine shipboard community as a symbol of transnationalism, labor unity, or creolization? Who benefits from a discourse in which women are bounded to an archaic nation-state? How do women enter history when it is produced by a migrant community of men?

By raising these questions, the first section highlights the ways in which the concept of a feminine sea is a vital metaphor to generate and sustain the ideologies of masculine reproduction on the ship. With its similar grammar of feminized flows and fluidity, one can extend this to the discourse of globalization as well.[26] Yet this creates a paradox. "The notion of feminine identity as relational, fluid, and without clear boundaries seems more congruent with the perpetual mobility of travel than is the presumed solidity and objectivity of masculine identity" (Wolff 1992, 31–32). Yet it is precisely the *lack* of ego fluidity in dominant forms of masculinity that makes it necessary to feminize travel as fluidity. By associating women with regeneration and (pro)creation, metaphors of femininity become essential to a masculinist paradigm of travel discourse that pathologizes female travelers themselves. As I explain in the first chapter, the rigid hierarchy of the ship and the vast fluidity of the sea are mutually constitutive elements of the transoceanic imaginary. By extension, the contained boundaries of the masculine subject operate in contradistinction to the vast fluidity of the feminized sea. The ship and the sea are necessarily gendered female so that a contained group of male travelers, a homosocial community, may maintain a heterosexual tidalectic associated with ocean space. Interestingly, the ship has not always been conceived as an exclusively masculine community contained by a feminized vessel; in England the term for ship was initially understood as male (Kemp, 1976, 780). Only in the sixteenth century was the ship attributed with feminine qualities and figureheads, and while we understand it as a homosocial space, it was as late as 1840 that women were banned from living aboard docked British Naval ships (Kemp 302, 800). The phrase "show" or "shake a leg" derives from the need to differentiate sailors from their female companions in the hammocks aboard ship (Kemp 800), while a "son of a gun" refers to the birth of (male) children on the gundecks of British Naval ships (Kemp 816). In most of the novels discussed in this section, actual women are not imagined on the ship, but as in Vega's story, symbols of femininity are vital to sustain the men's receptivity to intercultural contact and to maintain their mobile structure of the domestic. In other words, a symbolic grammar of feminized vessels and flows enables the homosocial community on the ship to maintain porous social boundaries and to reproduce, both narratively and as agents of history. If, as C. L. R. James asserts: "the ship is only a miniature of the world in which we live" (1978, 79), this suggests that the transoceanic imagination may reflect the gendered spatial logic of the nation-state.[27]

Although the transoceanic focus of the first section of this book seems to privilege routes, my examination of these literary works demonstrates that the discourse of diaspora is constituted in relation to the stabilizing notions of femininity, nation, and indigeneity. This is why it is crucial that we engage a tidalectic between land and sea, examining how indigenous narratives and epistemologies are essential to the constitution of dominant productions of diaspora. This tidalectic helps to complicate theories such as Anthony Appiah's notion of "rooted cosmopolitanism" (1998), because genealogical roots, in indigenous communities, are vital to ontological and legal claims against the colonial nation-state. Since postcolonial theories have tended to celebrate nomadism and cosmopolitanism without always addressing domestic issues such as cultural and national sovereignty, the second section of *Routes and Roots* departs from watery trajectories to focus on indigenous cartographies, exploring how island novelists nativize the literary landscape.

This book not only makes the claim that postcolonial and diaspora studies have tended to displace indigenous discourses, it takes one step farther to argue that the valorization of "routes" is constituted by a dichotomous rendering of native "roots."[28] Chapter 3, "Dead Reckoning: National Genealogies in Aotearoa / New Zealand," discusses the ways in which June Mitchell's novel *Amokura* (1978) charts native genealogies—the legacy of the dead—by reconfiguring the narrative structures of novel and nation through the use of Maori spiral time. Like the concept of "moving islands," which draws upon an indigenous "time sense" (Lewis 1994, 120) charted across distance, the spiral is a trope that symbolizes a dynamic interrelation between the temporal and spatial. As such, this challenges theories of nationalism by revealing that indigenous practices of national belonging are far more layered and inclusive than diaspora theorists would let us believe. This chapter contributes to recent discussions in Pacific studies about native epistemologies by exploring genealogy or whakapapa in Aotearoa / New Zealand, defined as an ancestral and bodily inheritance, a "meta-physics" or corporeal history. Although Maori literature is not associated with the practice of diaspora, I explore how Mitchell's rendering of an internal migration in nineteenth-century Aotearoa / New Zealand complicates the tidalectic between indigeneity and dispersal and literalizes the definition of whakapapa as to layer. By drawing Mitchell's spiral genealogies alongside Keri Hulme's Booker Prize–winning novel, *the bone people*

(1983), which also engages a rhizomatic layering of place, I foreground how Maori whakapapa is utilized as a paradigm of national settlement or native landfall. Ultimately, I define "dead reckoning" as an indigenous methodology that draws its foundation from the presence of the ancestors in the national landscape, rendering a literal body of history. Because Aotearoa/New Zealand, like many other islands in the Pacific, is understood to be a fish hauled from the sea by the demigod Maui, I explore how this concept of the pelagic or moving island complicates sedentary notions of land and soil.

"Adrift and Unmoored: Globalization and Urban Indigeneity" builds upon the previous chapter to chart how a fluid discourse of roots offers a model of native historiography in the destabilizing wake of the postmodern state. This chapter locates the process of globalization in the Pacific as vital to the unmooring of rural indigenous identities yet also crucial to the political consolidation of pan-tribal, regional, and urban sovereignty movements. I focus on Albert Wendt's dystopic novel, *Black Rainbow* (1992), which depicts homeless indigenous peoples who must revitalize their genealogies to resist a global capitalist state that emphasizes the "ever-moving present" over a native past. The novel responds to an unprecedented shift in the Pacific in which the global privatization of state territories catalyzed native migration as well as sovereignty movements that reconfigured the production of local historiography. His protagonist must "confess" his history to the government tribunal in order to be accepted into the "ever-moving present" of the capitalist state. I read this as Wendt's prescient warning about the ways in which historiography has become a lucrative business and an expanded domain of the state in the wake of land and resource claims submitted to the Waitangi Tribunal, an agency established to ensure the 1840 Treaty is honored. Depicting a protagonist of mixed heritage who attempts to sustain both family memory and national history, Wendt charts how Pacific diaspora might be usefully refashioned in terms of a creolized indigeneity that reflects global cosmopolitanism (routes) while maintaining genealogical continuity for land claims and sovereignty (roots).

Although Caribbean literary discourse has been traditionally mapped in terms of diaspora and "ex-isle," my final chapter expands the parameters of discussion by addressing how indigenous presence is excavated as a trope of terrestrial historiography in the anglophone islands, particularly in Michelle Cliff's *No Telephone to Heaven* (1987) and Merle Collins's *The Colour of Forgetting* (1995). Because British colonists arrived in the region after much of the indigenous population had been decimated, Carib and Arawak historical presence has not factored significantly in the anglophone Caribbean imagination until very recently. "Landfall: Carib and Arawak Sedimentation" investigates the ways in which writers such as Cliff, Collins, Jamaica Kincaid, and Wilson Harris have complicated the discourse of black nationalism to chart an indigenous Caribbean history in a dialogue with later arrivants. These efforts to localize and indigenize Caribbean history must be seen as a resistance to the ongoing pressures of outmigration from the region and as an effort to highlight the importance and viability of small island communities, or local roots in the wake of globalizing routes. They reflect a tidalectic engagement with routes and roots, upholding cultural creolization and offering a poetic corrective to materialist approaches to Caribbean historiography. Like Harris, Collins and Cliff forge complex alliances between African diaspora subjects and the traces of Carib and Arawak presence in their depictions of island colonization, with postcolonial nationalism inscribed as an ideal, but ultimately unattainable, landfall.

The title of this book, which borrows from James Clifford, highlights the central tenet of *Routes*: "Practices of displacement might emerge as *constitutive* of cultural meanings rather than as their simple transfer or extension" (1997, 3). As Davies observes, "Discourses of home and exile are central to any understanding of the politics of location" (1992, 20). The Caribbean and Pacific Islands I investigate here are characterized by a tidalectic engagement with settlement and migration. As I have discovered in the process of writing this book, the relationship between roots and routes is mutually constitutive and this can be imagined in historic and material terms. Writing about Vanuatu, anthropologist Joël Bonnemaison asks: "Can the tree, symbol of rootedness and stability, be reconciled with the canoe, symbol of unrestricted wandering?" (1994, 30). He determines that it can, since in that context the human is perceived as a rooted and fixed tree whereas the people represent a "canoe that follows 'roads' and explores the wide world" (30). Using seemingly contradictory terms such as "the land canoe" (43) and "territorial mobility" (48), Bonnemaison and other scholars have explained these indigenous spatial metaphors by emphasizing the profoundly circular patterns of both traditional and modern migration. Indigenous and diaspora epistemologies are crucial interests of this book, and the tree, a source of metaphysical roots and also a vehicle of transoceanic diaspora, represents that tidalectic crossing between space and time. This is why it's no accident that the opening scene of Walcott's epic poem *Omeros* depicts Caribbean trees as ancestral gods who must be felled in order for the Greek-inspired fishermen, Achille(s) and Hector, to fashion them into canoes and retrace their African routes to the sea. The transition from roots to routes suggests an imaginative return to origins in which "the logs gathered that thirst/for the sea which their own vined bodies were born with" (1990, 7). It is this tidalectic between land and sea, settlement and diaspora, that these postcolonial island literatures bring to the foreground, as we "catch the noise/of the surf lines," of the "sea's parchment atlas" (13).

PART I

The Sea is History

Transoceanic Diasporas

CHAPTER 1

Middle Passages
Modernity and Creolization

> The Atlantic is a rass of a history ocean.
> —Andrew Salkey, *Anancy, Traveller*

One of the most important Caribbean contributions to the conceptualization of space and time is an originary narrative of transoceanic diaspora. While scholars are increasingly turning to the Atlantic as a paradigm of transnational crossings and flows, the conceptual implications of this oceanic model have been deeply explored in the Caribbean, where tidalectics reconceptualize diaspora historiography. As I've explained, tidalectics foreground a cyclical model of history and resist the teleology of a Hegelian dialectical synthesis.[1] Drawing upon land/sea cartography, tidalectics foreground historical trajectories of dispersal and destabilize island isolation by highlighting waves of migrant landfalls into the Caribbean. This dynamic model is an important counter-narrative to discourses of filial rootedness and narrow visions of ethnic nationalism. This chapter explores the fluid metaphors of the Atlantic to theorize a Caribbean originary imagination and its engagement with the chronotope, or time-space, of narrative history. The shift in focus from terrestrial history to the transoceanic spaces that enabled African, Asian, European, and indigenous crossings to the islands complicates genealogical roots and destabilizes the colonial architecture that literally constructed the region as European. In this body of literature, water is associated with fluidity, flux, creolization, and originary routes.

The colonial balkanization of the islands into discrete language regions is destabilized by Kamau Brathwaite's contention that Caribbean "unity is submarine" (1974, 64). The history and geography of the Caribbean suggest a tidalectic engagement with land and sea and their associated narratives of empire, transoceanic diaspora, and postcolonial nation-building. While most scholars have focused on the slave plantation system as the originary mechanism of creolization in the Caribbean, they have neglected the ways in which the region's writers have mobilized a fluid oceanic imaginary, positioning the Atlantic as a shifting cultural origin of modernity and creolization—in the words of Jan Carew, "on an island your cosmos of the imagination begins with the sea" (1984, 34).

This concern with cognitive (re)mapping, or imaginatively occupying Caribbean and Atlantic seascapes, differs from other theories of reterritorialization because tidalectics are concerned with the fluidity of water as a shifting site of history and invoke the peoples who navigated or were coerced into transoceanic migrations.[2] As I have examined the regional maritime imagination elsewhere, this chapter addresses the literary trajectories of the middle passage and the ways in which the ocean functions as a metonymic history for the millions of Africans who were transported across the Atlantic.[3] I explore Derek Walcott's assertion that "the sea is history" in the first Caribbean novel set exclusively in the middle passage, John Hearne's *The Sure Salvation* (1981). Here the Atlantic Ocean is figuratively sounded as a space of black diaspora origins and world modernity.

This chapter is also concerned with the ways in which diaspora space is conceptualized in relation to modern time. Spatial theorists from David Harvey to Michel de Certeau have made important contributions to our understanding of time-space compression and how the movement of bodies transforms space into place. These theorists suggest that perceptions of time are constituted by physical and conceptual *movement across terrestrial space*. My intervention is to broaden this use of space to consider first, how immobility, or the lack of movement across space, can produce history, and second, how one's location in the perpetually moving ocean may produce alternative renderings of time-space. Turning from terrestrial landscapes to the alterity of the ocean raises questions as to how one may localize and thus historicize fluid space. Therefore the first section of this chapter sketches a history of how British colonial expansion sought to render the vastness of ocean space into temporalized place, while the second part turns to the transatlantic slave ship, building upon the work of Paul Gilroy (1993) and others to position the crossing as a time-space compression that helped constitute modernity.[4] To address the latter, I have adopted Bakhtin's notion of the chronotope to explore slave-ship narratives. He explains:

> In the literary artistic chronotope, spatial and temporal indicators
> are fused into one carefully thought-out, concrete whole. Time, as it
> were, thickens, takes on flesh, becomes artistically visible; likewise,
> space becomes charged and responsive to the movements of time, plot
> and history. (1981, 84)

Eric Sundquist has used this passage to explore the compressed time-space of Herman Melville's *Benito Cereno* (1855), a novel that mystifies a shipboard slave rebellion and has provided a structural and ideological template for *The Sure Salvation*. "Melville's story suggests the essential doubleness of the American ship of state . . . the ark of the covenant that authorized both liberty and slavery, leaving the national mission adrift, becalmed amidst incalculable danger" (1993, 143–144).[5] Hearne revises *Benito Cereno* to highlight the "doubleness" of the *British* "ship of state" as it sustains and criminalizes the slave trade after its abolition in 1807. In both novels, the slave ship's stagnancy, its paradoxical *immobility* in fluid oceanic space suspends and "thickens" perceptions of time. Hearne's text inscribes how time is rendered in the commodified and spatially compressed "flesh" of enslaved Africans and positions the middle passage as a fluid site of African and European modernity.

These transatlantic ships were unevenly situated within what Peter Linebaugh and Marcus Rediker refer to as the "hydrarchy," defined as "the organization of the maritime state from above, and the self-organization of the sailors from below" (2000, 144).[6] My intervention is to bring the literary inscription of African slaves in relation to the hydrarchy and ship-as-chronotope to gesture to the ways in which the material compression of slaves in the holds of ships may offer a different context for understanding Atlantic modernity and its nexus of space and time. Secondly, and vital to the aims of this book as a whole, I explore how localizing maritime space is the process by which one establishes that "the sea is history." Walcott's phrase has appeared as the epigraph to countless Caribbean texts and inspired Hearne's novel. While the ocean, perhaps more than any other space on earth, has been either ignored or read as a transparent, transitive, and asocial place by the vast majority of spatial theorists, ocean space and the Atlantic in particular contributed to the rise of the novel and its narrative encoding of modern time. For most of western Europe, the Atlantic has been the formative space of maritime imperialism and its literary counterpart, the castaway and nautical adventure narrative. This is why it is no coincidence that the ocean is the driving spatial mechanism of one of the earliest, most influential English novels: *Robinson Crusoe* (1719). As the British colonized territories across the Atlantic, Pacific, and Indian oceans, these bodies of water were interpellated as sites of muscular Christianity in nineteenth-century British literature. It was by adopting this template of transoceanic and masculine imperialism that many nineteenth-century Anglo-American nautical fictions helped extend the conceptual and geographic boundaries of the United States into the Caribbean and Pacific.[7] Thus Hearne's novel, which inscribes the ebb of British maritime expansion amidst the rising tide of revolutionary subjects in the nineteenth-century Americas, reflects how British nautical literature helped to constitute U.S. political and cultural production. At this point I would like to outline a heuristic genealogy of British maritime narratives, addressing the ways in which, if "space is a practiced place" (de Certeau 1984, 117), one may read a narrative "practice" of the Atlantic Ocean, specifically the middle passage.

Temporalizing Ocean Space

> Where are your monuments, your battles, your martyrs?
> Where is your tribal memory? Sirs,
> In that grey vault. The sea. The sea
> Has locked them up. The sea is History.
> —Derek Walcott, "The Sea is History"

In his introduction to *The Oxford Book of the Sea*, Jonathan Raban points out that the English language "is littered with dead nautical metaphors" (1992, 7), semantic remnants of transoceanic histories. Another maritime scholar contends that "no language in the world is so replete with nautical terms" (Batchelder 1929, 625). Words of spatial mobility such as navigate, traverse, launch, (a)board, course, moor, anchor, and wake all arose from British maritime activity and, while set adrift from their watery origins, function here as a marked "sea grammar" with which to address the language of ocean time and space.[8] As I will explain, these terms suggest a spatial philosophy, a telos of movement across water that subordinates time to space, rather than the more temporally inflected discourse of terrestrial knowledge.[9] In fact, the rapid emergence of seventeenth-century English nautical dictionaries suggests the necessity to translate a vocabulary of early modern globalization at the moment when Britain began to effectively compete with its European counterparts in transatlantic colonization.

Paradoxically, the expansion of empire led to more entrenched conflations of nation with race, a legacy that continues to nationalize scholarly boundaries, even in fields such as black diaspora and Atlantic studies. As Christopher Connery has shown, an "oceanic feeling" hardly precludes nationalist bias or the expansion of state capital in the service of empire. Because histories, like bodies of water, stream into one another, I want to foreground the complex system of economic and cultural flows from the

Mediterranean to the broader Atlantic. This is especially important given the nationalist contours of maritime studies that often relegate non-European subjects (and technologies) to the symbolic hold of transatlantic ships. This Mediterranean Sea complex, specifically the spatial logic of the Greek and Roman empires, was often mobilized in the discourse of British empire-building, while its non-European others were submerged.[10] While Atlantic studies are suffused with the language of newness and innovation, they all too often eclipse the contributions of other ocean histories. The maxim "Britannia rules the waves" was incorporated into a teleological narrative of *nationalist* empire, yet this process was made possible only through contact with more developed African, Arab, and Asian nautical technologies, including the astrolabe and the compass.[11] As such, the Atlantic histories invoked here arose from an earlier fluid space of trade and exchange. These adopted technologies of reckoning one's position at sea were integral to the ways in which the ocean (space) was harnessed to produce narrative (time).

Unlike terrestrial space, the perpetual circulation of ocean currents means that as a space, the sea necessarily dissolves local phenomenology and diffracts the accumulation of narrative. In other words, the ocean suspends and distorts terrestrial markings of temporality. Although one cannot simply disentangle space from time, the British struggle to establish longitude suggests that European conceptions of the ocean and its navigation were largely spatial until the modernizing (and thus temporal) transformations of the late eighteenth century. As Dava Sobel points out, reckoning latitude, a British inheritance from Ptolemy, is based upon natural markers such as the position of the stars or sun in a given place. Significantly, the Atlantic mapping of latitude was derived from Portuguese slave traders (and their Arab colleagues) off the west coast of Africa.[12] Longitude, particularly the zero-degree meridian at Greenwich, is a political construct, created to protect colonial trade and based on the difference in *time* between a British ship's departure and arrival point (Sobel 1995, 4–5). A nautical measurement first accurately calculated by the English clockmaker John Harrison in 1762, longitude is constructed almost exclusively in terms of time. In fact, Harrison's transatlantic crossing along the well-worn slave route to Jamaica enabled him to establish precise chronometry, contributing to the global homogenization of time-space and its transportability through the proliferation of pocket watches.

The Atlantic Ocean, specifically the routes of the maritime slave trade, was the constitutive space for our modern and global measurement of time. Longitude to this day is based upon the movement of eighteenth-century British ships traversing oceanic space. Thus the universalization of global space derives from Britannia's "rule" of the waves, a rule of both dominion and measurement that drew from the most fluid of earth's surfaces to standardize public space and time. While longitude to some extent reflects distance traveled, the ocean's propensity for distortion means that the spatial is subordinated to the temporal: "one degree of longitude equals four minutes of time [everywhere], but in terms of distance, one degree shrinks from sixty-eight miles at the Equator to virtually nothing at the poles" (Sobel 1995, 5). The conscription of the earth, and specifically the sea, into Euclidean geometries constitutive of modern linear time suggests a shift in cultural and political constructions of the ocean, a cognitive mapping that attempts to submit amorphous matter to the historical will of empires and nations.

Temporalizing ocean space was a vital objective to the British maritime empire because inaccuracies in time resulted in devastating losses of human labor and material resources through shipwreck. An error in a ship's chronometer of one minute could result in a spatial miscalculation of fifteen nautical miles—this proved especially deadly for laden ships returning to the rocky shores of Great Britain (Sobel 1995, 54). Anthony Giddens demonstrates that the eighteenth-century "invention of the mechanical clock and its diffusion . . . were of key significance in the separation of time from space" (1990, 17), but he neglects to mention that, paradoxically, the fluidity of ocean space facilitated the homogenization of time and, by extension, labor. The imbrication of transoceanic movement with successful timekeeping, the chronometers and hourglasses that measured distance and units of labor, dictated sailors' schedules "with a precision unknown to almost every other early modern worker" (Bolster 1997, 84). Accordingly, nautical speech is replete with temporal semantics: for instance, a sailor's "watch" reflects an assignment of labor (Bolster 1997, 84), while "dead time" and "slack time" describe a sailor's *terrestrial* unemployment between ocean voyages (Bolster 1997, 86); this suggests that the measured pace of linear time exists only at sea. While the dominant discourse of the British empire sought to mystify the relationship between slave and maritime labor, sailors coined the ironic term "Negro's holiday" to describe working Sundays (Kemp 1976, 589) and parodied "Rule Britannia" with the refrain that "on the waves . . . thy darling sons are slaves!" (quoted in Land 2001, 177). The rigid disciplining of nautical time and labor positioned the ship as "a prototype of the factory," an etymology that Linebaugh and Rediker trace to "factor," a West African trade representative "where factories were originally located" (2000, 150). As such, the eighteenth-century ship, a "machine of empire" and a "floating factory" (Linebaugh and Rediker 2000, 150) that brought Europe, Africa, and the Americas into uneven social and economic relations, was the means by which the homogenous, empty time of capitalist modernity was constructed. As Connery explains, "Movable capital is liquid capital" (1995, 40). This suggests the most compelling reason why, in the late eighteenth century, "flow" and "liquidity" suddenly became the "dominant metaphor[s]" for the circulation of capital, information, ideologies, and power (Illich 1987, 43–44).

Compared with the distance of its overseas territories, the encircling Atlantic provides Great Britain's most spatially proximate engagement with slavery and maritime colonialism; perhaps this geographic intimacy coupled with assumptions of *aqua nullius* help to explain why this ocean was a primary site of narratives of British ethnic nationalism and masculinity. In his reading of Hegel, Connery suggests that "ocean-going activates Western history" in ways that encode "a similar logic of master-slave" (1996, 296–297) and, I would add, a mystification of the vertical power relations that constitute the homogenizing nation-state. The British charting of a humanized, temporal ocean space was enacted across many registers in the eighteenth century, including the marshaling of a broad spectrum of Enlightenment sciences in the search for longitude and the incorporation of African slave traders like Sir Francis Drake and Sir John Hawkins into a genealogy of maritime nationalism.[13] The attempts to claim ocean space as territory caused multiple seventeenth- and eighteenth-century European maritime battles and generated legal debates over whether the ocean was essentially a closed (national territory) or open (internationally shared) space. A new legal grammar of the "freedom of the seas" ironically facilitated the passage of slave ships, contributing to the ways in which the Atlantic became a primary space of the dialectic between European colonial sovereignty and African subjection.[14] The eighteenth-century emergence of the nautical adventure novel, a symbolic effect of the ways in which the sovereignty of European male subjects was attained through a narrative temporalization of ocean space, can be understood as a modern product of the ways in which Britannia ruled the waves.

It is no coincidence that English novelists drew from firsthand accounts of transatlantic colonization and thus fictionally expanded a profoundly imperialist—and therefore historical—cartography of the sea. As Laura Brown explains, the rapid rise of British maritime shipping after 1660 contributed to a distinctive shift in the literature where "the sea [became] the national rhetorical topos" (2001, 63) to reflect and sustain British mercantile imperialism. This helps elucidate the extraordinary popularity of *Robinson Crusoe*, which, by the early twentieth century, had been adapted in over five hundred publications in England alone (Carpenter 1984, 8). As I explained in the introduction, the island-adventure genre, arising simulta-neously with the maritime novel, was vital to the expansion of British mus-cular Christianity. That these narratives conveniently configured islands and oceans as unpopulated only served to mystify the British formula for maritime colonialism: deserted islands were accidentally colonized by ship-wrecked children. The project of maritime empire was often reflected in a formulaic genre that marked the broad space of the transoceanic imagina-tion by narrative time through the use of chronotopic elements such as the tempest and shipwreck, punctuated by violent masculine encounters with pirates, buccaneers, or cannibals.[15]

By the nineteenth century, popular British sea fiction was already well entrenched in a mystification of transatlantic expansion, where boy-adven-ture narratives such as Charles Kingsley's xenophobic *Westward Ho!* (1855) and *Water Babies* (1863) were encoding a naturalized and infantilized tele-ology of Protestant maritime expansion. Once the late Renaissance cartog-raphers began to empty the Atlantic Ocean of imagined islands, antipodes, krakens, sirens, mermaids, and leviathans, it seems that the nautical adven-ture novel emerged to repopulate it, albeit selectively. The most important contribution to England's rise to modernity—the trade and enslavement of Africans—is peripheral to most maritime adventure novels of the nine-teenth century. This is particularly significant when we consider the Brit-ish novelist Frederick Marryat, whose popular maritime narratives gener-ally suppress the trade that enabled his familial, professional, and literary success.[16] The rise of a bourgeois readership sustained his writing career, but his father, a West Indian planter, slave trader, and chairman of Lloyds' (Eric Williams 1944,104), provided the material basis for it.

In gesturing to these broad narratives of the sea, I suggest that the radical economic and social changes brought about by transatlantic colo-nialism enacted a gradual sea change in conceptions of ocean space. While this may seem an obvious point, the colonial origins of this new sense of modern time-space have escaped the notice of most scholars working in the grammars of oceanic studies. As such, a metacritical apparatus for dis-cussing the ways in which colonialism constructed the sea as history has been lacking in Atlantic studies. For instance, Alain Corbin (1994) and George Ryley Scott (1939) detail how for centuries the French and English depicted the ocean as a hostile, ungodly place until the rise in therapeutic bathing repopulated European shores; this is the same time that nauti-cal novels reconfigured the sea as a space of romantic adventure and ref-uge. While both locate this conceptual shift in the late eighteenth century, neither connects this to European maritime imperialism and the ways in which the sea was rapidly becoming a temporal object of popular knowledge.[17] By turning to Raban's more recent work, which explores the ways in which the construction of the British literary canon is indebted to the maritime literature of Coleridge, Byron, and others, we can get a better understanding of literary histories of the ocean.

Raban's interesting chronology suggests that the first two centuries of British naval colonialism produced few narratives of the sea itself—rather, these works depicted the ocean as "merely a space to be traversed" (1992, 5), secondary to the teleology of arrival to exotic lands and material accumulation. With some exceptions, notably images of the tempest at sea, it was only in the eighteenth century that the sea itself emerged as a complex figure in British literature, depicted variously as a space of romance, gothic terror, reflection, the sublime, a "natural" counter to industrialized Europe, or a space of ontological abyss.[18] "The ocean pervades the popular print culture of the eighteenth century" (Laura Brown 2001, 62), yet there's a peculiar silence in both *The Oxford Book of the Sea* and British maritime literature in general about a black diaspora experience, or in Robert Farris Thompson's terms (expanded by Gilroy), a conceptual "black Atlantic." This is striking because the rise of maritime literature as a genre is coterminous with the development of nineteenth-century maritime technologies that led to an *increase* in the number of African slaves shipped to the Americas, even after all European states had abolished the trade.[19] Although Raban's collection includes excerpts from Charles Johnson's *Middle Passage* and Walcott's poem "The Sea is History," he does not acknowledge—to borrow the first words from Fred D'Aguiar's *Feeding the Ghosts*—that "the sea is slavery" (1997, 3).

The two-century gap between Britain's emergence into maritime colonialism and its belated epistemological engagements with ocean space suggest some of the conceptual difficulties of narrating the sea as a "practiced place." Since "no other area has manifested its interdisciplinary nature so clearly as marine studies" (Borgese 1975, 33), a broad range of narratives were engaged to remap the ocean as a template of British modernity. While the overlapping discourses of the expansion of empire and "freedom of the seas" were constituted by the practice of transoceanic slavery, their templates leave little room for a phenomenology of the sea that could incorporate the "souls/caught in the Middle Passage/limbo" (Nichols 1983, 16). Caribbean writers asking how to "eulogise/[the] names" of "the dead ones/who are not dead" (Nichols 1983, 17) have questioned the nautical genre's teleology of maritime progress. Even if "an African American concept of space had its beginnings in the holds of the slave ships during the Middle

Passage" (Diedrich, Gates, and Pedersen 1999, 8), its *representability* poses an obstacle due to the challenges I have outlined in temporalizing ocean space as well as localizing—and thus rendering historical—this violence of modern history. Brought together, ocean space and the middle passage pose ontological challenges to the representation of the historical process. The abjection of the middle passage may be characterized, to borrow from Julia Kristeva, as an "immemorial violence with which a body becomes separated from another body"(1982, 10). The inability to return to that lost object of attachment produces "a deep well of memory that is unapproachable and intimate" (1982, 6). The impossibility of a spatial return is symbolized by the Middle Passage Monument Project, which at best can only commemorate the losses of the crossing by lowering a memorial into the waters off the coast of New York, a synecdoche of "the world's largest, yet unmarked, graveyard, the Atlantic Ocean's infamous Middle Passage."[20]

To inscribe the sea as history raises questions as to how fundamentally *terrestrial* beings, unlike the Pacific navigators discussed in the following chapter, can construct a temporal and humanized ocean place. If "movement always seems to condition the production of a space and to associate it with a history" (de Certeau 1984, 118), how does one constitute a practiced place in uninhabitable space? If space is always relational, narrated, corporeally and socially experienced, traversed to be understood, collectively and individually remembered, made historic through cultural sedimentation, "constituted and constitutive" (Tilley 1994, 17), how might we produce a phenomenology of the sea? How do we begin to speak about the middle passage when the monuments that constitute space as a place are "locked" in "that grey vault," the sea?

The Middle Passage and the Quarrel with History

> I met History once, but he ain't recognize me.
> —Derek Walcott, "The Schooner *Flight*"

Alternately conceived as a spatial boundary or a frontier, the sea invokes both the fear of and desire for diaspora histories and practices. Yet even though transoceanic passages were the means by which most migrants before the mid-twentieth century traveled, the sea itself is rarely theorized as a diaspora space, even when it provides the primary spatial logic of interpretation. This is to say that as much as Atlantic scholars have modeled their work upon the Mediterranean model of Fernand Braudel, few have engaged directly with the *aquatic* aspects of transoceanic diaspora.[21] On the other hand, diaspora theorists, by and large, have focused primarily on the dialectical tension between the originary space of dispersal and the space of arrival without pausing to consider tidalectics, or the experience of movement *between* national/cultural spaces. My examination of Hearne's work attempts to weave both diaspora and spatial theories together, to foreground the fluid construction of diaspora space and its transoceanic itineraries. Here I've taken my cue from de Certeau, who warns that the same mapping process that "collates on the same plane heterogeneous spaces" also creates an "erasure of the *itineraries* which . . . make it possible to move from one to the other" (1984, 121, my emphasis). That these transoceanic itineraries are continually depicted in the middle passage novel as a distortion of linear time suggests the tautological nature of the memory of the crossing, a point often overlooked in diaspora scholarship.

The two words "middle passage" invoke some of the most abject horrors of modern history, yet the term itself is not subject to localization. Generally the middle passage suggests the claustrophobic "death ships" in the oceanic limbo between Africa and the Americas, connoting a transitional aquatic space of any given point in the 500-year history of the African slave trade. Yet etymologically, the term "middle passage" refers not to a geographic or even specifically historic space of African enslavement and transportation. As a "leg" of the triangular trade, a bodily metaphor that resonates with the term "limbo" and the tutelary god of the crossroads, Legba, the middle passage is defined as the baseline in the economic geometries of colonial relations.[22] In the simplest version of the triangular trade, European ships would travel to West Africa to trade goods for slaves, cross the Atlantic with human cargo to exchange for sugar products in the New World, and return to the northern Atlantic ports with rum, molasses, and sugar. Interestingly, there are few if any other language equivalents for the English expression "middle passage."[23] The phrase seems to have emerged from eighteenth-century British abolitionist discourse, where Thomas Clarkson's often-reproduced plan of the HMS *Brookes*, depicting the terrors of spatial and bodily compression, became synonymous with the middle passage experience.[24] As I will explain, the invocation of the unhealthy "flesh" of the contained slaves and the hold's unhygienic stench reflected not only abolitionist humanism but also a particularly modern dilemma about the contaminating effluvia of the masses.

This wave of humanizing the Atlantic by narrating slave experiences of the middle passage, while effective for the abolitionist movement, was rarely adopted by other genres. So while the shipment of African slaves to the plantation colonies by some accounts had doubled in the mid-nineteenth century, this violent peopling of the Atlantic is peripheral to the ubiquitous maritime adventure novel, which drew upon slave metaphors to advance naval reform for white sailors and grammars of oceanic naturalism that did not include the inhuman and "unnatural" containment of slaves at sea. Although British painters nationalized the Atlantic with depictions of naval captures of illegal slave ships, these images subsume an African experience of the middle passage to the glories of British maritime technology and its civilizing rule of law. Even painters such as J. M. W. Turner who were cognizant of the process of jettisoning live human "cargo" to elude naval capture, famously recorded in his *Slavers Throwing Overboard the Dead and Dying* (1840), subordinated this all-too-social seascape to the sublime naturalism of the sea, as Gilroy (1993) and Ian Baucom (2005) have demonstrated. Thus John Ruskin could displace the violence of the event by interpreting the painting to mean that the sea itself, rather than the human horrors of the middle passage, represented the "wild, unwearied, reckless incoherency, like that of an enraged multitude, whose masses act together in phrensy" (1903, 564).[25]

Even if the empire was belated in creating a terminology for the crossing, the African diasporan concept of "crossing the water" or "crossing the river" certainly has existed since the inception of the trade in human lives.[26] Although the term "middle passage" was in usage among abolitionists, it did not reemerge into *popular* discourse until the late 1950s and early 1960s. The rise of Atlantic diaspora studies coincides with the 1962 (re)discovery by oceanographers that this ocean is expanding.[27] This geographic and conceptual expansion in oceanic studies indicates a new spatial logic that can be said to derive from a number of overlapping factors, such as the Truman-inspired "scramble for the oceans," a shift in the terrain of area studies, and a global increase in migration that is being rediscovered in the fluid histories of black, labor, and anticolonial movements across the Atlantic and beyond. Due to these complicated contexts, recent scholarship has sought to destabilize genealogies of national purity and to emphasize black diaspora agency by highlighting the ways in which peoples and ideologies crisscrossed the Atlantic in a far less linear manner than middle passage trajectories.[28] While these interdisciplinary dialogues help construct vital new meanings for the conceptual history of the Atlantic and have greatly influenced this book, I suggest that the ideological contours of British maritime nationalism have made a larger impact upon the gendering of ocean space than has been recognized. Thus the mobility of north Atlantic metropolitan men continues to be the dominant metaphor for transatlantic migration, eclipsing the relationship to their often feminized homelands and minimizing the possibility of women's agency in transatlantic history. This problematic model of transoceanic diaspora often upholds a familiar colonial model of *aqua nullius* and obscures histories of abjection such as a violent peopling of the middle passage that may have less to say about a "counterculture of modernity" (Gilroy 1993, 36) than modernity's originary mechanism.

The literary production of the Caribbean, while absent from Gilroy's *The Black Atlantic*, has long been concerned with the ways in which the middle passage provides a complex historiography for creolization and new world modernity. Interestingly, the first Caribbean text to directly invoke the phrase in its title was V. S. Naipaul's *The Middle Passage* (1962), a travelogue that is decidedly not about the historic trade in African lives, but rather a work that inscribes an inverse trajectory of transoceanic diaspora, an account of tidalectic itineraries, exile, and return. This travel narrative of the author's return to Trinidad from England on a passenger ship includes Naipaul's notorious observation that "history is built around achievement and creation; and nothing was created in the West Indies" (1962, 29). By building upon the pro-empire historian and travel writer, James Anthony Froude, Naipaul's pessimistic account of the anglophone region's history was perceived as a slap in the face to a vital scholarly movement that, in the early years of independence, was busily excavating the subaltern histories of the region, particularly the creative and creolizing propensities of slave culture. Naipaul took the anticolonial and materialist framework to its most pessimistic extreme: if the history of the region was (over)determined by economic and epistemic colonial violence, then the potential for the creative reassemblage of cultural and political formations was impossible amidst the abjections of the British slave state.[29]

Naipaul's conflation of the materiality of British colonialism (its absentee planters and short-term architecture) with the *sign* of historiography was parodied in Walcott's poetic response. "The Sea is History" (1979) challenges the linear framework of Enlightenment progress by repeating the capitalized word "History" to foreground its unappeasable demands.[30] Like Froude and Naipaul, the poem's catechistic "Sirs" press the Caribbean subject for empirical proof of the Historical process: "Where are your monuments, your battles, your martyrs?" (1986, 364). In response, the poem's speaker guides the Historians through submarine depths and the "Genesis" of the middle passage, describes "the packed cries, / the shit, the moaning" (364), and historicizes the diaspora through Biblical chronologies such as "Exodus" and "Lamentations." In each case, the "Sirs" interrupt with their negation: "it was not History" (366).

Ultimately, Walcott's detemporalizing sea refuses to register a human-centered chronology: "the ocean kept turning blank pages / looking for History" (1986, 365). Consistent with many other works that inscribe the middle passage, Walcott decouples the relationship between space and time, calling attention to the ways in which narrative produces "History." Like Naipaul, he remains suspicious about the substitution of the progressive discourse of empire with ethnic nationalism, but he does not allow this model of progress to be replaced by a more "natural" narrative that would use the sea to chart an evolutionary chronology of human consciousness. After inscribing the "jubilation" and individualism of independence, when "each rock broke into its own nation" (367), Walcott charts a nationalist *devolution* to bureaucratic reptiles and insects. Resisting the Enlightenment telos of revolution and emancipation, he concludes the poem with an invocation of Darwinian "sea pools," not to uphold an evolutionist framework but rather to destabilize the human-centered chronology of History. By returning to the "salt chuckle" of the sea, the presumed origin of all life on earth, the poem completes an oceanic cycle, generating the unrepresentable "sound . . . of History, really beginning" (367).

Ironically, Naipaul's dismissal of the potential of Caribbean historiography in *The Middle Passage* catalyzed a creative exploration of transoceanic origins. At the time Hearne was writing *The Sure Salvation*, a pan-Caribbean dialogue on the "quarrel with history" was initiated at the 1976 Carifesta Forum in Kingston, Jamaica, where Edward Baugh presented his paper of that title.[31] In a conference that explored Naipaul's charges alongside Walcott's declaration that history is "irrelevant" to the region and that linear temporality must be tempered by myth, Hearne responded in his introduction to the *Carifesta Forum* by asserting that "history is the angel with whom all we Caribbean Jacobs have to wrestle." One way to reconceptualize how Caribbean subjects "occupy space but no time," he felt, was to "emerge from the great sac of amniotic fluid contained in the belly of the Americas" (1976, viii). Pursuing metaphors of oceanic space and time, Hearne advised Caribbean intellectuals to enter into the *"voyage of discovery across the longitude, and down into the parallel of a history that has not yet happened"* (ix, author's emphasis). Scholars have tended to overlook the importance of this conference, which I position here as a crucial turning point where the methodologies of Caribbean historiography shifted to transoceanic models of cultural origin.[32] As a conference participant and assistant editor of the collection, Édouard Glissant turned to the fluid genesis of the middle passage, characterizing Caribbean literature as *"the longing for the ideal of history,"* plumbed through an oceanic *"primordial source"*

(1989, 79, author's emphasis).[33] In this tidalectic examination of the Caribbean subject "in space and time" Brathwaite declared, in *Carifesta Forum*, that Caribbean "unity is submarine" (1976, 199).

Although writers such as Glissant, Brathwaite, Walcott, and others had been theorizing the poetics of the middle passage for decades, inscribing what Grace Nichols would term "the middle passage womb" (1983, 5), it was not until Hearne's *The Sure Salvation* that the crossing was fictionalized in the anglophone novel. This is comparatively late in the history of the region's literature, and I suspect it has much to do with pressing concerns about national sovereignty, rendered in terms of the "folk" and soil, and the ways in which the plantation system was shaping the racialized strata of emergent nation-states.[34] I've mentioned that the masculine and mobile bias of transoceanic diaspora studies needs to be examined in a tidalectic engagement with its feminized boundaries and epistemic borders. This relation between land and sea is characteristic of Hearne's work, which demonstrates how Caribbean theories of plantation creolization may be fruitfully positioned in a tidalectic engagement with transoceanic diaspora.

The Tidalectics of National Soil

Strangely, the first novel from the English-speaking region to explore the sea as history has been out of print since its initial publication, along with Hearne's five previous novels, which were first solicited for publication by T. S. Eliot. Hearne, a member of the first generation of post–World War II writers who migrated to and published in England, has been unevenly incorporated into the Caribbean literary canon and seems to have been a magnet for criticism in similar ways to Naipaul. Many of the region's primary literary figures, including George Lamming, Sylvia Wynter, and Wilson Harris, have all expressed distaste for the ways in which Hearne's earlier novels (published between 1955 and 1962) upheld colonial hierarchies or were unsuccessful in their representations of the Caribbean folk.[35] Historical context is crucial here. Hearne's first novels, explorations of pre-independence Jamaica, were published during an especially vibrant period of West Indian cultural activity. In an effort to destabilize the colonial hierarchies that valorized whiteness and English cultural hegemony, the region's intellectuals were turning to representations of what Lamming called "the peasant tongue" and experience. As such, Hearne was faulted for his presumed "dread of being identified with the land at the peasant level" and for not being "an example of that instinct and root impulse which returns the better West Indian writers back to the soil" (Lamming 1984, 46). Writing in London, Lamming concluded that "soil is a large part of what the West Indian novel has brought back to reading; lumps of earth: unrefined, perhaps, but good warm, fertile earth" (46).[36]

Lamming's invocation of national soil suggests a particular cultural coding of folk space that may be read alongside Liisa Malkki's explanation of the ways in which national ties to land are naturalized by the conflation of people with soil. Deconstructing the metaphysical "assumptions linking people to place, nation to territory" (1997, 56), she draws from Deleuze and Guattari to outline the ways in which arborescent metaphors underlie genealogical roots and validate national or ethnic rootedness. As the term "culture" is etymologically linked to "cultivation" (58), Malkki demonstrates why diaspora populations are positioned as so profoundly unnatural, outside the ontological "ground," so to speak, of being. The impetus to establish a genealogy of belonging to the land (through the folk) in Caribbean discourse must be read alongside Glissant's reminder that the forced cultivation of the plantation system created a lacuna where "nature and culture have not formed a dialectical whole that informs a people's consciousness" (1989, 63). Thus Lamming, Glissant, and others are part of a movement to reterritorialize the Caribbean landscape in ways that offer a less colonial and, by extension, a more "natural" dialectic between people and soil. The emergent literary elite of the anglophone Caribbean, often residing in British exile, sought to reconcile their spatial and social distance through the realist novel, a temporally driven narrative that often conflates the soil with the folk.[37] Generally speaking, questions about the representability of the subaltern were not in popular circulation at this time.[38]

It is only by engaging a theory of tidalectics, mutually inflective histories of the land and sea, that we can interpret Hearne's novels in a constitutive relationship between landscape, seascape, and the corporeality of social space. Like Aimé Césaire (1969), Hearne has often invoked his geography instructor as a major influence on his literary imagination, and his concerns with human spatial relations are evident in all of his novels.[39] *The Sure Salvation*, while it takes place entirely at sea, is equally informed by the spatial imagination. By breaking apart the metaphysical conflation of the folk with landscape, we can position Hearne's writing in a tidalectic context, with a decidedly ocular contour informed by his engagement with the visual arts.[40] As I will explain, Hearne's folk are not immediately recognizable along the lines of Lamming's valued "peasant" experience because they are represented at sea in the process of reformulating their diverse African experiences into a creolized aesthetic that will soon be transplanted to the Caribbean. The slaves' oceanic disconnection from any "good warm, fertile earth" results in a narrative of their hyperembodiment; their containment in the hold of a transoceanic slave ship produces the substitution of "fertile earth" by its cognates in dirt, soil, and human waste.

Reiterating the concerns of Hearne's previous novels, *The Sure Salvation* begins by invoking the nexus of time, space, and waste, interconnected narrative threads that are woven throughout the text. In the first chapter, significantly called "The poop," the novel begins in almost midsentence: "By the tenth day, the barque was ringed by the unbroken crust of its own garbage. And the refuse itself had discharged a contour of dully iridescent grease which seemed to have been painted onto the sea with one stroke of a broad brush" (1981, 7). This "clinging evidence of their corruption, which the water would not swallow" (7), disrupts the linearity of modern time by refusing historic absorption and symbolizes the larger transoceanic implications of this illegal English slave ship, bound for Brazil in 1860, for over three-quarters of the novel. The barque filled with 516 African, English, American, Irish, and Portuguese mariners and slaves is trapped in the transatlantic doldrums, running low on supplies, and sweltering in the windless south Atlantic heat. The ship is framed in "the still centre of a huge stillness: pasted to the middle of a galvanized plate that was the sea" (7). Narrative time, reflecting the stasis of the immobile ship, is particularly distorted. On the first page, between the invocation of the "tenth day" and present "now" time, eleven days have passed in less than a paragraph. The first 189 pages of the novel outline one nonchronologically narrated day on the ship—the final day before the wind mobilizes the ship/narrative. As such, the text undermines the adventure-driven maritime novel in ways that reflect back to Melville's *Benito Cereno*, supporting Glissant's observation that the novel of the postplantation Americas is characterized by a "tortured sense of time" (1989, 144). Hearne's decision to represent a densely packed English slave ship in 1860, decades after the British abolition of the trade and of slavery in its colonies, pinpoints the failures of linear chronologies of progress, sovereignty, and liberation, a critique also embedded in the novel's ironic title. The final thirty-five pages then recount a slave insurrection orchestrated by the African-American cook, Alex Delfosse, the murder of some of the primary European characters, the ship's capture by a British naval steamship off the coast of the Americas, and their escort to a riverside settlement in the Guianas where the slaves are released and the Europeans await trial and probable hanging.

I am intrigued by Hearne's inscription of the temporal/spatial nexus of diaspora because it flatly refuses the chronotope of masculine spatial motility so evident in maritime narratives and studies. Hearne's model of diaspora inscribes extreme immobility, stasis, and timelessness, a literal waste of feces, blood, vomit, and sperm that envelops both the ship and the middle passage experience. As such, he inscribes an oppressive spatial logic that attempts to unite with the temporal; a particular challenge I have already noted in the conceptualization of ocean space. For if, as de Certeau and others have observed, our ability to process space is constituted by our movement through it—and a return to a specific point to practice it as a locality or place—this poses a challenge to middle passage narratives in general and more specifically to the stasis of this ship. In other words, like Walcott, Hearne raises the question as to how to mark—and thus materially make meaningful—ocean spaces that were traversed by slave ships when one cannot locate the exact coordinates of the places where, for instance, Africans died in the passage or drowned at sea. In response to Walcott's question, "Where are your monuments, your battles, your martyrs?" the *terrestrial* practices of making space meaningful, Hearne's narrative must extend beyond the sea as metaphor and immobilize the ship in one specific place for three weeks, thus marking time by the growing mass of human waste that encompasses and embodies the social practices of the ship. Paradoxically, the ship's stasis provides a unique opportunity to capture the illusiveness of the narrative present even though the spatial movement required to produce time is entirely lacking. This is why the only present-time writing occurs in the novel's first pages, where the captain locates the ship in a static Euclidean nexus of time and space: *"Noon, May 17, 1860—Lat 1° 14" S, Long 32° 16' W. No distance. Calm continues"* (12, author's emphasis).[41]

Unlike the maritime discourses of empire that construct a homogenous, universal, and natural oceanic plane as a template for (expanding) human space and time, Hearne refuses to render the ocean as a transparent metaphor for human desire. Nor does he support the empire's conflation of a universalized sea with homogenized human history. Therefore the ocean's ontological challenge frames the first page of the novel. In response to the three-week stasis, the multiethnic crew has been struck by "a vague and debilitating panic" (7). The seamen are plagued by "a curious sense of expectancy," and it "was if each man were trying to fashion for himself some memory of the world's tumult" (7). Their inability to contextualize both time (memory) and space (the world), suggests not only a lack of recognition of the ways in which the transatlantic slave trade was a globalizing process, but the dehumanizing experience of oceanic stasis and the dependence upon *movement* to conceptualize local place and subjectivity itself. Hearne continues:

> In this prison of silence and immobility *their only proofs of being* were the writing edge of the sun and the nightly fattening of the moon. They were tantalized by the conviction that immediately beyond the walls of opaque blue—on the horizon's edge, if only they could get there—they would find waves running before the wind, curling at their crests with a hiss of spray, and a sky loud with swooping birds that shrieked beautiful and reassuring discords. (7, my emphasis)

The natural markers of latitude, the "writhing" sun and the "fattening" moon, appear to threaten rather than facilitate human orientation, rupturing the foundations of natural metaphor and thus destabilizing the crew's ontology. Unlike Gaston Bachelard's suggestion that natural matter, particularly water, aids the human subject to "plumb the depths of being" (1983, 1), Hearne's ocean remains a horizontal plane of garbage, refuse, and corruption (1981, 7). Although metaphors of "depth" may have arisen from maritime experience (Springer 1995, 22), the *Sure Salvation*'s crew remains trapped in a lateral "prison of silence." Deprived of their own itinerancy and agency, a profound challenge to their sense of being, the crew fantasizes a telos of knowable ocean space (the ubiquitous "running" and "curling" waves of so many maritime narratives) rather than, for instance, arrival in the terrestrial Americas where they will reap the profits from the journey. Their disorientation shows that ontology is naturalized by *movement* across ocean space. Since they are trapped between "the walls of opaque blue," the crew struggles to come to terms with the human markers of Atlantic time and space: "the clinging filth" (18) that marks the "tenth day" and the "third week" does not represent the temporality of their voyage from Angola (distance) but rather their immobility. Consequently, the *time of stasis* is signified by the spatial expansion of human decay and waste. Their inability to experience movement through ocean space and therefore produce a phenomenology of time renders the spatial logic of the boundless ocean, even for these seasoned mariners, entirely illegible.

Although nineteenth-century imperialists like Froude exclaimed that "the sea is the natural home of Englishmen; the Norse blood is in us, and we rove over the waters . . . as eagerly as our ancestors" (1886, 18), Hearne's sea resists universalizing metaphors and the naturalizing claims by one genealogical root. Like all bodies of water, the Atlantic here is socially inflected and experienced across a number of broad registers. The ship's captain, William Hogarth (an invocation of the eighteenth-century satirist of the bourgeois will to property), views the ocean in far more metaphorical terms than his crew, as "a huge mirror bursting off his face . . . it was if the ship had sailed into the core of the sun" (16).[42] Ivan Illich observes that "[a]s a vehicle for metaphors, water is a shifting mirror" (1987, 25), yet Hearne's ocean resists its humanizing reflection. Hogarth's social privilege allows him to produce a series of oceanic metaphors, but these remain personal abstractions that cannot signify beyond his individual desires. Like his crew, he remains oblivious to the process of modernity, segregating his moral dilemma—the betrayal of his wife Eliza—from the ethics of running an illegal slave ship. While the "barque lay in the dead sea like a needle caught in a bowl of molten silver," the captain makes parallels between the ship's failed itinerary and that of his personal life. He determines that both represent "failure," which "had been waiting for him like an uncharted sargasso here in the open ocean" (17). This is a complex series of social, spatial, and intertextual metaphors. To be positioned in the core of the sun suggests such an extreme *interiority* to truly universal time that one cannot register the way humans mark natural temporality—from the revolution of the earth. The metaphorical collapse of the sun/sea is associated with the melted needle of the compass, amorphous and unable to signify within a vessel of "molten silver." The trajectory of his life, as an English aristocrat, a title without property or capital, is likened to the spatial entrapment of the Sargasso Sea: a mariner's nightmare, a space of aquatic weeds located between the Old and New Worlds that signifies impenetrability, stasis, and in the words of the online *OED*, a figurative "confused or stagnant mass." This term enacts an intertextual chain that stretches back to Jean Rhys's novel that popularized this uninhabitable space, *Wide Sargasso Sea* (1966). Rhys, in her "prequel" to *Jane Eyre*, had been concerned with Bertha Rochester's entrapment in the Victorian attic and, like Hearne, the overall inability for the Caribbean writer/subject to locate herself within the larger narratives of racialized British domesticity and soil. Tracing a genealogy of the Sargasso between these two texts suggests a diasporan aporia, a morass of uninhabitable space for European, African, and Caribbean transatlantic subjects. Trapped among his failed metaphors, in the atemporal core of the sun, amidst an ocean that refuses to reflect, and without a directional needle to guide, one could place Hogarth in the same ontological mire that affects his crew.

European phenomenologies of the sea here are neither homogeneous, nor are they easily categorized by social class or maritime experience.

Although the crew is plagued by the moral repercussions of their participation in the slave trade, and Hogarth sublimates his doubts about the
ethics of the trade into an obsession with his betrayal of his wife, these
intertwined perspectives function in stark contrast to the philosophy of
the ranking officer, George Reynolds, a trickster figure who represents
the uneven epistemologies of Atlantic modernity. Consequently, Reynolds
manifests an overt critique of the crew who raise moral doubts only once
they are trapped in the narrative center of the middle passage and a destabilization of the narrative structure that seeks to create meaning-laden
ocean space. In this way Hearne seems to anticipate the textual destabilization that occurs in the conclusion of his good friend Walcott's epic poem
Omeros. After richly inscribing nearly 300 pages of "the sea's parchment
atlas" (1990, 13), Walcott dissolves his transoceanic imaginary by determining that the sea "was an epic where every line was erased" and relegates
it to "a wide page without metaphors" (296). In a similar vein, Hearne's
misanthropic Reynolds, self-defined by "a hate so consuming that . . . [he]
is made ethereal by [his] regard for the truth" (82), has this to pronounce
about the sea:

> We cannot distort it into lying shapes as we do the land. No parks,
> no palaces, no fine cities fashioned from the miserable stunted flesh
> of the many so that the few may write each other encomiums on their
> achievements. How many slow deaths to build and keep a gentleman's
> manor! . . . But the sea will not be moulded into our excremental
> falsehoods. It will not record the shape of any keel. Christ could walk
> it to the end of time and leave no more mark of his passage than will
> this floating barracoon we choose to call a ship. (82–83)

Being the devilish character that he is, Reynolds concludes his monologue
by declaring that once he comes into his "small fortune" from this illegal
trade, "the world shall learn the purifying terror of the sea's indifference.
. . . *The world shall learn*" (83, author's emphasis). Hearne responds to his
character's deconstruction of his oceanic metaphors by decapitating him
during the slave insurrection, fashioning Reynolds into a "severed head
(with every feature of it broken horribly)" (194). After detailing Reynolds'
misogyny and his proclivity for the young "flesh" of certain women slaves,
the author has him figuratively castrated by Tadene, a "dry, thin, oldish"
African woman (194). In this case Hearne's metaphors have the last vindi-
cating word, placing a liberating and violent corporeality at the fluid center
of oceanic modernity.

The Contingencies of Atlantic Modernity

To overemphasize the transparency of oceanic metaphor in this text would be to overlook the ways in which Hearne has depicted maritime space, the intentionality of social resistance, and modernity itself as profoundly contingent. *The Sure Salvation* destabilizes the discourses that have temporalized the Atlantic, such as the Euclidean geometries of latitude and longitude, the construction of homogenous time through the "watches" of maritime labor, and the telos of movement across ocean space that is deemed necessary for the ontology of the human subject. The immobility of the ship results in the stasis of labor itself—the sailors cannot function in their usual capacity as the faceless "hands" of the "floating factory" and therefore time cannot be measured by labor (see Bakhtin 1981, 207). Moreover, the connection between the plantation system and the slaves' forced "irruption into modernity" (Glissant 1989, 146) is complicated by a population that, while captive, has not yet entered the degradations of New World labor. While the novel records a slave mutiny, it deconstructs the heroics of the maritime adventure narrative and suspends "adventure-time" itself (Bakhtin 1981, 87), sharing Walcott's distrust of forms of ethnic national literatures that encode "the hallucination of imperial romance" derived from the nautical "literature of exploration remembered from Captain Marryat" and others (Walcott 1998, 58).

Hearne doesn't substitute the maritime grammar of colonial heroics with its subaltern reversal; he adopts the genre of the realist novel to implode its chronotopes and fracture its humanist teleology. Accordingly, the slave insurrection does not derive from any subaltern consciousness or black diaspora unity; in fact, the novel repeatedly inscribes the slaves' mutual intranslatability and their description of the African-American cook as a "white man" (1981, 141). In turn, Delfosse denies a "sense of kinship" (57) with the Africans; while he supplies the slaves with arms, he intends to take them, not back to Africa as they request, but rather "up the Amazon ... to start a kingdom" with himself as self-appointed ruler (199). Delfosse is not a modern Toussaint L'Ouverture, liberator of Saint-Domingue, whose name signifies the potential of "the opening." Although Delfosse was also born a slave, he does not epitomize "the concrete realization of liberty, equality and fraternity ... which overflowed their narrow environment and embraced the whole of the world," as C. L. R. James has characterized Toussaint and the Haitian Revolution (1963, 265). In the languages of the European nations engaged in the slave trade, "del fosse" translates as the cesspool, gulf, gap, or grave. These terms highlight the lack of translatability within and across the African diaspora, similar to the ways in which discourses of fraternity and unity among the English seamen on Hearne's ship are contradicted by their overt racism towards their fellow Portuguese and African "brothers." As such, Hearne resists the universalizing and homogenizing discourses of Atlantic modernity and their twentieth-century legacies in maritime and diaspora studies, which necessarily construct a shared sense of motility and purpose. Consequently, it becomes far more challenging to speak of the ways in which this ship may represent a particular containment of class, racial, or even gendered unity. Instead, history itself actively disrupts any unifying discourse. As a character from one of Hearne's previous novels observes: "'History dig a gulf between us . . . an' it don't fill in yet'" (1962, 248).[43]

Hearne's critique of the heroic and revolutionizing discourses of the black Atlantic reveals how these tropes often construct ocean space as a universal template for masculine history. Unlike diaspora discourses that naturalize masculine movement at the expense of women's immobility, Hearne encompasses all of his subjects, male and female, in a modern stasis. Far from segregating women from history and modernity, Hearne's female characters are always vital to the political process (Figueroa 1972, 75). While theories of Atlantic modernity often uncritically position the "ship as a world" despite its absence of women, Hearne includes Hogarth's wife Eliza on the *Sure Salvation*, uniting issues of national and private domesticity alongside the presumably more public and political ambits of shipboard life. By bringing together these forms of domesticity on the ship, Hearne helps us to consider how traditional maritime narratives often uphold the ship as a nation by segregating this masculine sphere from the feminized shore and, more importantly, demonstrates that the polarization of the genders is the product of modernity itself. Through the representation of Tadene and her niece Mtishta (Reynolds's sexual captive), the novel positions women slaves as more vital to the execution of Delfosse's mutiny than he realizes. Although Delfosse interpellates her as "that dried-up old bitch" (Hearne, 1981,142), Tadene and a boy described as a "woman-man" (141) are integral to his control of the ship. This is not because women are simply reversed from the sign of reproduction and cultural generation to a destructive opposition to European hydrarchy. Just as he problematizes homogenizing discourses of race that conflate diverse African ethnicities with Delfosse's "kin" or "brother[s] in blood" (57), Hearne suggests that allegiances across gender (an unstable concept in itself) are also contingent.

Unlike British maritime novels, social and spatial motility—the movement of the wind, ocean currents, or a slave mutiny—neither drive this narrative forward nor constitute its temporality. There are no tempests or battles against nature that would incorporate the ocean as a participant in the human historical process. Rather, Hearne introduces "real time" through the recognition of contingency itself. As mentioned, the first three-quarters of the book are rendered in what Bakhtin might call "extratemporal hiatus" (1981, 91), similar to *Benito Cereno* where the ship/subjects lack temporal depth and mobility. Hearne inscribes European, American, and African subjects trapped in an oceanic abyss, a space devoid of a recognizable relationship to the temporal. The narrative histories of the ship/subjects are not rendered until Delfosse refutes Hogarth's assertion that his role in the slave trade is not "by choice." Hogarth explains, "Had the world been different it would have found a different use for me, and I for it" (1981, 136). Delfosse responds, "Had the world been different, cap'n, you'd have been where you are now . . . like me. . . . . We'd have come up on it a different way is all" (136). Delfosse's response shocks the captain and catalyses the temporal movement of the novel. Hogarth receives this tautological pronouncement like "the strokes of a funeral bell," which made him "feel helpless; as if [he] had been carried bound to this time and this place to watch over the interment of all purpose and endeavor" (146). Paradoxically, this realization of extreme immobility and the contraction of time and space then opens the narrative into a wider temporality and social place; the novel then inscribes a contractual geography of the Atlantic trade world that connects England, West Africa, the Caribbean, and North American ports.

Immediately after Hogarth's realization of Atlantic contingency, we become privy to his secret betrayal: by initially refusing to marry "below his station," he has contributed to Eliza's miscarriage and has never regained her trust; she continues to deny the exchange of her "flesh" for this marriage. Although he attempts to subvert the privileges of his aristocratic birth through the merchant trade and through sexual exchange with the middle class, Hogarth's inability to embrace the consequences of bourgeois modernity results in betrayal of those bodies that surround him on the ship. Readers also become privy to the previous itineraries of the merchant ship, *The Sure Salvation*, Hogarth's role in securing the East India trade for British aristocrats, and the complex historical relationship between Hogarth and Delfosse commencing with their first meeting in Cuba. Only after this exchange does the wind pick up, the ship begin to travel, and the mutiny take place. While Hearne's text departs from *Benito Cereno* by placing the mutiny in the present time of the narrative, its formal description prevents its interpretation as a causal event. In phrasing devoid of sentiment, the narrator recounts flatly: "At the slaves feeding time on the second day of the southeaster, Alexander Delfosse shot dead Boyo Dolan and the young Portuguese who together had charge of the culverin pointed into the slaves' hold" (194). The impact of the mutiny on the reader is restricted given its rendering as the shortest chapter in the novel. It is not the shipboard revolution, but rather the revelation of spatial and temporal contingency, a mapping of the oceanic abyss by chance, which leads Hogarth to recognize that his "life has been a *waste*" (146, my emphasis). The invocation of this term is not accidental, and it reiterates my earlier contention that space, time, and waste are constitutively, if not contingently related.

Contingency, like the nation, is a "Janus-faced" ideologeme (Nairn 1977) that invokes the complex process of modernity itself. As a term synonymous to tangentiality, proximity, and chance, it also encodes a conceptual contradiction: an occurrence defined by its dependence upon a prior event in history. The duality of the term becomes vital to understanding the conflict between Hogarth and Delfosse and highlights their unequal relations to modernity. At their first meeting in Havana, when Delfosse offers his services to coordinate the ship's supplies, Hogarth responds with the liberal paternalism characteristic of Amasa Delano in *Benito Cereno*. Like Delano, who "took to Negroes . . . just as other men to Newfoundland dogs" (Melville 1990, 73), Hogarth condescends to do "what [he] had never done before," to shake a black man's "paw" (Hearne 1981, 158). He resents Delfosse's fine clothing, his fluency in Spanish, his ability to command respect from the dockworkers who had exploited the ship's cache, and he struggles to come to terms with the first black subject who does not approach him with "deference" (148). When Delfosse throws Hogarth's tip into the harbor for local children, Hogarth thinks, "Had Alex proposed marriage, then, to the daughter I did not have—had he suggested that we claim descent from a common ancestor—he could not have done a greater violence to my sensibilities than his contemptuous disposal of my guineas" (153). His inability to interpret the nature of their relationship within the modern discourse of fraternity resurfaces as an epistemic crisis after the mutiny. Delfosse's suggestion that they were fated to arrive to this point fills Hogarth with "dread and *awe close to terror*, almost close to *superstition*" (146, my emphasis). Invoking the very terms of tradition that modernity seeks to supplant, Hogarth adopts the role of victim, concluding that since the voyage was Delfosse's idea, Hogarth has always been his "slave" (147). In an inversion of the Hegelian dialectic, Hogarth refuses to recognize his companion's pursuit of modernity—the birth of the sovereign individual.

Delfosse's facility with multiple European languages and his fluency in the social grammars of Atlantic trade allow him to justify the mutiny in terms of historical contingency, as a descendant of slaves adopting Enlightenment ideals of progress tinged by social Darwinism. Arguing that "there ain't nothing owing to a man that he don't take when it offers" (143), he's the only character with a sense of futurity, a plan to "take back" the "kingdom" from the white man (142). Significantly his sense of modernity and history is derived from his youthful travels with his white "brother," Louis Delfosse, who was killed in the midst of a rape in their quest to conquer "the women and the gold and the silver" of the U.S. frontier (53). In Louis's words, their inability to be rewarded for the violent participation in manifest destiny is attributed to history: *The man is nothing without the time. And this isn't our time. We're kings without a crown because of your black skin* (53, author's emphasis). Delfosse's earthy lexicon, referring to the slaves as cattle, comparing Reynolds to "any Pawnee or Dakota buck" (121), and carrying a wallet he carved from the "belly-skin" of a "young Apache who figured that he or me was one too many for that whole goddam' Mex border" (159), demonstrates the violent entanglement between diaspora and indigeneity and positions him as an active agent in a brutal and self-conscious historical process of expansion across the continent. As a complement to the domesticity represented by the women on board, Delfosse's terrestrial imaginary adds a tidalectic contour to the maritime grammar of this ship. His experience of the "wrong" temporality of the terrestrial frontier catalyzes his decision to take to the sea, perhaps assuming that the spatial logic of the nineteenth-century Atlantic will facilitate his mutiny and his eventual rule of an El Dorado dream—a colony in the Guianas. Yet Delfosse, like Hogarth, is unable to predict the ways in which the era of steam mechanized the Atlantic into increasingly rigidified and disciplinary technologies of time. As many theorists have shown, the civilizing process of modernity, at land and sea, was constituted by corporeal disciplinarity and the hierarchy of social bodies. To clarify this point I must turn to the hydrarchy of the ship.

The "Smells of the Hold"

Ocean space is conceptually replete with contradictions, perhaps necessary aporiae. Therefore it is difficult to envision the vastness of the ocean, a place of ontological limitlessness and fluidity, a space that cannot be captured by the panopticon, without the constraints of the shipboard hydrarchy. This tension between the ship and the sea means that transoceanic diaspora space is limitless and bounded, naturalized and socially stratified, and is constructed by the telos of home and the anticipation of arrival. The profound entanglement between perceptions of the oceanic and the hydrarchic—a tidalectic flow between the limitless and the structural, the natural and the social—is constituted and constitutive of western discourses of the Atlantic. This is the driving mechanism of fictional and historical narratives of the maritime mutiny, which often evoke social Darwinism as originary naturalism at sea. Thus a troubled modernity becomes enacted in narrative constructions of the sea, where the presumed atemporal and self-determining idiom of traversing ocean space is continually contested and constrained by social hierarchies and the material structure of the ship. Perhaps this is why the middle passage poses such a challenge to seafaring literature that celebrates masculine motility at sea as a metaphor of positive social and cultural expansion—to sustain this Enlightenment ideologeme, one must suppress the shackled passengers in the hold.[44] And perhaps this is why, for all their vital contributions to our understanding of multiethnic communities aboard ships that crisscross the Atlantic, Linebaugh, Rediker, and Gilroy reclaim a subaltern masculine agency in their visions of a revolutionary and black Atlantic. And perhaps, ultimately, this helps explain why the vast majority of literary revisions of the middle passage pursue a telos of mutiny.

In the western narrative tradition, the ship is a profoundly domestic—in the broadest definition of the term—and transnational social space, a place of practiced masculinity, labor, and uneven fraternity. Theorists of the Atlantic who position the ship as a fluid and nonhegemonic space, an alternative to the conservative nation-state, might well be reminded of a tradition of depicting the ship as the republic that dates back to Plato's *Phaedrus*.[45] Ships also signify religious, epistemological, and cultural journeys. Many syncretic African religions have adopted a Biblical conflation of ship/church as a structural vessel for black cultural unity, and Afro-Caribbean rituals often invoke a Legba-like, culturally and ontologically transformative enactment of the middle passage limbo.[46] While these narratives are diverse, they share an investment in the ship as a vessel of ontological and social transformation.

I want to focus specifically on the chronotope of the ship as both domestic/national space and the attendant corporeal polity that must constitute this as a place. This is particularly evident in the destabilizing language of gender, a sign of modernity that Hearne inscribes in *The Sure Salvation*. I have alluded to the ways in which Hearne's characters—the "woman-man" translator, the "feminine deftness" of the Portuguese sailors (17), and castrating Tadene—undermine gendered binary axioms. Hortense Spillers has raised the question as to whether we can gender the enslaved persons who were dehumanized as "flesh" in the middle passage experience.[47] Because of the dismantling of African kinship practices, Spillers determines that "the cargo of a ship might not be regarded as elements of the domestic" (1987, 72). Here I quote her at length as she succinctly encapsulates some of the spatial and temporal epistemologies examined in this chapter:

> Those African persons in the "middle passage" were literally suspended in the "oceanic," if we think of the latter in its Freudian orientation as an analogy for undifferentiated identity: removed from the indigenous land and culture, and not-yet "American" either, these captive persons . . . were in movement across the Atlantic, but they were also *nowhere* at all. Inasmuch as . . . the captive personality did not know where s/he was, we could say that they were the culturally "unmade," thrown in the midst of a figurative darkness that "exposed" their destinies to an unknown course. . . . [N]avigational science of the day was not sufficient to guarantee the intended destination. We might say that the slave ship, its crew, and its human-as-cargo stand for a wild and unclaimed richness of *possibility* that is not interrupted, not "counted"/"accounted," or differentiated, until its movement gains the land. . . . Under these conditions, one is neither female, nor male, as both subjects are taken into "account" as *quantities*. (72, author's emphasis)

The prequantifying language of enslaved bodies is inscribed in Hearne's novel as an undifferentiated and tautological "stench of the hold," abject corporeality, "waste," and bodily fluid. Since it is a fictional account, it is not, as Spillers suggests, "ungendered." In his imaginative vision of the transatlantic crossing, in an immobile space unmarked by time where the oppressive heat threatens the lives of both crew and slaves and thus forces them to circulate on the ship, Hearne has constructed a tiered yet permeable social layering, a profoundly domestic space of the (proto-national) ship, which is most visible in his gendered spatial logic.

By examining the architecture of the ship, we can see that Hearne suggests that European gendered norms arose from transatlantic colonization and were constitutive components of Atlantic modernity. His use of a fluid imaginary that draws from bodily waste rather than the ocean is effective because it facilitates the *dissolution* of the disciplinary boundaries between public and private domains. Women, the most obvious subjects marked by the domestic, are rendered corporeally present in both the "head" and "belly" (to borrow two shipboard terms) of social and material hierarchy. For instance, Hearne contains Eliza with her husband in what he terms "the poop." Tadene resides within the spatial abyss of the hold but emerges to bathe, eat, to assist her niece Mtishta, and to eject Reynolds's severed head in a scene that symbolizes this space as *vagina dentata*. Finally, Mtishta is spatially and socially trapped in the strata between these two older women, chosen by Reynolds from among the slaves to be his "little black beauty, [his] heathen bunkmate" (92). She resides in his private cabin and is taught Reynolds's version of the master's language, with emphasis on the ways in which it is racialized, sexualized, and gendered. In Hearne's parody of Prospero and Caliban of *The Tempest*, a text often claimed as a founding (masculine) narrative of Caribbean literature, Mtishta's first lesson is to interpellate herself as a "bitch," and to sexualize her body as "cunt" and "tits" (94). Mtishta functions in a binary but interdependent relation to literate, asexual, "lilac-scented" Eliza who, without any recognition of the slaves that buttress her social position, teaches literacy to the cabin boy, Joshua, through Biblical narratives of the horror of the (sexual) flesh. Interestingly, Hearne locates the nineteenth-century cult of domesticity and its racial codes as a specifically middle passage construction of social space.

Unlike most maritime novels, Hearne's hydrarchy does not encode a naturalized masculine motility grafted upon either a feminized sea or ship—in fact the ocean and ship are not gendered in this text—and women are not external to the historical process by being relegated to distant national shores. Hearne's "ship is a world" caught in the modern process of being "refashioned" (195) into new meanings of the domestic, foregrounding the racialization of sexual violence and language itself. In returning to Spillers' question about the production of oceanic "flesh," one could say that the contained slaves in Hearne's text are a corporeal mass *and* quantified as "four hundred and seventy-five bodies" that frighten the sailors with their "moans of bewildered protest" (25). In attributing agency and interiority to a number of the Africans, a type of access rendered impossible by the flattened historical "account" of the trade in "flesh," Hearne positions these characters as subjects and by extension, as gendered beings. As a structure of containment, the ship, like the nation, represents the architecture of gendered and racial stratification, but its stasis in the ocean of history ultimately forces these structural boundaries to dissolve through the exchange of bodily fluids.

The architecture of Hearne's ship, and by extension his characters, is determined by the literal production of bodily labor and waste. The first eight of his ten chapters are labeled after socially segregated spaces of the ship such as "The poop," "Officer's mess," "The forecastle," and "The midshiphouse." The slaves aren't located in a specifically titled space since they are corporeally or imaginatively present in all social spaces with the exception of "The poop." But this term, the most scatological of all the labeled spaces on the ship, brings the abstracted captain and his wife in direct relationship to the flesh of their corporeal cargo. The prevalence of physical metaphor here is not surprising when we consider that, to draw from the appendix of Peter Jeans's maritime dictionary, "Nautical terms related to the human body" represent the ways in which threats to sailors' survival were incorporated into the semantic and lexical body of the ship. This resonates with Philip Curtin's reminder that Atlantic sailors died at rates that in some cases exceeded those of the slaves, and that workers' compensation was often determined by the loss of limbs, digits, and other body parts (1968). Like Reynolds's instruction in the reification of the sexual and laboring body, the maritime conceptualization and labeling of shipboard space produces an itemized corporeality of terms that range from buttocks to breast, arse to brow, cheeks to bosom, and poop to crotch (Jeans 2004, 403–409). In his rendering of the corporeality of the ship, its workers, and its slaves, Hearne emphasizes the bodies that produce and are produced by Atlantic modernity.

The segregation of the ship into discrete bodily parts, its spatial compression and its clear racial hydrarchy are ultimately dissolved by the copious production of human waste, which seeps across all social boundaries. The narrative frame of the captain's space, "The poop" is "ringed by the unbroken crust of its own garbage" (Hearne 1981, 7), and smells that arise from the hold extend outwards of a mile at sea. When Reynolds takes the crew out in the "jolly boat," attempting to pull "clear of the ever-widening, dully-shimmering band of waste," he is unable to escape and fears *they'll smell us clear to the Admiralty*" (101, author's emphasis). The production of bodily waste that might attract the disciplinary apparatus of the naval state can be set alongside Mary Douglas's assertion that conceptions of dirt and pollution arise from social spaces that are constituted by exaggerated notions of hierarchy and control (1966, 4). "Dirt offends against order" (Douglas, 1966, 2), so its presence viscerally foregrounds the ways in which the hydrarchy of the slave ship constructs a fragile rationality over a permeating ethical and corporeal pollution. Waste, while related to the majority population on the ship, the slaves, is also produced and circulated by the high-ranking European officers. In keeping with the modern bourgeois "campaign to deodorize bodies and space" (Corbin 1986, 105), a hierarchy of toilets has been established: a "privy" for the officers, a "little booth" for the crew, while the "slaves urinated and defecated where they lay below" (Hearne 1981, 100). When Reynolds emerges from the hold "with a small lump of yellow excrement grained with dark streaks" and carries this on a spatula to the captain's "poop" for examination (42), we are given an almost visual testimony to the ways in which bodily waste permeates the social strata of the ship, and a reiteration of how the civilizing practices of modernity "authorized the strategy of continual surveillance" (Corbin 1986, 94–95). Like the racial hydrarchy that enables Eliza's cult of domesticity, the production and circulation of waste signifies the ways in which the middle passage was constitutive—rather than external to—a socially tiered modernity.

The term waste, derived from the Latin *vastus*, signifies uninhabited or uncultivated space and has been semantically linked with European conceptions of the ocean. Waste is also historical; as Alain Corbin has shown, western modernity was coterminous with a new "importance accorded to the circulation of liquid masses" (1986, 91) to maintain the health of the body politic. Laura Brown has detailed the etymological link between "sewer" and "shore" and how this contributed to a shift in British literatures that conflated water with waste during the rise of its maritime empire. Over time, the concept of waste developed symbolic and material connotations with sewage, enacting a disciplining code of hygiene that resulted in the urban sewers built in London in the 1860s (Corbin 1986, 225), the temporal frame of Hearne's novel. As such, Walcott's assertion that the "sea is history" is interpreted through the logic of "the sea is waste." Hearne temporalizes ocean space through the production of human bodies, and waste becomes the only localizable product of transoceanic history as well as the primary signifier of modernity. The antonym to waste, value, is materially constituted by the bodies of the slaves, whose feces are constantly monitored for impurities so that Reynolds and the crew may accumulate a "small fortune" (Hearne 1981, 83). The desire of capital is doubly linked to the slaves by Hearne's continual references to the exchange of gold "guineas," a term that arose from the African slave trade itself. Most of the crew are unable to make the semantic and material connections between waste, value, and the transatlantic exchange of African bodies. When they are visibly repelled by "the stench of the hold," Reynolds retorts, *"Don't you like the smell? Inhale it. . . . Wallow in it. It's your fortune you're sniffing, you block-head"* (39–40, author's emphasis).

82   Although he overlooks the empire's racialization of bodies, Corbin historicizes the modern process by which "the stench of the poor" was constructed (1986, 142). In the late eighteenth century, an emergent bourgeois concern with the deodorization and discipline of the masses reflected a fear of corporeal proximity, a construction of "the fetidity of the labouring classes" (143), particularly sailors. This discourse of the corporeal waste of the masses is reminiscent of my earlier discussion of the "folk," if we consider the semantic resonance between waste and soil. In fact, Illich points out that the term "shit" derives from the same etymological root as "earth" (1987, 29). This connection between the corporeality of the "folk" and the nation-building process has long been a concern in Hearne's writing. His second novel, *Stranger at the Gate* (1956), describes urban Jamaican poverty in bodily terms that invoke what the geographer Brian Hudson has categorized as a "smellscape" (1992, 187). Hudson demonstrates that Hearne's middle- and upper-class spaces and bodies are rendered in normative, acorporeal terms that are constituted in unequal relation to the hyperembodied Jamaican poor. In *Stranger*, Hearne writes, "Forty thousand people lived in the Jungle [the "Dungle," in Kingston], and five hundred of them had jobs to go to in the morning . . . . [T]he people gave off the sweetish stink of bodies which don't get enough food, and it's like smelling from a distance the room where a man is ill with jaundice" (1956, 74). Here the bodily language of the urban folk, when read against the depiction of slaves in his final novel, suggests that the latter function as a proto-national mass in the hold. For in *The Sure Salvation*, Hearne describes the middle passage abyss in remarkably similar terms:

> The smells of the hold seem to have congealed into one substance
> denser than the air in which it is suspended: an exudation, foul, tepid
> and almost phantasmagorial, that clings to the face, hands and nostrils
> like mucus. Something that does not rise from only the gross dis-
> charges or urine puddles, oozing shit, splashed vomit, the constant
> farts and belches, the sweat, mingled oils and furious heat of near five
> hundred living bodies packed on shelves as close as corpses from an
> epidemic heaped into a pit of quicklime. (1981, 137)

Although Hearne's works need to be positioned in the nation-building era of Jamaica and the broader Caribbean, I do not want to simply assert that the ship here is the *Republic*, to follow the metaphor of Plato's *Phaedrus* and Charles Johnson's *Middle Passage*. Rather, I want to deepen this parallel by suggesting that the constitutive components of modern nation-building can be traced back to the hydrarchy of the slave ship itself. This marks Hearne's break from Caribbean scholars who situate the pigmentocracy of the plantation as the origin of creolization and the postcolonial nation-state. By extension, Hearne places the middle passage as an originary narrative of creolization and modernity, even as the novel problematizes its temporality and foregrounds its historical alterity. By exploring the antinomy between waste and value, Hearne makes a vital contribution to materialist historiographies of Caribbean modernity which, in Marxist terms, have traditionally drawn from the exploitation of slave labor and the economic expansion of empire. By exploring the (nonlabor) production of bodies, configuring the ocean as waste, and tracing the semantic value of transatlantic "guineas," Hearne connects economic history to a corporeal Atlantic modernity.

Orifices of Creolization

Maritime historians have long argued that "civilization" is "the product of the activities of seamen sailing in ships across the seas," positioning the ocean as "the great medium" of "dissemination" of "the seminal fluid and the lifeblood of civilization" (Waters 1967, 189; see also Connery 1996, 296–298). These metaphors of fluidity and movement often encode a sexually virile and masculine motility of (etymologically) spermatic "dissemination" of "seminal" waters. Hearne's emphasis on the *viscosity* of middle passage waste, a "congealed" substance described in the novel as "denser than air," which "clings" like "mucus" (1981, 137) positions transoceanic history as an unstable and feminized substance that cannot flow towards a linear futurity (see Douglas 1966, 38; see also Grosz 1994, 194). The novel's corporeality positions the ship as a body politic, but resists the maritime telos of progress and mobility. *Pace* Freud, Hearne explores how "dirtiness of any kind seems to us incompatible with civilization" (Freud 1961, 44), but his novel positions the "dirty trade" (1981, 35) as the inassimilable "waste" of civilizing narratives. Thus the "clinging evidence of their corruption, which the water would not swallow" (1981, 7), registers more than an oceanic sublime characterized by Connery as a recognition that "the ocean is *too* external: its assimilability... is always in doubt" (1996, 290). As in Andrew Salkey's epigraph to this chapter, the Atlantic is a "rass" of a history ocean—a Jamaican creolization of "rat's ass"—that suggests that abject corporeality of the middle passage is sanitized from the history of civilization as both event and narrative. Perhaps this is why of all the animals likened to human subjects on board, rendering the ship as a Conradian bestiary, "sea dog" becomes the most privileged metaphor in Hearne's novel.[48] As Freud has shown, dogs are unevenly incorporated into the civilizing process due to their association with a developed olfactory capacity "which has no horror of excrement, and that is not ashamed of its sexual functions" (1961, 52).

In *The Sure Salvation* the "smells of sweat and heavy sleep, like a coma, of faeces, menstrual blood, baby's vomit, of closely packed flesh [that] thickened in the air above the hold" (Hearne 1981, 36) pose, in Reynolds's words, a palpable "problem for the world's digestion" (37). Just as Hearne resists the homogenizing metaphors of the oceanic, his invocation of waste is specific to the age and gender of particular bodies. The culinary "spatula" that Reynolds carries to "the poop," described as "a load of yellow waste ringed by pale yellow gravy" (43) is tied to cycles of bodily consumption, remarkably like the crew's unpalatable food of "stringy meat" and "yellow grease" (31). As a result, the civilizing process of western capital is shown to be characterized by "immediate hunger, lust and ruthless preservation of the self" (63), particularly for the novel's underclass and racialized characters. Unlike the folkloric novel examined by Bakhtin, Hearne suggests that "consumption" and "productive labor" can be decoupled, rendering *waste* as their unspeakable result (207). The *Sure Salvation*'s immobility, its entrapment in the corporealized present, implodes the temporal registers of Bakhtin's chronotope, which, he explains, is more heavily encoded by time than space. Thus the immobility of the ship and its surrounding waste cannot be "responsive to the movements of time, plot and history" (Bakhtin 1981, 84). As such, Hearne's middle passage is mired in the end-products and consumptive discharges of its own history, destabilizing linear temporality and infusing the present with the viscosity of bodily presence. The bodies "packed" out of historical view into the "shelves" of the hold invoke what de Certeau has noted as the disciplinary quarantine of "ob-scene" bodies, "censured, deprived of language," and "unnamable" (de Certeau 1984, 191) in the telos of transparent, fluid, civilizing history.

To position the middle passage as a site of historical origins for Caribbean modernity, one must limit the totalizing implications of the "sea as waste." Waste in this context may also be read as a position of "exile" beyond signification where an imperial rule of law is not overly inscribed on bodies (de Certeau 1984, 191). Since European histories of the middle passage emphasized the crossing as a "social death," positioning Africans in the New World as a *tabula rasa* upon which to inscribe colonial modernity, Hearne's generation was pursuing a logic of creolization that argued for the existence of cultural residue and survivals, a history of endurance rising from the horrors of the "civilizing" process.[49] The folk culture of the slaves thus became a vital symbolic resource for postwar nationalism and creolization itself. So while Hearne's invocation of waste must necessarily include the loss of subjects in the middle passage—a narrative attempt at a return to memorialize the unspeakable—it also utilizes the metaphor of waste as a sign of social margins or frontier. As Douglas reminds us, the fluids and substances emitted from the body necessarily highlight the permeability of social and corporeal structures, positioning human refuse in terms of power and danger (1966, 120). Hearne's inscription of the sea as waste positions the middle passage as the site where corporeal and social boundaries are transgressed. Since "any structure of ideas is vulnerable at its margins" (Douglas 1966, 121), the expansion of capital—a sign of the civilizing process itself— becomes radically decentered from its Euro-American continental frame and placed in an Africanized Atlantic.

Abject bodies have always been a problem to the metanarrative of modernity because they elude logical rationality (Kristeva 1982, 65). Since spaces of the margin, those "orifices" of the social and corporeal body, signify vulnerability to pollution and permeability (Kristeva 1982, 121), the mouth and "cunt" become Hearne's privileged metaphors of the violence of the creolization process. I have discussed the ways in which Mtishta enters the master's language through the process of shipboard rape and her interpellation as a racialized "bitch" (Hearne 1981, 95). As Corbin points out, the response of bourgeois modernity to the perceived filth of the masses was to purify the social body through instruction (1986,148) and through the deodorization of language (1986, 214). In terms of the body of Africans, Mtishta becomes the first self-conscious, speaking subject of Atlantic creolization. An Irish sailor remarks on the ship's polyglossia, ironically complaining, "'It's as hard to get an exchange av dacint English on this tub as in the jungles av Africa'" (Hearne 1981, 31). Like the majority of Europeans on board, he seems oblivious to the ship's modernizing process. In contrast, the sexual and linguistic exchange between Mtishta and Reynolds configures them as uneven but active agents of transatlantic creolization. Far from suppressing Mtishta under the weight of her own sexual victimization, Hearne places her narrative in the literal center of the novel, providing brief access to her interiority and her interpellation of her rapist as "*Elegwa:* evil without a purpose, accidentally embodied; a spirit without a role in the complex exchanges of good and bad; a thing outside the decent order of worship and propitiation" (83). Significantly, she refers to him by a New World (Cuban) name rather than West African (Eshu, Legba). Since Reynolds is "outside knowledge" and "beyond explanation," she determines that he is worth "no more than a few expiatory gestures" (83). Although Reynolds has "planted" his penis in "the moist darkness where its new roots might grow and find purchase," Mtishta ultimately considers herself "safe" from "being consumed" (83). Hearne omits Reynolds' voice in this violent exchange, so Mtishta's narrative predominates, exceeding the consuming logic of capital and the exploitation of human bodies. In fact, this violent sexual "moment of passage" catalyzes her memories of home, capture, and exile, her critique of the slave trade as secular consumption without "proper ceremony," and her commitment to inform the women of Reynolds's "people" that "a purpose for a woman's mouth" is not to "uselessly swallow . . . seed and eat . . . children" (93). Admittedly, Hearne's inscription of Mtishta's agency is deeply problematic—his indirect narrative voice renders her relations with Reynolds as "making love" (93)—and she and Tadene disappear from the narrative after the mutiny and are absent from New World futurity. One might interpret her terror of forced oral sex, a practice she finds worse than death and slavery (93), as a desire for insemination. Nevertheless, her critiques of the unproductive cycles of capitalist consumption and secular individualism, coupled with her piercing insight into "what his people called woman . . . *Bitch*" (95), generate a vital counter-narrative to the civilizing process as well as an epistemic site of creolization itself.

As Mary Douglas points out, discourses of bodily pollution are metaphysically conflated with sexual "perversion" and rigidify the boundaries between the sacred and profane. Thus the figure by which Mtishta recognizes Reynolds, Elegwa, signifies a syncretic African deity of the crossroads—a generative sign of the creolization process and the (sexual) initiation into Atlantic modernity. Known as Legba in Dahomey, this figure represents the divine linguist and trickster, illicit and "perverse" sexuality and was often conflated by Christian missionaries with the devil (Herskovits 1938, 225). In the form of the Yoruba trickster Eshu-Elegba, he is the *agent provocateur* of "change and transition" (Wescott 1962, 337); he is irreverent towards social and sacred boundaries and is also an explorer (340–341). Similar to Reynolds, he is a figure of "flagrant orality" (Thompson 1983, 32), associated with the spoon (or spatula) and an "insatiable hunger" of the libido (Wescott 1962, 347). Like the transformative codes of creolization, Elegwa ushers in the spirit of change (Thompson 1983, xv), is "the ultimate master of potentiality" (19), and is "one of the most important images of the black Atlantic world" (19). As a deity associated with trade and commerce (Pelton 1980, 89), his transference to the middle passage, a western border of Africa, suggests that "the limits of this world can be horizons" (88). He highlights middle passage modernity as "a principle of fluidity, of uncertainty, of the indeterminacy even of one's inscribed fate" (Gates 1988, 28).

In keeping with Glissant's suggestion that creolization is a mutual process that implicates Europeans and Africans, Mtishta characterizes Reynolds (and his aristocratic ilk) as originary mechanisms of the slave trade and its associated violence. Reynolds is one of the few characters who is unimpeded by the hypocritical boundaries of bourgeois morality and is a gleeful participant in a middle passage modernity that is constituted by the semantic and material exchange of waste and value. He embraces and embodies the abject, that underbelly of modernity, by recognizing that "the sea will not be moulded into our excremental falsehoods" (Hearne 1981, 82). Although he hopes that upon arrival Mtishta will present "one of those yellow Brazilian swells with a blue-eyed mulatto boy" (89), a challenge to the creole planters who he feels "drone on interminably about [their] Visigothic forebears" (89), his decapitation/castration ultimately terminates his patronymic claims on New World futurity. Highlighting the ways in which diaspora is etymologically derived from sperm, Hearne provides a subtle critique of culture models offered by Caribbean theorists such as Denis Williams who have argued that the filial concept of the "ancestor might fittingly be replaced by that of the donor—the donor of the sperm," reducing Caribbean creolization to "African sperm in various states of catalysis" (1969, 12). Reynolds's alliance with the patronymic is visible in his anticipated production of a "blue-eyed . . . boy," a white masculinity that literally frames and occludes the central sign of creolization: "mulatto."

Hearne's novel provides a critique of masculinist genealogies of diaspora and creolization, even those secured through mutiny and revolt.[50] This might explain why Delfosse's plot of mutiny is shown to have a problematic origin (his adaptation of Enlightenment individualism) and ultimately results in failure. This allows creolization, the only generative process to arise from oceanic waste, to become the only remaining narrative of futurity in the New World. Delfosse, who models his future kingdom up the Amazon on the likes of Hernándo Cortés, Francisco Pizarro, and the "Emperor Christophe" (Hearne 1981, 200), has only two days of rule at sea before he is intercepted by the HMS *Beaver*, a British naval steamer that signifies a "revolution" in technology, patrolling for illegal slave ships (204). Lieutenant Michael Honeyball, an adherent of technology as a tool of empire, is "obsessed" with the machinery of "steam and steel" (205) and its disciplinary rule. This phallic "power throbbing through the connection rod to his twin screws" is what allows him to intercept the *Sure Salvation*, a ship lost to time and nautical technologies (205). Honeyball also ushers in an age of lost intimacy with the sea and an illusory ideologeme of the temporal conquest of ocean space through science. Although his engine fails while he's accompanying the slaver to the Guianas, and he is nearly outrun by the wind-driven power of the *Sure Salvation*, Honeyball believes:

> He had learned how to use the sure power of steam against the immemorial energy of the sea that had now become random and helpless against the mind that could demand any direction or make any assertion with absolute assurance of the tireless, utterly obedient servant it was now able to command on a moment's decision. (205)

In prose almost as torturous as his logic, Honeyball reflects a radical shift in the nineteenth-century maritime world, where the emergence of new technologies feminized the sea and subjected its currents and depths to military science and a new discipline of oceanography. The HMS *Beaver*, the name of one of Marryat's transatlantic ships, also invokes Darwin's *Beagle*, a vehicle best known for its contributions to an evolutionary rendering of deep historic time. The temporal frame of Hearne's novel—May to June 1860—is contemporaneous with the publication of the first U.S. edition of *Origin of Species* and the debate at the British Association for the Advancement of Science between Thomas Huxley and Samuel Wilberforce over special versus natural selection. Publications from the *Beagle*'s voyage contributed to the rise of U.S. nautical fiction by adapting Darwin's account of an oceanic origin of life to uphold the genre of naturalism and its chronotopes of violent evolutionary struggle.[51] Importantly, the *Beagle*'s voyage also catalyzed the field of oceanography, the rise of maritime studies, and the establishment of the first transatlantic submarine telegraph cable (1866), the "spinal cord of the British empire" (Headrick 1988, 101). As a vehicle of imperial measurement and rule, the *Beagle*'s mission included the surveillance of the Argentine coast, to secure the Falklands as a territory for the empire and, with twenty-four chronometers on board, to tighten the temporal precision of longitude (Browne 1992, 464). This mechanistic rule of the sea is a radical change from Columbus's attempts to measure the speed of his ship by the pace of his own heartbeat (Gerbi 1985, 22).

Honeyball's maritime nationalism and his investment in the modernizing technologies of empire are depicted, like Amasa Delano of *Benito Cereno*, as a dangerously cloaked liberal paternalism that seeks to distance itself from the "filthy, barbarous trade" (Hearne 1981, 223) it sustains by deflecting that history through the valorization of Atlantic surveillance and corporeal discipline. His "precise command of the oceans he patrolled and protected" for the nation-state is undermined by the nakedness of the newly liberated Africans; their lack of clothing threatens him with "a sense of order overthrown, of blatant challenge to all proper and civilized progress, more serious than the smells and other evidence of slavery that still clung to the vessel" (213). In stark contrast to Hogarth, Honeyball is later "consoled" in "moments of guilt" (211) by Delfosse's pronouncement that "'you an' me could no more help meetin' up the way we done than we could help bein' born the way each of us was. It had to happen this way'" (212). On the one hand, Hearne may be suggesting the ways in which this narrative of interception is already predetermined by the maritime genre itself, particularly *Benito Cereno*. On the other hand, this verbal exchange also demonstrates how quickly Honeyball interprets contingency as absolution from historical responsibility. This is evident in Honeyball's decision to dump his "prize" in a coastal village of British Guiana that is ill-prepared for its new African residents and has no precedent for legal proceedings against the Europeans. As an Amasa Delano figure who is unable to fathom or "cut the knot" (an image also prevalent on Hearne's ship), Honeyball remains oblivious to black agency and subjectivity beyond the dialectic of master-slave. As Delfosse explains, "'I'se black an' free an' you don' really like neither condition'" (209). It doesn't occur to Honeyball that he has intercepted a ship that is completely under control of agents of the black Atlantic and, given the free movement of all bodies, can no longer be interpellated as a slaver.

Even if he abandons his "prize" in the Guianas, Honeyball and his claim to patriotic progress and social liberalism are no less dangerous. Hearne destabilizes the maritime adventure novel by minimizing Honeyball's capture of the *Sure Salvation*, denying the chronotope of a dramatic pursuit and battle at sea when Delfosse surrenders voluntarily. Nevertheless, Honeyball still attempts to derive his narrative of technological progress from a patriarchal legacy of maritime nationalism. Although Honeyball had read and dismissed Darwin's thesis, Hearne's narrator describes him as

> a new species—all the more terrible in his potential to alter the development of his kind for good or ill, because he was utterly unaware that his youthful understanding of the new [steam] power he

had inherited . . . made him as different a creature from the heroes of his boyhood (Nelson, Wellington, Rodney, Cook, Columbus, Drake and the great reformers of the Anglican Church) as they had been different from the apes to which that damned Darwin had recently suggested they were linked. (206)

Honeyball, a bourgeois subject who concedes to Hogarth's aristocratic privilege (refusing to contain him in the forecastle with the common sailors), is all the more dangerous because he idealizes a patriarchal genealogy of empire, entirely English "voyagers of history." In contrast, Hogarth's adopted maritime forebears had little investment in religious or secular nationalism. Although both men's visions of history uphold a masculine genealogy of empire, Hogarth does not feminize the ship and sea as submissive objects like his replacement, who introduces a newly gendered grammar of the oceanic. For example, Honeyball's response to Eliza's presence on the ship is to call for a disciplinary "fumigating" of her feminine contamination (207), and he denies African women any subjectivity—Mtishta, discovered in Reynolds's cabin, is simply "black and naked." By interpellating the slaves as uncivilized objects, visibly resenting Delfosse's claims to equality, and invoking a patriarchal genealogy of the sea, Honeyball fashions himself a liberator precisely through his own failure to recognize his complicity in the violent social hierarchies of maritime nationalism. Only by homogenizing transoceanic history can he inscribe a genealogy of aristocratic and patriarchal heroes of the state, an "imagined community" or sperm bank of "seamen" forebears who are sanitized from the trade in flesh.

Although scholars have often cited the 1890 publication of Alfred Thayer Mahan's *The Influence of Sea Power upon History* as a catalyst for American transoceanic expansion, an era when a "Hegelian oceanic elementalism" became "fused with American manifest destiny" (Connery 1995, 182), Hearne's novel and its precursor in *Benito Cereno* suggest an earlier collusion between science and the military to sustain the Anglo-American dominance of ocean space. Like *Benito Cereno*, Hearne's novel encodes transoceanic expansion under the veil of a liberal humanism that attempts to cloak the rising tide of revolutionary subjects in France, Haiti, and the Americas. But as a palimpsest, *Sure Salvation* interjects an African-American subject in a historical era and genre that is primarily dictated by Euro-American characters. As a character and symbol, "Del fosse" signifies the historical aporia rendered by benevolent narratives of historical progress that emphasize the civilizing banishment of the trade and the liberation of the slaves rather then the European construction of these systems themselves. Just as Melville aligned the slave revolt in *Benito Cereno* with the Haitian revolution (see Sundquist 1993), Hearne shifts his narrative of Atlantic modernity to the eve of the American Civil War; both position the sea as a constitutive space of the liberated subject who emerges only to be immediately subjected to the transoceanic reach of an imperialist nation-state.

The sea change Hearne inscribes in these transoceanic narratives may be better understood if we consider Honeyball's masculinist claim to technological power as a reflection of the emergent ideologies demonstrated in Matthew Fountaine Maury's bestselling *The Physical Geography of the Sea*, first published in 1855. Inspired by the voyage of the *Beagle* (although, like Honeyball, offended by Darwin's evolutionary thesis), Maury is often cited as the "father" of oceanography. He was a significant organizer of an international effort in 1853 to increase the speed and profit of transoceanic trade by universalizing marine science. He encouraged naval and merchant ships to expand the rule and measurement of the sea by using their instruments to produce a "floating observatory" (1857, xiii) and envisioned the Atlantic as a "great highway" that needed to be latitudinally expanded for trade, filling those oceanic "blank spaces" on hydrographic maps just as "civilized man" might expand into the "solitudes of the wilderness" in the western migration to Oregon (x). By connecting nationalist expansion across the land and sea as manifest destiny, and flattening both topoi into homogenous resources for the expanding empire of science, Maury anticipated an oceanic "harvest" of knowledge for "the benefit of commerce and navigation." Similar to Honeyball's idealization of Anglican reformers, Maury claimed the knowledge was for "the good of all," but targeted the "maritime states of Christendom" (xiii).

Honeyball's sea of science, technology, and national discipline is reflected in Maury's attempt to prove the ways in which the ocean "has its offices and duties to perform," natural "machinery" that is likened to the "mechanism of a watch" (1857, 53). By de-spatializing the oceanic through the temporal registers of longitude and steam ships, the "clockwork of the ocean," a synecdoche of "the machinery of the universe" was scientifically determined by "order and regularity" (169). Since the rise of oceanographic surveillance was a national and commercial endeavor, it is no surprise that Maury conscripts the natural rhythms of the sea into "laws of order," creating a transparent sea grammar. In Maury's "hand-book of nature, every fact is a syllable," legible to the (male) subject who is destined to "read aright from the great volume" of the sea (69). This connection between the perceived legibility of the sea, the rise of oceanography in the service of the U.S. military, and the development of the American maritime novel are inextricably connected. They are all dependent upon a disciplinary Atlantic modernity that subjects its laboring and abject bodies to the mechanism of linear time, dominion, and rule.

Hearne positions Honeyball as "all the more terrible in his potential to alter the development of his kind" because, unlike Hogarth, his social Darwinism is too naturalized to be recognized as a distinct historical development in the trajectory of maritime empire. Although both men are oblivious to the ways in which they have participated in and contributed to Atlantic modernity and slavery, Honeyball, like his name, may seem all the more sweet and natural for his benign intervention. Maury reminded his readers that these new claims to knowledge/power over the ocean meant that we must "cease to regard it as a waste of waters" (1857, 53), but Honeyball's character makes it clear that the rise of oceanography was engaged with a metaphysical cleansing of the "dirty trade" and the "stench of the masses" from maritime history. In fact the new era of oceanography was seen as an instructive tool for the masses, a practice that would "induce a serious earnestness" in sailors' work and "teach [them] to view lightly those irksome and often offensive duties" on the ship (Maury 1857, xiv). Marine sciences were pedagogical in their deodorization of the masses and, as I explain in the next chapter, also helped to provide a natural bodily metaphor for economic circulation. This is how oceanic "circulation" became a metaphor for blood in a universalized human body, "complete" and "obedient to law and order" (Maury 1857, 154). Although the ocean, as Connery has shown, has been deemed radically exterior to human comprehension, the fluid metaphors of blood and circulation ultimately provided the way in which it was internalized as ethnicity and nation. Through the new oceanography represented by Honeyball and Maury we can see that the rise of masculine sciences relegated feminized nature, "the womb of the sea" (Maury 1857, 248), to the regulation of measurement and rule. The ocean's violent and diverse human history was submerged, like the slaves in Turner's painting, by a scientific naturalism hinged to commerce, producing a sea grammar that has no vocabulary for articulating the sea as slavery.

Between Land and Sea: Limbo Gateways

> The journey over water: middle passage: time's river: was a
> new initiation: lembe: limbo: legba: god of the crossroads.
> —Kamau Brathwaite, "Gods of the Middle Passage"

In the real history that haunts *Benito Cereno*, the slaves who revolted on the *Tryal* were tortured and killed by the crew, and the survivors were resold into slavery. Melville's novel neglects to mention these details and does not inscribe their futurity. In contrast, Hearne provides a narrative space for his characters that is not overdetermined by Honeyball's "liberating" regime of discipline and surveillance. By placing the Africans in an English colony, Hearne circumvents the claims on their bodies that would have been made by the neighboring South American slave-states. Ironically, the ship is left in the Guianas, the land of "the Golden Kingdom" (Hearne 1981, 219) that Delfosse had sought as El Dorado. Significantly, Hearne empties the entire village of its European population on the day of the *Sure Salvation*'s arrival; the local whites are in the interior, celebrating a birthday of a monarch whose name they have forgotten. Since Hogarth and his crew are incarcerated and Honeyball has departed, Delfosse and the Africans are left to navigate their own process of acculturation, facilitated by the local "mulatto" Weddington, a transplant from Barbados. The absence of Europeans places the arrivants in a direct dialogue with the Afro-Caribbean residents. Importantly, the Africans disembark onto "the *stelling*," a Dutch word for pier and the title of Hearne's first published short story (1960). On the middle of "the great iron-heart stage," they begin to dance, unevenly "since they were culled from such a variety of tribes, nations and peoples" (222). Hearne writes:

> And the sound of their feet—stamping into the planks of the land-
> ing tacked onto the edge of this new land which they could not even
> begin to comprehend—made a curious harmony, as of different
> tongues trying to discover the few important words by which they
> might discover essential exchange. The black people of Abari, all
> fifteen thousand of them, gathered at the edge of the *stelling*, and
> watched with incomprehension, resentment, and visibly mounting
> interest the dances that were being danced before them by people
> who looked like them but with whom they could not exchange one
> meaningful word. (222)

Caught between land and sea, the arrivants are no longer routed, but not yet rooted; the movement of their feet on the ship-like *stelling*, a structure of iron and wood that suggests the transitionary regime of the oceanic, highlights a moment of possibility rather than completion. As they are not yet interpellated by the English language and the residual hierarchies of the plantation system, their first movement as a unified body occurs only when they depart the hydrarchy of the ship and are placed on the lateral footing of the *stelling*, a symbol of the potential of this new world.

Hearne's decision to conclude the novel on the *stelling*, a limbo space at the gateway between the Atlantic and the vast Guyanese interior, metonymically invokes the colonial utopian drive towards El Dorado and the possibilities of reformulating a new understanding of the past in the Caribbean present. Although the "proper" speech and English uniform adopted by the Barbadian Weddington (whom Honeyball repeatedly misnames as "Washington") suggests the dangers of assimilation, encoding the ways in which "Little England" has taken root,[52] Hearne seems to hope that these arrivants will learn from the indigenous inhabitants "who understood that the relationship between the huge, nurturing land and those who lived on it was not one of possession" (219). In this novel, history, as Roberto Márquez points out, will provide no "sure salvation" (1983, 270). But highlighting the creative, diverse, and tidalectic process of creolization offers a different temporal trajectory of possibility.

We may see the dance of these New World Africans in terms of the generative potential of limbo, first theorized by Wilson Harris in his *History, Fable and Myth in the Caribbean and Guianas*. The limbo dance, "born, as it is said, on the slave ships of the Middle Passage" (1995b, 157), resonates with the deity Legba, encoding a "pun on limbo as a shared phantom limb" for diaspora communities seeking to remember the losses of the crossing (157). The phantom limb, an absent signifier of a lost corporeal unity brought into being through memory rather than History, offers a bodily trace and memorial of the middle passage crossing.[53] The "limbo dance becomes the human gateway which dislocates (and therefore begins to free itself from) a uniform chain of miles across the Atlantic" (28), a counter-memory to the homogenous temporality of longitude and universalized maritime history. To Harris, the dance also encodes "a profound art of compensation which seeks to replay a dismemberment of tribes . . . and to invoke at the same time a curious psychic re-assembly of the parts of the dead god or gods" (28).

Unlike most theories of Caribbean creolization which root the process in the plantation system, Hearne places his subjects at the shores of Guyana, "land of many waters," at a moment of uneven recognition between the arrivants and black residents, performing a dance that does not insist upon a unity of the social body but rather is a fledgling attempt at diversity of expression before they enter the social and linguistic grammars of colonial plantation culture. In a text that destabilizes the desire to fix the ocean and these shores as cultural origin, the *stelling* is not the privileged site of creolization and modernity. To begin to locate the first symptoms of modernity in this novel we would have to turn to the women characters, Mtishta and Tadene, who have undergone the process of displacement and reassemblage first in Africa when kidnapped from their villages, then in the coastal trading ports, and finally in the middle passage itself. Hearne's novel is far more visionary than his counterparts of the time, who often de-temporalized African culture by locating modernity in the ships and plantations of the western Atlantic as if the continent were outside of the historical process of the middle passage and slavery. In Hearne's vision, Africa was already modern before its subjects entered the Atlantic, and thus his characters represent not so much a counterculture of modernity as its driving mechanism.

By reading *The Sure Salvation* tidalectically in the complex relationship between land and sea, we see that the novel maps a process of modernity and creolization that is not fixed or rooted in any one place. Thus metaphorically and historically, the middle passage, a process more than a place, signifies that violent and regenerative way in which the sea is history. To fathom the middle passage, we might trace its signifying wake in the aquatic metaphors of *Modernity and Its Futures;* the authors describe the process of time-space compression as a point when "identities become detached—disembedded—from specific times, places histories, and traditions, and appear 'free-floating'" (Hall, Held, and McGrew 1992, 303). Or, to draw from Anthony Giddens's definition, modernity entails a "'lifting out' of social relations from local contexts of interaction and their restructuring across indefinite spans of time-space" (1990, 21). By inscribing the sea as bodily waste, *The Sure Salvation* warns of the dangers of dehistoricizing a "free-floating" subject who has been forcibly removed from "social relations" by a disciplinary oceanic regime that "thanks to the liquid element itself, leaves no borders, furrows, or markings" (Connery 1995, 177). Hearne suggests that only by forcing chronological movement to stagnate, to examine those places where time might be "tricked, frozen by violence" (1981, 47), will we get a glimpse of its diverse spatial bodies in those limbo moments of possibility and change.

CHAPTER 2

Vessels of the Pacific
An Ocean in the Blood

> We are sixty-five percent water. . . . Our brains are eighty
> per cent water. We are more water than blood. So our
> water ties to one another are more important than our
> blood ties! We carry within us the seas out of which we
> came.
> —Albert Wendt, *Ola*

A tidalectic methodology of reading island literatures brings together
the rooted discourse of terrestrial belonging with the fluidity of
transoceanic migration, foregrounding the process of diaspora
and highlighting the complex relationship between national and regional
identities. Although Pacific Island discourse is generally associated with
indigenous sovereignty and a historic relationship to the land, to read these
cultural productions tidalectically one must engage with the vital counter-
narrative of transoceanic routes and diaspora. In fact, this chapter shows
that contestations over land sovereignty in the Pacific are often mitigated
through maritime origins; thus regional aquatic routes often sustain local
roots. Like their Caribbean counterparts, writers from the Pacific Islands
(Oceania) have turned to the genealogies of transoceanic migration in an
attempt to remap the national boundaries imposed by western colonialism.
Unlike the enforced Atlantic crossings examined in the previous chapter,
ancient Pacific voyaging represents the voluntary settlement of the largest
region on the globe, coordinated and orchestrated with indigenous technology. Although their experiences of diaspora and migration are radically
different from the Atlantic context, many Pacific Island writers have destabilized myths of island isolation through a transoceanic imaginary that
highlights vast kinship networks and the agency of the first indigenous
settlers.[1] Here I explore how the histories of Pacific voyaging, symbolized

by transoceanic vessels, have been engaged in different ways by the military, anthropology, and indigenous literatures. I argue that the discourse of routes encodes not only an oceanic imaginary but also the *vehicles* and *vessels* of Pacific historiography. Whether rendered as a voyaging canoe, a naval ship, a drifting raft, or metaphorically as ethnic blood, the concept of the *vessel* is integral to territorial claims of indigenous sovereignty as well as (masculine) ethnic regionalism.

The foundation of this chapter is inspired by Epeli Hauʻofaʻs vision of "a sea of islands," a regional imaginary that stresses fluidity and interconnectedness rather than isolation (1993b, 7). By invoking the settlement of Oceania by ancient voyagers, Hauʻofa explains that these historical migration patterns can be used as tropes for a more "holistic" understanding of an increasingly mobile and globalized Pacific. His conceptual mapping of the region has been tremendously influential, cited by scholars across the disciplines as a way to indigenize a regional imagination that is still subject to the colonial legacy of cultural and economic belittlement.[2] Yet this invocation of a particular ethnic migration, generally imagined as masculine Polynesian voyagers, raises important questions about navigating the intersections of ethnicity, gender, and class in the contemporary Pacific. Hauʻofaʻs vision was originally published as a book-length dialogue in *A New Oceania*, but its subsequent circulation in the United States as an isolated article has deflected attention from its original critiques. Importantly, Derek Walcottʻs poem "The Sea is History" served as the frontispiece for this Pacific dialogue, but the contributors demonstrated that the best methodology of engaging that history was deeply contested. While agreeing that a new vision of the region was needed, Hauʻofaʻs colleagues at the University of the South Pacific (USP) reminded readers that Oceania was still characterized by continuing colonialism, ethnic and racial tensions, gender inequities, and the exploitation of island labor by transnational capital. Ultimately the respondents warned that a romantic recuperation of ancient "people from the sea" (Hauʻofa 1993b, 8) should not eclipse a rigorous examination of contemporary globalization in the Pacific.[3]

To understand the reasons for Hauʻofaʻs intervention and how these tensions over regional identity developed across time one has to turn to the spatial mapping of the Pacific. I do so by exploring how indigenous narratives are often relegated to a feminized "Basin" by the military and economic dominance of the northern "Rim" through the symbolism of the transoceanic vessel. A focus on the vessel helps to foreground the Rim/Basin tidalectic that undergirds the transnational economic utopia known as "Asia Pacific." Moreover, since ideologies of national belonging operate by conflating women with land, it is surely no coincidence that this era of globalization has drawn from a maritime grammar of flows, circulation, and fluidity, which are constituted by discursive constructions of a feminized and increasingly territorialized ocean. This discourse of diasporic fluidity has not been examined in terms of how the ocean and the male-populated boats that are imagined to cross its expanse reiterate the gendered logic of national belonging. The Pacific, a region interpellated into the desiring flows of twentieth-century global capitalism, is thus an important place from which to begin such an analysis (Connery 1995; Wilson and Dirlik 1995a and 1995b, Dirlik 1993).

The Rim's construction of the Pacific Basin as *aqua nullius* or empty ocean is founded on a remarkable spatial collapse of the world's largest geographic region to bring the powerful northern economies into a neighborly alliance. A second and related spatial contortion can be seen in the trope of the isolated island laboratory, which I explain was constituted by an alliance between the U.S. military and its subsidized anthropologists. This island isolation theory could be sustained only by denying the agency of indigenous maritime technology that connected the islands for millennia before the arrival of Europeans. Reduced to a basin, the Pacific was symbolically emptied as a vessel of sovereignty. I then turn to the colonial problematics of Thor Heyerdahl's *Kon-Tiki* expedition, which undermined ancient Polynesian voyaging histories to uphold a white patriarchal genealogy of the Pacific, ideologically sustaining postwar Rim expansion into the Basin. In the second part of this chapter, I turn to the revitalization of voyaging histories, evident in the region's literature as well as the reconstruction of double-hulled vaka (sailing canoes), such as the Hawaiian vessel *Hokule'a*, which, since 1976, has sailed over 50,000 miles across Oceania using the wayfinding system of etak. As explained in the introduction, etak represents a complex methodology of navigating space and time, rendering land and sea in dynamic and shifting interrelation. Building upon the work of Vicente Diaz and J. Kehaulani Kauanui, I explore this concept of "moving islands" as the most salient counter-narrative to the belittling colonial stereotypes of isolated, ahistorical isles positioned outside the trajectories of modernity (Diaz 1996; Diaz and Kauanui 2001). By rendering the voyaging canoe as a metonymy of a moving island, this chapter positions the circulation of these indigenous vessels as a tidalectic engagement of routes and roots.

Through the lens of these voyaging canoes, the discourse of Pacific Island indigeneity may be brought in closer focus with a subtext of diaspora and migration that has powerfully emerged in recent decades. These migratory narratives recuperate the history of voyagers who crossed the tremendous expanse of the Pacific and settled nearly every island in the cartographic triangulation known as Polynesia, between Hawai'i, Rapa Nui (Easter Island), and Aotearoa/New Zealand. Interestingly, in the most colonized Pacific Islands, indigenous activists have emphasized the long history of land occupation (roots) in an effort to maintain local sovereignty amidst a powerful resurgence in transoceanic migration narratives (routes). The ethnic contours of this native-diaspora intractability are nicely summarized by Hawaiian scholar and poet Haunani-Kay Trask: "The light of our dawns, like the color of our skin, tells us who we are, and where we belong. We know our genealogy descends from the great voyagers of the far Pacific. And we cherish our inheritance" (1999, xv). Although tensions exist between local and diasporic identities in the Pacific, I suggest that they are not as polarized as they may seem when we consider that *contemporary* trajectories of migration are often mitigated and expressed through the symbolism of *precolonial* voyaging canoes.[4] Interest in originary migrants, a discourse that James Clifford terms "indigenous cosmopolitanism" (2000, 96), has heightened in a context in which the economic and political contours of the region are shifting through the tentacles—and I use this word deliberately—of late capitalist globalization.

These voyaging histories are vital to cultural sovereignty in that they highlight indigenous technology and agency, yet are also imbricated in the globalizing shifts in ocean governance. As I mentioned in the introduction, the very language that Hau'ofa employs to articulate "the ocean in us," conceptualized as "our pathway to each other" as well as "our common heritage" (1997, 124, 148), is derived from an unprecedented remapping of global sovereignty and common space: the United Nations Convention on the Law of the Sea. The notion of an oceanic "common heritage" has been in circulation in different yet overlapping epistemologies of the Pacific, and it is intrinsically linked to the feminized, watery metaphors used to characterize this postmodern era of fluidity, flows, circulations, and currents. The very terms with which we categorize this era are entangled in the shifting conceptions and territorializations of seas.

Since the ocean is historically tied to the vessels that help connect it as a region, this chapter traces the ways in which the Pacific voyaging canoe has been utilized by agents of colonialism *and* indigenous sovereignty. The systematic erasure of the vaka, a native vessel of sovereignty, has been integral to interpellations of the Pacific as an empty basin or a series of isolated islands. This is why regenerating the transoceanic vaka has been so vital to reconnecting transnational indigenous communities and conceptualizing the vessel as a "moving island." Concentrating on the tidalectic between land and sea highlights metaphors of movement and fluidity that ultimately are embedded in the etymology and semantics of the term diaspora itself: sperm and blood. By tracing the connections between these fluid metaphors of dispersal across the ocean, I explore three contiguous forms of Pacific regionalism. First, I turn to late-twentieth-century efforts to consolidate the economic exchange across Asia Pacific through the imagery of a capitalist space of fluidity and flow, a softened product of American military discourses that interpellated the islands as remote and isolated. Second, I explore how the construction of ethnic genealogy, or blood ties evident in some contemporary Polynesian voyaging narratives, reproduce culture by literalizing diaspora as the dispersal of male seed through the motif of what Eric Leed calls the "spermatic journey" (1991, 114). In the final section I turn to what Albert Wendt calls "our water ties," a language of fluidity that reflects a new era of Pacific Island literature in an ocean of globalization.

An Empty Vessel: The Basin of Isolated Laboratories

To trace a genealogy of oceanic regionalism one must necessarily engage with the vessels that made it possible for human beings to undertake their travels. The Pacific Islands region was first imagined and mapped by its earliest human inhabitants, who by 1500 BCE were well on their way to navigating across the largest ocean in the world; at nearly 7,000 miles in width, this is farther than the distance between northernmost Europe to the southernmost tip of Africa. As befitting a region of such size and complexity, there is no one indigenous name for the Pacific Ocean, even in Polynesian languages, where it is known as moana, the realm of Tangaroa, the Great Ocean of Kiwa (and Hine Moana), as well as the vast or supreme marae of space.[5] To Europeans, the region was interpellated as the South Seas and claimed for Spain by Vasco Nuñez de Balboa as he waded into the Gulf of Panama in 1513. A few years later it was rather inappropriately named the Pacific by Ferdinand Magellan, who crossed the ocean with a mutinous crew and, in a historic first contact between Europeans and Pacific Islanders in Micronesia, killed seven Chamorros before landing on Guam, where he raided their village and burned down their houses in retaliation for the theft of items from his ship.[6] In fact, this startling recognition of the Pacific and its uninterrupted connection to Asia was the last stage, for Europeans, in mapping a complete sphere of the globe. The remoteness of the Pacific Ocean from Europe and its vastness have been the cause of its belated interpellation into modernity, despite the fact that knowledge of this ocean provided the materials for modern measurement and imperial rule. Over the next two centuries, naval, merchant, and whaling vessels crisscrossed and mapped the Pacific, particularly Enlightenment-minded explorers such as James Cook, who marveled at the Polynesians' navigational abilities and characterized them as "by far the most extensive nation on earth" (quoted in Finney 1994, 7). Although countless studies have been dedicated to these "Vikings of the Pacific," peoples who, in the words of Sir Peter Buck / Te Rangi Hiroa, surpassed the achievement of Phoenician, Mediterranean, and Norse sailors to become "the supreme navigators of history" (1938, 13),[7] most scholarship either positions Asia as a metonymy for the Pacific or sidesteps these navigational histories by locating the concept of the region as an economic and political byproduct of the Cold War. Even scholars attuned to the indigenous history of the Pacific insist that the region is a Euro-American construct.[8]

Focusing on the history of transpacific vessels helps elucidate the ways in which regional studies contributed to the erasure of precolonial indigenous histories by substituting the Pacific vaka with the naval vessels of imperial nation-states. The development of region or area studies is conceptually and historically tied to Commonwealth, postcolonial and diaspora studies. After World War II, geopolitical paradigms such as Immanuel Wallerstein's world systems theory and the categorization of First, Second, Third, and later Fourth Worlds contributed to a new understanding of the uneven economic, social, and geopolitical layerings of humanity.[9] Like postcolonial and diaspora studies, the concept of the region has the theoretical potential to challenge national boundaries by focusing on the ways in which people and products flow across diverse spaces. If one considers how European colonialism carved the world into discrete nations that were then politically and economically eroded by the policies of the World Bank and the International Monetary Fund (IMF), it becomes understandable why a regional "imagined community," such as the Pacific, Africa, or the black Atlantic could pose a vital alternative to national, colonial, and corporate hegemonies. Yet in its efforts to dismantle the ethnic and political boundaries of the nation-state, postcolonial regionalism shares characteristics with the telos of transnational capitalism. Thus Pacific scholars might be mindful of Misao Miyoshi's warning that regional studies is "part of the Cold War strategy" (1995, 80), and that has produced disturbing "parallel and cognate developments between economy and scholarship" (81).[10]

While regional studies are often framed in geopolitical terms, economic and cultural contributions to the constituency of a region must be considered alongside one another if we are to simultaneously recognize the vessels of native sovereignty and transnational capital. Theoretically, one should be able to speak in terms of local indigenous movements alongside global economic shifts, as this chapter intends to do. Oceania provides a particularly paradigmatic space for these entanglements, given the ways in which the larger, late-capitalist metropoles of the northern Rim quite literally circumscribe the region and determine its monetary and labor flows. As Rob Wilson and Arif Dirlik have shown (1995a), Asia Pacific has been the dominant modality for understanding the region. The Islands, erased from the teleology of the celebrated "Pacific Century" and relegated to a geographic and economic Basin, are producing a differently inflected discourse of migratory flows through the reclamation of Polynesian voyaging histories. My point here is not to draw a simple distinction between the flows of economy and culture, as the division between the Rim and Basin might suggest. Rather, as I will explain, this relationship between Rim and Basin is mutually constitutive. The modernizing Rim is dependent upon historic claims to vessels in the Basin, while conversely, ancient voyaging narratives of the Basin have adopted the globalizing tropes of the Rim to navigate in the economic wake of late capitalism.

Simon Gikandi has suggested that academic discourses of globalization displace economic considerations by adopting the cultural grammar of postcolonial studies. Had he included the Pacific, he would have found that the cultural production of the Islands has been largely subsumed by economic "Rim-speak." This is not from any lack of effort to complicate the Rim-Basin binary. Wilson and Dirlik's collection, *Asia/Pacific as Space of Cultural Production*, represents a vital attempt to destabilize these spatial hierarchies and to remap the Pacific to include the millions of Islanders who reside within the largest ocean in the world. This important volume includes a reprint of Hauʻofa's "Our Sea of Islands," which helped broaden its distribution and concludes with a Micronesian poem that also invokes voyaging canoes. Although the editors assert that cartographies of the region "need not belong exclusively to the circulations of hegemonic power" (1995a, 11), they contend that the Pacific is "dominantly a Euro-American formation" (2). As such, they reiterate Dirlik's earlier assertion that "EuroAmericans were responsible not only for mapping the Pacific, but also for attaching names to the maps" (1993, 5). By gendering the ways in which the *"global deforms and molests the local"* (Wilson and Dirlik 1995a, 8, authors' emphasis), and encoding binary Rim-Basin relations in terms of mobile masculine economies overlaid upon feminized local cultures, this influential collection was not able to fully explore the efficacy of indigenous forms of regionalism and the Pacific vessels that sutured these cultural and economic histories together.

Paul Sharrad has usefully demonstrated that the perceived newness of 103 Asia Pacific was a palimpsest over colonial mystifications of an idyllic South Seas that had interpellated the Pacific Basin as a vast, empty (feminized) ocean to be filled by masculine European voyagers. In strikingly gendered language, Sharrad argued that the Basin suggests "something more akin to a sink than a bowl; a container, a vessel that exists to be filled or emptied" (1990, 599). In terms that resonate with the Caribbean, Hauʻofa warned against the scholarly tendency to describe Oceania as "a Spanish lake, a British Lake, an American Lake, and even a Japanese Lake" (1993, 10). Yet scholars have tended to amplify rather than deconstruct the gendered economic and geopolitical imaginaries of the region. In surveying the Caribbean and Pacific, continental Rim powers often translate "vessel" as an empty Basin rather than an alternative navigation of sovereignty.

Given the importance accorded to the economic and cultural "flows" of the Pacific, I would like to turn to Christopher Connery's work, because his observations on the emergence of regional studies concur with Miyoshi's concerns and include a prescient warning about the epistemological underpinnings of Rim/Basin relations. He writes:

> [R]egionalism's origination in the binarisms of developed/underdeveloped, expansion/contraction, or growth/stagnation is significant. The concept of region, arising as it does within a binary logic of difference, is a semiotic utopia, a "spatial fix" for those faced with analyzing the always differentiating but always concealing logic of capital. The region, less encumbered by the various ideological or mythical mystifications that pervade the state, will be where history and analysis takes place. (Connery 1996, 286–287)

Connery connects Pacific Rim studies with U.S. imperialism as it continues to fulfill its manifest destiny across the Pacific towards Asian capital, reflecting a similar teleology to that which allowed the United States to invade the sovereign territory of Hawaiʻi in 1893. His comparison of late nineteenth- and twentieth-century imperialist discourses of the Pacific-as-destiny suggests that the ocean Basin is "the void that gives substance to what surrounds it" (1996, 288). Thus the logic of capital erases itself through its most elemental metaphor: the ocean. Connery traces a genealogy of ocean modernity by outlining how the simultaneous emergence of capitalism and transoceanic imperialism gave rise to Euro-American perceptions that the ocean was at once the mythopoetic source of evolutionary origins as well as economic destiny. Since the ocean has "long functioned as capital's myth element" (289), the economic and oceanic sublime are mutually constitutive axioms, newly displaced onto the late-twentieth-century emergence of high capitalist Pacific Rim economies.

I would like to build upon Connery's ideas to explore how the ocean is placed, as argued in the last chapter, in a complex constitutive relationship with the hydrarchy of the ship. In configuring an empty Basin to erect the Rim, Pacific area studies often eclipse the vessels that make its regionalism possible, neglecting to consider the ways in which transoceanic ships construct the region through migration and settlement, colonialism and violence, as well as cultural and economic trade and exchange. Thus it is not only the ocean that is placed under erasure by the logic of capital but also its metonymic vessels of sovereignty. These vessels include indigenous vaka such as the *Hokule'a*, the transoceanic container ships that sustain the flow of transnational capital, as well as the naval craft that claimed the region for Euro-America and brought their cargo, including nuclear weapons. Although the links between area studies and militarization are well known, scholars have not fully acknowledged the ways in which Pacific studies arose out of U.S. naval militarization during and after World War II. This is a crucial erasure because the naval and technological colonization of this vast region are constitutive elements in the fashioning of an Asia Pacific discourse that immobilizes the vessels of island historiography.

Although its transoceanic routes are often obscured, an international Pacific studies first emerged in the early twentieth century and solidified as a postwar discipline that largely reflected British and American naval interests in the region.[11] As John Terrell, Terry Hunt, and Chris Gosden have shown, initially the field was coordinated and funded by the U.S. military under the aegis of the National Research Council's Pacific Science Board (PSB), which declared its intent to address the "glaring lack of scientific knowledge" that "hampered military operations" and "the pressing need of the Navy for basic information" (1997, 156).[12] PSB-coordinated anthropologists working in Micronesia perpetuated the idea that the Pacific Islands were "isolated" from modernity, ideal "laboratories" for the study of bounded cultures, and that their populations had partaken in no deliberate inter-island voyages in the recent or ancient past. As Terence Wesley-Smith's genealogy of the field has shown, area studies funding was concordant with federal military interests while a "laboratory rationale" partitioned the islands and elided the complexities of regional exchange (1995, 122). These "insular" Pacific Islands that historian Oskar Spate found "'so splendidly splittable into Ph.D. topics'" (quoted in Kirch 1986, 2), were segregated from modernity in ways that mystified western naval expansion into the region.

The island laboratory paradigm was a pernicious erasure of the ways in which the region was enmeshed in the violent "Pacific theater," particularly when we consider that Micronesia was the launching point for Japan's attack on Pearl Harbor as well as the base from which *Enola Gay* and *Bock's Car* departed for Hiroshima and Nagasaki. As a region of more than 2,200 islands, Micronesia was anything but isolated from the effects of the war and hosted some of the most important transportation bases. An incredible expanse of the western Pacific, having already experienced German, French, British, Japanese, and Spanish colonialism, became deeply militarized from the Philippines to the Solomon Islands. In fact, the term "island hopping" was coined by the U.S. Navy to describe the establishment of a system of communications, supplies, intelligence, and transport that involved nearly every archipelago across the 7,000-mile-wide region. The same Pacific region categorized as "isolated" by anthropologists hosted the largest naval war in human history. For example, in only the last six months of the war, the U.S. Navy reported over "17,000 sailings of vessels large and small through the six million square miles of Western Sea Frontier waters" (E. King 1945, 199). The terraqueous nature of the Pacific demanded a new "amphibious" naval strategy from the United States that linked islands as stepping stones, formulating the eastern Pacific as "the most heavily traveled military highway on and above the sea" (E. King 1945, 199). The legacy of these transpacific vessels is still dangerously present: over 1,000 sunken warships, including destroyers and oil tankers weighing over 3 million tons, are poisoning regional waters, while some waterways of northern Australia are still off-limits due to floating mines.[13]

The regional imaginary of Asia Pacific configures the islands as a Basin by erasing the history of naval battles that ranged from the Aleutian Islands of the Bering Sea to the southern reaches of Port Moresby. As one historian observes: "It proved impossible to draw a line on the map to say where the war should stop"; the desire for transpacific military communications "seemed to dictate the invasion" of any island deemed strategic to Allied interests (I. Campbell 1992, 183). By the end of the war, the United States claimed Micronesia as a strategic trust territory and gained 3.5 million square miles of sea area which, according to a U.S. Army-funded study on Oceania, was "roughly equivalent to the size of the continental United States" (Bunge and Cooke 1984, 295). I suggest that the amnesia in postcolonial studies about the extent of U.S. imperialism is precisely because the Rim configures the Pacific as *aqua nullius* and its islands synonymous with isolation.

The construction of isolated islands derives from the erasure of the sea as a highway and its traffic in maritime vessels. The discourse of insular islands, sustained by many anthropologists, not only helped to validate nuclear testing in the region but in some cases suppressed its dangerous effects. The U.S. militarization of the Pacific was, by necessity, a naval endeavor, yet these fleets rarely appear in regional scholarship. Operation Crossroads, a mystifying name for the nuclearization of two supposedly isolated islands, was made possible by naval technologies: over 90 ships were sent to the Bikini Lagoon and used as targets for the two atmospheric detonations, while over 150 additional naval vessels surrounded the site for support services. Precisely where anthropologists mapped isolation, the United States detonated sixty-six atomic and hydrogen bombs on Enewetak and Bikini Atolls between 1946 and 1958 (Robie 1999, 143). Pacific Science Board scholars were employed to report their contamination levels.[14] Two years after the United States dropped a fifteen-megaton hydrogen bomb over Bikini (1,000 times more destructive than in Hiroshima), causing the irradiation and diaspora from the surrounding islands, Ward Goodenough's article, citing the PSB and framed with Margaret Mead's approving introduction to "Polynesia as a Laboratory," argued that Oceania "provides . . . instances of 'pure' cultural radiation unaffected by external contacts" (Mead 1957; Goodenough 1957, 54; Terrell, Hunt, and Gosden 1997, 157). Goodenough specifically argued that the ocean proved a barrier to Islanders and, against all evidence to the contrary, suppressed its role as a naval highway (150–151). Moreover, his use of the terms "pure" and "unaffected cultures" constituted by "radiation" are particularly meaningful when we consider that the United States, Britain, and France were rapidly nuclearizing the region and that reports had recently been issued that Rongelap Islanders, having been covered with over five centimeters of nuclear fallout from Bikini, were diagnosed with fatal chromosome damage (M. King 1986, 7).

Together, the nuclear powers and many anthropologists categorized the Pacific Islands as remote laboratories and therefore ideal contained spaces for the execution of cultural and radioactive experimentation, testing, and research.[15] Others have alleged, with convincing evidence, that the United States deliberately exposed Rongelap Islanders to nuclear radiation because their contained island environment facilitated a controlled study of its deadly effects (see O'Rourke 1986). K. R. Howe explains that since colonial contact: "The Pacific and its peoples were both a *laboratory* for the study of human prehistory and a major *testing ground* for Enlightenment and subsequent science" (2003, 23; my emphasis). As a whole, the concept of a wartime or nuclearized Pacific region is notably absent from most metropolitan discourses of Basin and Rim, evidencing an amnesia not only in terms of the "cognate developments between economy and scholarship," but between scholarship and militarization.[16] This lack of historical depth should not, perhaps, come as a surprise, given the ocean's role "as capital's myth element," and the Pacific's recent appropriation into the utopian telos of late capitalism, which cloaks its dystopian form in nuclear eschatology.[17] As Connery warns: "Pacific Rim Discourse—perhaps the most obvious articulation of Paul Virilio's notion of the disappearance of space and time as tangible dimensions of social life—will resist the attempt to historicize it" (1995, 56). To sum up, Asia Pacific studies have tended to erase the Basin by configuring the Rim as its metonym; this is made possible by the reluctance to speak in meaningful ways about the region's militarization, which is mystified by the colonial trope of isolated isles. The myth of isolation can only be sustained by suppressing the long historical presence of maritime vessels—both indigenous and foreign. As such, the transpacific voyaging histories of the Polynesians that connected the island region became one of the first casualties of isolationist axioms. As I will explain, the transoceanic vaka was the focal point of Rim-Basin contention, integral even in its erasure to the regional imaginary.

The White Chief-God: Military Drift and Accidental Landfall

In order to substantiate this theory of island isolation, scholars were posed with a particular problem in terms of the enormous size of a culture region named by eighteenth-century Europeans as "Polynesia," or many islands.[18] It is well known that Cook and other explorers of this period were astonished by the region's maritime technology and double-hulled voyaging canoes (vaka), which often dwarfed European ships. Because these eastern Pacific cultures were recognized as the product of transoceanic migration, countless studies were devoted to tracing Islander origins. Well into the twentieth century, amateur and professional ethnologists interpellated Polynesians as one of the lost tribes of Israel, a model of Christian diffusionism that was later adapted by Orientalists as an Aryan genealogy that led back to India.[19] Thus even in its earliest racial theories, European discourse constructed human presence in the Pacific in terms of a global network of family—a shared diaspora of Aryan Christian kinship. While this European fascination with Islander origins and mobility positioned Polynesians as technologically savvy agents, it also justified European occupation of the region by positioning indigenous peoples as settlers and thereby undermining native sovereignty.[20] These Polynesian origin theories also had the rather dubious distinction of suggesting that the Islands themselves could not generate the seeds of culture, which were perceived as the birthright of Europeans. As Patrick Kirch points out: "Little consideration was given to the possibility that Polynesian cultures had developed within the Pacific" (2000, 208). This suggests a European ideologeme of *aqua nullius*, upon which continental peoples overlaid their presumably more developed cultures. For roughly 200 years, the European notion of culture dispersion across nearly 7,000 miles of the Pacific held sway with academics, even when in 1947 Thor Heyerdahl attempted to prove that Polynesians came from South America by drifting on prevailing currents from Peru to the Tuamotu Archipelago (French-occupied Polynesia) on his raft, the *Kon-Tiki*.[21] While his journey gripped the popular imagination, few scholars took his experiment seriously, given the cultural and linguistic studies that historicized Pacific Island dispersal from Southeast Asia. Yet Heyerdahl's famous accidental-drift theories, and his originary vessel of Aryan racial origins, mark a radical shift in the approach to Pacific Island mobility and agency, which has not been conceptually linked to the militarization of the region and its disciplinary byproduct, area studies.

Heyerdahl's *Kon-Tiki: Across the Pacific by Raft* contributed to the erasure of Polynesian subjects, based as it was upon a western arboreal model of genealogical succession that invests ontological authority in originary founders. In this case, deliberate ocean-voyaging Polynesians are preempted by the *idea* of Incans on a balsa raft, drifting aimlessly on the prevailing currents across 4,300 miles of open sea. In his experiment to prove that proto-Incans settled the Pacific Islands, Heyerdahl is suspiciously silent about Polynesian vessels, substituting the intentionality of the double-hulled sailing vaka for the far less maneuverable log raft, even when native outriggers in the Tuamotu group had to rescue the *Kon-Tiki* from dangerous reefs. I draw attention to this suppression of indigenous watercraft because the ship, as I have explained in the previous chapter, generally functions as an important metaphor of the people—a vehicle of the collective will in the past and present. To dislocate the connection between Pacific seafarers and their originary vessels is to deny the region's material and cultural history as well as its capacity to navigate the future. Thus I shift the concept of the *vessel* from its Rim definition as empty Basin, absence, and lack, to a crucial bodily metaphor of a people's connection to their genealogy, history, and sovereignty. A focus on the vessel renders tidalectics visible—it is the principal way in which roots are connected to routes and islands connected to the sea.

While scholars often point to the error of Heyerdahl's theory, citing **109**
the ample evidence of an eastward rather than westward trajectory of the
region's settlement, I am less interested in examining *Kon-Tiki*'s empiricism (after all, migrations are always far more complicated than their
theories), than in positioning the text as a cultural artifact of the war in
the Pacific in which a Euro-American regionalism was already operative.
Through the best-selling narrative *Kon-Tiki*, which was translated into
sixty-seven languages and made into an Oscar-winning documentary, the
Allied powers were given genealogical authority of the Pacific in a way that
undermined *Asian antecedents* of the region. Heyerdahl's erasure of Pacific
voyaging capacities and the materiality of double-hulled vaka reflects
colonial and twentieth-century militarization of the region; in both cases,
western powers were particularly threatened by Islander mobility. Alfred
Crosby has demonstrated that European empires in the Atlantic developed
their island colonization skills by limiting native mobility (1986). Across
the Pacific, long-distance indigenous voyaging was discouraged and criminalized by nineteenth-century European missionaries, traders, and colonial administrations who had a vested interest in maintaining a local tax-paying, church-going, and plantation-working population.[22] The remnants
of voyaging practices were further circumscribed by German, Japanese,
British, French, and U.S. prohibitions during the Second World War.
Discouraged by the wartime powers and finding an acceptable alternative
in motorized vessels, double-hulled vaka production became increasingly
rare. Heyerdahl's shift of attention from the purposeful vaka to the drifting
balsa raft reflected the waning of many indigenous inter-island exchange
systems.[23]

This is a genealogical sketch of how military and academic discourses
converged to construct an isolated Pacific in the midst of a global war,
an ideology constituted by the erasure of Pacific vaka. It is not surprising
that a tight military circle funded and supported Heyerdahl's misconstrued
attempt to posit a white patriarchal genealogy of the Pacific region. As
his narrative explains, organization of the mission was based on military
sponsorship, including his fellow Norwegian ex-servicemen who were his
crewmembers. Heyerdahl received an audience at the Pentagon in order to
solicit contributions from the American War Department, who enthusiastically supported his "courage and enterprise" by providing his crew with
field rations and equipment from the Air Material Command (1950, 49).
Describing the project as a "minor military operation," Heyerdahl prom-

ised to test and report on the equipment's performance in severe maritime conditions (47). His meetings with the Naval Hydrographic Institute, the British Military Mission, as well as discussions with British, Norwegian, Peruvian, and U.S. Air Force and Navy officers, resulted in funding, communications, supplies, maps, and the connections that were necessary for him to construct and launch the *Kon-Tiki* from the naval yard in Callao. When the crew anticipated landfall on a small atoll of the Tuamotu group (Angatau), they hoisted the Norwegian, French, American, British, Peruvian, and Swedish flags for the benefit of villagers who spoke no western languages. The *Kon-Tiki* expedition seemed far less about anthropology than about a particular mission to rediscover the region in terms of an Allied victory, dressed in the flags of Euro-American military occupation of the Pacific.

The *Kon-Tiki* expedition gained its historical authority by positioning Euro-American presence in the Pacific as the originary narrative from which all subsequent genealogies must derive. Although almost every popular account of his voyage suggests that Heyerdahl was trying to prove that the early Incans migrated across the Pacific, his book specifically argues that a pre-Incan civilization of Euro-Americans, "mysterious white men with beards" (1950, 24), created the stone structures at Lake Titicaca, settled the Pacific Islands, and brought their technology to the temples in Rapa Nui, the Marquesas, and Tahiti. By racializing Polynesian and Incan oral narratives, Heyerdahl determined that both populations were speaking of the same figure when they mentioned "the white chief-god Sun-Tiki," whom he claimed "the inhabitants of all the eastern Pacific islands hailed as the original founder of their race" (25). His appropriation of native genealogical systems struck at the epistemic core of Polynesian identities. Interestingly, his categorization of racial phenotypes and his narrative of Aryan antecedents for the Pacific Islands, while not new to anthropology, have been promulgated by the Mormon Church, which has broadened his Incan origin story into a white American genealogy for the region. Moreover, some church scholars have attributed the importance of ships and genealogy in the indigenous Pacific to the Book of Mormon.[24] As such, Heyerdahl's imagined *vessel* of Pacific history reinvigorated old colonial models of blood purity and racial descent, validating western political power through a fabricated history of Aryan diaspora.

To his presumed western audience, Heyerdahl translates the cosmological significance of native genealogy and the deification of founding ancestors. This is a necessary frame because the racial origins that the *Kon-Tiki* will establish for Polynesians must fit neatly with indigenous genealogies, while allowing Heyerdahl to invest his own arrivant body as the material manifestation of "the white chief-god Sun-Tiki." As such, his narrative is strikingly reminiscent of what Gananath Obeyesekere has called the "myth model" of Cook's deification as the god Lono in Hawai'i, where indigenous cosmological systems were configured with such structural rigidity that "the natives" presumably could not differentiate between a European explorer (or a bearded Norwegian) and their own gods. Heyerdahl consciously draws upon the Enlightenment explorer model in his narrative of events in the Tuamotu group (Raroia), yet he circumvents the structural telos of Cook's demise by transporting the genealogical origin itself: the vessel *Kon-Tiki*. Thus his account is a deft blending of purported native superstitions alongside western civilizing benevolence: he contends that his crew's shipwreck on the reef is understood by Raroians as a supernatural visit from Tiki, "the long-dead founder of their race" (1950, 269); he lectures Islanders about their presumed ancestor and the reason for his voyage; he saves the life of a boy by administering penicillin; he amazes with his radio; and he rechristens the island Fenua Kon-Tiki (Kon-Tiki Land) (272). Since European voyaging narratives and the South Seas fiction they inspired were primarily concerned with a system of (sexualized) exchange, Heyerdahl borrows freely from narratives of Cook, Melville, and other discursive fashionings of the region when he recounts the Raroian's contributions: the seductive hula-dancing women, "the natives'" desire to possess their material goods and their dazzling white bodies and, predictably, the local chief's blessing of Heyerdahl with the name of the Island's founding ancestor. Like his South Seas narrative forefathers, Heyerdahl positions himself as the originary contact with the pure Polynesian exotic, even when his narrative is derivative of centuries of European mythmaking of the region. Barely two years after a devastating war, he determines "this was the South Seas life as the old days had known it" (1950, 283). The revitalization of the romanticized eighteenth-century South Seas, even more visible in Heyerdahl's contemporary, U.S. naval officer James Michener, suggests a Euro-American alliance in the coding of an increasingly exoticized and touristed regional entity known as the "South Pacific."[25]

If ritual was thought to provide the means by which Cook was deified and integrated into native cosmology, then Heyerdahl uses it to position himself as an originary presence in the Pacific. As Mary Douglas argues: "Ritual focuses attention by framing; it enlivens the memory and links the present with the relevant past" (1966, 64). Heyerdahl appropriates ritual for racialized ends; after participating in a ceremonial drama with Islanders and his crew, he adopts the deified genealogy of Kon-Tiki by concluding, "once more there were white and bearded chiefs among the Polynesian people" (1950, 289). Heyerdahl's self-aggrandizement, narrated on behalf of the western Allies symbolized in the flags that deck his voyaging raft, suggests a recolonization of the Pacific, coded in the typological terms of discovery narratives but with the important added twist of denying any indigenous claims to nonwhite history. As Obeyesekere observes of the colonial myth-model, "this 'European god' is a myth of conquest, imperialism, and civilization—a triad that cannot easily be separated" (1992, 3). Heyerdahl revised and even improved upon Cook's narrative; through the powerful metaphysical symbolism of the vessel *Kon-Tiki*, he invested himself and his Allies with the originary founding narrative of the region, as well as the (colonial) *vehicle* of the destiny of the people.

Given the metaphysical and political claims associated with Pacific vessels, it is not difficult to determine why so many western military institutions were ideologically and financially invested in this experiment, which culminated with Heyerdahl and his crew receiving an audience with President Truman, where they presented the American flag under which *Kon-Tiki* had sailed. By that time Truman's administration had just annexed most of Micronesia. The President's support of this transoceanic venture should also be seen in relationship to the international criticism he was facing for greatly extending the littoral state by declaring in 1945 that the continental shelf contiguous to the United States was under exclusive national jurisdiction, a violation of the freedom of the seas doctrine that was immediately followed by a "scramble for the oceans" on the part of many other nations, including *Kon-Tiki*'s launching hosts, Peru.[26] The Pacific war had proved lucrative for oceanography, and naval experiments had revealed tremendous oil and mineral reserves on the ocean floor. Combined with the scramble to militarize the seas with submarine atomic weapons and to use *aqua nullius* for the dumping of nuclear waste, Truman's proclamation catalyzed a radical new territorialism of the oceans. Although Heyerdahl was an active environmentalist, his voyage on the *Kon-Tiki* became a locus of vital military and corporate interests due to the ways in which the ocean and island space of the postwar Pacific were being carved into discrete territories.

Heyerdahl's grandiose journey upholds a division in time-space in his polarization of the Pacific Rim and Basin. He constructs a close temporal and racialized genealogy between white America and the indigenous Pacific to validate his theory, yet separates them spatially so that the expedition will seem all the more extraordinary for locating what he repeatedly refers to as "isolated" and "primitive" islands. The largest ocean on the planet is charted in exceedingly narrow terms; it must serve as a barrier to civilization and a highway to the *Kon-Tiki* crew, but never the reverse. This is why Heyerdahl is thrown into a panic that the Royal New Zealand Air Force (based in Rarotonga) may send a rescue team out to Raroia before he can be welcomed by "the natives"; the culmination of his voyage would certainly have been far less romantic had he been greeted by a relative of the military institutions that facilitated his journey. His need to cognitively and spatially separate the urban militarized Rim from the tropical "South Seas" anticipates the divisive logic of Asia Pacific studies, which has been slow to account for the ways in which the northern Rim militarized the Pacific in the 1940s, and through a network of cable, radio, submarine, naval, and air communication systems, connected the region more regularly and hegemonically than ever in history. The military globalization of the region, often neglected in area studies scholarship, authorized itself through the suppression of the earliest form of Pacific cosmopolitanism— the Polynesian kinship and trade systems that linked communities across thousands of miles through transoceanic vaka. Consequently, one might map a historical palimpsest of the region in which Polynesian voyaging was overlaid by military globalization that, following the logic of capital, inverted its eschatology into the utopian economic entity known as the Asia Pacific. The coterminous erasure of Pacific vaka with the rise of naval militarization has produced jarring effects when one positions these two vessels of contesting authority alongside each other. This is why, many decades later, Pacific Islanders and their supporters delivered a powerful anticolonial message by sailing fleets of modern vaka and outriggers to Moruroa, surrounding French nuclear ships with indigenous vessels.

The rise of indigenous labor, sovereignty, and decolonization movements that followed on the heels of the Pacific war, often symbolized by the cultural vehicle of the people, the vaka, were frequently circumscribed by the collusion of militarization and academic scholarship. Military-funded disciplines like anthropology, through projects like the *Kon-Tiki*, often undermined indigenous histories by projecting the wartime waning of vaka navigation back to the ancient past. These isolationist theories of the Pacific were dependent upon the "accidental" and "drift" voyaging theories that flourished in the postwar Pacific, depicting Islanders as mere "castaways," despite the sailing experiments that demonstrated the intentionality of Polynesian transoceanic navigation.[27] Soon after the *Kon-Tiki* voyage, other scholars rushed to uphold island isolation theories by denying vaka navigation technologies. For example, Ward Goodenough, citing the Pacific Science Board, found his episteme of island isolation in an "impressive analysis of Polynesian geographical knowledge" which concluded that precolonial Islanders "were often lost at sea, wandering with the prevailing winds and currents" (1957, 148), having accidentally settled the far reaches of the Pacific. Following on the ideological heels of Heyerdahl, Goodenough was referring to *Ancient Voyagers in the Pacific* (1956), a notorious dismissal of indigenous navigational capacities authored by the New Zealand Civil Defense Officer Andrew Sharp. In this influential book, Sharp conceded the viability of inter-island voyages in central Polynesia (Samoa, Tonga, Fiji, and the Tuamotus), but by confusing European difficulties in transoceanic navigation with Pacific practices, and dismissing the possibility of deliberate landfall without instruments, determined that successful settlement of islands beyond the 300-mile range was entirely "accidental" (1956, 14). Sharp concluded that early "Polynesia comprised a number of little worlds, inaccessible except through accidental migration" (14). While he has been critiqued for his Eurocentrism, his lack of maritime experience, and his inexpert handling of historical materials, Sharp's work has not been placed in the context I am trying to outline here—an embattled Pacific, in which the Euro-American and Polynesian maritime vessels were vital symbols of sovereignty, vying for historical authority through contested articulations of the past.

We should note that while Sharp was theorizing accidental Polynesian travelers, a rapidly industrialized Auckland was attracting a major immigrant population of Pacific Islanders, particularly from the New Zealand-administered Cook Islands and Niue. When *Ancient Voyagers* was published, Auckland, with over 10,000 new Pacific Island and Maori immigrants, was well on its way to becoming the "Polynesian capital" of the world.[28] This was also an era of unprecedented native urbanization that witnessed the establishment of the Maori Women's Welfare League and other organizations which, gaining momentum from Maori battalions returning from the war, were building an important political platform in which the sovereignty of the nation's tangata whenua was powerfully articulated.[29] Sharp's dismissal of Pacific navigational abilities is especially important when one considers that many Maori tribal identities are derived from a founding waka (or vaka, of which hundreds exist in oral tradition), or navigating ancestor of Aotearoa/New Zealand.[30] Because some voyaging ancestors and waka are shared between Maori and Cook Islanders, this poses a compelling symbolic imaginary of Pacific regionalism that was being rearticulated in postwar migrations. Explaining how indigenous "seafaring traditions lived on in the cultural symbolism of the waka," Ranginui Walker explains "the waka of ancestral forebearers took on new meaning as the symbol for tribal identity, territorial ownership and political relations" (1990, 28).

Importantly, just as contemporary Pacific indigeneity was being revitalized through waka symbology, Sharp interjected with this regional theory of "separate worlds" only tangentially connected by "isolated canoes" (1956, 14). His semantic slippage from "isolated islands" to "isolated canoes" suggests the colonial discomfort with what Vicente Diaz has pinpointed as another important oxymoron of the region: "restless natives" (2000, 10). Just as the visibility of mobile, self-determined, and modern Polynesians increased in Aotearoa/New Zealand, Sharp suggested indigenous peoples were unable to navigate their collective vessels of the past and, by extension, their symbolic future. Put in this context, Sharp's "accidental voyage" theory, like Heyerdahl's white-bearded gods, disenfranchised native sovereignty by destabilizing the ontological ground on which their claims rested: first—and deliberate—settlement of Oceania.

While Sharp's attempt to correct the romanticism of the "Vikings of the Pacific" model outlined by his predecessors, S. Percy Smith and Peter Buck, was not unilaterally accepted,[31] *Ancient Voyagers* was profoundly influential. Like *Kon-Tiki*, the work rendered a passive historical body of Pacific Islanders, caught in the vagaries and flows of the ocean, subject to currents and storms; overdetermined by their seascapes, they "were often lost at sea, wandering with the prevailing winds and currents." If we consider Albert Wendt's contention that the literature produced by westerners about the Pacific Island region is "more revealing of papalagi [white] fantasies and hang-ups, dreams and nightmares, prejudices and ways of viewing our crippled cosmos, than of our actual islands," (1993, 18), then we might conclude that *Ancient Voyagers* is far less about precolonial Polynesians than Sharp's postwar Pacific nightmare. New Zealand, which gained full sovereignty from Britain in 1947, felt particularly vulnerable to the rapid military Americanization of Oceania after its colonial "motherland" was defeated by the Japanese in Singapore (Sinclair 2000, 283–284). Although the country was experiencing an economic boom, the nation and broader region were undergoing rapid change as Samoans, Cook Islanders, and Maori negotiated with the New Zealand state for decolonization. Unlike Heyerdahl's intimation that the "Pacific theater" of the war had left Island cultures untouched, Sharp seems to suggest that the militarization of the Pacific precluded regional unity. Approaching Sharp's theory through the methodologies of etak, we can trace the "refracted current" back to the originary disruption. That is to say, his images of skeletons in canoes, his inventory of travelers who cannot navigate the stormy Pacific, his frustration at narratives that consist of "confusions and inventions" (1956, 127) and finally, his invocation of the "ghosts of two hundred thousand ancient voyagers who sank beneath the waves" and who "cannot speak," (127) reflect the deadly, consuming, and disorienting anxieties of the postwar Pacific. Sharp's narrative of oceanic chaos and consumption sounds like a skeptical precursor to Gilles Deleuze and Félix Guattari's celebration of the postmodern, where "everything commingles," all becomes "drift that ascends and descends the flows of time," and where "spaces and forms are undone" to construct a "new order" of the globe (1977, 84–85).

Part Two: Blood Vessels and Regional Circulation

> We sweat and cry salt water, so we know
> that the ocean is really in our blood.
> —Teresia Teaiwa, quoted in Hauʻofa, "The Ocean in Us"

The vaka that crossed Oceania were integral to regionalism before European contact and offer a historical counter to the ways in which Rim-speak interpellated the Basin as *aqua nullius* and a feminized vessel. Overall we can describe Rim-Basin tensions as competing claims to the region that are validated through originary and racialized narratives of diaspora. In both cases the semantics of the terms "vessel" and "vehicle" are historically and symbolically operative. To the Rim, the ocean functions as a feminized Basin or vessel to be filled (or penetrated) by the vehicle of white patriarchy that displaces the historic and purposeful trajectories of transoceanic vaka. Yet in the past few decades the resurgence of indigenous inter-island voyaging has offered an originary regional genealogy for Oceania as well as a naturalized precursor to late twentieth-century diaspora practice. The biggest contribution Andrew Sharp made to Pacific seafaring, much to his dismay, was to catalyze efforts to prove the possibility of long-distance voyaging by using traditional navigation systems such as etak and sailing vast distances across the region without instruments. A revitalization of voyaging canoes, oral histories, and the native identities that are powerfully associated with these vessels arose from the Polynesian Voyaging Society's 1976 project: the building of an oceangoing vaka (waʻa), *Hokuleʻa*, and its noninstrument navigation from Hawaiʻi to Tahiti. American anthropologist Ben Finney was vital to the conceptualization of the project, and he recruited Mau Piailug, an initiate of Caroline navigational traditions, to guide the canoe across 2,400 unfamiliar ocean miles with the system of etak. Due to the tensions and violence that erupted between some haole (white) and Hawaiian men over their claims to the vaka, Piailug refused to guide the vessel back from Tahiti and reportedly abandoned the crew in disgust.

The lynchpin (to use a nautical term) of this debate hinged on divergent interpretations of the purpose of this vessel and its genealogical relation to the broader region. As such, "blood" became the operative codeword for past and present ethnic belonging, broadening the semantics of "vessel." I have mentioned that narratives of the nation, rooted in the soil of the "motherland," shift to the language of bodily fluids and flows when invoking transoceanic regionalism. As I have discussed in the previous chapter, the soil, while symbolically and materially invested with human history, is conceptualized more as a *product* of the national body—its excess—than the *internalized* and circulatory semantics of the sea. Laura Brown's work has shown how the ocean became a vital and ubiquitous trope of the flows and torrents of British expansion and trade in the English poetry of the early eighteenth century, but it had not yet been associated with racialized blood-streams. According to Ivan Illich, the semantics of the circulation of corporeal *and* social fluids became connected through images of blood, water, and economic goods in late eighteenth-century Europe. Just as western medical practitioners rediscovered that human blood *circulated* in the body (400 years after their Middle Eastern counterparts), the social came "to be imagined as a system of conduits," where the "liquidity" of bodies, ideas, and products arose as a "dominant metaphor after the French revolution" (Illich 1987, 43). Through a complex historical process, ethnic genealogies became coded in what Gaston Bachelard calls the "valorization of liquid by blood" (1983, 60) or, in Michel Foucault's terms, "sanguinity," a process whereby "power spoke *through* blood" (1980, 147, emphasis in original).[32]

Literally and metaphorically, social and racialized bloodstreams and flows expanded from national estuaries into imperial seas.[33] The grammar of the corporeal fluidity of sperm and blood—rendered here as an outpouring of the ethnic national body into the seas—is an integral metaphor of diaspora. Rather than dispersing their ethnicity into the dissolving oceanic, British imperialist discourse claimed a diaspora in the blood, a bodily metaphor based on the restriction and control of global flow through their ethnic blood vessels. This is why, for example, countless nineteenth-century British travel narratives such as James Anthony Froude's *Oceana* identify Anglo-Saxon "blood" as the originary impetus for transoceanic expansion. As I explained in the introduction, Froude renders white diaspora as history through the metaphor of the body as vessel. "The sea is the natural home of Englishmen; the Norse blood is in us and we rove over the waters, for business or pleasure, as eagerly as our ancestors" (1886, 18). Through the metaphor of blood vessels, white British bodies became naturalized as the empire that ruled the waves.[34]

Although European discourses of oceanic sanguinity provided natural and corporeal metaphors of the imperialist project, there are correlations to the contemporary Pacific and this broader discussion about the (blood) vessels of sovereignty. Pacific Islanders often trace ancestry to transoceanic voyagers to uphold genealogical networks of sovereignty and to historicize and make meaning out of the modern migration of the descendent. Commenting on her Samoan and European heritage and migrancy to the United States, poet Caroline Sinavaiana-Gabbard determines that "distance and travel are in my blood, in the genes" (2001, 13). Teresia Teaiwa's epigraph to this section suggests that "the ocean is really in our blood" because it is corporeally and visibly produced through sweat and tears. This invocation of the ocean, unlike "capital's myth element," is invested with the legacy of specific cultural and ethnic origins, in similar ways to the middle passage narratives discussed in the previous chapter. Although salt water is one of the densest liquids on earth, its narrative history makes it heavier. "This water, enriched by so many reflections and so many shadows, is *heavy water*" (Bachelard 1983, 56; author's emphasis). Read tidalectically, the "heavy water" of the transoceanic imagination is constituted by the practices of the land; Pacific routes are entangled with ethnic roots. Even though "water draws the entire countryside along towards its own destiny" (Bachelard 1983, 61), one might say that the first voyage of the *Hokule'a* also drew Pacific waters—and their contested narrative histories—into the language of this (state's) countryside.

Hokule'a: (Blood) Vessels of Sovereignty

I argued in the previous chapter that the vast fluidity of the ocean seems to demand a conceptual opposite in the containment of the ship. Here I have demonstrated how the concept of Asia Pacific has been constituted by the erasure of native vessels of sovereignty, and I would like to explore what these shipboard metaphors signify about indigenous regionalism. The contestations over the early voyages of the *Hokule'a* (1976) are particularly instructive because one can pinpoint a paradigmatic shift whereby indigenous activists subverted the configuration of Oceania as an empty vessel and reclaimed this vaka as a vehicle of extended kinship relations across the eastern Pacific. As I will explain, this epistemology of the ship encodes the vessel as both body and blood, constructing a pan-Pacific genealogy of kinship networks as an alternative to colonial regionalism.

As cofounders of the Polynesian Voyaging Society in Honolulu, Ben **119** Finney, a white American anthropologist, and Herb Kane, a Hawaiian artist, coordinated the building of a historical replica of a Hawaiian vaka (waʻa) in preparation for the U.S. bicentennial celebration. According to Finney's account, the Kanaka Maoli sovereignty movement configured *Hokuleʻa* as an object of cultural nationalism which overshadowed its scientific goals to counteract Andrew Sharp's caustic thesis. In his summary of the events in *Hokuleʻa: The Way to Tahiti*, Finney recounts how his attempts to integrate Hawaiian customs, blessings by kahuna (priests), and the broader community into the project threatened the itinerary and objectives of the voyage. He traces the origins of the problem to his decision to allow Kane "to take the canoe to the Hawaiian people" on a two-month cultural odyssey through the archipelago that rekindled ancestral pride, facilitated short trips on the canoe, and raised general awareness about the voyage (1979, 32). According to Finney, Kane's "sailabout," a term I borrow from Maria Lepowsky (1995) to reflect the kinship networks that sustain Pacific diaspora, generated arguments over proprietorship of the *Hokuleʻa*. After one of many incidents of conflict Finney reflects:

> [L]ittle did we know that, within the context of modern Hawaii, to join cultural revival with experimental voyaging was to create an explosive mixture, and that so seemingly innocent an effort as trying to launch the canoe in a culturally appropriate way had tapped into a reservoir of jealousy and long-repressed resentments that would threaten to keep us from ever sailing to Tahiti. (1979, 6)

Finney has been a vital contributor to the regeneration of indigenous cultural traditions in Oceania and his groundbreaking work has been crucial to my own understanding of Pacific voyaging histories. Thus my point is not to question his valuable and ongoing legacy but rather to explore his textual interpretation of these events in the 1970s and their implications, decades later, for an understanding of Pacific regionalism. As an artifact of that era, *Hokuleʻa: The Way to Tahiti* documents the confusion over the politically coded "*Hokuleʻa* for Hawaiians only' movement" (Finney 1979, 35) and reflects broader tensions about Hawaiian and Pacific regional sovereignty. In his description of the claims to the vaka, Finney's narrative tends to erect a spatial and racialized hierarchy of authentic and inauthentic subjects, rendered along lines between "genuine canoe kahuna" (33) versus spiritual charlatans, "shallow-water men" versus deep-water sailors (56), and young urban "half-Hawaiians" versus less Americanized, older Polynesians. Thus Finney and the newspaper accounts of this time racialize Polynesian ancestry by demarcating percentages of Hawaiian blood while putting whiteness under erasure. In an effort to resist mutually constitutive discourses of blood that would mark whiteness and its own historical trajectories of diaspora, Finney's language shifts to spatial hierarchies. As a result, indigenous distance from urban centers becomes proportional to native authenticity in a way that is not applied to white subjects. Consequently, experiential knowledge of the deep sea and rural Hawai'i becomes the legitimizing criteria of a depoliticized indigeneity, where "modern change . . . robs Polynesians of their former virtues" (1979, 274).

Finney's account of the first *Hokule'a* voyage reflects an important shift in how the vessels of Pacific regionalism are represented and a more conscious racialization of white and indigenous diaspora. Unlike Heyerdahl's grandiose narrative of a white genealogy of the region, Finney's account of the thirty-five-day trip to Tahiti is probably the least romantic of any American text produced in the Pacific. While the all-male, multinational crew face stormy seas, unmitigating heat, boredom, spoiled food, sharks, a loss of bearing, illness, and a near mutiny, these dramatic components of the sea story are detached from their narrative tropes because of Finney's contested claims to the *Hokule'a*. He explains that a "sea drama" erupts between Hawaiian members of the crew over the haole Voyaging Society members due to their hierarchical likeness to "the colonial administration and administrators" (181). While the voyage had been characterized by animosities throughout, it erupts into violence on the last night at sea. Anchored off the coast of Tahiti, and timing their arrival into the harbor to coincide with the holiday that has been declared in their honor, the tensions over racialized blood are manifested in bloodshed when one of the younger "part" Hawaiian men, attacks Finney and the "non-Hawaiians" on board (Haugen 1976, A2). When they arrive the next day to tens of thousands of anticipant Tahitians (including Bengt Danielsson of the *Kon-Tiki*), Finney is sporting a black eye and their local sponsors become concerned about the fractious behavior of the crew. Voyaging Society board members fly in from Hawai'i to mediate, Mau Piailug departs hastily, the crew is sent home, and an entirely new group is flown in to guide *Hokule'a*, the name for Hawai'i's zenith star of joy, back home.

Finney explains that it was "naïve . . . to think that scientific research and cultural revival could be easily combined in today's Hawaii" (1979, 37), segregating the temporal trajectories of science and indigeneity. This masks a more striking incongruity: the celebration of the bicentennial anniversary of the United States by reawakening one of the most important cultural symbols of precolonial regionalism in Hawai'i. The bicentennial itinerary, which reenacts a historical and genealogical trajectory between two Polynesian archipelagoes under continuing colonial rule, apparently did not seem problematic to the Voyaging Society and its federal U.S. sponsors until struggles over *Hokule'a* made media headlines. This national celebration, articulated along the racialized lines of "part," "pure," and "non" Hawaiian identities, is particularly striking when one considers that Hawai'i, deemed by some white Americans as too multiethnic to integrate into the union, had at that time experienced less than twenty years as a state. Thus Finney's repeated use of the term "cultural revival," the presumed antithesis of U.S. patriotism, is notable in this context of self-conscious statehood, increasing tourism, and sovereignty activism. Haunani-Kay Trask has commented upon the mystifications of "cultural revival" narratives, arguing that "anthropologists and politicians readily use this term because it has no political context: the primary emphasis is usually on trivializing quaint practices and beliefs rather than on supporting conscious Native resistance to cultural imperialism" (1993, 115). The racial language in which these narratives interpellate degrees of authentic Hawaiianess draws from a colonial grammar that J. Kehaulani Kauanui has called "blood logics." She explains that this is not only a matter of "deracination" but a "logics of dilution" that delegitimizes genealogical claims to land, resources, and sovereignty (2002, 118). "Blood quantum inherently mobilizes racial categories as a proxy for ancestry" in ways that disenfranchise Hawaiians from ancestral *and* contemporary presence (120).[35]

Although the *Hokule'a*'s route from Hawai'i to Tahiti retraced ancient genealogical and political allegiances between Pacific Islanders, Finney's narrative does not actively engage an anticolonial regionalism that links these archipelagoes in the present. Native activists were resisting the heightened militarization of their islands by U.S. and French naval vessels, but the text does not reconcile contemporary political sovereignty activism with the genealogies rekindled by the voyaging canoe. This gap is important because the first voyage of the *Hokule'a* occurred precisely when Pacific Islanders were articulating a counter-narrative to colonial balkanization through an indigenous regionalism called the Pacific Way, visible in institutional bodies organized around economic, political, antinuclear, and environmental concerns.[36] While postwar Islanders lobbied their respective colonial administrators for independence, Hawaiians faced severe "militourism," a term Teresia Teaiwa borrows from Louis Owens and

121

defines as "a phenomenon by which military or paramilitary force ensures the smooth running of the tourist industry, and that same tourist industry masks the military force behind it" (1999, 251). By turning Hawai'i into its Pacific Command Center, the U.S. military was already putting a strain on land and water resources. Increasing transnational corporate investment led to concern that the 600,000 acres of Native Trust lands that had been confiscated by the military during World War II, as well as lands appropriated during the Vietnam War, would be transferred from state to corporate hands without consideration of Kanaka Maoli claims (Trask 1993, 91–92). Rapid development of tourist complexes, hotels, and golf courses compounded the land alienation that had begun with the militarization of the state in the late nineteenth century. That *Hokule'a* was launched as a bicentennial canoe is all the more poignant when we consider that July 4th is also the anniversary of the 1894 establishment of the (illegal) provisional government by white plantation interests and their seizure of 1.8 million acres of Kanaka Maoli lands. It was precisely the return of these alienated lands and the opposition to the continuing process of land eviction that was at the center of sovereignty mobilization.[37]

Trask pinpoints 1976 as the moment when Hawaiian "concern had exploded over Kaho'olawe Island," which had been used as a U.S. Navy bombing practice site since World War II (1993, 91). The continued destruction of this island was considered an affront to its sacred history (and a palpable threat to nearby Maui residents), so activists petitioned for its return to Kanaka Maoli guardianship. Read tidalectically, terrestrial U.S. military expansion and the subsequent land evictions of Hawaiians increased attention to the legitimacy of sovereign vessels of the sea. Since naval activities on Kaho'olawe were under intense scrutiny, one might categorize this as a contest between radically different vessels of cultural, political, and state authority. Given the widespread colonial suppression of indigenous mobility, it is not surprising that precontact Kaho'olawe was considered to be the center of navigational and priestly training for transpacific voyaging, and it is the only island in Oceania named for the Polynesian deity of the ocean, Kanaloa.[38] The sea channel leading from Kaho'olawe to the open Pacific is called "Ke Ala i Kahiki"—the way to Tahiti invoked in Finney's title—which *Hokule'a* was to rechart. As potent symbols of a indigenous Pacific revival, the "age of ethnicity," and the vitality of ancestral roots (Kanahele 1982, 6), the *Hokule'a* and Kaho'olawe were positioned as the frontispiece and framing images of what George Kanahele has termed the *Hawaiian renaissance*.[39]

A week before they were to set sail for Tahiti, the crew was asked if the *Hokuleʻa* would transport Kanaka Maoli elders to Kahoʻolawe to protest military violence and naval occupation. Finney remarks that the activists provided a "fiery appeal to Hawaiian patriotism that gripped the crew" and apparently "set the slight amount of Hawaiian blood in first mate Dave Lyman's blood racing" (1979, 85).[40] One crewmember declared that "going to Kahoolawe will really make *Hokuleʻa* a Hawaiian canoe," but Finney refused due to his fear that media headlines would report "Hawaiian Bicentennial Canoe seized Liberating Island" (85). Because the Coast Guard had already threatened Finney with *Hokuleʻa*'s confiscation if it were used to protest U.S. Navy operations, tensions about maritime sovereignty, coded in terms of indigenous versus nation-state vessels, became the focal point.

Thirty years later Finney concedes that it seems questionable to what extent the voyaging canoe, a precolonial vessel of sovereignty, could represent a multicultural and creolized Hawaiʻi amidst a decolonization movement that was not only Pacific but global in scope. Consequently, my question as to why a Polynesian vessel should have been expected to symbolize the U.S. nation-state might be better understood if we consider the ways in which indigenous icons are often appropriated as markers of national identity, coextensive with the state's boundaries as long as they are relegated to the past. This is obvious in white settler spaces such as Hawaiʻi and Aotearoa/New Zealand because indigeneity is a unique cultural difference often amplified to generate historical distinctiveness from the colonial homeland and to sustain the tourist economy. Yet the presence of modern, active indigenous subjects often challenges the temporal segregation of native culture from the colonial state.[41] This often positions white settlers, and haole voyagers on the *Hokuleʻa*, uneasily within a state that is purportedly celebrating its national bicentennial while also distinguishing itself through the native past. The inability to reconcile these positions is evident in a 1976 editorial of *The Honolulu Advertiser* that declared, in the midst of a vital Kanaka Maoli movement, that "the canoe trip reminds us that we are all immigrants here in Hawaii" (June 4, 1976, A12). As Trask has famously declared: "Native land belongs to Native people; they are the only residents with a genealogical claim to their place. . . . We are *not* all immigrants" (1993, 174). While Finney's text categorized the voyage in terms of a linear itinerary between Hawaiʻi and Tahiti that would revitalize indigenous seafaring technologies, his narrative seems challenged by the present/presence of native activism. Thus the movement across ocean space results in a direct conflict with a deeper indigenous time, precisely because the canoe, as a *vessel of the people*, cannot contain the competing histories, knowledges, and practices of 1976 Hawai'i.

The spatial and temporal complexity symbolized by indigenous seafaring vessels helps explains why, six days after the arrival of the *Hokule'a*, anticolonial demonstrations erupted in Tahiti. The French occupation of Te Ao Ma'ohi has been vital to their transoceanic empire; French nuclear vessels have benefited from the Truman-generated expansion of the littoral state, which increased colonial claims to Pacific waters. Yet French defiance of the 1966 Partial Test Ban Treaty spurred a series of anti-nuclear conferences, declarations, and constitutions across the region and beyond. By rendering Oceania as *aqua nullius* and by denying inter-island networks and sovereignty, the French could conduct massive nuclear detonations at Moruroa and Fangataufa atolls, islands chosen for their "remote" and "isolated" location. And yet by 1974, radiation contamination was registered 2,000 miles away in Samoa where it contributed to local casualties. As a demonstration of the power of their maritime vessels, the forty-six atmospheric explosions conducted from 1966 to 1974 were primarily orchestrated and launched from French naval ships and barges.[42]

As a historical reenactment and as an expression of indigenous political solidarity, the *Hokule'a* represents an essential vehicle for regional sovereignty. Finney's text observes that the success of the Tahitian demonstration "and the political reforms that have followed owed a debt to *Hokule'a*'s grand entrance into Papeete Harbor and her uplifting impact on the Tahitian people" (1979, 271–272). *Hokule'a* regenerated oral traditions that connected Hawaiian and Tahitian voyaging genealogies, reinvigorated precolonial forms of regionalism, inspired over 200 Tahitian songs, and catalyzed indigenous activism against European and U.S. imperialism. Inspired by the Voyaging Society, Tahitians established similar vaka organizations that sponsored flotillas of indigenous vessels to protest nuclear testing at Moruroa. As a vessel of Hawaiian and Tahitian sovereignty, the *Hokule'a* became a vehicle of genealogical history, regional identity, and an important symbol for contemporary political struggle.

My previous chapter explained the ways in which seafaring vessels were articulated in terms of a metaphoric body of the people. Just as Atlantic sailors conceptualized the ship in terms of discrete body parts, from ribs to the head, an analogous language exists in many parts of the indigenous Pacific that conceptualizes the material components of the vaka in corporeal terms; these often symbolize the present and future trajectories of the local or national community. For instance, according to David

Malo, the "body of the canoe" in Hawaiian tradition is described as the topknot of hair or neck (maku'u), the mouth (waha), and the bones (iwi kaela) (1903, 128–129). Other Pacific languages similarly conceptualize the vaka in terms of a material human body, a social body, and as a metaphor of the community's ancestry and leadership.[43] Over 200 tribal identities in Aotearoa/New Zealand and the Cook Islands are derived from an originary voyaging canoe, reflecting a social structure of routed roots that is remarkably similar to Vanuatu, thousands of miles away. While it is crucial to note, as Vanessa Griffen and Margaret Jolly have, that many Pacific Islanders do not have transoceanic genealogies, in the cases where this mode of travel was vital to communal history, the vaka is invested with the metaphysics of origins, leadership, autonomy, and destiny.[44] Like the grammar of diaspora, canoe metaphysics also draw from fluid metaphors of kinship and blood. As Joakim Peter points out of the Chuuk Islands of Micronesia, "waa," the cognate of "vaka," operates dually as "blood vessels that carry life through the body and as canoe, the centerpiece of navigation traditions that moves islands" (2000, 266). Drawing from navigator Celestino Emwalu, Vicente Diaz remarks that "like veins in our body, the canoe is the carrier of life."[45] As a vehicle of history, a vessel of blood, and a moving island, the voyaging canoe represents diaspora origins and the capacity to navigate the future. Read in this way, the Pacific is not simply the planet's originary ocean; for its first peoples, its generative fluidity is essential to the grammar of indigenous ontology.

As a vehicle of movement and flow that links the past to the future, the voyaging canoe continues to be a marker of genealogical and historical continuity. Although Pacific seafaring vessels are profoundly diverse, even when they are superseded by introduced technologies they continue to be vital to the symbolic economy of many Island identities and are crucial to rendering the sea as history. In many Island languages the cognate of "vaka" translates as "vessel" and is applied to airplanes, automobiles, submarines, and satellites, suggesting an indigenization of modernity and technology that does not minimize its traditional invocation as a powerful metaphor for the people. As such, the airplanes, steamboats, and passenger ships that connect the Pacific Islands are semantically incorporated into metaphors of regionalism. In this sense the vaka becomes a far more historical and spatial vehicle of multiple communal interests, from ontological and metaphysical discourses of blood and body to the globalizing and diaspora contingencies of Pacific migration. This is why it is significant that when Tahitians genealogically connected some of the *Hokule'a* crewmen as "long-lost relatives" (Finney 1979, 270), Finney observes that whaling vessels and other western vehicles facilitated these ancestral migrations. The familial networks of kinship, blood, and sovereignty activism that connect Pacific peoples are rendered through ancient *and* modern trajectories of transoceanic vehicles. Nevertheless, Herb Kane reported that even "if the biggest French warship and the supersonic Concords landed in Tahiti at the same time as the *Hokule'a*, there is no question about what the Tahitians would go to see. The canoe" (*Honolulu Star-Bulletin*, June 18, 1976, C7).

By comparing two Honolulu newspaper articles printed the day the *Hokule'a* arrived at Tahiti, we can see that on the one hand, the voyage reproduced the sea as history by regenerating indigenous trade and kinship networks across Oceania. On the other hand, the Rim's claims to the Basin symbolically empty this vessel in the interests of U.S. expansion. In a piece entitled "Hokule'a & our Pacific," the editors of *The Sunday Advertiser* printed a detailed political map of the region and argued that the vaka's voyage would encourage stronger economic investment between French and U.S. territories. Belittling the *Hokule'a* as "a nice emotional glow for Hawaiians and others in the Islands," the article emphasized U.S. political and economic expansion couched in proprietary terms as "minding the store" to counteract "Communist giants" looming on the other side of the Rim (August 1, 1976, B2). This replicates the logic of *aqua nullius* that bolstered Truman's annexation of Micronesia and the (nuclear) militarization of Oceania, literally and figuratively supplanting the vaka with the wartime vessels of the U.S. Navy.

In the same edition, columnist Sammy Amalu posed an alternative vision of regionalism: the *Hokule'a* as a (blood) vessel of Hawaiian and Polynesian sovereignty amidst an era of Cold War expansion exacted between Rim powers in the Pacific. Imagining Oceania as a brotherly network of kinship, he encouraged the vaka to "sail the seas of Kanaloa as if they are our own—which they are" (A15). Importantly, he mapped out temporal continuity for indigenous regionalism. While citing the opposition to French, British, and U.S. colonial and military activities in Polynesia and Micronesia, Amalu reminded readers that the precolonial kinship networks rekindled by the *Hokule'a* had already been utilized by Hawaiian monarchs such as King Kalakaua in his nineteenth-century vision of "an empire of Oceania." Although largely forgotten by historians, David Kalakaua, the first monarch to circle the globe and a key figure of Hawaiian cultural revival, responded to the rising threats of German, American, British, Spanish, and French annexation of the Pacific Islands in the 1880s by attempting to establish political ties with the kingdoms of Japan, Samoa, Tonga, and the Cook Islands and to consolidate a "Polynesian Federation." He described it as a mission of philanthropy in response to "repeated calls" from Samoa and other islands for a "Confederation or solidarity of the Polynesian Race" (Kalakaua in Kuykendall 1967, 339). His first and only naval vessel, *Kaimiloa*, was dispatched to Samoa, yet while a treaty of federation was signed, the trip was a political disaster. The scandal it created was a precipitating factor in Kalakaua's concession of sovereignty to white American businessmen in the 1887 Bayonet Constitution.[46] In referencing this incident, Amalu offers an alternative regionalism that has been overlooked in the Rim-speak of Asia Pacific: he suggests that the *Hokule'a* might reawaken "one vast empire not of conquest or of political power but one of culture, and of common ancestry" (Amalu 1976, A15).

    Since I have argued that one cannot segregate regional political power in the Pacific from culture and "common ancestry," I now turn to how the (blood) vessels of sovereignty have been used to signify an indigenous regionalism in contemporary literary texts. This destabilizes the idea of the region as a Euro-American construct and engages with the complex mapping of a watery network of blood vessels and history to inscribe what Trask calls an "ancestral ocean" (1993, 51). This complement to terrestrial-based identities leads her to describe Pacific Islanders as "more the children of the sea than the land" (69). As a tidalectic engagement between land and sea, this upholds the roots of indigenous sovereignty as they are routed through the watery metaphors of diaspora as an "ocean in the blood."

Vaka Pasifika: Regional Identity and Other Cargo

Since the *Hokule'a*'s initial noninstrument navigation to Tahiti, the Pacific voyaging canoe and its navigational system of etak have provided vital and sustaining metaphors of indigeneity in Oceania. In those areas that are marked by long oceanic histories, the voyaging canoe has figured prominently as an icon of indigenous renaissance. As a symbol that registers ethnic, national, and regional identity and history, the canoe features in multiple flags (French Polynesia, Guam, the South Pacific Commission) and seals (Solomon and Marshall Islands). As an embodiment of this living tradition, the *Hokule'a* has inspired many other voyaging replicas across the Pacific and is considered a "floating classroom." The vessel's revitalization of regional knowledge and indigenous science led to the "Seafaring Pacific Islanders" theme chosen by Cook Islands premier Sir Albert Henry for the 1992 Festival of Pacific Arts. An early architect of Pacific Way practices and policies, Henry emphasized the "great ocean voyagers" at a festival which featured the gathering of *Hokule'a* and seventeen additional vaka in Rarotonga (Cook Islands).[47] Since the 1970s, voyaging canoes and etak navigational modes have provided the inspiration for a new generation of Pacific cultural production, including poetry, novels, music, visual arts, film, methodologies for Pacific regionalism (Hau'ofa), and a Native Pacific Cultural Studies (Diaz and Kauanui).

Although the metaphors produced by indigenous maritime traditions are complex, it is not difficult to determine why they are so appealing to regional and local identities. As icons of native movement, of rooted routes, the voyaging canoe naturalizes migration and avoids the pathologizing language reserved for refugees that Liisa Malkki has documented in the grammar of diaspora. Except by Andrew Sharp, ancient Pacific travelers are not depicted as rootless "boat people," but rather as cosmopolitan "people of the sea." Just as the English language demarcates positive progress through metaphors of self-determined movement, indigenous seafaring provides an imaginative reservoir for "charting," "navigating," and "plotting" a course that is not overdetermined by the trajectories of western colonization. Moreover, the etak concept of moving islands destabilizes the myth of isolation and renders the indigenous peoples of Oceania as active participants in the world historical process. The semantics of the canoe itself encode the body of the ancestors, providing a genealogical rendering of place as an alternative to colonial historiography in a way that is conceptually tied to the continuity of the social body. Moreover, the fluidity of the ocean allows for a dynamic mapping of social and political territory and a shared regional unity based on the decolonizing ideology of the Pacific Way.

With the decolonization of many island nations, the notion of a "Pacific Way" arose to encourage the viability of precolonial history, native communal and familial values, consensus building, reciprocity, indigenous arts, and inter-island cooperation and unity (see R. Crocombe 1976). Gathering postcolonial and regional momentum, this movement was vital to the literary arts movement generated by Ulli and Georgina Beier's writing seminars and publishing venues at the University of Papua New Guinea which, due to their connections to Nigeria, were already in a dialogue with African writers.[48] The Pacific Way ideology informed the construction of the regional service and outreach model for the University of the South Pacific (USP), established in Fiji in 1968 and modeled after that other inter-island educational center, the University of the West Indies. According to Marjorie Crocombe, institutional support for Pacific literature was lacking until a broad spectrum of Melanesian literary initiatives was showcased in Fiji at the first South Pacific Arts Festival in 1972. In response, Crocombe and others, inspired by the Beiers, established the South Pacific Creative Arts Society and helped steward an incipient literary movement with support from scholars such as Ken Arvidson, Satendra Nandan, Albert Wendt, and many others.

Just as transatlantic literature was forged through the process of maritime expansion, many Pacific narratives are characterized by this complex entanglement between transoceanic voyaging and cultural identity. The nautical vessel has been a (literal) vehicle for transpacific travel and helped catalyze and conceptualize a regional "way" in the cultural and literary arts. In fact, Wendt suggested the indigenization of the term "Pacific Way" as "Vaka Pasifika," to highlight the regional translation of "vaka" as causative prefix and vessel or vehicle of Pacific identity (see R. Crocombe 1976, 1). The decade of the first *Hokule'a* voyage was characterized by a tremendous expansion in regional literary production, a movement, in Wendt's words, "towards a new Oceania." By the mid-1970s, the first creative writing journals, novels, poetry collections, Pacific Island anthologies, and a regional literature conference were established.[49] The vaka, and the transoceanic imagination that it represents, are key to placing these emergent literatures in history. As Paul Sharrad has shown: "Polynesian navigation has supplied what has perhaps become a master trope for Pacific literary production" (1998, 97).

Just as Euro-American literature of the "South Seas" was a maritime endeavor, established by naval officers and sailors in their "island hopping" across the region, the first wave of indigenous fiction was also deeply informed by the movement of ships and the ocean, establishing a tidalectic between land and the sea. The fact that these early fictions were also collaborative helps us sketch a genealogy between the construction of nautical South Seas fiction after World War I and the use of maritime vehicles and tropes to "craft" the region's native literature. One of the region's first indigenous texts, the autobiography of Cook Islander Florence "Johnny" Frisbie, was cowritten with her white American father and detailed her shipboard travels with her family across a wartorn Pacific (1948 and 1959). Frisbie's compatriots, Tom and Lydia Davis, coauthored the region's first published indigenous novel, *Makutu* (1960), a story of white maritime travel to Polynesia that centers on the character Tangaroa, the deity of the ocean. These early texts present a maritime narrative legacy that, in addition to raising more localized concerns, can be directly connected to the South Seas nautical adventure genre that Frisbie's father adopted from his predecessors, Robert Louis Stevenson and Herman Melville.[50]

Thus, well before Hau'ofa's theory of a "sea of islands," Pacific writers were using ships and the ocean to conceptualize regional identity. In Samoa the first literary journal was entitled *Moana*, while in Fiji, Sano Malifa mapped the region from an airplane in his poetry collection *Looking Down at Waves* (1975). Wendt's groundbreaking regional anthology *Lali* was "nursed," he felt, "by the warmth and love of our mother, the Pacific" (1980, xviii–xix). Similarly, the cover of the first issue of the regional journal *Mana* featured a carving from the prow of a Solomon Islands canoe. In the second issue, Marjorie Crocombe declared "the canoe is afloat.... *Mana* is just a vehicle to help carry the rich cargoes of individual talent" across the Pacific (1974, n.p.). This transoceanic imagination has often been sustained by those whom Albert Wendt describes as "scholar-shippers," who have crossed the region for educational reasons. In fact, Wendt's first novel, *Sons for the Return Home* (1973), emphasized what he called the "pelagic" nature of the region's literary figures. More recently, Hau'ofa noted approvingly of a USP student journal called *Wansolwara*, "a pidgin word . . . translated as 'one ocean—one people'" (1997, 139–140). It is this entanglement between regional literary production and a continuous history of transoceanic migration that Sharrad describes, in his meticulous survey of Pacific literature, as a "pelagic post-colonialism" (1998).

Yet while the tidalectic between land and sea has helped to constitute the regional imagination, little attention has been paid to the ships and the seas that are so often a vehicle for Pacific literary production. In this early "wave" of Pacific writing, Vincent Eri's novel *The Crocodile* (1970) is particularly significant because it employs maritime vessels to signal the transition from sovereign to colonized island status. As one of the first indigenous novels of the region and a tremendous influence on subsequent literary production, the narrative inscribes a coming-of-age story in Australian-governed New Guinea during World War II in which temporal movement is directed by the trajectories of ships. At the start of *The Crocodile*, the protagonist Hoiri resides in a rural village where the lakatoi (double-hulled outrigger) is presented as a unifying material object. In his vision of the inter-island networks rendered famous by Bronislaw Malinowski's *Argonauts of the Pacific*, Eri emphasizes how building the canoe unites members of the community in shared labor, just as the canoe's long sea voyages connect island villages through trade and exchange networks (kula). These canoes provide sustaining goods and materials and when one lakatoi is retired, its hulls are transformed into the floors of the community meetinghouse and the coffin of Hoiri's mother (1970, 25). Hoiri's first voyage includes a stop in Port Moresby, the center of colonial modernity, where he is disturbed by the overwhelming presence of steel ships and the incomprehensible practice of white people who withhold the cargo sent to him by his "dead ancestors" (46). This new association of the ship with injustice and material inequity is then developed in later scenes when Australian colonizers force Hoiri and his companions to labor as cargo carriers for the difficult upriver trips to the diamond mines. Indigenous watercraft and labor are appropriated without compensation, particularly in the Allied effort against the Japanese invasion.

Caught between the racialized "white" and "yellow" people's war, Hoiri's community is pressed to help Australia win so that "the brown men would be treated as brothers and would sit at the table with the white men" (1970, 140). Hoiri is forced to unload cargo from Allied barges and to help build a military base where, significantly, he supplements his meager income by carving "toy canoes" for American troops as souvenirs (159). This dramatic reduction of the community-building lakatoi to a child's toy of militourism becomes all the more devastating when an Australian officer confiscates his supplemental funds, and Hoiri is accused of lying and stealing. While his maritime travels with the Allies open his perspective to a broader regional understanding of what will become the 600-island nation of independent Papua New Guinea, his last sea voyage is described in terms of bewitchment and terror.[51] Although he has been informed of the approach of massive American ships, when one does appear on the horizon he cannot assimilate it as a vessel, describing it instead as a "dark green island" with "thick black smoke" (163). This "moving island" becomes "a metal cave," a "sinister version of Noah" and the Ark, where he and his fellow Papuans become "the creatures" that are "watched" and "counted" as they board like "human cargo" (165, 167). As a closing frame to the novel, the massive steel ship transports them to their home villages after three years' absence working for the Allies; this is a stark contrast to the equitable trade relations of the kula ring that open the book.

The ship's overwhelmingly industrial presence signals a new era of reification of native labor in New Guinea. After exposing the closely linked apparatuses of colonial, capitalist, and military occupation of the Pacific, Eri neither resuscitates the voyaging canoe nor accepts its substitution by these steel vehicles of a violent modernity. Reading the novel in terms of the tidalectic relation between roots and routes, we see that the men's forced migration away from their home has greatly disturbed the economic and social equilibrium of the village. Hoiri's absence has contributed to the death of his wife and father, and Eri concludes the novel with the community's neglect of their own gardens and their dependence on imported capital rather than the indigenous kula ring that was symbolized and facilitated by the voyaging canoe. As an important transitionary text of native literary production, *The Crocodile* records the epistemic violence of western military expansion in the Pacific, demonstrating how its naval power appropriated and supplanted native vehicles to configure *aqua nullius*.

Eri's novel is significant because it foregrounds why the maritime vehicle is a crucial icon of territorial claims between Rim and Basin, just as it details the process by which indigenous sovereign vessels were substituted for the steel machinery of naval occupation. At the forefront of discussions about the Melanesian and Pacific Way, Eri's configuration of voyaging culture in western Oceania reflects an era of a vibrant regional dialogue and its placement here helps to counter a recent trend, in literature and cultural studies, of focusing exclusively on Polynesian seafaring and cultural production.[52] In the decades after the publication of *The Crocodile*, attention has shifted towards indigenous literary production in white-settler-states such as Hawai'i and Aotearoa/New Zealand, eclipsing the formative and historic influence of the western Pacific. Because Polynesians represent only 15 percent of the total indigenous population of the Pacific Islands and Australia (R. Crocombe 1992, 6), I would like to make an effort to sustain a dialogue across the region, even if, as I will explain, emerging etak islands such as Hawai'i and Aotearoa/New Zealand are becoming new centers of regional activity. In order to maintain a regional tidalectic, I want to turn to Fiji as a vital crossroads of Pacific political, cultural, and academic exchange and one that, tectonically and historically, has linked the eastern (Polynesian) Pacific with its western (Melanesian and Micronesian) counterparts.

Hau'ofa's theory of a new Oceania has been promulgated as a model for theorizing Pacific cultures, but in an effort to sustain the breadth of this regional dialogue, I would like to highlight its dialogue with an earlier era of the Vaka Pasifika, its Melanesian sources, and its contemporary Fijian contexts. As a Tongan raised in Papua New Guinea who resides in Fiji, Hau'ofa was certainly aware of the publication of Bernard Narokobi's *The Melanesian Way* (1982), a series of articles and dialogues between the writer and fellow Papuans about the vitality of precolonial history, the need for regional unity, the problems of colonial belittlement and small island size, and the natural metaphors of land and seascape that sustain postcolonial models of identity. Although this connection has not been noted, Hau'ofa published *A New Oceania* ten years after Narokobi's text with the same press, and he addressed remarkably similar concerns (Waddell, Naidu, and Hau'ofa 1993). In fact, like *The Melanesian Way*, his text incorporated the challenges of his compatriots about theorizing inter-island identity in the wake of regional inequities of gender, class, and ethnic privilege. In their responses, writers suggested that "the reality is that Epeli's Oceania is characterised not by pan-Pacific unity but by intense national and subnational ethnic divisions" (Borer, 1993, 86). Like the Melanesian Way, the Pacific Way ideology was eventually complicated by internal divisions along the lines of ethnicity, political status, social class, and chiefly privilege.[53] The 1987 coups in Fiji, where an indigenous military elite overthrew its democratically elected government to disenfranchise Fijians of Indian descent, cast a pall over utopian regional initiatives and brought into sharp relief the conflicts of ethnicity that threatened the Vaka Pasifika. On the heels of these coups, Subramani's pioneering *South Pacific Literature* warned of a "strong jingoistic accent [that could] nullify the 'ideology' of regionalism and the 'Pacific way'" (1992, xiv).

Although Hau'ofa now refers to the Pacific Way as "a shallow ideology that was swept away by the rising tide of regional disunity in the 1980's" (1997, 127), "Our sea of islands" has to be contextualized as an antidote to that disunity, reflecting an engagement with Melanesian theories of the Vaka Pasifika to counteract the fragmentation engendered by the Fijian coups. By 1990 the Fijian constitution had been rewritten in ways that were deemed discriminatory to nonindigenous residents, and by 1992 the leader of the coup, backed by the chiefly elite, was elected prime minister. Violence against Indo-Fijians created a rift in the Vaka Pasifika, leading the region's intellectuals to question how the Pacific Way might invoke a unifying past that contributes to contemporary discrimination.[54] These events are vital to consider in contextualizing the creation and circulation of "Our sea of islands," and another self-conscious attempt to uphold the unity of regional identity, Tom Davis's novel *Vaka: Saga of a Polynesian Canoe* (1992b). Here I position Fiji and the coups as absent signifiers that are vital to understanding a new era of regionalist discourse that represented an indigenization of the utopian and globalizing contours of Asia Pacific as well as the shifting ethnic divisions between Pacific Islanders.

Vaka Pasifika: Ethnic Blood Vessels and the Spermatic Journey

Nicholas Thomas asserts that voyaging projects "recover tradition, but they are special because they do not affirm particular peoples in a nationalist mode as much as they celebrate the connections between people" (1997, 5). In the narratives of white and Polynesian diaspora discussed here, these regional connections have generally been articulated in terms of masculine ethnic kinship, blood vessels, and political alliance. Yet as alluring as diaspora and regional identifications may be in providing a fluid alternative to the terrestrial limitations of the nation-state, they often present, as Connery has shown about the ocean, a utopian "spatial fix." Destabilizing western notions of the Pacific as an empty vessel to emphasize indigenous vehicles of sovereignty does not necessarily lead to a unifying model for regional identity. In fact, the concept of the region, even when stitched together by the transpacific vaka, cannot provide a panacea for the ethnic and gender hierarchies that flow over from colonial and national frameworks. In this context it is helpful to remember the common metaphor of the nation as a ship; a semantic connection relevant to some Pacific narratives of the transoceanic vaka.[55]

As I will explain, configuring the voyaging canoe as the vehicle of an anticolonial Pacific Way has resulted in a rescripting of imperialist histories that, in some cases, naturalize contemporary political and social hierarchies by projecting an originary model of ethnic purity onto the region's past. By upholding a chiefly masculine elite as the progenitors of the region, these narratives demonstrate remarkable parallels to a type of anticolonial nationalism that Partha Chatterjee has shown was characterized by the gendered segregation of time and space (1989). He demonstrates that women represent tradition and purity through their presumed isolation from the corrupting (yet dynamic) public realm of transnational trade, colonization, and exchange. Restated in terms of this project, Pacific women function as the roots to stabilize transoceanic masculine routes. This is why it is no coincidence that the voyaging canoe in these modern narratives is often referred to as "she," even though Polynesian languages are not gendered. By turning to Davis's *Vaka: Saga of a Polynesian Canoe*, I interrogate how the text displaces the anxieties about contemporary ethnic migrations in the globalized Pacific onto a fictive historiography of the transoceanic (blood) vessel. This line of inquiry raises questions about relations of power in the Pacific and problematizes the concept of the region as a gendered utopian space that transcends the limitations of the nation-state and ethnic nationalism.

Written by the former prime minister of the Cook Islands, *Vaka* represents the only historical novel that attempts to chart Polynesian settlement of Oceania.[56] As a genre and a discursive mode of decolonization, historical novels are integral to postcolonial literature, but they serve a specific function in indigenous communities by outlining an ontology that is vital for contemporary social and political allegiances and for sustaining sovereignty. In a paper delivered at the Pacific Historical Association, Davis spoke of this forthcoming novel, explaining that it was an attempt to excavate the oral traditions of the region (1992a, 69). Arguing for the importance of those oral voyaging histories transcribed by early anthropologists but dismissed by Sharp and others as fabrications, Davis positions his novel and the Pacific narrative process in a lineage with tumukorero, "expert keepers of the records of history and its fragments" (70). By turning to the voyaging histories narrated by "Polynesian elders" and anthropologists such as Te Rangi Hiroa, Davis described *Vaka* as an effort to "write a history of a people who did not consider it isolation to live on an island surrounded by an ocean which to them was a highway to everywhere" (1992a, 70). Emphasizing the cultural, political, religious, and especially genealogical commonalities between Polynesians, Davis's paper made an argument for intercultural contact that contributed to a regional "oneness" (71).

I take up the layering of indigenous genealogy and history in subsequent chapters, so here I will merely emphasize the fluid network of kinship that buoys the regional imagination, the Vaka Pasifika. These filial networks are vital to precolonial as well as globalized Oceania and are manifested in myriad formulations which cannot be represented in all their complexity here. What I would like to question is a practice, to borrow again from Kauanui, of "blood logics" that reduces the history of transoceanic voyaging into a story of racial purity; this utilizes colonial ideologies of race as a mystified proxy for Pacific genealogy. Overall, my work seeks to foreground Islander-based recovery projects and native histories, knowledges, and narratives of unity. Yet I concur with Nicholas Thomas that when indigenous discontinuities are suppressed in favor of a homogenizing racial "oneness," then those projects require some scrutiny, particularly when these texts bear a discomforting relationship to western romance narratives that are the antithesis of "decolonizing history" (1997, 46).

As a meticulously researched and documented account of precolonial Polynesian cultures, *Vaka* is at once an ethnographic and historical rendering of ocean origins. The author's foreword lists dozens of archives, printed texts, and sources of oral history, and the book includes Davis's illustrations of material objects, an orthography and pronunciation guide, genealogies of the principal characters, and an index. The cover represents the author's illustration of a fully manned double-hulled vessel at sea, and the novel is dedicated to those whom Davis describes as "descendants of the principle characters who brought this great canoe through twelve generations of history" (1992b, v). Like the Pacific texts discussed in the following chapters, the novel represents a weaving together of genealogy and history that decolonizes the hierarchy between objective and subjective narratives of the past. Although it is the first indigenous Pacific maritime novel, it is not the first text written to destabilize Euro-American visions of the region by upholding the genealogical origins of the Polynesians. Structurally, Davis borrows much from Maori anthropologist Te Rangi Hiroa, who dedicated his epic ethnography, *Vikings of the Pacific* (1938), to his "kinsmen in the scattered isles of Polynesia." Davis's text shares with Buck an effort to "draw [Polynesians] together in the bond of the spirit . . . for we come of the blood that conquered the Pacific with stone-aged vessels" (Buck 1938, xi).

The presence of these vessels of sovereignty, whether "stone-aged" or contemporary, is crucial to interpreting ontological claims to the region. Just as Europeans in the Pacific authenticate their presence through familial narratives of "founding fathers" like Magellan, Tasman, Bougainville, and especially Cook, indigenous writers of the region can destabilize these claims by excavating originary navigators and vessels. Davis, president of the Cook Island Voyaging Society and a respected mariner who sailed his yacht from the Pacific to New England to attend Harvard University, understandably places the Pacific vaka at the center of his novel. In fact, its first words assert that "Polynesians are people of the outrigger canoe" (1992b, xvii). Unlike the bildungsroman that traces the trajectory of one *individual*'s development, this novel inscribes the history of one *vaka* as it was passed down from father to son during the height of Pacific voyaging and settlement from 1000–1300 CE. As a protagonist, the canoe is humanized—the nineteen chapters of the novel are organized around its "conception," "birth," "taming," "migration," and "death." Although the novel does not pose one central human protagonist, it does offer a succession of masculine heroes, who embody chiefly leadership and who represent the canoe's human progeny. Overall, the individualist contours of historical narrative are altered because the vaka provides continuity across 300 years; this is extended farther through the genealogical relationships the book establishes with its Pacific author and his indigenous readers. The canoe literally becomes a (blood) vessel of Pacific history. As a mobile vehicle of history, its significations are dynamic and its placement shifts over space and time. The vessel changes names nearly ten times depending on its owners and circumstances, and it travels widely from its origin in Upolu (Samoa) to Fiji, Tonga, Tahiti, Rarotonga, and then it is retired as the well-known founding waka *Takitumu* in Aotearoa. Held together by the "roots" of its "conception" forest in Upolu (where the trees are felled for its construction according to the well-known story of Lata / Rata), this vaka establishes an originary Pacific cosmopolitanism of transoceanic routes.

Published a year before Hau'ofa's "Sea of islands," Davis demonstrates that "Polynesians living on islands never feel isolated because Te Moana Nui a Kiva is perceived as a highway to everywhere" and that the vaka has been integral to Islander communication for over three thousand years of history (1992b, xviii, 274).

For all of its investment in decolonizing history and offering an indigenous model for Pacific regionalism, Davis's novel has been largely ignored, perhaps because it tries too self-consciously to inscribe "explorers, adventurous reading freebooters, and the restless wanderings of our canoe people" (1992b, 6). I agree with the otherwise indefatigable Paul Sharrad, who concedes that "it reads like an interminable school history text" (1998, 97). The Davises' first novel, *Makutu*, was accused of drawing too heavily from romantic South Seas fiction (see Subramani 1992, 14), and we can extend that claim to *Vaka*'s inscription of the maritime adventure novel which valorizes masculine motility over feminized stasis and constructs racialized others for narrative tension. Consequently, *Vaka* does less to decolonize history than to construct regional identity by literalizing the etymology of "diaspora," producing the voyaging canoe as a vessel of what Leed calls the "spermatic journey" across space and time. Moreover, its partitioning of Oceania into hierarchies of Polynesia over Melanesia mitigates Thomas's argument that the divisive "ethnic typifications that have been generated over the past two centuries" by Europeans "have had a negligible impact" on cultural production in the region (1997, 155), suggesting a larger rift in the Vaka Pasifika.

Activating the metonymic relationship between the (blood) vessel and ethnicity, Davis inscribes "heroic adventurers" whose migrations, like Froude's, are generated by the bodily presence of "the ancestral salt of the sea strong in their blood" (1992b, 172).[57] It places "Samoa and Tonga" as the "seat of the Polynesian race" and conceives of the region as "one large extended family throughout Te Moana Nui a Kiva" (173). Although Davis's prologue concedes that not all Islanders were aristocratic ocean voyagers (xviii), the novel, like its chiefly protagonists, seems to be a "stickler for the protocol of purity of blood and lineage of royalty" (227). This is literalized at the end of the canoe's voyaging life when it sails with the "Great Fleet" to settle Aotearoa/New Zealand. After a succession of chiefly owners across twelve generations, the last guardian, the priest Ta'u Ariki, sanctifies the vaka's burial in Aotearoa with his own blood and founds the Ngati Ta'u (Ngai Tahu/Kai Tahu) community.

To fully engage with the vessel's gendered symbology of bodily fluid, we have to turn to the ways in which the grammar of diaspora often invokes blood and sperm as originary essence. Davis's depiction of an ancient Pacific diaspora draws on many causes for the migrations, such as family disputes, political turmoil, boredom, and resource limitations, but the vast majority of his voyagers reflect the telos of the "spermatic journey," defined by Leed as travel "stimulated by a male reproductive motive, a search for temporal extension of self in children, only achievable through the agency of women" (1991, 114). In this way the "blood of their sea-going ancestors" that "surged hotly" in their bodies (Davis 1992b, 8) may be seen as a substitution for those other bodily fluids that are etymologically linked to diaspora. Leed derives these observations from the oral epics of Greek and Viking travel, whose voyagers have been valorized as determining "agents of history" and civilizing empire (1991, 15, 115). Significantly, these same texts inspired Malinowski's "Argonauts," Buck's "Vikings," and Davis's "Saga." In fact, Buck referred to these men who "surpassed the achievements" of the Phoenicians, Mediterraneans, and Vikings as "the supreme navigators of history" (1938, 13). In the "spermatic journey," travel "broadcasts the male seed that founds lineages" and simultaneously determines the "boundaries that contain women" (Leed 1991, 114). Thus in *Vaka*'s detailed inscription of 300 years of Polynesian voyaging in a canoe that transports over 100 people at a time, women are never represented on board. It is not that women do not voyage on the vaka, they occasionally do, but Davis neglects to depict them textually, preferring to inscribe a homosocial community of seafarers.

This reflects an unfortunate legacy derived from Pacific anthropology in which the settlement of Oceania was configured as an adventurous masculine endeavor with spurious arguments that women were not allowed on board, which of course begs the question as to how new settlements reproduced without them.[58] For instance, fifty years before Heyerdahl's bearded white gods, J. Macmillan Brown (a teacher of Peter Buck) theorized Aryan diffusion to the Pacific as a "masculine expedition." Brown argued "a few hundred miles of sea were sure to daunt primitive woman from venturing her children and her household gods upon so dangerous an element; the thousands of miles between resting places in Polynesia made such ventures impossible for them" (1907, 261). To Brown, reproduction derived from the "masculine infiltration" of islands that, mysteriously, were already populated with women (Brown 1907, 263; see Howe 2003, 135–136).

This gendered segregation of space, projected ahistorically onto the past, also informed debates over whether the presence of women onboard the *Hokule'a* would contaminate the canoe's sanctity. The infrequent representation of women in Pacific maritime narratives is not an accurate reflection of the region's orature. In fact the scholarly archive records countless Pacific women travelers including sea deities (Hine Moana, the wife of Kiwa), female voyaging companions (of Tangi'ia, Ru, Tane, and Rakanui), autonomous women voyagers (Hineraki, Pele, and Nafanua), and a few female navigators (Hine, Nei Nim'anoa). These women appear in Davis's original sources, directing and organizing transoceanic voyages, yet he excludes them from his historical novel.[59] I am not concerned with representing the historical accuracy of female presence in transoceanic voyaging, as that is self-evident. Instead, I ask why are women's routes suppressed? What is gained by these deliberate efforts to masculinize Pacific seafaring?

One way to approach these questions is to deconstruct the land-sea binary and engage tidalectically with the complex gendering of space. This approach refuses the homogenization of *aqua* and *terra nullius* and foregrounds the ways in which specific places in the land and sea (the mountain, lagoon, or deep ocean) may be gendered relationally and historically, destabilizing the assumed synecdochic relationship between place and space. To pursue the complexity of place one would recognize that a tree in a forest, for instance, might be gendered female, only to be masculinized once it is refashioned into a voyaging canoe, as Shirley Campbell's research suggests about Vakuta.[60] On the one hand, this may suggest that the sea is associated with mobility and masculinity while the land represents femininity and heaviness (S. Campbell 2002, 154–156), a symbolic arrangement sustained by the conceptualization of the "long" canoe as phallus in multiple Pacific contexts.[61] Yet this masculinization of the vessel needs to be considered alongside the fact that the sailing canoe is often interpellated as a female witch (147) and in other cases as a bird.[62] I suggest that the western homogenization of space has tended to suppress the more complicated and dynamic vehicles of gender relations in the Pacific.

In fact, women's bodies are not exclusively rooted to the land when we consider that *aspects of the feminine* are generated and indeed integral to men's successful routes at sea. To pursue the trace of mobile women subjects, we must examine how they are transformed and transported into feminized objects of desire. For example, early in Davis's novel, the young chiefly male, Te Arutanga Nuku of Samoa, pursues his father's voyaging canoe, *Tarai Po*, as a love interest, demonstrating the way in which penetrating masculine subjects often reduce women to symbolic vessels (or basins). Described as a "beckoning temptress" (1992b, 17), a vessel with "a shapely hull," he determines that it was "love at first sight" (24). In his gaze, the canoe "took on the physical qualities of a beautiful beckoning woman and his desire for her grew immensely" (25). Conveniently, he remembers that his father secretly desires his wife, Te Pori, so he arranges her sexual exchange for the canoe. Once he obtains the vessel, he names it after his wife and thereafter the narrator must refer to her as "the woman" to differentiate her from the new subject of the novel, *Te Pori*, the voyaging canoe. Arutanga is "stimulated" by the sight of his new property in the lagoon; "he realized that the canoe had the same effect on him as that of a woman" (42). He returns to his sleeping wife, sees that she is "as beautiful as the canoe" and that sexually, she can "give [him] what the canoe cannot" (42). Although his wife "was not able to follow his demanding passion, [she] was happy to satisfy it, for she sensed that the canoe had aroused him" (43). In this incident Davis rather helpfully outlines the conflation of heterosexual desire for women with a need to possess and master this vessel. This demonstrates the ways in which the circulation and exchange of that desire leads to the substitution of an actual woman for the wooden vehicle and how the animation of that vessel (or vehicle of history) is obtained by sexualizing her body. Therefore it is not surprising that Te Pori ("the woman") feels sexually competitive with her new namesake, the canoe (43). Like maritime novels in general, the homosocial decks of the voyaging canoe maintain a precarious hold on their heterosexuality by gendering the ship as an accessible female body.

Like the trees that are felled, uprooted, and transformed into the wooden voyaging canoe (Davis 1992b, 14), the sacrifice of a woman's body makes the vaka—and the subject of Davis's novel—possible. This is upheld in another oral tradition in which the well-known Tahitian voyaging hero, Iro (Hiro), murders his wife underneath his docked canoe and buries her under its wood shavings. Davis justifies this gynocide by suggesting that Iro's protofeminist wife questioned his virility.[63] We might interpret the trope of sacrifice as the originary mechanism by which nature is transformed into culture which, as Sherry Ortner has shown (1974), generally occurs through the agency of women (as vehicle). But in this Levi-Straussian transition from the raw to the cooked, Davis attributes the lifeblood of the vessel to cultured masculinity. His narrator argues that it is "craftsmen . . . who build part of the soul that goes into a vessel and makes her a living being. It is the men who command and sail her who complete the process. If these men are good at their jobs and are in empathy with her, a boat comes to life and evokes a soul and personality of her own" (1992b, 48). Davis upholds a familiar process of gendered cultural generation in which women, like the trees, provide the raw primitive materials for the vessel while masculine artistry and history refine the vehicle into a meaningful form. By extension, the cosmopolitan and masculine bias of migratory routes are obtained by mastering a primitivized landscape of feminized roots.

If we pursue this broader network of regional exchange, we begin to comprehend *Vaka*'s investment in constructing masculine maritime histories. After obtaining *Te Pori*, Arutanga and his wife ("the woman") determine they will participate in a malanga, a visiting tour across the Samoan Islands. Te Pori is interested in reestablishing her kinship connections, to see "their royal counterparts" (52), while Arutanga looks forward to the trade. The malanga, Davis emphasizes, entails a tidalectic relationship between land and sea in which the visitors must transport vast quantities of gifts for their hosts, who must respond with "unstinting generosity" in kind (57). As he explains: "In Polynesian terms it was generosity—each side must outdo the other in free giving, but in effect it was barter or trade. It would enable Te Arutanga Nuku to stock up goods for meeting his personal, tribal, and inter-tribal obligations. This should do wonders for his mana [power]" (57). Interestingly, of all the goods traded, Davis emphasizes that "fine mats were the currency of the region" that "determined individual and community wealth" (57). In anticipation of receiving these particular goods, Arutanga "inwardly thanked his wife for obtaining the canoe for him" (57). He benefits from the fact that her sexual sacrifice has been recorded in songs and "made the canoe's fame spread more rapidly" (55), opening broader channels of trade. In terms of women's participation in these trade networks, Davis mentions that women weave the sails of the vaka, with "care, gossip and chanting" (23). He neglects to explain that women are also responsible for the creation and production of these fine mats, of transforming nature into one of the highest valued objects of culture. If we isolate how gender functions in this regional exchange, we see that the protagonist exchanges a woman (his wife) for a feminized vehicle of inter-island bartering (the canoe) in order to acquire the valuable product of women's domestic labor (fine mats). Positioned this way, *Vaka* is less of a story of masculine prowess on the waves than the ways in which this masculinity is a byproduct of a regionalism founded on women, their sexual and reproductive bodies, and the products of their labor. In essence, the object of desire, Arutanga's mana, is obtained by accumulating the domestic products of women's labor. The impetus for his voyage, like that of the many men in this novel who sail for sexual relations and to spread their seed, is valorized, but it is a mystification of the ways in which women truly "weave" the region together.[64]

Read in these terms, Davis's masculine voyagers appropriate women's power by feminizing the canoe and depicting their travels in terms of mastering this feminine vessel or body. This explains why the canoe and its master represent a heterosexual hierarchy; this deflects from the canoe's signification as a more powerful—and perhaps consuming—*maternal* object. Seen this way, transoceanic voyaging is not so much about the exchange of women's bodies that Davis wants to suggest, even if Arutanga's trade "amassed a fortune in his warehouse." Instead, like the twentieth-century globalization that informs the novel's transoceanic imagination, the novel is about an *exchange of masculine bodies* across the region. Men are thus positioned as "routed" objects of exchange between feminized "roots"; they enter history and genealogy only by appropriating and collecting women's power and productions (from mats to children). This is significant when we consider that Davis exaggerates the virility of travel at the expense of the Polynesian tradition of hospitality, a practice that was not, historically speaking, feminized.

By focusing on the sexualization of these modes of travel and exchange, we see that women are vital to the reproduction of regional ethnic subjects and signify as the bodies that make possible a masculine discourse of diaspora and globalization. These semantic connections are embedded in the term "diaspora" and arise from a complex metaphysical association between sperm, blood, and spatial dispersal (for trade and racial regeneration). In her exploration of the gendered metaphors of nature and industrialization in Europe, Carolyn Merchant demonstrates how seventeenth-century medical sciences (facilitated by the raw materials of colonialism) established new theories of heterosexual reproductive relations (1983). This new empiricism attempted to validate the Aristotelian logic of the passive female whose womb is activated by the dynamic male along the lines of culture's transmogrification of nature. With William Harvey's (re)discovery of the circulation of the blood, a new language emerged to describe a sexual economy of bodily fluids. Semen, as Thomas Laqueur has shown, was already semantically imagined in terms of oceanic metaphors of water, foam, and froth (1990, 46, 120, 146). In Harvey's theory of generation, masculine sperm functions as the "spirit" or "logos" in its god-like act of (pro)creation (Laqueur 1990, 146–147). Although modern ideas of sexual difference had not yet formed, even Aristotle's theory of the one-sex body of masculine and feminine ejaculate was gendered—the male produced a "thicker, whiter, frothier quality of . . . semen" (Laqueur 1990, 38). Despite its whiteness, Aristotle argued that the sperm represents that first fluid of the body; it "is made from the purest part of the blood, from the essence of life" (quoted in Laqueur 38). Later writers sought to explain the contrast between whiteness and sanguinity by suggesting that "the semen of the male is the foam of blood according to the matter of water, which, when beaten against rocks, makes white foam" (Isidore quoted in Laqueur 56). This "fungibility of fluids" means that semen may "stand in the same relationship to blood" (40), just as their perceived saltiness may connect both to the ocean (103).

This notion of a gendered economy of fluids—or, in Elizabeth Grosz's terms, a "sexualization of ontology," (1994, 103), is relevant to *Vaka*'s own mediation of the region's transition to modernity. Here I explore two further connections that elucidate this complex entanglement between blood, sperm, and transoceanic diaspora. Laqueur has demonstrated that the fungibility of fluids contributed to the modern notion of sexually distinct bodies, of gendered difference. *Vaka* demonstrates not only a gendered regionalism but one that constructs female "roots" in order to ensure a type of racial purity, engaging the voyaging canoe as metaphoric "blood" vessel or, to borrow from Laqueur, a "vascular pathway" (1990, 105). Thus scrutinizing Davis's construction of the region as gendered difference reveals this is a proxy for *racial difference*, a sign of that regional problematic of "blood logics" that bifurcated the Pacific Way in the 1980s. Secondly, I want to explore Merchant's suggestion that the grammar of sexual fluids and exchange established by Harvey and others reflected a larger colonial and commercial context of mechanical philosophy in which "the passive role . . . assigned to both matter and the female in reproduction is consistent with . . . the trend towards female passivity in the sphere of industrial production" (1983, 156). As I will explain, Davis projects the "tentacles" of these globalizing shifts of an emergent economic and political entity—Asia Pacific—back onto Polynesian voyaging history.

Feminist scholars have demonstrated the ways in which women's reproductive bodies are made to bear the responsibility of ethnic and racial regeneration. This suggests a second reason why Davis overlooks the histories of women migrants and associates almost all of his female characters with the land. Like the Euro-American beachcomber narratives that constructed an idyllic "South Seas," Davis fabricates his Pacific on the migratory routes of men who depend upon the welcoming arms of receptive women to acculturate them into their new island homes. This is visible in the way Arutanga's travel companions "left behind some girls and gained some new ones" in their "profitable voyages" (1992b, 66), which place a sexually receptive woman in every port. Te Pori and Arutanga's male descendants inherit the canoe and construct a masculine regionalism based on sports (traveling to compete at inter-island regional "championships") (78), elite voyaging societies (85), to "assist in the chiefly wars" (94), and to respond to the "urgent call of adventure" (97). Like the fictional Polynesian women who always seem to swarm Euro-American ships with their desire for unwashed sailors, Arutanga's traveling son, Rangi, finds on arrival to Tonga that he is "sought after by the royal young ladies, for it would be considered a matter of envy if one of them conceived a child from this handsome affluent cousin from Upolu" (101). Although he has a wife at home, he exchanges sexual fluids with local women as readily as he accepts lavish gifts (102). Since he is on a "spermatic journey," spreading the seeds of diaspora, Rangi "hoped the alliances he made with his female hosts would bear positive results" (106).

Definitions of the region, like the family, nation, and ethnicity, necessitate the demarcation of borders. In constructing a regional web of kinship through the voyaging vessel, Davis's text demonstrates severe anxiety about crossing the western frontier of the Polynesian Triangle. The European partition of the region into racialized culture regions of Polynesia, Melanesia, and Micronesia is tied to a long history of what Bernard Smith has shown as an ideological hierarchy between "hard" and "soft primitives" of the indigenous Pacific.[65] But such divisions work only if one categorizes the region in terms of isolated islands rather than exploring the complex process of trade and exchange that was made possible by maritime vessels of history. Ethnographic histories of the Pacific interpellated the "soft" primitives of Polynesia into a familial narrative of Aryan diaspora, but the eastward trajectory of this migration posed a racial problem in terms of incorporating the "dark" islands and peoples of Melanesia as stopovers in this telos of a white civilizing migration. As a result, the western boundary of the Polynesian Triangle, popularized by the nineteenth-century mapping of Jules-Sébastien-César Dumont d'Urville, has isolated Fiji from its neighbors, Tonga and Samoa. This rigid cartography also pathologizes those Polynesian "outliers" to the west of the triangulated border, as if they lost their way in island Melanesia. Although arguments can be made for a shared history that has produced a relatively culturally unified Polynesia, the Melanesian Pacific is far too diverse to signify much beyond a geographic rubric. Although it is generally ignored by the metropoles of the eastern region, a remarkable 80 percent of the Pacific population consists of Melanesian people, and one-third of all the world's languages are found there (Kirch 2000, 211, Lal and Fortune 2000, 58). Since the early works of Malinowski's *Argonauts*, this diversity has been vital to the construction of modern anthropology and its mapping of culture and space. Sailing into this region of ethnic difference causes tremendous anxiety in Davis's novel, because the first stop, Fiji, like its series of coups since 1987, poses a challenge to the unifying family ethic of Vaka Pasifika.

Gender and ethnic difference are key determinants in understanding the mapping of culture regions in the Pacific. The racial partitioning of the region was popularized by d'Urville, who, in 1832, described Melanesians as "much closer to a barbaric state than the Polynesians and the Micronesians . . . , [who] have no governing bodies, no laws, and no formal religious practices. All their institutions seem to be in their infancy. Their aptitudes and their intelligence are also largely generally inferior to those of the copper-skinned race" (2003, 169). Melanesian women, d'Urville contended, "are even more hideous than the men, especially those who have suckled children, as their breasts immediately become flaccid and droopy" (169). Gender was key to European racialization of the Pacific just as it has been crucial to Davis's mapping of Polynesia. Harriet Guest and Margaret Jolly have shown that women were essential to the "racial plots" constructed by eighteenth-century European explorers who fabricated an idea of a progressive Polynesian civilization that they opposed to a degenerating Melanesian savagery (Guest 1996). Pacific women's receptiveness to European sexual advances was interpreted as "an index of civilization" just as the agency of Pacific women was seen as "catalytic to the process" of the European civilizing mission (Jolly 2001a, 36–37). Consequently, the stereotype of the sexually accessible "dusky maiden" of eastern Polynesia helped European men position these islands in a racial hierarchy over the women of Melanesia who, in their lack of receptivity to European male advances, were substituted by that colonial icon of fear and otherness: the dark-skinned cannibal male. It is precisely this fear of corporeal consumption and the lack of women's sexual receptivity in Melanesia that constructs its ethnic difference, posing a genealogical challenge to Davis's model of familial regionalism as his protagonist enters the waters of Fiji.

For a novel that relies so extensively on regional history and ethnography, we may find Davis's stereotypes and inaccuracies about Fiji surprising until we recognize them as part of the colonial legacy about Melanesia. Like the South Seas fiction that derives its narrative tension from the threat of racialized others, Davis warns us that his Polynesian hero Rangi is sailing "into the gruesome territory" of Melanesia, known for its "stories of savage cannibalism, endemic in all of the Fiji Islands" (1992b, 93). As he approaches the islands, Rangi becomes increasingly agitated, wondering if "the warlike propensity of Fijians" has been "exaggerated" (108), and fearing that their phallic "big canoes" might be "bigger and faster than *Te Pori*" (107). Upon meeting the Fijian tui or ruler, he confirms that the stereotypes are correct and that this reputation of savagery and violence is well founded (108). Reiterating the treatment of women as an index of civilization (or its lack), Rangi is positioned as the noble foil to a nation of warmongering rapists (138). We are told repeatedly that Fijians systematically crushed human beings as rollers for their voyaging canoes (36, 39, 93), indulged in cannibalism, and were bloodthirsty savages who spared neither women nor children (138). Far from an arrival narrative in which Rangi may disperse his reproductive seed and depart with valuable goods, he is terrorized by the idea that his host nation may literally consume his bodily fluid (and organs). Like the Robinsonades that deflected the violence of European land and resource consumption onto indigenous cannibalism, Rangi's narrative constructs racial difference through a grammar of inequitable consumption. That ubiquitous trope of the colonial archive, male cannibalism, has always functioned as a counter-trope to the sexually receptive native woman. This explains why Rangi never encounters Melanesian women in his many years in Fiji. They are substituted by either sexually receptive women of Tongan descent or, more commonly, by Melanesian male anthropophagists.

By regenerating the gendered colonial myths of "hard" and "soft" primitives", Davis faces a particular problem in that he is constructing the region through kinship relations that are stitched together by the voyaging canoe. The character's anxiety is less a plot device than a signal of the strain on kinship relations posed by asserting a blood relationship between his Polynesian heroes and these "savage" Melanesians. Thus he places the action of the novel in Bau, a small eastern island called the "stronghold from which Polynesian influence spread to Fiji" (97). The tui of Bau claims Tongan blood, thereby establishing kinship to Rangi through Polynesia and sidestepping the thorny question of racial admixture. Thus, like South Seas fiction, the novel benefits from its adventurous peppering of savagery and bloodshed without contaminating the genealogies or cultural practices of its Polynesian heroes. In order to ensure there is no ethnic cross-contamination, Davis fabricates a division between the "Melanesian Fijians" and their elite "Polynesian rulers." This reflects back to an inaccurate partitioning of Fiji that many anthropologists, including Peter Buck, used to circumvent the question of racial hybridity. In order to control the contaminating effect of the black-skinned masses, Davis adopts a colonial model for Fiji where "Melanesian people [are] ruled by chiefs of

Polynesian descent, mostly in a Polynesian way" (1992b, 93). To ensure these transplanted Polynesians would not degenerate (as Robinsonades and anthropologists once feared), Davis insists that they "did not indulge in human sacrifice as did the Fijian Melanesians" (39).

We must ask why Davis manipulated the historical record to reflect not only the superiority of Polynesian culture but its civilized distinction from Melanesia. This inquiry helps us to understand a vital component of imagining Oceania: that like its colonial (and anthropological) antecedents, Davis's novel upholds a progressive eastern culture of Polynesia that depends for its advance on a Melanesian primitivism. Thus the space of the eastern Pacific is constituted in terms of a temporal and cultural telos towards a deracialized civilization. This imbrication helps to explain why Davis reiterates so many of the racial mythologies of Fiji. His protagonist Rangi, like later Methodist missionaries, argues that addiction to cannibalism was the "cause of continuous strife" in Fiji, and that peace was not possible since the "need for bokola [was] constant and murder, strife and war were the means of its supply" (115). Bokola, or edible human flesh, becomes a synonym for Fiji itself, a site of blood violence and terrible "consumption" (115). In a page drawn from the civilizing *Robinson Crusoe*, Rangi intervenes to stop the Fijians from this practice (130). Traditions of Polynesian cannibalism are deliberately excised from his revision of the region's history, even those that appeared in his primary sources, such as the narrative of Tangi'ia and Tutapu. In that story, Davis racializes the maritime battles between these famous half-brothers as an epic struggle between Polynesia and Melanesia. In his version, the dark-skinned Tutapu, a descendant of a lowly commoner, is configured as the cannibal consumer of his light-skinned foe, who ultimately settled Rarotonga and from whom many Cook Island families, including Davis's, derive their genealogy.[66] Borrowing much from S. Percy Smith's Aryan vision of Polynesian history, including the legend of the "Great Fleet" of canoes that settled Aotearoa, Davis denigrates Melanesian difference and denies regional kinship by posing Polynesians as their rightful colonizers.[67] In racializing these tensions, Davis unknowingly extends the semantic registers of the vaka to suggest a violent rupture in the familial "blood vessel" that ordinarily should "flow" like the ships and waters that link the region in a vast network of kinship.

Given the importance of the vaka to cultural, historical, and genealogical relations in the Pacific, and Davis's extensive experience in maritime history, we must be troubled by the fact that he denies that Fiji is an originary source for the double-hulled voyaging canoe (drua). Despite the evidence of his own sources, he attributes the body and sail design of this vessel to Tongan (Polynesian) history and positions the Fijians as simply the suppliers of timber and other raw materials (132).[68] Although he has adopted the well-known beachcomber myth that Fijian autocrats used men for canoe rollers, Davis neglects to mention that the same practices were also attributed to Polynesians in Tahiti.[69] Fiji's role as an indigenous center for pan-Pacific trade and exchange is minimized by Davis denying "Melanesian Fijians" their agency in this process. Against all evidence to the contrary, Davis even erases Fiji as the originary dispersal point for that vital communal drink of the eastern Pacific: kava. His depiction of the island region resonates with d'Urville, who, in conceding the long history of exchange with Fiji, had difficulty in justifying its cartographic segregation from its eastern neighbors. Consequently d'Urville's admission of some vestige of civilization among (male) Fijians, like Davis's, is attributed to the "proximity of the Tongan people" (2003, 170).

To summarize, Davis's novel reiterates the ways in which European cartographies of the region used women as the index of civilization to uphold their ethnic partitioning of Oceania. Fiji, with its long history of trade and exchange, has always challenged these ethnic maps of the Pacific, a position that became more salient after its series of racialized coups. While Davis was writing his novel, the Vaka Pasifika was challenged by the ways in which the discourse of Pacific indigeneity was taken to a disturbing extreme in Fiji. This is why *Vaka*, I believe, spends so much textual space inscribing this island nation, only to utilize colonial history to reduce it to a site of violence and primitivism. The way that *ancient* Fiji becomes a proxy for the ethnic strife of the *contemporary* Pacific is an important reminder of the ways in which discourses of regionalism are no substitute for the hierarchies of the nation-state. Moreover, the anti-Asian sentiment that has characterized some mappings of the Pacific region (from Heyerdah's postwar denial of Asiatic origins to the diaspora from Fiji of its citizens of Indian descent) is indicative of the palpable tensions emerging out of the economic rise of Asia Pacific and its migration across the Island region. In order to understand why Davis would reinscribe the colonial and especially Aryanist models for masculine migration, we have to position his novel in the context of a rapidly globalizing Pacific. Consequently, I turn now to the intersections of race and gender in the regional imaginary, exploring how the radical socioeconomic shifts signified by diaspora catalyze the valorization of masculine agents of history.

Hawaiki: Hubs of the Globalizing Octopus

I have argued that migration theories of the Pacific, from Heyerdahl and
Sharp to Finney and Davis, often reflect more about regional shifts in the
socioeconomic power of the writers' contexts than the past they wish to
inscribe. To this end I would like to turn to a paradigmatic image of migration in the eastern Pacific (Figure 4). Taken from Te Rangi Hiroa's *Vikings
of the Pacific*, this visual representation of the inter-island octopus also
encapsulates some of the challenges of regionalism and gestures towards
its globalizing potentials. Like Tupaia's map, drawn two centuries earlier,
it represents an indigenous cartography of the region based on relations of
trade, narrative, and kinship. This untitled picture of Polynesian migration represents the legendary homeland of Hawaiki (Havaiki, Hawai'i) as
the head of an octopus in the Society Islands (Te Ao Ma'ohi), with its
eight tentacles radiating across eastern Oceania. Like the routes charted

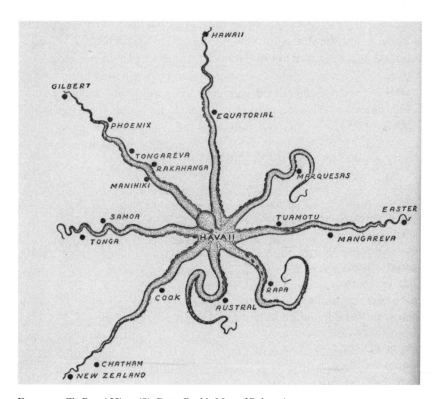

FIGURE 4. Te Rangi Hiroa/Sir Peter Buck's Map of Polynesia.

in Davis's novel, the limbs of the octopus stretch to the far corners of the Polynesian Triangle, connecting Aotearoa, Hawai'i, and Rapa Nui into one unified body rather than an abstract geometric symbol. While Fiji is not included in Davis's or Buck's labeled map of Polynesia, it is signified by the unnamed endpoint of the limb that stretches eastward past Samoa and Tonga.

Buck's choice of an octopus to represent the movement of the pre-colonial Pacific is significant in multiple ways. First, like Davis's novel, it naturalizes migration and highlights how the islands are genealogically and corporeally connected, much like the arboreal metaphors of ancestral roots and branches. Although he does not comment on the image, Buck was certainly cognizant of the complex symbolization of the octopus to Polynesia, particularly in Samoan and Hawaiian cosmologies, where it was seen as the god of fishing and the sea (Tangaroa/Kanaloa), as the divine ancestor of priestly navigators at Ra'iatea (Havai'i), as a symbol of navigation and its teaching centers such as Kaho'olawe and Opoa, and finally, its importance as a navigating symbol whose movement has been likened to that of a canoe.[70] Like the stories throughout the region that depict the land as a fish that must be hauled out of the sea by demigods (Tahiti-nui, Aotearoa, Aitutaki),[71] the octopus also foregrounds the movement and dynamism of islands as they rise and fall through geological and political change. This brings us back to the concept of etak, in which the islands are dynamic and moving and, like Hawaiki, represent both the origin and destination of the traveler. As Albert Wendt has written, "We are all in search of that heaven, that Hawaiki, where our hearts will find meaning" (1993, 9).

The process of constructing an origin and hub of the Vaka Pasifika is a constitutive part of regionalism. Te Rangi Hiroa places the head in the Society Islands, the Tahiti group which was "the nucleus for exploration and the dissemination of learning throughout central Polynesia" (1938, 66). Drawing from the work of Teuira Henry, he argued that Hawaiki (a former name for Ra'iatea) was the "mother of lands" and "the hub of the Polynesian universe" in terms of the training in arts, religion, and navigation sciences (87). In his poignant recounting of his 1929 visit to the sacred marae there (Taputapu-atea), Buck configured this temple as the vital center of Hawaiki, "the head of the octopus of Ta'aroa," the place where canoes were built and navigation was taught. In fact, the first voyage of the *Hokule'a* made a pilgrimage to this exact spot to reinvigorate the historical and genealogical connections that this "hub" facilitated across Polynesia and, with the help of Tom Davis, it returned in 1992 for the South Pacific Arts Festival and celebration of voyaging culture.[72] In his day Te Rangi

Hiroa remarked that his own attempt to visit the originary space of his Maori ancestral "seed" was dependent on a New Zealand naval vehicle. The double-hulled vaka was replaced by "a steel-clad British man-of-war" that, like the steam ships of the previous chapter, "controlled" the seas and regulated the exact hour of arrival (1938, 82). Faced with "a modern French village," unattended stone ruins, and indigenous peoples celebrating "the fall of the Bastille," Buck mourned that "it was all wrong." (83). In his search for a Polynesian Hawaiki, he concluded that "Taputapu-atea was a mute symbol. It was something that we Polynesians have lost and cannot find, something that we yearn for and cannot recreate" (85). Despondent about the literal and symbolic "foreign weeds" (85), Te Rangi Hiroa concluded his chapter about this Pacific "hub" by attempting to "keep down the riding tide" of despair by responding "briskly in the American vernacular, 'Let's go'" (86).

151

Diaspora narratives, like precolonial histories, are often characterized by nostalgia for an originary homeland, and this is apparent in Buck's configuration of French-occupied Polynesia as a cultural origin, a Hawaiki that he hoped would produce the *monumental* evidence of precolonial history that he felt was lacking in his own deeply colonized home. As a Maori scholar trained in Aotearoa/New Zealand and employed by the Bishop Museum in Hawai'i, Buck's transnationalism provided an alternative interpretation of that globalizing octopus and its broadening tentacles across the Pacific. Given the radical postwar shifts in the Pacific Islands, it is not surprising that metaphors likening corporate globalization to an octopus were already circulating in Buck's context. The alarming consolidation of U.S. corporate control of Hawaiian plantations and politics (ushered in under the aegis of the statehood movement) led Te Rangi Hiroa's contemporary, Fred Buckley, to refer to the Bishop estate as a "landed octopus," likening it to the other capitalist "tentacles of the 'Big Five' octopus of King Sugar's oligarchy" (quoted in Daws 1968, 334). In fact, Buck's shift to the American vernacular while visiting a precolonial Pacific hub is significant when we consider that in his personal correspondence from Honolulu, he remarked that American-occupied Hawai'i was "really the hub of the Pacific" (Sorrenson 1986, 1.75).[73]

As a figure who adopted S. Percy Smith's model of an Aryan Hawaiki for Polynesians and who, ironically, was later denied American citizenship because the United States categorized Polynesians as Asians (Howe 2003, 192), Te Rangi Hiroa serves as an important example of the ways in which diaspora narratives presuppose an idealized origin that can be only partially recovered in that complex tidalectic relationship between home and migration, roots and routes. Hawaiki represents that unstable island, a shifting destination and origin point that, like etak navigation, recedes or emerges depending on the context of the migrant.[74] *Vikings* and Davis's *Vaka* are texts that engage western models of historiography and diaspora in order to reestablish Polynesian kinship relations across the region in dynamic relationships of governance and administration.[75] In his correspondence, Buck imagined a type of "Ministry of Polynesian Affairs," a pan-Polynesian entity much like Kalakaua's vision, except it would be administered by Maori liaisons to New Zealand's inherited colonies, such as Samoa and the Cook Islands.[76]

These narratives of locating an originary Hawaiki often reflect political struggles over which masculine migrants can claim to be the subjects of history. Because some Polynesian migration histories mention an originary homeland of Hawaiki, many have pondered where this location may be fixed. Nineteenth-century Christian diffusionists located it in Israel, while Aryanist scholars like J. Macmillan Brown and S. Percy Smith turned to India to posit Caucasian origins for Maori and Polynesians in general. In his theory of a transoceanic Aryan globalization, Macmillan Brown argued vigorously that "the only section of mankind" that is truly "maritime is Caucasian" (1907, 7) and incorporated Polynesians as part of this "Robinson Crusoe of a race" (262). Like migration theories that claimed the Americas as Hawaiki, these models of history were inspired by a refusal to naturalize Asian presence in the Pacific. As M. P. K. Sorrenson points out, the rise of these Aryan origin stories occurred at the moment when a "vicious anti-Chinese campaign" was lobbied to uphold a "'White New Zealand' immigration policy" (1979, 29). Aryan origin theories often interpellated indigenous peoples as settlers in the same vein as British colonists, destabilizing native land and resource claims against the white colonial state. Moreover, incorporating Polynesians into an ancient narrative of prehistoric Aryan diaspora minimized European anxieties about racial degeneration in the antipodean Pacific colonies (see Sorrenson 1979, 29). Overall, any fears generated by racial mixing might be alleviated by these origin stories—as Sorrenson quips, "What better myth could there be for a young country struggling for nationhood and for the amalgamation of its races than this reunification of the Aryans?" (30).

Buck's adaptation of the Aryan migration model for Pacific settlement led him to argue that the ancient Polynesians sailed thousands of miles northwards into Micronesia in order to avoid the direct route through Melanesia. When faced with contradictory archaeological evidence, Te Rangi Hiroa created a secondary and illogical migration route for plants through Melanesia in order to prevent any racial contamination of the Polynesians from Melanesians (see Buck 1938, 43–51; Howe 2003, 55–56). The discredited southern route through Melanesia, he argued, would have **153** had to conclude that Fiji was "the rallying place of the Polynesians, from whence they scattered east, north, and south to explore and settle the far-flung islands within the Polynesian triangle" (Buck 1938, 43).

Aryan diaspora theories reflect a deep resistance to considering a Fijian Hawaiki, a dynamic space of Polynesian and Melanesian exchange, despite the fact that these islands were one of a few "strong genetic bottle-necks" of eastward migration (Kirch and Green 2001, 73). These regional theories formulate vaka historiographies of the Pacific Way in which the *originary* space of Hawaiki might be charted in terms that are congruent with its political and ethnic *destination*. Just as the shifting tentacles of colonial power were reflected in Buck's image of the Pacific octopus and were vital to theorizing a space of origins, Davis's novel adopts precolonial trajectories to map the globalizing routes of migrant destinations. Drawing from *Vikings of the Pacific*, Davis's *Vaka* inscribes regional history as performative genealogy, emphasizing those figures, migrations, and set-tlement routes that partially engage his own family ancestry. Outside the bounds of the novel, Davis performed and revitalized these histories by organizing the building of an ancestral replica canoe, the *Takitumu*, which sailed to Taputapu-atea and other regional festivals.[77] Just as the *Hokuleʻa* charted "Ke Ala i Kahiki"—a vehicle of return to the ancient homeland or Hawaiki—Buck and Davis were also mapping routes of return, spaces of origin. Like the term Hawaiki, the trajectory and definition of "Ke Ala i Kahiki" is not fixed. Although it is commonly defined as "the way to Tahiti," scholars have pointed out that "Kahiki" or "Tahiti" may refer to any island outside of the speaker's orbit, just as it may reflect the way to "Iti," or Fiji (Viti). And while much has been written about the ethnic hierarchies that led to the segregation of Fiji from its Polynesian neighbors, and scholars have shown the vital role this archipelago played in shaping eastern Pacific cultures, the works discussed here have not pressed the boundaries of these colonial maps. My intention is not to uphold Fiji as *the origin* but rather to ask what it would mean to consider a deeper, more ethnically complex model of the Vaka Pasifika, to produce a regional imagination that does not uphold Hawaiki as a narrowly defined model of belonging.

Hawaiki represents an unstable place of origin that changes depending on the population and context in which it is used, as well as the destination place for the transmigration of the human spirit.[78] It is this point of destina-tion, in what Stewart Firth has pinpointed as a second era of globalization in the Pacific, which informs Davis's cartography of the region and helps us to understand the racialized "seeds" of diaspora that he is sowing. A large part of *Vaka* details the settlement of Davis's home, Rarotonga, while the conclusion describes the congregation of Islanders there who decide to settle Aotearoa. While Te Rangi Hiroa and others have discredited the idea of a "Great Fleet" to New Zealand, it is important to consider why Davis would regenerate this particular model of history decades after it had been dismissed as a homogenization of Maori genealogies and oral histories.[79] To do so we must consider the circumstances in which Davis was writing, when more Cook Islanders were living overseas than at home, and nearly 70 percent were residing in Aotearoa / New Zealand (R. Crocombe 1992, 7). As subjects who retain dual citizenship, Cook Islanders may be considered as some of the *original* migrants to Aotearoa as well as active participants in contemporary transoceanic globalization. In fact, Davis's upholding of a fleet of mobile Pacific Islanders not only anticipates the 1992 South Pacific Festival of the Arts, but also becomes a way of *unifying* and *naturalizing* trajectories of migrant labor towards emerging Hawaiki or etak destination points in a globalized Oceania. The model of kinship networks suggests the reality of MIRAB (migration and remittance) societies and helps to naturalize a process that in its contemporary context is about the scattering of families as they seek a Hawaiki of economic opportunity. Thus the "strife" over "territory and power" that pushes Davis's precolonial Polynesians into "a migration to the new world" of Aotearoa (1992b, 287) creates a new generation of "canoe people" (288) that anticipates late twentieth-century Cook Island migration patterns. In many ways, Davis's novel naturalizes Polynesian migration to Aotearoa / New Zealand and deflects the racial hierarchies that may posit indigenous migrants as "aliens" in their own sea of islands.

Towards a New Vaka Pasifika: Our Water Ties

In this genealogical sketch of the Vaka Pasifika, I conclude with a gesture to the ways in which a new era of Pacific literature has revisioned the regional imagination to chart alternative vehicles of sovereignty. By emphasizing "water ties" over "blood vessels," these works destabilize an ethnic partitioning of the region and engage with more dynamically imagined spaces of origin and destination. For example, in an effort to rethink the masculine trajectories of Pacific migration, Teresia Kieuea Teaiwa's poetry collection, *Searching for Nei Nim'anoa*, calls upon "one of only a few female figures in the male-dominated field of Pacific Island navigational traditions" (1995, ix) as she moves between the Gilbertese, Fijian, and Hawaiian Islands, placing women at the center of these origin stories. Similarly, the narrator of Sia Figiel's *Girl in the Moon Circle* defines her modern Samoan community as "Sea people. Sea clan. Travelling from Samoa to Tonga. To Fiji. To Aotearoa. To Rarotonga. To Tahiti. To Hawai'i. To other parts of the Moana. Guided by stars. Guided by the moon. The sun. Birds. Sharks. Different fish" (1996, 104). As a text charting the American globalization of the Pacific Islands and the networks of kinship that extend to the United States and New Zealand, Figiel's narrative of coming of age in Samoa offers a challenge to the island isolate model of Margaret Mead and, like Davis and Buck, maps the region as genealogy.

155

A playful and creative interpretation of the meanings of vaka, vessel, and vehicle is visible in Robert Sullivan's *Star Waka*, a collection of 100 poems from Aotearoa/New Zealand named after voyaging vessels. Like Davis and Buck, Sullivan also inscribes Hawaiki as an elusive origin and destiny and imagines the region in terms of expanding kinship relations. Similar to Teweiariki Teaero's poetry collection *Waa in Storms*, Sullivan's text is conceived as a waka, a vehicle of exploration, memory, and indigenous history of the region. In his preface he explains, "This sequence is like a waka, members of the crew change, the rhythm and the view changes—it is subject to the laws of nature" (Sullivan 1999, n.p). Drawing upon the broad range of metaphors associated with the term waka and vessel, Sullivan inscribes "Honda waka" (8) and "computer waka" (59); he imagines waka as "a great living Library of people" (74) and declares they are "vehicles for a revival" (28). The waka is conceived as a vehicle for sovereignty in Aotearoa and in a broader, regional sense of the globalized Pacific.

In a similar vein, *Alchemies of Distance* (2001), Caroline Sinavaiana-Gabbard's collection of poetry, structurally adopts the metaphor of the voyage, utilizing Pacific vaka in her modern migration from the U.S. South to Pacific metropoles in California, Honolulu, and Amerika Samoa. This circular pattern of departure and return is invoked through originary narratives, freed from their material and literal interpretations. Past and present, poetry and myth, land and sea are all dynamic and constitutive elements of the writer's genealogy, a term defined not as a simple racial lineage but as the presence of the past in the present. Sinavaiana-Gabbard imagines subjectivity through the metaphor of the vessel, explaining in her preface of "hard years with the feel of crossing strange seas in a smallish boat. Still afloat in my memory, this boat has sails of frayed pandanus, woven strips of fala battered by the crossing, makeshift patches straining to hold until landfall" (2001, 11). Explicating that "culture itself is the boat that can cross the va, the space between then and now, here and there, the distances between time and space" (24), Sinavaiana-Gabbard regenerates the Samoan woman warrior, Nafanua, whose function as leader and vessel represents a female-centered voyaging tradition in which she "consents to act as a vessel for the divine . . . she's not only the traveler and the vehicle, she becomes the path as well" (25, see also 43).

While there are creative new visions of the wakes left by ancient voyaging canoes, I would like to conclude by turning to the possibilities also generated by "our water ties," the terms that formulate the epigraph to this chapter and that will bring us back to Hau'ofa's notion of "the ocean in us." In "Sea of Islands," Hau'ofa outlines a connection between ancient voyaging trajectories and migrant globalization:

> The new economic reality made nonsense of artificial boundaries, enabling the people to shake off their confinement and they have since moved, by the tens of thousands, doing what their ancestors had done before them: enlarging their world as they go, to Australia, New Zealand, Hawai'i, mainland United States, Canada and even Europe, they strike routes in new resource areas . . . , expanding kinship networks through which they circulate themselves, their relatives, their material goods, and their stories all across the ocean, and the ocean is theirs because it has always been their home. (1993b, 94)

Uncannily predictive of Hau'ofa's vision of the Pacific process of "world enlargement," Albert Wendt's novel *Ola* (1991) inscribes his Samoan woman protagonist as a "world traveller" who visits Japan, Israel/Palestine, Aotearoa/New Zealand, and the United States—some of the broadest migrations of any Pacific Island novel. This maps a global cartography and, like Johnny Frisbie's autobiography, also includes Asia (Japan) in this vision that brings Oceania to Asia Pacific. The Christian pilgrimage to Jerusalem described in the novel can be seen as a challenge to diffusionist models of Polynesian origins. This positions an alternative mapping of colonial relations that includes Palestine and suggests that models of diffusionism may contribute to the rendering of a Christian Hawaiki and generate a new trajectory of pilgrimage.

As a "Permanent Traveller," Ola admits she's "permanently in motion, a pelagic Samoan" (Wendt 1991, 155). Her experience of travel reflects Hau'ofa's "world enlargement," particularly because Wendt employs the sea as the source of her fluctuating identity. Ola comes to recognize herself as a subject in a Lacanian moment when she sees her reflection in the ocean. She observes, "Yes, it was me, I existed, I am, I am separate. I was myself" (1991, 35). Years later, on the coast of Aotearoa/New Zealand, she explains that she "felt at home, remembering: the sea which cups my islands, washes each night through my dreams, no matter what shore I reach" (76). These same "water ties" encourage Rawiri, the narrator of Witi Ihimaera's *The Whale Rider* (1987), to return from his visit to Papua New Guinea, articulated through a seashell that whispers *"hoki mai, hoki mai ki te wa kainga"* (1987, 59), return to your home.[80] Although Ola's complex journeys are facilitated by modern vehicles such as airplanes and automobiles (which figure heavily in the text), Wendt relates these to early colonial and aquatic migrations. Like Hau'ofa, he privileges water as the site of transcultural connection. His character observes: "We are sixty-five percent water. . . . Our brains are eighty per cent water. We are more water than blood. So our water ties to one another are more important than our blood ties! We carry within us the seas out of which we came" (1991, 124). This reflects what Hau'ofa will later describe as a "regional identity that is anchored in our common inheritance of . . . the Pacific Ocean" (1997, 124). In an effort to move away from the ethnic hierarchies of belonging, Wendt seems to be upholding Hau'ofa's sentiment that "all of us in Oceania today, whether indigenous or otherwise, can truly assert that the sea is our common heritage" (Hau'ofa 1997, 142).

In writing about Pacific regionalism, Hau'ofa explains the process of his own complex migration through the region and highlights the importance of roots in the wake of globalizing routes. He emphasizes that most Polynesians "have Havaiki, a shared ancestral homeland that exists hazily in primordial memory." But its location, like the floating islands of etak, cannot be fixed in either time or space. Like Walcott's far Cythera, "it, too, is far and feverish,/ it dilates on the horizon" (1986, 481). To Hau'ofa, Hawaiki is "far into the past ahead, leading on to other memories, other realities, other homelands" (2000, 470).[81] Hawaiki is at once the past and the future, it is originary rather than origin, a gateway rather than destination.

PART II

Indigenous Landscapes
and National Settlements

CHAPTER 3

Dead Reckoning
National Genealogies in Aotearoa / New Zealand

Trace out your ancestral stem, so that it may be known where
you come from and in which direction you are going.
—Maori proverb

Let us remember our ancestors, Let us remember the land,
especially the land lived upon,
The new land gained, and the old land forsaken.
—June Mitchell, *Amokura*

This chapter explores the role of whakapapa, or genealogy, in contemporary Maori discourses of Aotearoa / New Zealand, a corporeal
historiography or "meta-physics" that offers a dynamic and relational approach to the nexus of space and time, often symbolized by the
spiral. This book focuses on these epistemologies of space-time because
the recent scholarly emphasis on discourses of diaspora and globalization
(routes) have largely overlooked indigeneity (roots). More alarmingly, it
has become increasingly common to dismiss sedentary and rooted conceptions of space and nation and to define them as necessarily conservative and
essentialist discourses that produce ethnic violence.[1] This is a dangerous
conflation of roots with ethnic nationalism which has far-reaching consequences. While some scholars have pointed out how postcolonial and
diaspora studies have ignored indigenous discourses, this chapter takes that
position one step farther by arguing that these fields celebrating routes
are partially constituted by a dichotomous rendering of native roots. As a
result, I argue that the historicity of space and place has been eclipsed in
the growing disciplinary split between diaspora and indigenous studies. My
exploration of whakapapa is also intended to shift the discussion beyond
this polarizing tension between the postcolonial and indigenous subject by
foregrounding Maori epistemology as a starting point. As such, this chapter is committed to dialogues across Oceania in terms of how indigenous

epistemologies may be usefully engaged at the center rather than endpoint of Pacific, postcolonial, and cultural studies.

"Dead Reckoning" is the most profoundly localized chapter of this volume, exploring renderings of Maori epistemology at the level of iwi (tribes) in order to elucidate the ways in which localism itself is often produced in response to broader contexts of intra-national and international diaspora. In order to simultaneously engage with indigeneity and diaspora, this chapter discusses the ways in which particular New Zealand novelists chart native genealogies, the legacy of the dead, by reconfiguring the narratives of novel and nation through the use of Maori spiral time. Like the concept of "moving islands," which draws upon what David Lewis calls an indigenous "time sense" (1994, 120) charted across distance, the spiral is a trope that symbolizes dynamic interrelation between the temporal and spatial. As "the major symbol for New Zealand and for Maori people," it encompasses both national history and cultural memory. As novelist Witi Ihimaera explains, "The double spiral . . . allows you then to go back into history and then come out again. Back from personal into political and then come out again" (Jussawalla and Desenbrock 1992, 242). Adopting the form of the spiral, Maori whakapapa mobilize corporeal historiographies, political and familial mediations of space that are vital to indigenous sovereignty.[2]

As I have written elsewhere about Patricia Grace's inscription of the spiral,[3] here I will focus on the novel *Amokura* (1978), a work produced by her contemporary June Mitchell, that has escaped the notice of literary critics. Writing in the early years of what Ranginui Walker terms the "Maori Renaissance" (1996, 176) and amidst intense indigenous activism of the 1970s, Mitchell employs whakapapa as a paradigm of national settlement or native landfall. One can define "dead reckoning" as an indigenous navigation system that draws its foundation from the historical and spiritual presence of the ancestors as they traverse and settle the national landscape. Although theorists have lauded the ways in which "the idea of diaspora" will simply "offer a ready alternative to the stern discipline of conceptions of identity rooted in primordial kinship" and naturalized soil (Gilroy 1997, 328), Mitchell's novel reveals how kinship reckoning, botanical metaphors, and even the soil itself are dynamic, historic, and shifting metaphors of culture that are anything but essentialist and exclusionary. In this historical novel about her nineteenth-century ancestor, Mitchell has adopted Maori women's flax weaving as a way to mediate the epistemological interstices between the hierarchies of national genealogy and the more rhizomorphic and corporeal contours of indigenous whakapapa. It is through her rendering of dynamic and mobile Maori subjects that I bring together the rather polarized discourses of indigeneity and diaspora as they are contested and negotiated in a particular historical space. Interestingly, Mitchell offers a compelling critique of patriarchal nationalism that resonates with other arenas of postcolonial feminism, but like Keri Hulme's Booker-prize winning novel, *the bone people* (1983), she employs Maori epistemology as key to theorizing a more nuanced layering of indigenous and diasporic settlement. This layering may be likened to the tidalectic of land and sea that has functioned as a methodological frame to this book. My concluding pages examine *the bone people* to demonstrate how, like *Amokura*, these novels destabilize essentialist discourses of ancestry and rootedness through a rhizomatic genealogy of place.

Whakapapa: Exploring Meta-Physical Genealogies

James Clifford has asked, "How is 'indigeneity' both rooted in and routed through particular places?" (2001, 469). The key to responding to this difficult question is to examine the intractability of the situatedness of indigenous identity with the nexus of time and space, expressed in terms of land and genealogy. In elucidating possible frameworks for Pacific studies, scholars such as Vicente Diaz, J. Kehaulani Kauanui, Teresia Teaiwa, David Welchman Gegeo, and Manulani Aluli Meyer, to name only a few, have pinpointed "place and genealogy" (Meyer 2001, 125) as vital to indigeneity, as long as we recognize that "place is portable" (Gegeo 2001a, 495) and that the process of diaspora does not necessarily signal familial, genealogical, or ontological dispossession. In fact, transplanting also "marks the possibilities in taking root and growing in a different soil while continuing to maintain an originary location and emphasizing indigeneity as a central form of identification" (Diaz and Kauanui 2001, 320).

In Aotearoa/New Zealand, whakapapa has become an increasingly important conceptual tool and epistemology to situate and theorize Maori identity at the local, regional, and global levels. Although there are similarities between western notions of genealogy and Maori whakapapa, the two systems of historical reckoning differ in their translations of space and place. Whakapapa are produced in both arboreal and rhizomatic forms; defined as a layering of ancestry and orally transmitted, they have been historically produced in far more complicated ways than the vertical descent modalities that were introduced with written technology to Aotearoa.[4] In fact the English words "descent" and "ascent" suggest, like written genealogical trees, a corporeal history that is rendered from top to bottom, signifying a linear human trajectory from past to present. Gilles Deleuze and Félix Guattari have likened these western tree symbologies to "dictatorship theorems" (1987, 17), explaining that arborescent typologies "are hierarchical systems with centers of significance and subjectification, central automata like organized memories" (16). As oral productions, whakapapa Maori trace "descent" rather as "ascent," from the originary ancestor to the current top layers, with roots in the originary ground of being, Papatuanuku, the Maori earth deity/mother (Salmond 1991, 345).

Unlike the noun "genealogy," which signifies an originary moment or ancestor, whakapapa, an intransitive verb and noun, suggests a *performative* rendering of meta-physical history rather than a static or essentialist lineage system. Its connotations of layering and movement suggest Deleuze and Guattari's rhizomorphous system of relation, based upon lateral and multiple ruptures that incorporate connections between all life forms and inanimate matter. I emphasize the rhizomatic aspect of whakapapa here because many anthropological studies have focused rather conservatively on patriarchal cognatic (blood) systems throughout the indigenous Pacific in a way that suppresses more dynamic relations. But the mutually constitutive aspect of these two structural systems should not be overlooked: Deleuze and Guattari concede that "tree or root structures [exist] in rhizomes" and vice versa (1987, 15). If "the rhizome is an anti-genealogy" (Deleuze and Guattari 1987, 11) in that it destabilizes one specific genus, it can be likened to the situational modalities of Maori whakapapa. For instance, an individual may employ a variety of whakapapa, including different founding ancestors, depending on the kinship relations that are to be established in each context.[5] Although print culture has somewhat fixed Maori genealogies, and rendered some arboreal and patriarchal, whakapapa can be challenged or revised, incorporate new honorary members, "slough off" members who have let the fires of their ancestral lands go cold, or revise hierarchical birth orders.[6] This is not to suggest an astructural process, but rather to emphasize that the performative and contextual aspects of whakapapa existed long before contact with Europeans.

Defining the system of whakapapa has generated a tremendous amount of recent scholarship in Aotearoa/New Zealand, but it has not yet been explored in terms of literary production.[7] Tipene O'Regan describes whakapapa as a human and cosmic "taxonomy" (1992, 14), Te Ahukaramu Charles Royal has usefully employed it as "a research methodology" (1999, 80), and Joan Metge defines it as a system of "genealogical knowledge" (1995, 90). Cleve Barlow refers to whakapapa as "the basis for the organization of knowledge in the creation and development of all things" (1991,

173), which encompasses the gods, animal and plant forms, topoi, and creatures of the sea. To O'Regan and others, whakapapa is synonymous with indigenous identity and cannot be divorced from the political context in which Maori are framed unequally within a white-settler nation-state. As the "key to who we are," he explains, "it carries both the past and the present and is the vehicle of our future. . . . It is the testament to our sense of being indigenous. It lends a possessiveness to our view of the past" (1993, 340).[8] O'Regan echoes the activist Donna Awatere in her famous statement, "To the Maori, the past is the present is the future. Who I am and my relationship to everyone else depends on my *Whakapapa* . . . on those from whom I am descended" (1984, 29). Rendering the past in terms of personal and collective history/memory is a vital tool of decolonization and demands political responsibility. Hence the editors of *Te Ao Marama* write, "For us, the past is not something that is behind us. The past is before us, a long, unbroken line of ancestors, to whom we are accountable" (Ihimaera et al. 1992, 18).[9] Because British colonization disenfranchised Maori from ancestral lands, whakapapa have become central to sovereignty; they historicize a connection between indigenous people and national place. In fact, some anthropologists suggest that tracing and performing genealogies became more far more important after European colonization in the Pacific (Schwimmer 1990, 305).

Since whakapapa are generally articulated in corporeal and spiritual terms that invoke ancestral presence in the experienced present, they are profoundly "meta-physical," a term I orthographically detach in order to highlight the historical dialogue between "meta" and "physical" phenomenology. This is in keeping with the vital work on Pacific epistemologies in which theorists such as Linda Tuhiwai Smith (1999) and Manulani Meyer (2001) among others have emphasized an integrated, phenomenological approach to knowledge that may be reinvigorated as a decolonizing project. Temporally, whakapapa function in terms of a spiral, what novelist Patricia Grace calls a "now-time," simultaneously past and present, which is 'rooted' in the ancestral-descendant in his or her experienced place.[10] The emphasis on the phenomenology of place marks a vital difference between whakapapa and western conceptions of genealogy. As Christopher Tilley points out, "Whereas in the West there is a tendency to privilege temporal relationships between events in narrative accounts, typically in [the indigenous Pacific] it is spatial relationships that are emphasized" (1994, 59). Thus "landscape may act powerfully *as* memory, a template in the process of memory work that is not fixed and static, but something drawn upon in social encounters and disputes over land" (ibid.). Whakapapa then function as historical, communal, and familial memory, vital counter-narratives to colonial accounts of linear progress and modernity. Because whakapapa trace cosmogenic ancestry to the founding mother deity, Papatuanuku, they can take on strategic importance by encoding European colonialism as both unnatural and ahistorical. This is a vital if overlooked strategy of indigenous epistemology—*in theory*, British appropriation of land then becomes a violation of the natural, familial, and meta-physical order of Aotearoa / New Zealand.

Scholarly interest in whakapapa as a methodology and metonymy for identity emerged in the late 1970s, in a large part due to Maori land and resource claims against the breached Treaty of Waitangi (1840), a controversial contract between British settlers and most Maori tribes. The Waitangi Tribunal was established in 1975 to process land alienation claims as the government began to privatize national resources in its embrace of corporate globalization. Hundreds of Maori claims have been brought before the tribunal, and in every case the key to the reclamation process resides in whakapapa—a native historiography mobilized in the western court system that poses a counter-memory to the colonial order. The treaty claims have provided an intense arena of bicultural navigation of the colonial past and the national future, which have been complicated by Maori urbanization and subsequent loss of some tribal affiliations. In many cases the legal system has rendered an arborescent system of whakapapa that excludes contemporary, "detribalized" urban Maori from claiming land and resources and has also ossified and "rooted" historic, nineteenth-century indigenous identities and whakapapa relations. Following this logic, many scholars have presumed that recent urbanization has destabilized an *a priori* coherent system of whakapapa that was based on iwi (tribe) rather than hapu (subtribe) relations and never deeply contested. By adopting a more spiral approach to time, I contend that the urbanization process itself allows us to see more clearly the complicated genealogical relationships of the past. This is why it is not a coincidence that June Mitchell's *Amokura*, written during the tumultuous years of Maori migration to urban centers that led to vital intertribal allegiances, has been chiefly concerned with historic questions of migration and the politicization of Maori identities. Mitchell's novel examines the ways in which complex intertribal relations in the early nineteenth century, particularly the southern migrations initiated by the Ngati Toa (a North Island tribe) diplomat and politician, Te Rauparaha, created a complex genealogical palimpsest of the Kapiti coastal areas of Aotearoa / New Zealand. Mitchell's novel literalizes the definition of whakapapa as to layer, particularly in relation to Maori land occupation and resettlement. Her complicated depiction of indigenous historiography positions Maori as simultaneously native to Aotearoa/New Zealand as well as subjects of an internal diaspora. This is a crucial and relatively unexplored aspect of Maori literary historiography: due to the land-claims process, the language of *indigenous* presence has taken political and social prevalence over the intra-national *diaspora* histories that are integral to the novels I explore here. While *Amokura* is framed by a discourse of internal Maori migration, the narrative attempts to nativize these new settlers to the Kapiti region through the methodologies of human and botanic whakapapa, instituting a complex and rhizomorphic genealogy of place.

Weaving Flax, Family, and Narrative

To my knowledge, literary studies have not turned their attention to the diverse and often contested historiographies between iwi as they have been recorded in the Maori novel. While postcolonial studies is generally concerned with the recuperation of local histories, I suspect that the reason some Maori texts do not "travel" is because they insist upon a type of local engagement that is not easily translatable to a national and/or postcolonial rubric. Engaging with the localizing and historic contours of intertribal relations works against the grain of assimilationist national paradigms, while some postcolonial studies have eclipsed temporal complexities in the overriding concern with broad geographic comparisons. Following the lead of Édouard Glissant, my approach seeks to interrogate simultaneous renderings of "diversity" and "sameness." As many scholars have pointed out, the word "Maori" itself, the preferred term for indigenous New Zealanders, came into existence through colonial contact, and while it has been vital to the anticolonialist movement in its consolidation of pan-tribal identifications, it can also subsume the specific local histories that I explore here. Therefore I view this chapter as a way to complicate Maori/Pakeha (white) social binaries, most visible in grand national narratives of New Zealand biculturalism, which often suppress creolization and polarize each population into discrete racial histories, divided along the lines of colonizer/colonized, diasporic/indigenous, and white/black (or brown). Indigenous claims against the hegemonic aspects of the white-settler nation-state have only recently begun to be redressed, and for this reason there is still ample justification to emphasize pan-tribal unity. Yet given the complex creolization process that informs nearly all island populations, and given how Maori novels of the past forty years have been gesturing towards complex tribal identities, a discussion of the ways in which these claims to history are narrated through genealogical heritage and migration is long overdue. Here I highlight the narrative process of localizing cultural historiography to complicate dominant theories of the sedentary and botanical metaphors of cultural roots.

Perhaps due to its profoundly local and historically specific rendering of Maori whakapapa, *Amokura* has received little scholarly attention, and it has been out of print since its first publication in 1978.[11] This is surprising because it was one of the first novels by a Maori woman to be published, and it anticipates many of the thematic concerns such as kinship, Maori/Pakeha marriage contracts, migration, sovereignty, and land dispossession that are so evident in the works of celebrated authors such as Patricia Grace, Keri Hulme, and Witi Ihimaera. Grace's *Mutuwhenua* (1978), lauded as the first Maori woman's novel, was published the same year as *Amokura*. Interestingly, both texts explore the struggle for cultural retention when Maori women marry Pakeha men, suggesting a thematic concern with biculturalism in the form of nation and genre itself. The greenstone "mere" (weapon), so prominent an image in Grace's novel as a representation of suppressed ancestral and cultural heritage, is also the foundation of Mitchell's title. "Amokura," Mitchell explains, was the greenstone mere given by her Ngati Raukawa grandfather to Te Rauparaha; "the significance of this gesture was that he gave to Te Rauparaha at the same time the military leadership of his people" (1978, 194). This transference of power from one tribe to another suggests a dynamic alternative to anthropological tracings of genealogy by cognatic or blood descent to a larger and more complicated methodology of political alliance, migration, and settlement. In another context, Chadwick Allen has referred to a similar mode of indigenous political efficacy as a "meta-bloodline" (2002, 245).[12]

Mitchell's novel is also significant because it represents an important juncture in national literature; until the 1960s, Maori writing in English consisted predominantly of autobiographies, nonfiction ethnographies, and cultural and regional histories. *Amokura* draws upon all of the preceding genres in a fictionalized history of her Ngati Raukawa heritage as told by her ancestor Te Akau Meretini Horohau of Otaki, known as Mere. The novel can be described as a regional history, an ancestral autobiography, an ethnography, and ultimately—in recreating the author's whakapapa—a corporeal historiography of the early contact period in Aotearoa/New Zealand. The novel's engagement with the past, as a "historiographic metafiction" (Hutcheon 1988, 105), is self-conscious; it concludes with over forty pages of bibliographic footnotes, written and oral histories, archival materials, two maps of the region, a facsimile of a land purchase, and her narrator's (selective) whakapapa. As such, it brings Maori whaka-papa in a dialogue with poststructural genealogies. To Foucault, the latter refers to "the union of erudite knowledge and local memories which allows us to establish a historical knowledge of struggles and to make use of this knowledge tactically today" (1977, 83). Like Ihimaera's later novel, *The Matriarch* (1986), *Amokura* weaves together nineteenth-century newspaper articles, letters, battle accounts, songs, and family history in a way that nar-rates early New Zealand nation-building as a complex exchange between Pakeha and Maori. The visibility of nineteenth-century print culture in these historical novels suggests the ways in which both the New Zealand novel and its print media antecedents have been mutually constitutive com-ponents of national "imagined communities."

Mitchell has selected Mere to narrate this national narrative, I believe, because her lifespan, from the early 1820s to 1897, reflects some of the most radical changes in Aotearoa/New Zealand, including the signing of the Treaty of Waitangi in 1840 and the establishment of the Native Land Court in 1865. Mere's position is also significant because she represents the last "full-blood" Maori of Mitchell's whakapapa; her marriage to a British settler thus parallels the imbrication of Maori in Pakeha social and trade relations. In Mere's lifetime, the colonization of Aotearoa/New Zea-land resulted in the loss of the indigenous demographic majority as well as the British appropriation of 17 million acres of the North Island alone. British whaling communities and traders who settled in this era introduced both disease and muskets, thereby increasing Maori tribal warfare causali-ties and fundamentally changing the location and power balance between iwi. Access to this new technology was one of the primary reasons why Te Rauparaha, although a fifth-born son of a relatively small iwi, became one of the most powerful and in some cases, feared, figures of the time. Although he has been vilified by countless British historians, Te Rauparaha was an exceedingly adroit politician, cultivator, warrior, and leader, who was able to unify a large number of North Island tribes and convince them to migrate, on foot, hundreds of miles from their homes on a heke (migra-tion) to settle on lands he had secured through warfare and alliance along the Kapiti coastline. Te Rauparaha was well known to the British traders of the region—in fact their presence had been one of the primary rea-sons the Ngati Toa leader had decided to migrate south. Through the flax exchange, he was able to establish a thriving trade as well as arrange a number of voyages on British vessels.[13]

Although Te Rauparaha is the best-known historical figure of the novel, Mitchell presents her own whakapapa in a way that highlights the communal aspect of national historiography. Unlike the western bildungs-roman, which traces the development of an individualized subject, Mere doesn't enter her novel until after her elders have spoken about the ardors of migrating south with Te Rauparaha. These accounts are one founda-tion of the novel and subsequent genealogical layers are built upon them. The first section serves as a literal narrative whakapapa that informs and sustains Mere's first-person narration. After the ancestors' voices, Mere states, "Thus in this manner as I grow towards my womanhood I hear the old ones speak to us, bemoaning in their groups together, recalling the past" (1978, 3). The single subject transforms into a community where the narrator, reader, and writer become "us." Mitchell's historiography, orga-nized through the methodology of whakapapa, brings together discourses of diaspora and indigeneity, migration and settlement. *Amokura* constructs a cognitive mapping of New Zealand history that destabilizes the individu-alist bildungsroman by placing both the author and narrator's subjectivities in a complex spatio-temporal genealogy.[14]

While Mere's coming-of-age is inseparable from the voices and experi-ences of her ancestors, they in turn represent diverse origins, destabilizing the "genus" in traditional arborescent definitions of genealogy. Because the peoples who migrated to the Kapiti region represented a variety of tribes from the central and western areas of the North Island of Aotearoa / New Zealand, the narrator draws upon a diverse net of ancestry—more defined by their involvement in this historic event (the largest migration of its time) and their loose kinship affiliations with Te Rauparaha—than by "blood" alone. This is a significant gesture, given some (arborescent) Maori traditions of determining tribal identity by an eponymous founding ances-tor, thus constructing kinship around ideologies of descent.[15] *Amokura*, on the other hand, suggests that the narrator's whakapapa is determined as much by internal diaspora as by land settlement. In other words, this is a far more complicated negotiation of indigenous identity than many schol-ars have allowed, emphasizing a dynamic phenomenological relationship between tribal members and the accumulative experience of place. From the beginning Mere explains, "We love the stories the old people tell us. . . . We learn from the old people, we revere them" (Mitchell 1978, 3). The multiple voices of the novel's past and present often take precedence over a single, present-tense, narrative voice, positioning the novel's protagonist as a mediator of complex diasporan histories. By sanctifying her communal narrative, Mitchell positions the elders—and by extension her text—as an embodied whakapapa.

As an encoding of indigenous epistemology, Mitchell's tribute to her narrator/ancestor calls attention to the gendered botanical metaphors that constitute national and familial whakapapa. In the preface she writes, "How often I have needed to say to her: My tipuna [elder] . . . I gathered the flax with care. I sought the blessing necessary for the work. Forgive where my weaving feels uneven to your fingers . . . . I know the design clearly in my heart, and the sun's journeys pass uncounted while I work—but I need a finer skill to discipline the threads" (vii). The New Zealand flax plant (*phormium*), or harakeke, has been employed in Maori tradition as a metaphor for whanau, or extended family (Metge 1990, 56), and more recently as a metonymy for Maori women's writing; by extension this is women's work. Weaving flax appears frequently throughout *Amokura* to indigenize the narrator's struggle with the abstraction of writing in English. As Metge observes, "Maori use the flax bush . . . as a favourite metaphor for the family group . . . they identify the rito [new shoot] in each fan as a child . . . emerging from and protected by its parents . . . on either side" (1995, 16). Mitchell has harvested the older shoots from the flax/human family to weave her narrative. By imagining her novel as a creative employment of one of the most vital plants of Maori culture, and one of the central trade goods for the early colonial economy, she suggests that her narrative is historically implicated in national and global trade networks that depend on indigenous production. After a series of anecdotal reminiscences, her narrator comments, "These were all the bright strands I found for my taniko [dyed flax] weaving before the sun went down today" (1978, 102). Because Mitchell is necessarily reliant upon British historiography of the early contact period to envision her ancestor's life, she indigenizes the process of writing through the flax-weaving metaphor and highlights the relationship between historical genealogy and whakapapa. As both weaver and writer, Mitchell makes a clear relationship between the process of scripting a national genealogy and women's traditions of constructing "te aho tapu," or the sacred thread. According to Merimeri Penfold, "The female in Maori society is a sacred element in maintaining lines of descent" (quoted in Pendergrast 1987, 5), which suggests a constitutive relationship between artistic and biological (re)production that is broadly encompassed by whakapapa.

Although diaspora scholars have tended to separate natural metaphors from human histories, Mitchell highlights the ways in which the flax trade helped make the southern migration possible, just as this plant served as a metaphor for the extended kinship of the migrants. Hence flax, like most botanical metaphors, is rooted in the soil of Aotearoa as well as transplanted or rerouted in a new set of familial, social, and trade relations. National attachments to land are naturalized according to the conflation of people with the soil. Arguing that "assumptions linking people to place, nation to territory are . . . metaphysical" (1997, 56), Malkki examines the botanical metaphors that are embedded in national discourse. Building upon the work of Deleuze and Guattari, she deconstructs the arborescent metaphors that underline kinship ties, genealogical roots, and cultural branches, as they validate national or ethnic rootedness. She argues that these botanical metaphors highlight the "powerful sedentarism in our thinking" (61). But Malkki, like Paul Gilroy and other diasporan theorists, tends to over-emphasize the ways in which botanical metaphors code diasporic subjects as profoundly unnatural. Assuming that the hegemonic nation-state is the only arena in which naturalizing discourse is employed, Gilroy asserts, "Diaspora is a valuable idea because it points towards a more refined and more worldly sense of culture than the characteristic notions of soil, landscape and rootedness" (1997, 328). Mitchell's employment of the flax plant as a metaphor of indigenous culture, extended and dynamic kinship, as well as an emergent colonial commodity, complicates Gilroy's reductive definition of naturalizing and fixed "rootedness" and demonstrates how even the flax plant contributes to a "worldly sense of culture."

Although Deleuze and Guattari may argue that "history is always written from the sedentary point of view . . .what is lacking is a Nomadology" (1987, 23), *Amokura* suggests a far deeper historical articulation of the relationship between diaspora and indigeneity and the production of place. Because the novel is framed in terms of intra-national migration, one cannot accurately categorize this text as "lacking" a "nomadology" in this sense. Although she is concerned with the process of migration, Mitchell does not construct this in binary opposition to a "sedentary point of view" that is conflated with feminized stagnancy. The botanical images of this novel, particularly the rhizomatic flax plant,[16] suggest a protonational moment in nineteenth-century New Zealand history, a far more fluid exchange of flora, a complex process of roots and routes, and a gendered inflection of the ways in which women, often positioned metonymically to nature, are integral to the production of masculinist diaspora.

Although the metaphors of family and flax have specific indigenous and precolonial modalities, their importance as vital nation-building commodities is evident in the sections of the novel that foreground the relationship between botanical metaphors and women's bodies. Early in the novel Mitchell recounts Te Rauparaha's giving his granddaughter Mere as a "present" in marriage to the Pakeha Tom Cook "because [Te Rauparaha] want[ed] more trade" (1978, 4). Since Mere's name is a homonym for the mere, or weapon, bequeathed to Te Rauparaha, Mitchell suggests a masculine system of exchange that predates Pakeha arrival. Although Mere seems somewhat reconciled to the marriage arrangement, Mitchell imagines a more radical alternative for her character. Mere has "worshipped the chief Te Rangihaeata," nephew of Te Rauparaha, whose open resistance to Pakeha settlement, topographic surveying, and land acquisition caused considerable damage to early British imperialism. Alignment with this anticolonialist, something Mere had "dreamt" as her future, would have positioned her in relation to some of the more overt resistance to British hegemony in this century and within an alternative cartography that opposed colonial appropriation. While posed as an alternative, this trajectory is not pursued and Mitchell depicts her ancestor as traded like a flax product into a masculinist system of desire. Although she does not mention Maori traditions of arranged marriage, which might characterize this exchange in an alternate trajectory of history,[17] she does invest her character with some agency. Mere decides she will "love this man" but "not because [she was] made a present for him by Te Rauparaha's order" (7). Thus, early in the novel, Mitchell signals some tension regarding one of her central historical characters, a man whom she will later critique for his "habit of using an unsuspecting tribe—or a person—as a bait to help his schemes" (131). While Mitchell's narrative is implicated in a construction of cultural and national roots, she is deeply ambiguous about positioning a "founding father" as a tribal icon or as the patriarch of this exodus.

Entangled Roots: Layering Whakapapa

The multiple tribal migrations with Te Rauparaha and the increasing pressure of British settlement fundamentally changed the relationship between the people, the land, and by extension, whakapapa. The tribes who migrated south, including Mere's Ngati Raukawa, did so in a precarious relationship with the Ngati Toa leader. Since arborescent forms of leadership at that time were determined by the senior lines of a genealogy, for the Ngati Raukawa to "follow" the "junior" tribe Ngati Toa was perceived by some migrants as problematic, even though Te Rauparaha was related to Ngati Raukawa through his mother. Ngati Raukawa resisted Te Rauparaha's appeals to migrate for many years; in the words of Te Kanae, we "'will not go to you, a common person'" (quoted in Burns 1980, 95). Ultimately many members of the tribe did migrate, but only after local wars had threatened their place of residence and after their own chief burned down their homes in frustration (126).

The familial relationship between Mere and Te Rauparaha is fraught with tension in *Amokura* because it doesn't fit into the traditional notion of whakapapa outlined in anthropological models of cognatic descent groups.[18] Put in Deleuze and Guattari's terms, Mitchell seems to be resisting the arborescent and hierarchical structures of patriarchal genealogies in favor of a far more rhizomatic genealogy of place. Te Rauparaha is the best-known and documented figure in the novel and responsible for the great migrations south, but Mitchell resists his celebrity for a number of reasons, including conflicts of rank, gender, and the trauma of diaspora. I mentioned earlier that whakapapa is central to land sovereignty and to historicizing a people's relationship to a particular landscape. Metge asserts that whakapapa "is almost inseparable from that of traditional history" (1967, 127). But if whakapapa is a taxonomy, or system of genealogical knowledge based on the history of space and place among other things, its ontological basis is destabilized in the Ngati Raukawa tribe's separation from ancestral land. In *Amokura* we are told that Te Rauparaha led the migrations; Mere's ancestors define this intra-national diaspora in terms of terrible loss when they explain, "We left the graves of our ancestors. Weeping we came; with pain across the heart we came. We left . . . all of that land known to us in every part and blessed by the names our history has given it" (1978, 2). Mere's tribe is displaced from their meta-physical history and consequently need to reposition and renarrate their whakapapa in a new landscape. Significantly, Mitchell ignores the violent tribal disputes over land that contributed to the southern migration. Instead, Te Rauparaha's quest for muskets, weapons, and greenstone are given causality, particularly his intention to establish "supreme power over all tribes" and Pakeha settlers (2). Thus the intertribal warfare that catalyzed the migration recedes into distant history; Mitchell is more interested in depicting Te Rauparaha and his associated tribes pursuing the modernity of capital through their southern migration to Pakeha trading centers. Just as Mere and the flax plant enter a new phase of commodification, Mere's immediate family incorporate western ideologies of property and ownership. For instance, in one important scene, her (British) husband Tame (Tom) confiscates his schooner-racing trophy from the hands of his children, declaring, "That's my cup." Immediately his young son starts "chanting cheekily . . . 'That's-mine-I-built-it. That's-mine-I-bought-it. . . . *That's mine I inherited it!'"* (author's emphasis 48). Given my previous discussion about the importance of ships as symbolic vessels of sovereignty, it is particularly telling that this conflict is focused on Tame's schooner trophy, which we might read as a successful Pakeha substitution for the waka, the vehicle of the people. Their son anticipates the individualist claims that dominate the later court scenes, which seek to establish Te Rauparaha's leadership and material inheritance within a capitalist philosopheme. As I explain, the relationship between inheritance, land, and identity is disrupted by the state machinery of the Native Land Court.

Because western legal structures require an arborescent genealogy to validate land claims, Mitchell's text provides a patriarchal whakapapa at the same time that it subsumes it under her matriarchal heritage. The complication of inheritance is apparent in that Mitchell presents Te Rauparaha as a somewhat problematic figure in contrast to his wife, Te Akau, Mere's biological grandmother.[19] The end pages of *Amokura* document the whakapapa of the Ngati Raukawa iwi, the tribe with whom Mere most identifies. I believe it is not by accident that Te Rauparaha appears in the literal center of the whakapapa; he is incorporated into Ngati Raukawa although he is generally associated with Ngati Toa. This is a significant gesture in that it subsumes Te Rauparaha's patriarchal lineage under his *matriarchal* whakapapa, complicating traditional printed historiography for this figure. Mitchell's use of genealogy here is in keeping with my earlier suggestion that whakapapa represent dynamic processes, deeply informed by context and place. Since the Kapiti and Otaki land court claims must testify to the southern diaspora under Te Rauparaha's leadership, he is maternally incorporated into the spatial history of Ngati Raukawa.

In *Amokura*, whakapapa exist in multiple, rhizomorphous, and selective forms: the introductory scene of migrant elders; the printed diagram that follows the structure of a genealogical tree but that offers a feminized whakapapa of place; the capitalist inheritance mimicked by Mere's son; and a matrilineal counter to Te Rauparaha in the oral form recounted by his wife, Te Akau. Although Te Akau is by descent of another tribe, her exogamous marriage and migration south with her husband enable her to construct complicated whakapapa for her granddaughter/narrator, and these are offered as an alternative genealogy to Te Rauparaha's diaspora. In Mere's words, Te Akau "would call back the names one by one, on and on through the lines of this and that descent, until the mists parted and showed you the Arawa canoe, and showed you the Tainui" (1978, 138). Te Akau's voice and body mobilize Maori settlement history in a way that suggests that pan-tribal alliances such as those consolidated under Te Rauparaha are part of both the past and present destiny. In other words, this is a broad, meta-physical, and familial narrative of history—the Tainui and Arawa canoes reflect the ancient settlement of northern Aotearoa/New Zealand by water, while Mere and Te Akau's presence represent a later southern migration by land.[20] This suggests a dual migratory history that still positions *all* Maori as tangata whenua, or first people of the land. Similar to Patricia Grace's later novel *Potiki* (1986), Mitchell's narrative of Maori migration history enacts the dynamic movement of a spiral; tribal epistemologies are replicated through ancestral bodies and knowledges that embody and enact the past *and* future. Hence the ancient migration to Aotearoa is seen to precipitate the later, more modern diaspora with Te Rauparaha. Te Akau teaches Mere to realize she is "made of the past, of what my people have been before me." Mere learns, "I am all of them as well as myself, and I am all they have done in spite of what I have not done. What a burden then of honour I carry, what a treasure of inheritance I hold in my memory" (138). In this way Te Akau mobilizes the proverb, "The mana [prestige] of a person's ancestors are not lost; they are gifts passed down to him (or her)" (Metge 1995, 228).

Te Akau's whakapapa not only resists patriarchal genealogies but also offers a larger historical and meta-physical scope than Te Rauparaha's diaspora; her legacy also preserves the memory of tension over land and resources produced by Maori migration. According to oral history, the Tainui and Arawa canoes left Hawaiki—an ancestral homeland examined in the previous chapter—due to familial disputes and warfare. Although Mitchell does not mention this, the disputes between the arrivants "traveled" to Aotearoa—in some accounts a Tainui chief orchestrated the burning of the Arawa canoe due to competition over resources.[21] Since Te Akau represents Mere's Arawa ancestry and Te Rauparaha the Tainui (separate voyaging canoes from which some Maori derive tribal identity), Mere is left to weave together these two iwi across historical/familial time and space. The "mists" that part for Mere reveal a diasporic genealogy that extends to Hawaiki, replicated on a closer historical scale through the leadership of Te Rauparaha's heke. Thus Te Akau's whakapapa functions as a vehicle of history in which the routes of migration to Aotearoa anticipate a secondary migration over land. This is rendered in spiral time, condensing the meta-physical associations between the voyaging canoe and iwi as dynamic vessels of Maori history.

I have dwelled on Mitchell's rhizomatic employment of whakapapa for a number of reasons. First, most analyses of Maori literature sidestep the complex tribal relations that inform cultural production, and I have attempted to mitigate this with some historical context. Second, it is clear that although most anthropologists suggest that genealogical complications among Maori iwi occurred after twentieth-century urbanization, in this historical novel, the number of exogamous marriages between migratory populations of Te Arawa, Ngati Raukawa, and Ngati Toa suggests that complex alliances were visible well before Pakeha had become a majority population. If we extend the metaphor of the flax plant as whanau, one can draw comparisons between the tribally entangled family of *Amokura* and Joan Metge's comment that the flax plant has rhizomorphous roots that "are so entwined that they cannot be separated except with a sharp spade" (1995, 15). Finally, to suggest that only recent urbanization has fragmented Maori tribal relations is to ignore the ways in which, in the nineteenth century, introduced commodities like the musket and state apparatuses like the land court had already set the scene for cultural alienation.

The Sharp Spade: Native Land Court

In *Amokura* the sharp spade that breaks so many tribal roots appears as the Native Land Court, established in 1865. Anthropologist Hugh Kawharu states that the Native Land Court decisions facilitated "a major break in the traditional way of life . . . and struck at the roots of [Maori] political systems" (1975, 7). In the words of historian James Belich, "This notorious institution was designed to destroy Maori communal land tenure and so both facilitate Pakeha land buying and 'detribalise' Maori" (1996, 258). By forcing communally held land into individual properties, the Native Land Court assured not only that Maori would lose their turangawaewae, or place to stand, but their direct links to ancestors, whanau, and the tribe itself. The rifts caused by the heke arise in the Native Land Court scenes of the novel, which take place after Te Rauparaha's death. The entanglement between land occupation, tribal identity, and whakapapa is rendered most visible during the courtroom scenes, which are the focus of three chapters of the novel. Some sections are transcribed verbatim from the Otaki Maori Land Court Minutes. In one case, Mere's aunt, Pipi Kutia, testifies against Mere's family and tribe. The daughter of Te Akau (and later the wife of Te Rauparaha), Pipi Kutia, like all the witnesses in court, must show some type of relationship to Te Rauparaha in order to be legally recognized as a trustee to the land. Due to the court's employment of an arborescent genealogical structure, the more rhizomatic articulations of whakapapa discussed earlier are discarded, highlighting the ways in which whakapapa may function as profoundly contextual and historical performances.

The court scenes facilitate two new definitions of whakapapa, and, if we follow Deleuze and Guattari's advice to "follow the rhizome by rupture" (1987, 11), we are provided with a historical account of the ways in which competing epistemologies function in the Native Land Court. First, Te Rauparaha, although of a "junior" tribe to many of those in the courtroom, must be invoked as a benefactor and leader—almost an ancestor—in order for anyone to claim the conquered territory. Second, the "detribalization" Belich observes is rendered as a selective, often misleading testimony of kinship relations and whakapapa. This becomes evident in a number of examples, such as when Mere's brother deliberately misdefines the relations between two subtribes and then claims a different iwi than his sister. Pipi Kutia testifies disparagingly about a man who everyone but the Pakeha judge knows is her brother. Mere explains that these are recognized tactics when "siding with" other tribes in court. The Otaki Maori Land Court records will not reveal the strategic use of whakapapa, but Mere's narrative does. She explains that Pipi Kutia "was never friendly with her brother my father . . . because she has been Te Rauparaha's wife sometimes she will be reminding us of that" (92). In the courtroom each witness makes some type of familial claim to Te Rauparaha, undermining assumptions that whakapapa follow strict cognatic rules of ancestry and rank. When Mere testifies, she does not reveal the relationship between her aunt and father. Instead, she attempts to defend her whakapapa, but due to the courtroom context, she is caught between rhizomatic and arborescent definitions of human relations. As with the other claimants, she must testify to the mana of Te Rauparaha without diminishing her own parents and extended family. Pipi Kutia had suggested that her father was a coward and that "Rauparaha had no confidence in this man" (1978, 92). Mere responds in conflicting ways, "My parents did not come under the authority or protection of Te Rauparaha. My ancestors and parents had authority. When they arrived here, my father and Te Rauparaha killed the people on this land. My father was not a slave that they should direct him! This land was conquered by Te Rauparaha—and I have a claim to this land therefore" (98). The arborescent structure of the western legal system places Mere in a precarious position—claiming the whakapapa recounted by Te Akau would diminish her chance of legal entitlement to the land; yet by upholding Te Rauparaha as leader of Ngati Raukawa, she undermines her parents' authority. While she may be defending the mana of her ancestors, it is probably not a coincidence that of all the Ngati Raukawa present in the printed whakapapa in the novel, Mere's parents are conspicuously missing.[22]

While most acknowledge that whakapapa were somewhat fixed with the introduction of writing, the land court testimonies and Mitchell's commentary suggest that they are far more fluid, selective, and performative—that is, constructed in the sense that they serve a particular purpose.[23] Lest the reader believe that the land courts did successfully "detribalise" Maori claimants, Mitchell follows the court scenes with an image of pan-tribal unity—a new meetinghouse is built where the "supports of ancestry are justly chosen, all significant to us who are of the Tainui and Te Arawa canoes" (1978, 120). As such, we are given a literal architecture of the ways in which the disparate routes of voyaging culture are joined and rooted in the land of Aotearoa. Scholars have called attention to the ways in which the iconography of Maori meetinghouses embodies tribal history.[24] In *Amokura* this is represented in a literal way; at the new meetinghouse, an elderly Mere explains that "we old women feel that memory is like the shawl each wears on her head as we talk together: the memory of our history keeps us tidy and warm." The women observe the young, whose faces, voices, and body language, Mere states, "remind us of our relations and our elders" (121). In this scene, the past is literally embodied through kinship and ancestry. While embracing a relation, Mere asks, "How does a brusque pakeha understand? This is not merely a touch from the flesh of today: it is also a spirit encounter with all the forebears we represent" (122). *Amokura* suggests that metaphysical genealogies offer an approach to history that is not homologous to western epistemes and cannot be fully replicated in court procedure. Mitchell's image of pan-tribal community building represents an alternative to the alienating land court scenes, a supplement to the other history where, forty years later, Maori of this region retained only 20 percent of their lands.

Naturalizing Whakapapa and Maori Settlement

I have outlined some of the intertribal complexity that informs the novel, a focus on human whakapapa rendered in the meeting house's wooden sculpture, Te Akau's oral tradition, Mitchell's printed genealogy, and legal discourse. I turn now to the ways in which *Amokura* defines whakapapa as a practiced relation to place. I mentioned earlier that whakapapa include the human, animal, plant, and meta-physical worlds. Thus, in order to naturalize her subject's acculturation into a new landscape, Mitchell draws upon nonhuman relations with both natural and supernatural elements. For example, her Maori glossary provides the names of nearly thirty plants, trees, birds, and varieties of flax that function prominently in the novel as rhizomatic companions to Mere. Immediately after her marriage to her Pakeha husband, Mere calls out a greeting to Rangi, her "father the sky" (1978, 8), as well as to the hills that represent Papatuanuku, likening her marriage to the union of her primordial ancestors. After a visit from her sisters, she turns to the world of Tane, god of the forest and her "tall tree brothers" (35).[25] She states, "I breathe again the breath of my mother the earth: heartbeat by heartbeat I melt back." She "sleeps as a baby sleeps, fastened to [her] nourishment inside the womb" (36). Her meta-physical rebirth, in a location that has only recently been settled by her extended family, suggests the ways in which, following Michel de Certeau, *"space is a practiced place"* (author's emphasis 1984, 117).

Other examples of her naturalized relationship to the new landscape are woven deftly throughout the text. With her children on her hip, Mere likens herself to "a tree of fruit" (1978, 37), she finds the "land is a voice singing through [her] feet," and gives birth to her son on a flax mat while calling on the blessings of Tane (15). When Mere's daughter later tries to "wither the roots of [her] children in this land" (147) by not relating their Maori heritage, Mere recites her whakapapa: "I am the past and future, I and my ancestors and descendants, and loyalty is due to life beyond myself" (148). Her daughter's denial of her Maori heritage and her initial refusal to pass this legacy on to her own children is one of the central crisis moments of the text, a rupture in the regeneration of sacred historiography. Since whakapapa is also constituted by nonhuman historical presence, Mere can turn to the meta-physical world to sanction her settlement in the new land-scape. The nonhuman world, historicized through Maori phenomenology and Pakeha settlement, provides an alternative and more positively coded "poetics of Relation" (Glissant 1997, 34) than that provided by her daughter or the alienating land court.

I mentioned earlier that Maori tribal relations are usually centralized around genealogical connections to a common ancestor, who may embody the historical migration from Hawaiki (see O'Regan 1992). The terms iwi (defined in English as bone, or tribe) and hapu (conceived in the womb, or subtribe) reflect a corporeality, a meta-physical history that characterizes the loose boundaries of each community. As stated earlier, these group-ings are usually established by ancestral occupation of land. But since the Ngati Raukawa of *Amokura* are migrants uneasily positioned under Te Rauparaha's legacy, and displaced from their northern homelands/history, Mitchell turns to a broader conception of whakapapa in order to natural-ize this resettlement. This broader whakapapa is in accordance with tradi-tional Maori rendering of human and cosmic interrelation, but I suggest that in some sections of *Amokura* it functions as an idealized alternative to intertribal dispute, Pakeha assimilation policies, and the alienation of the land court.

Whakapapa articulate the discourse of ontological belonging in terms of land and family, drawing a network of kin and ancestry that extends far beyond the human world. Therefore Mere, who positions herself as a diasporic subject, is able to secure a series of meta-physical kinship relations by turning to the maternal deity of Aotearoa, Papatuanuku, the originary layer of all whakapapa. Powhiri Rika-Heke describes Papa as "the primary source of our cultural identity and our spiritual being" (1996, 174).[26] To assert that Papatuanuku is an ancestor for all Maori is to broaden the descriptors of indigenous kinship and naturalize settlement. In this sense it has been argued that all Maori are genealogically connected. While this pan-tribal and meta-physical philosopheme has gained momentum from the Maori sovereignty movement and ecological strains on Aotearoa / New Zealand, it is also a vital component of whakapapa epistemology in that it is dynamic and relative to the nexus of social and political relations. In other words, whakapapa function in a series of simultaneously held local (tribal and subtribal), national (pan-tribal), and natural identifications. Mitchell's meta-physical extension to the natural world circumvents some of the colonial and intertribal pressures experienced by her Maori characters, who are tangata whenua of Otaki or Kapiti but not in the sense of *first* people.[27]

Since I have differentiated between western notions of genealogy and Maori whakapapa, I would also like to caution against conflating traditional western interpellations of the natural world with Maori epistemologies of the land and seascape. My point is not to erect a facile binary between western and indigenous practices by instituting New Age axioms that romanticize indigenous cultures for their ecological sensitivity. In no way does this chapter suggest an essentialist construction of environmental ethics, even as I recognize that Maori have been at the forefront of ecological conservation in Aotearoa. In fact, some of the first cases brought before the Waitangi Tribunal were to protect rivers and harbors from corporate waste. My point is to make a historical differentiation between the ways in which whakapapa codes the precapitalist, natural world and the nineteenth-century imperial expansion that constituted a philosopheme of *terra nullius*, where the colonized landscape was interpellated as an "uncultivated" blank slate and native peoples were characterized, by extension, as "uncultured." As many scholars have observed, this ideology was one of the least subtle justifications for western appropriation of indigenous land

and resources.[28] Because Maori oral tradition has a long history of anthropomorphizing the landscape of Aotearoa, where flora and fauna, mountains, rivers, the sea, and atua (gods) are narrated in active social and political terms, the natural world does not function as *terra nullius* onto which Maori human settlement can be simplistically grafted. *Amokura*, like the Caribbean novels discussed in Chapter Five, constructs a phenomenological narrative of landscape, a dynamic relationship between humans, flora, and fauna that reflect the shifting social geographies of nineteenth-century Aotearoa / New Zealand as this colony transformed from a rural to an increasingly urbanized merchant economy. Thus Mitchell seems to share Wilson Harris's objective to "visualize links between technology and living landscapes in continuously new ways that [take] nothing for granted in an increasingly violent and materialistic world" (1999, 43).

Mitchell's inscription of whakapapa encodes landscape as constituted and constitutive of human history; natural forces of Aotearoa play as much a part in the plot as the human residents. For example, Mere and her husband lose their home due to an earthquake, the Tarawera eruption destroys some of Mere's Te Arawa kin (and the touristed Pink Terraces), a river taniwha (spirit) claims the lives of two of her children, and the Manawatu River floods due to Pakeha deforestation. These phenomenologies of landscape, as corporeal and narrative histories, are woven alongside the introduction of steam engines, flour, flax and corn mills, the English language, Pakeha settlement, alienation from ancestral land, and capitalist commodification. In this way the indigenous world of Aotearoa / New Zealand experiences a seismic cultural slippage akin to the great earthquakes and volcanic activity of this era. Ultimately, Mitchell's topos encodes whakapapa as deeply engaged with "te ao hurihuri," the changing world.

Pakeha Arrivants as New Kin: Arborescence and the Soil

I have argued that the multiple forms of whakapapa in *Amokura* reflect dynamic rhizomatic systems and, if I may borrow from Joan Metge again, can be likened to the flax plant where, according to one Maori proverb, "The flax flowers; new shoots fill the empty gaps" (1995, 290). Since whakapapa is as much about the past as it is about the future, I will conclude this section on *Amokura* with a few comments on the ways in which arrivant Pakeha and their plants (the "new shoots") are adopted as kin and how, by extension, the newcomers are positioned as younger siblings. Mitchell contributes to an ever-growing whakapapa in order to reconcile the human conflicts exacerbated by Pakeha colonization by demonstrating how her character embraces new plant commodities like potatoes and onions, and cultivates an English flower garden. Although I mentioned earlier that *in theory* whakapapa Maori could render British settlement as unnatural, Mitchell's narrator, married to a Pakeha, a mother of eight children, and a grandmother of twenty mokopuna of mixed heritage, spends a tremendous amount of time cultivating new arrivants and seeds. Since the etymology of diaspora encodes the dispersal of seed, Mitchell seems to be narrating the multiple layerings of diasporic settlement to naturalize New Zealand biculturalism. While she is critical of Pakeha attitudes to the land as a commodity, claiming that they clear the land with "no sacred awareness of their action . . . they bite the feet of the tall trees of Tane" (110), some Pakeha settlement is naturalized by the introduction of flora. While indigenous plants may have a genealogical link to Maori, especially the totara tree that is associated with Te Rauparaha and some Maori voyaging traditions (1978, 49, 61, 90), the new imports are embraced like family. Mere explains that while "a garden of coloured flowers is not a Maori idea," she asks her aunt, Pipi Ipurape, to teach her the new imports (12). In her tour of her aunt's garden, Mere is introduced to lavender, sweet pea, snapdragon, and other varieties. Mere "meets the hollyhock, who is high and staring like Pipi Kutia." Like the hollyhock, Mere claims the wallflower as family, calling it "affectionate . . . its scent as dear as a loved relation" (13). At the end of her life, Mere reflects back upon "all the fruits and vegetables we have grown for food since the pakeha brought us the new seeds," the peach trees that were imported to her land, the wheat fields, and her "English garden plants" (116–117).

Amokura presents a multiethnic national whakapapa based on layered genealogies of place for the broader Maori population and Pakeha arrivants. Mitchell incorporates both arborescent and rhizomatic components of genealogy, articulated in a profoundly spatial phenomenology of diaspora and settlement. This is most evident in the scene when Pipi Ipurape dies, and Mere prays for her family at her local church. While the meetinghouse suggests a structure of pan-tribal Maori identity, Mitchell also turns to Rangiatea, the church built under Te Rauparaha's direction, which suggests "trust with pakeha"(60). Mitchell writes that the "shell of the church is pakeha, the lining is Maori." Since the Maori meetinghouse is often depicted in terms of extended kinship or whanau, Mitchell extends this structure of kinship to the church, as space that incorporates British settlement—symbolizing two houses of this bicultural nation. In their church, "pakeha and Maori harmonize words together" (60). Rangiatea is a Christian structure that is literally built upon historic Maori sediment. Mere comments, "Under this altar we laid our trust with the trust of the pakeha; under his shape of altar we buried the treasure-box of earth, brought with us centuries of summers ago from our ancient shrine at Hawaiki in the vast ocean of Kiwa" (60).

Mitchell's inscription of the creolized church Rangiatea might be read as a response to the questions posed in the previous chapter about trying to locate a space of origins or roots in a long history of transoceanic voyaging and routes. The church reflects a real place of worship in Aotearoa and a testament to the well-known Maori proverb, "I can never be lost; I am a seed sown from Rangiatea." Like Benítez-Rojo's concept of the repeating island, Rangiatea (Ra'iatea) has traveled and spread to many locations throughout the Pacific. It is generally understood as a figurative Hawaiki; reflecting spiral time, it is both the symbolic origin and destination of the traveler. In fact, this brings us back to Te Rangi Hiroa's octopus map of Oceania, which places Ra'iatea, the presumed center of Polynesian navigation, at the hub of the Pacific. (See Figure 4.) In Mitchell's context, Rangiatea is invoked as both an origin and end point, a figurative Hawaiki that reflects the space of departure for ancient voyaging canoes and the ultimate place of destination for the travelers of Te Rauparaha's heke.

Mitchell's invocation of this buried "treasure-box of earth" adds new dimensions to theories that claim the intrinsic "sedentary" nature of both soil and roots. First, it claims Papatuanuku, the earth, as the primary Maori ancestor. By extension, Maori (and broader Pacific) cosmology, migration, settlement, and genealogy function as the literal foundation of the church and the architecture of the nation. This suggests that since Maori were originary migrants to Aotearoa, they are entitled to full sovereignty over land and national resources. Just as ancient Tainui and Arawa peoples made claims to specific areas and resources of Aotearoa by displaying more weathered and aged artifacts to substantiate first arrival,[29] *Amokura* suggests that the founding soil of the nation—transplanted from Hawaiki—validates the mana and whakapapa of tangata whenua. Mitchell is well aware of the importance of positioning Maori as literal carriers and guardians of "national soil" in the nineteenth century, given that the 1862 Native Land Act had prevented Maori of less than "half-caste" from claiming ancestral land.

I have emphasized Mitchell's rhizomorphous conception of genealogy in that it incorporates new landscapes and peoples in a familial structure. If we approach this novel as a national family tree, then clearly *Amokura* suggests a particular originary authority should be assigned to Maori based on their prior occupation and narration of Aotearoa. Overall, Mitchell has

184

contributed a gendered critique of masculinist theories of diaspora and has complicated the assumption that both "roots" and national "soil" are *a priori*, sedentary essences. Here those very icons of rootedness—soil, plants, and indigenous identities—are strategically positioned as routed in complex transoceanic networks. Yet just when it seems she has completed her sacred, bicultural, and domestic architecture, the natural—and particularly arborescent—world seems to gain control of Mitchell's narrative and resist the futurity of her aspirations by returning to precolonial time and space.

If Maori spiral narrative, like the nation, demands sacrifice for its regeneration, Mitchell's text concludes on a profoundly ambivalent note about the national and natural costs. While praying in the Rangiatea church, Mere "reflects on the years of growth that have matured Pipi's garden; how everything at present is thriving with leaf and blossom." But the "sadness of remembering" her deceased aunt and her Pakeha garden cause Mere to "dream that the three pillars" that support the church "become huge totara trees again. And that slowly all kinds of smaller trees and looping vines and fern families gather to grow here also" (61). This is a radically different image than the Maori meetinghouse, where Mere admires how the "supports of ancestry are justly chosen, all significant to us who are of the Tainui and Te Arawa canoes" (120). In this Rangiatea scene, Mitchell dismantles the bicultural architecture by returning it to its natural and decidedly nonhuman form. Since totara trees function in the novel as a naturalized symbol of Maori history—as precolonial ancestors—the hierarchy and mana of Maori whakapapa remain intact, and Pakeha settlement becomes ahistorical. In fact Mere's dream of a *depopulated* landscape suggests the only tribal and national reconciliation possible—a space beyond recognizable human history. Here she finds the seeds of the future, "O the surge of life there is from rootlet to leaf tip—the pulse, the need, the fulfillment that travels even the entire height of the forest tree and reaches to everywhere within it. I live as a plant lives. The light draws me to keep opening" (61). Perhaps it is no coincidence that after Mere visits Rangiatea, she has an argument with her husband about the ways in which he is discouraging her children from maintaining Maori traditions and his involvement in encouraging her whanau to sell their land. She attests to this destruction by lamenting, "Again you take the bark from the sunless side of me, Tame. Again I must attend to my healing. The lonely healing" (63).

On the last day of her life, Mere looks upon a young Maori/Pakeha couple and says, "You children of so remote mothers, you embrace not simply each other but the life of the land. From your flesh could grow a kauri [tree] strength for unity . . . it could" (163). The ellipsis and the word "could" suggest that her effort to include Pakeha in her narrative of metaphysical origins and in the broader framework of whakapapa is still an unfulfilled possibility. The kauri tree, like the totara, suggests indigenous whakapapa as well as the preferred materials for Maori voyaging canoes, perhaps invoking the phrase, "He waka eke noa," or "a common cause, a canoe for all people" (Nelson 1991, 25). To mark this shift from roots to diasporic routes, Mitchell concludes her novel by attempting to naturalize Maori and Pakeha migrants, turning from the complex entanglement of human roots towards the whakapapa of the natural world, scattering hope in her grandchildren, whom she calls "the seeds of our future" (1978, 60).

Amokura, researched and written during an intense decade of Maori activism, reflects as much of the nineteenth-century land alienation, diaspora, and resistance as its twentieth-century counterpart. Just as Mitchell's ancestors contested duplicitous land acquisitions in the courtrooms of the late nineteenth century, Maori of the 1970s were preparing evidence for the Waitangi Tribunal hearings, often drawing upon their antecedents' testimonies in the Native Land Court.[30] *Amokura* was being completed when the activists Nga Tamatoa petitioned Parliament for Maori language to be recognized under New Zealand's bicultural agenda in 1973 and is deeply informed by the 1975 Maori Land March and the Bastion Point protests. In these circumstances, which continue to reverberate today, Mitchell's uneven bicultural weaving of a national whakapapa can be better understood. More than two decades after *Amokura* was completed, many Maori have not yet been granted alienated lands, and the nation continues to unravel and reweave its complex whakapapa. Or as Mere describes her union with her husband, "Life with Tame is many times a cry across my heart. We are different. Different. The plaiting we make together is not evenly smooth. It has errors—they are seen by the eye and felt with the fingertips" (1978, 37).

National Beginnings: Keri Hulme's *the bone people*

> Other bones lie deep in mine
> Within these lie other bones,
> It matters not where I turn.
> —Arapera Hineira Blank, "Bone Song"

In this discussion of literary representations of whakapapa, it is appropriate that I conclude with Keri Hulme's *the bone people*, not only since it is the text that catalyzed both my travel to Aotearoa/New Zealand and this course of research, but because Hulme became a magnet for criticism by those who felt that her whakapapa was not substantial enough to justify her novel being awarded the Pegasus Prize for Maori Fiction in 1984. Literary figure C. K. Stead initiated this hotly contested debate, insisting that Hulme could not rightfully claim indigenous identity based on one Maori grandparent (1989, 180). Albert Wendt and others countered this argument, asserting that Stead had adopted a colonial taxonomy of race designed to artificially partition indigenous subjects and homogenize Maori under Pakeha assimilation.[31] Certainly there is a long colonial history of legal blood quantum requirements in Aotearoa/New Zealand that inform Stead's critique; until 1981, claims against the Crown required specific "fractions of origins" to retain Maori land (Stewart-Harawira 1993, 30). Interestingly, Hulme's novel anticipated this debate about who can and cannot define Maori identity, and in fact *the bone people* is largely concerned with examining the implications of whakapapa in terms of contemporary New Zealand relations. By confusing Hulme with her protagonist, and by neglecting the *spatial* and often contingent aspects of whakapapa, critics like Stead have grafted a rigidly defined genealogy over a far more dynamic system of rhizomatic relations.

Hulme's character Kerewin, when confronted with those she perceives as "brown faces [who] stare at her with bright unfriendly eyes" in a local bar, thinks "as always, she wants to whip out a certified copy of her whakapapa, preferably with illustrated photographs (most of her [relations] are much more Maori looking than she is). 'Look! I really am one of you,' she could say. 'Well, at least some of me is. . . .'" (K. Hulme 1983, 112). Kerewin, a flawed character, is not the spokesperson for Hulme's theories of ethnic relations here; the author is well aware that a "certified" whakapapa is not the means by which one "proves" Maori identity. At another point Kerewin comments on how ancestry has been quantified in terms of notions of racial purity and suggests the spatial modalities of racial categorization. As she observes, "'If I was in America, I'd be an octoroon'" (61). Importantly, these observations occur early in the novel, when Kerewin is still caught in an epistemic "limbo" (28), using transatlantic discourses of miscegenation and creolization to demonstrate that "Maoritanga," or the Maori way, has been "lost in the way [she] lives" (62).

Like *Amokura*, *the bone people* addresses issues of national belonging by unevenly incorporating the multiple ethnic settlements of Aotearoa/New Zealand under a loose rubric of whakapapa. And like Mitchell, Hulme attempts to reconcile competing cultural epistemologies by incorporating Pakeha into Maori tradition based on a layering of diaspora that positions Maori as the authoritative first-nation people. The text explores the relationship between the British-Maori protagonist Kerewin Holmes (the author's pun: Keri win home), an eccentric and bookish painter who has retreated from human companionship into her South Island tower, and the arrivant Pakeha boy/child Simon Peter, who literally breaks into her home/heart, eventually bringing with him his adoptive, abusive, and loving Maori father, Joe. Although also concerned with the nation's entangled history of love and violence, *the bone people* is far more radical in terms of destabilizing romance narratives and the presumed heterosexual union that initiates the chain of whakapapa. Unlike Mitchell's protagonist, Kerewin resists the maternal role expected of her and refuses to join into a sexual relationship with Joe (who proposes marriage), suggesting an alternative to the heterosexual family triptych evident in Mitchell's conflation of biological and artistic (re)production. As these three main characters also draw upon diverse ethnic and epistemic genealogies, they struggle to create a new definition of the family/nation. They do so by undertaking separate meta-physical journeys that bring each character close to death, but are then regenerated in Maori spiral time to renew their relationship. Layer by layer, the novel discards gender and ethnic hierarchies in its reconstruction of the family, weaving a lateral whakapapa of the newly formed nation.

As I have mentioned, the spiral gestures to the past while moving into the future, positioning historical events in the present so that time becomes coeval or simultaneous. As Kerewin remarks, "It was an old symbol of rebirth, and the outward-inward nature of things" (45). This allows Hulme's Maori ancestors, segregated into the linear past by critics like Stead, to take on profound importance in her practiced claims to indigeneity. Since Maori historiography is positioned as both indigenous and diasporic, this lends a unique and complex dimension to discourses of space, time, and national belonging. Interestingly, both Mitchell and Hulme situate Maori migration as a vital point on the spiral historiography of the nation, complicating James Clifford's contention that "diasporas are caught up with and defined against (1) the norms of nation-states and (2) indigenous, and especially autochthonous, claims by 'tribal' peoples" (1997, 250). Instead of segregating empirical and literary discourses of diaspora and indigeneity, the novels I discuss here articulate a more complicated and entangled history. Rather than simply turning to the prior occupation of land in order to validate first-nation status, both authors destabilize the boundaries of the nation itself. If "the nation-state, as common territory and time" can be "subverted by diasporic attachments" (1997, 250), as Clifford asserts, then Mitchell and Hulme's spiral claim to both an indigenous and a diasporic presence/present has profound ramifications. This is why it is not an accident that Hulme locates the historic (and somewhat unrecognized) core of the new nation as an ancient voyaging canoe that signifies prior Maori arrival to Aotearoa, invested with mauri or the land's life force. In similar ways to *Amokura* and its "treasure-box of earth," this destabilizes colonial Pakeha claims to land/nation and rescripts national genealogies in a tidalectic relation between land and sea, indigenous and arrivant. Significantly, Hulme's new national community is structured by a rhizomatic and contingent whakapapa, drawing upon the narrative spiral, suggesting a complex nationalism that cannot be simply reduced to "blood" ties.

While historic Maori migration is not directly depicted, the novel positions the Polynesian voyaging canoe as the literal and spiritual center of the novel. This is made apparent when the three main characters are separated by emotional and physical violence. Joe has beaten Simon so severely that the boy ends up in the hospital; denied access to his son, Joe travels across the country until a Maori elder, a living remnant of the precolonial past, rescues him. Meanwhile, Kerewin develops a tumor in her puku (belly) (a cancer of her meta-physical being)[32] and retreats to her cabin on the shore, anticipating her death. The elder who takes Joe in explains that the ancestors predicted his arrival, suggesting his incorporation into spiral time. When the elder dies, Joe is bequeathed guardianship of the canoe, called "the spirit of the islands . . . one of the great voyaging ships of our people." This great voyaging waka (vaka), "the heart of Aotearoa" is "asleep" because of the "mess the Pakeha have made" of the land (K. Hulme 1984, 364). Joe's quest for origins is posited as a meta-physical journey, the attainment of which can redeem both the land and the bicultural nation. The mysterious origins of Simon, the young Euro-Irish trickster of the novel, are discovered in the same chapter, when the heroin-dealing ship that brought him to Aotearoa/New Zealand is dredged from the ocean. The juxtaposition of two voyaging ships, one for an illegal trade associated with European capitalism and violence, and the other, a living facilitator of the ancient migration of Maori peoples and associated with the redemption of the land, are brought together to metonymically invoke the complex, transoceanic origins of the nation.

Like the buried "treasure-box of earth" beneath Rangiatea, Maori taonga (treasures) must be narratively recovered as foundations of national whakapapa. Both Hulme and Mitchell deconstruct what Henri Lefebvre refers to as the "illusion of [spatial] transparency," constitutive of colonial capitalism and philosophemes of *terra nullius*. He explains "the illusion of transparency goes hand in hand with a view of space as innocent, as free of traps or secret places. Anything hidden or dissimulated—and hence dangerous—is antagonistic to transparency, under whose reign everything can be taken in by a single glance" (1991, 28). By unearthing the complex, sacred and "hidden" foundations of Aotearoa/New Zealand, both Hulme and Mitchell disclose the ways in which the nation-state's panopticon, which renders both natural space and national ideologies as transparent, fails to recognize the opaque layerings of multiethnic, national, and natural soil.

In Hulme's novel, only when the "heart" of Aotearoa is recuperated and regenerated can the broader national family be woven in the fabric of whakapapa. This is apparent when an earthquake awakens the ship, conveniently relieving Joe of his isolated guardianship and facilitating his reunion with Kerewin and her now legally adopted son. Simon explains that his new family "only make sense together . . . if we are not, we are broken. We are nothing." He observes, they are "not family, not whanau . . . maybe there aren't words for us yet?" Hulme is clearly searching for a definition of whakapapa that offers a less heteronormative and reproductive modality. Her pun, "*E nga iwi, o nga iwi*" (author's emphasis 1983, 395), also visible in the novel's title, comes closest to defining such new familial/communal groupings that are not circumscribed by western linear time. Hulme translates her pun as "O the bones of the people" (the ancestors) and "O the people of the bones (i.e., the beginning people, the people who make another people)" (450). This brings the past and present together in a corporeal way that highlights the dynamic process of nation-building rather than a linear and cognatic genealogical trajectory. The national unification of multicultural bodies is suggested in Hulme's corporeal language—she describes that any dualist "pairing" will merely result in "nothing more than people by themselves . . . . But all together, they have become the heart and muscles and mind of something perilous and new, something strange and growing and great" (4).[33]

As lateral as these corporeal images may appear, *the bone people* suggests that multiethnic settlers must draw upon the Maori "heart of Aotearoa" before successfully regenerating the island nation. In an interview with Elizabeth Alley, Hulme explains, "You must respect all aspects of your ancestry. You cannot choose one and raise it to a superiority over the other" (Alley 1992, 143). While this is evidenced by the polysemic, creolized Kerewin, the invocation of the voyaging canoe functions as the originary foundation of whakapapa, which in turn precipitates a differently inflected architecture of the nation than Mitchell's meetinghouse and church. Interestingly, after Kerewin recovers from her illness, she immediately starts "rebuilding the Maori hall because it seemed, in [her] spiral fashion, the straightforward thing to do." She's assisted by anonymous Maori characters who wonder "why [she] was playing with their relic" (1983, 431). Importantly, Hulme avoids any direct description of its architecture, a significant break from her literary counterparts who have invested the meetinghouse with indigenous historiography. Unlike the specific Arawa and Tainui supports of *Amokura*, Hulme narratively re-erects "old gateposts" that are undescribed, unnamed, and thus bereft of a particular history. Having "relit" the symbolic "fire," Kerewin "sinks gracefully into oblivion" (1983, 432) and returns to her tower. Like the unnamed and thus detribalized voyaging canoe, *the bone people* avoids specific or localized historiography in an effort to establish a broader and more lateral network of relations.[34]

The novel is rather ambiguous about centralizing sacred Maori structures as the symbolic architecture of Aotearoa/New Zealand and hence constructs an alternative vision that draws upon both European and indigenous epistemologies. This is underscored by Kerewin's partial destruction of her isolated (phallic) tower and the rebuilding of a populated, spiral home. Or as she describes it, "a shell-shape, a regular spiral of rooms expanding around the decapitated Tower . . . privacy, apartness, but all connected and all part of the whole . . . it will be a studio and hall and church and guesthouse . . . but above all else, HOME. Home in a larger sense than I've used the term before" (434). At the conclusion of the novel, the reunion of "nga iwi" takes place in Kerewin's new spiral house and importantly incorporates her previously estranged "blood" relatives, suggesting a nationalist imaginary that assumes cognatic, arboreal, and rhizomorphous relations of whakapapa. Hulme's redefinition of national identity situates Maori arrival as the primary site of origins, yet incorporates later settlers in this new architecture of the nation.

While Hulme has been criticized for what is perceived as assimilationist ideology, few critics have pointed out how European history in this novel is subsumed by Maoritanga, or the Maori way.[35] For instance, Simon is a combination of multiple Maori and western myths: at various times he represents Simon Peter in the New Testament, Caliban of *The Tempest*, and the trickster demigods of Celtic and Polynesian lore. Yet the spiral structure of the novel clearly prioritizes originary Maori whakapapa as a founding narrative. Rather than allowing Maori to "sink into the white potato and no longer exist as a race" (1984, 39), as Donna Awatere describes

New Zealand bicultural practices, Hulme reverses the terms: Pakeha must accept Maori migratory history and primary arrival upon the islands before successful nationhood is achieved. Because Simon's Euro-Celtic origins and language are severed, European claims to New Zealand settlement are subsumed by the ancient, "breathing" (K. Hulme 1983, 364) presence of the Polynesian voyaging canoe. This entails a different conception of national, western time. As Ranginui Walker explains, "On a genealogical time scale extending to the mythological time of the gods, historic events in Maori thought are as fresh in the memory as if they happened only yesterday. To the Pakeha, events of a hundred years ago are considered ancient history" (1987, 212). In *the bone people*, the living canoe, invested with mauri, becomes the nexus of the national past and future.

Both Hulme and Mitchell offer a vital challenge to so-called minority discourses that rely far more on modern diasporic historiography than is generally acknowledged. For instance, Homi Bhabha's "Dissemination: Time, narrative and the margins of the modern nation," poses an informative reading of the "double-time" inscribed by the "minority" writer, who destabilizes the "pedagogical . . . [narration] of national authority in a tradition of the people" (1994, 147). In other words, "double time" deconstructs western hegemonies that institute a monolithic formation of national identity that dispossesses minority populations. While Bhabha argues that the racial minority's "performative" time of the nation is overlaid upon an "archaic, atavistic temporality of Tradition" (149), these layerings of time and space are destabilized by indigenous presence. Since native history and ontology is prior to European settlement, there are "alter/native"—and more originary—models of national tradition that dismantle "pedagogical" authorities. Rather than posing Maori time, tradition, and modernity against Pakeha narrations of the national imagined community, Hulme and Mitchell assimilate Pakeha tradition within the former, thereby neither evoking, nor even acknowledging, a "pedagogical" national trajectory. In fact, Bhabha's reading of "minority" discourse cannot be applied to indigenous writers whose histories necessarily predate the arrival of subsequent settlers. Juxtaposing theories of "minority" discourse against an indigenous narration of place highlights the dangers of defining migration as a phenomenon of (post)colonial modernity. This also confirms my suspicion that much of the so-called minority discourse theory produced in the United States and United Kingdom neglects indigenous historiography in favor of transatlantic diaspora. The suppression of indigenous nationalisms discursively erases precolonial narratives of time and space.

Routes and Roots in the "Pacific Beyond"

Due to the economic, political, and social changes brought about by the
European Economic Community, the institution of an antinuclear policy
in the early 1980s, and increasing Pacific Island and Asian immigration,
Aotearoa/New Zealand has been consciously constructing a separate identity from its colonial "motherland" and aligning itself with its geographi-
cally closer neighbors in the Pacific. For European-identified New Zealanders, this represents a radically different paradigm, which destabilizes
previous attachments to the British colonial past. As many scholars and
artists have pointed out, a less Eurocentric vision is needed to cognitively
and economically remap Aotearoa/New Zealand in relation to the broader
Pacific. Ranginui Walker explains, "Pakeha New Zealanders are no longer
European. They are adrift in the South Pacific and must come to terms
with that reality. They have to learn to become Pacific people" (1987,
228).

193

The bone people anticipates Walker's contention that Pakeha are culturally "adrift"; this is signified by Simon's accidental arrival. Hulme positions
him as human jetsam, "goods thrown overboard to lighten the ship" (1983,
82). In the prologue of the novel, entitled "The End at The Beginning,"
the origins of Kerewin, Joe, and Simon are explored. The adults are already
somewhat "rooted" and caught in a network of (fractured) personal relations, but Simon is quite literally unmoored. Hulme describes his genesis
in terms derived from the Old Testament: "In the beginning, it was darkness, and more fear, and a howling wind across the sea" (3). Although both
peoples must dredge their diasporan origins into the national presence/
present, there is a marked historiographic difference between the illegal
jetsam of Pakeha arrival, and the voyaging canoe "that knifed across the
great Kiwa [Pacific] centuries ago ... guided by stars, powered by the wind
and by the muscles of stronghearted women and men" (366). Like the British schooner that brings Mere's husband to Aotearoa in *Amokura*, these
two novels suggest a diasporic and specifically transoceanic formulation of
national and, by extension, regional belonging, provided that Pakeha "learn
to become Pacific people."[36] When read alongside the Pacific voyaging literature discussed in the previous chapter, Mitchell and Hulme's texts are
ultimately more concerned with national cartographies than "recharting
Polynesia." Both novels echo Ihimaera's proposition that "as far as New
Zealand is concerned, we must come to terms with the Pacific within us
before we can grapple with the Pacific beyond us" (1991, 140).

In conclusion, I'd like to expand this discussion of "the Pacific beyond" by aligning Mitchell and Hulme's telos of national whakapapa closer to the methodologies of etak navigation. David Lewis suggests that this indigenous and polydimensional system of reference is an important alternative to the necessary distortions of European cartography, which reduce the complexity of a sphere into a flat plane (1994, 142). Many scholars have shown how nineteenth-century British cartography—an attempt to inscribe and thus ideologically fix colonial territories and cultures—reflects the spatial contours of empire and, by extension, the nation-state. In a similar fashion one might position etak as an indigenous cognitive mapping that is homologous to the nationalist cartographies of both *Amokura* and *the bone people*. Like each novel's inscription of national time-space, etak allows for the direct participation of indigenous subjects in a nexus of temporal and spatial dimensions.

Unlike the western system of navigation that fixes one narrow target or telos, etak relies upon an "expanding target" destination, which "expand[s] the range at which islands may be located, a concept quite foreign to exact instrumental navigation, and one most unlikely to owe anything at all to Western influence" (Lewis 1994, 207). This "expanding target" paradigm relies upon oral histories of navigation, dead reckoning, star compasses, and the successful interpretation of environmental phenomena; systems of national navigation that I have traced through both novels. Importantly, the texts examined in this chapter offer an alternative and polydimensional reckoning of both time and space in ways that destabilize the conflation of botanic metaphors with sedentary roots. The voyaging canoes of Hulme and Mitchell's novels evoke national routes, while the transported soil from Hawaiki suggests oceanic roots. This is not surprising when one considers the narratives of Maui, the trickster demigod who "fished up" the North Island. Among many Maori, the North Island is referred to as "Te Ika a Maui" (Maui's fish), while the South Island is conceptualized as Maui's waka, or canoe. Thus Aotearoa's indigenous cartography utilizes a far more fluid series of metaphors than any of the arboreal philosophemes examined within postcolonial or diasporan studies. As such, this offers an important alter/native to the homogenizing discourses of the terrestrial nation-state.

Significantly, one can map a broader Pacific conceptualization of destabilized routes and roots by examining the semantics of navigational "swell pattern analysis" (Lewis 1994, 207). Marshallese navigators refer to these wave patterns in terms of the body and land: swells from the east are referred to as the "backbone" (194), while a series of intersecting pairs of swells are termed a "root." Following the watery "root" leads to trees (the arboreal) and the land (national soil) (198). This fluid arboreal system of routes and roots, or watery roots, can be likened to Mitchell and Hulme's collective images of relocated soil, diasporic metaphors, feminized transplants such as flax, as well as the ancient voyaging canoes that function as indigenous foundations of the new nation. Because the navigational telos of etak conceptualizes "expanding" rather than narrow homogenous targets, this system has particular resonance with the ways in which both novelists literally expand the definition of the nation's whakapapa, from the hierarchical and colonial nation-state to a more dynamic and fluid conception of natural and national reckoning.

Adrift and Unmoored
Globalization and Urban Indigeneity

I am both indigenous and one of the newcomers.
—Albert Wendt, "Pacific Maps"

While the last chapter examined the natural and botanical meta-phors invoked by the roots of Maori diaspora and resettlement, here I focus on the repercussions of the presumably unnatural routes of indigenous urbanization and globalization in Aotearoa / New Zealand. The terms "globalization" and "indigeneity" may seem to be diametrically opposed. On the one hand, globalization invokes a specifically unnatural formulation of fractured, heterogeneous, and hierarchical social spaces that are constituted by the logic of transnational capital. Discourses of indigeneity, on the other hand, seem inextricably bound to natural, rooted, precapitalist, and communal formations that are at once constituted by the objectives of national sovereignty while simultaneously suppressed and romanticized by the nation-state. Generally speaking, one might trace a series of ideological oppositions between globalization and indigeneity along the lines of individualist/communal, unnatural/natural, urban/rural, transnational/national, and migratory/originary. This is why, it seems to me, that most of the research focused on the "time-space compression" (Harvey 1989, 147) of globalization is primarily concerned with recent migrations of capital and labor to the transnational metropole. These discourses that emphasize the material and social flows of the postmodern city seem epistemologically ill-equipped to engage with indigeneity due to its association with spatial continuity as well as protonational presence.

With the preponderance of spatial theories circulating in academic circles, one might assume that this would be an appropriate milieu in which to interject indigenous epistemologies of space. But this has been far from the case. As the introduction to this book has explained, postcolonial studies has increasingly embraced diaspora and globalization, so that indigenous presence, discourses, and practices, if noticed at all, are relegated to a footnote or are subsumed under the frameworks of African, Asian, and other migrant subjects. As James Clifford (1988), Arjun Appadurai (1988), and Johannes Fabian (1983) have pointed out, the anthropological "native" continues to be ideologically "incarcerated" in a homogenous, atemporal space. Conflated with a presumably passive and ahistorical landscape, the indigenous subject is rarely associated with modernity, unless it is to propose an essentialist critique of modernization. For example, in the 1970s United States, the most popular image of the modern indigenous subject derived from the influential Keep America Beautiful, Inc. television commercial. Building upon the assumed ontological divide between the modern and premodern subject (and deflecting corporate environmental destruction onto individual agents), the advertisement depicts an American Indian in "traditional" garb, traversing a polluted urban landscape. As a car speeds past him, ejecting litter at his feet, the camera zooms in to capture the silent (glycerin) tear he sheds over the nation's environmental destruction. I rehearse this image not to undermine indigenous communities who have been historically at the forefront of environmental conservation, and in fact have suffered disproportionately in terms of nuclear, industrial, and biotechnological waste, but rather to point out the near intractability of the indigenous-modern dyad. This actor, "Iron Eyes" Cody, could no more have been replaced with, say, an Asian- or European-American, than he could have been depicted as a mobile, modern subject in his own automobile. This is one reason why allegations that Cody was not Cree and Cherokee, as he claimed, but rather the son of Italian immigrants, have been so contentious. In this example the "Eco-Indian" functions as an ethical foil to white modernity.[1] In the rare instances when the popular imagination positions the indigenous subject in urban space, cultural death and "fatal impact" are assumed.

Yet theorizing an urbanized and/or diasporic native subject has also posed significant ontological crises in indigenous circles, particularly among populations who depend upon histories of continuous presence in order to substantiate land and resource claims against the colonial nation-state. For instance, heated debates have arisen in Pacific anthropological circles between critics who argue that identity is a process of intricate social construction, and native sovereignty theorists who utilize familial genealogies to authenticate cultural identity in settler nations such as Hawai'i and Aotearoa/New Zealand. The conflict hinges on the difference between historiography as a discursive symbolic mediation, and indigenous genealogies that prioritize corporeal relationships in, as I explained in the last chapter, "meta-physical" terms. As my reading of particular Maori novels has suggested, Pacific genealogies articulate dynamic systems of relation in both arborescent and naturalizing, rhizomatic forms. While I want to foreground what J. Kehaulani Kauanui refers to as "the contingency of genealogy" (1998, 692), I would like to examine the repercussions of abandoning the naturalistic metaphors that express Pacific kinship relations such as the flax plant (or, as Kauanui demonstrates in Hawai'i, taro) in urbanized indigenous spaces. Discourses of social construction often have undermined the epistemological foundation of indigenous sovereignty, yet the debates against it have also tended to suppress genealogical contingencies that have constituted Pacific relations long before European arrival. In this chapter I have chosen to navigate between the rather polarized positions expressed in this debate by examining Albert Wendt's dystopic novel, *Black Rainbow* (1992), which depicts a socially constructed and globalized indigenous urban subject who reflects a profoundly creolized identity. While discourses of creolization in the Caribbean context can be traced to the earliest stages of that region's colonial history, in some parts of Oceania, claiming multicultural antecedents may undermine indigenous claims to ancestral land. Since most settler nation-states require some type of blood quantum to authenticate identity, destabilizing native ancestry has significant material consequences. Creolization also poses a challenge to the legal and ontological bases upon which many tribal identities are formed. Given the entwined histories of institutional and indigenous discourses of ipseity, one cannot *simply* position a free-floating, deconstructed, and landless indigenous nomadism in the popular vein of academic cosmopolitanism.

These concerns have impacted the literary production of Albert Wendt, a Samoan who resided for decades in Aotearoa/New Zealand and was the chair of the English Department at the University of Auckland. As one of the most prolific and best-known writers from the Pacific Islands, Wendt's early novels, *Sons for the Return Home* (1973), *Pouliuli* (1977), and *Leaves of the Banyan Tree* (1979), examine the impact of colonial, especially Christian, modernity upon Samoan familial and communal structures. Ironically, given Wendt's sustained critique of anthropology in the romanticized "South Seas," these early novels were featured more often in departments of anthropology than literature (Sarti and Evans 1998, 212). Although his work is now central to Pacific literature courses, most attention has focused upon his early, more modernist-inflected novels than his later "postmodern" texts, which include *Black Rainbow* and *Ola* (1991). Critics seem to be far more comfortable with Wendt's earlier narratives, which critique colonialism (and its handmaiden, anthropology) through a fragmented yet historically and culturally coherent narrative subject, than his recent novels, which are far more radical in terms of destabilizing the authenticity of narrative form and voice.[2]

I suspect that this discomfort with urban and, by extension, globalized indigeneity can be traced to the radical changes that took place in Aotearoa / New Zealand in the 1970s and 1980s, which placed indigenous subjects in potentially liberating but also tenuous spatial and social positions. During the World War II era, 75 percent of Maori lived in historic, generally rural, tribal areas. By the 1970s, 80 percent of Maori had migrated to the nation's urban centers due to the expanding manufacturing sector and the centralization of industry in the cities (Durie 1998, 95). While urban Maori migration often destabilized familial and genealogical connections, it also contributed to productive pan-tribal allegiances. The activism, land occupations, and marches of the 1970s gradually brought New Zealand to recognize what is now referred to as the "founding document" of the nation: the 1840 Treaty of Waitangi, a contract of mutual sovereignty between Maori and British settlers. The shifting of regional trade blocs in the 1970s and 1980s, particularly Britain's move into the European Economic Community, led the New Zealand Labour government in 1984 to abandon its Keynesian welfare-state policies and embrace its Pacific (Rim) neighbors in expanding relations of trade and immigration. The state's deregulation of industries, coupled with increasing Maori, Pacific Island, European, and Asian immigration to the cities, contributed to the globalization of Aotearoa / New Zealand at the same moment that Maori began negotiating an unprecedented number of financial, political, and conceptual claims against the British Crown, represented by the New Zealand government.[3] Similar to the globalization of Hawai'i described in Chapter Two, the process of offering New Zealand resources, labor, and services into the world marketplace catalyzed a renewed wave of indigenous activism. The establishment of the 1986 State-Owned Enterprises Bill, which attempted to privatize state-held lands and assets, would have transferred alienated Maori resources directly to corporations without judicial consideration of tribal claims (Durie 1998, 182). After two years of negotiations, the Treaty of Waitangi State Enterprises Act introduced safeguards to protect Maori claims before domestic and transnational corporations could appropriate alienated land and fisheries (184). As I will explore in more detail later, the same act also provided funding and resources for the Waitangi Tribunal, a part-time investigative body first formed under the Treaty of Waitangi Act 1975, which registers, researches, and writes recommendations regarding Crown inconsistencies in honoring the principles of the Treaty with its Maori partners.[4] Recognition of the Treaty in the 1980s as a politically and legally binding document of Maori and Pakeha (white) partnership catalyzed an extraordinary number of legislative rulings that reconfigured the environmental, social, and financial spaces of the nation.

While I will return to these transformations to the sociopolitical fabric of Aotearoa/New Zealand, my point here is to give some context for Wendt's dystopic novel and to suggest the ways in which state and global hegemonic forces have constituted Maori discourses of space-time continuity *and* discontinuity. As I have already explored the epistemological importance of tracing indigenous genealogies, or whakapapa, in the last chapter, one can see how the recent urbanization and social reconstitution of the majority of Maori has posed challenges to the traditional histories that must be performed for both the Waitangi Tribunal and the Office of Treaty Settlements. In other words, just as many Maori became urbanized and in many cases alienated from their whakapapa, the treaty claims process has required that they provide authentication of their "traditional" indigenous status, rendered along familial and spatial genealogies as well as tribal affiliations. This is hardly the arena in which to glibly deconstruct the history of indigenous presence.[5]

Given this context, it is not a surprise that Wendt's *Black Rainbow* directly engages with the forces of corporate globalization and urban indigeneity in Aotearoa/New Zealand. He destabilizes essentialist discourses of "native blood" by presenting urban characters who are constituted by multiethnic genealogies and complex, often competing global discourses. While the novel has often been categorized as postmodern, a complex term glossed by David Harvey as a destabilization of "eternal and immutable elements" (1989, 44), *Black Rainbow*'s recovery of urban genealogies poses an alternative narrative of temporal and spatial continuity. As a result, Wendt repeatedly uses the term "deconstruction" as a synonym for the death of his characters.

Wendt's futuristic novel opens with his protagonist completing his oral history "confessions" to the significantly named state "Tribunal." After deeming that he is a "Free Citizen," the New Zealand state then relocates his wife and children to an unknown place, provides the unnamed hero with a series of written and verbal clues, and structures a quest around the board game Monopoly, with financial compensation for each successfully fulfilled segment of his mission. The Tribunal employs "Hunters" to help the protagonist "enjoy" this artificial "Game of Life," convincing the protagonist that the game is "real," and "full of risk" (Wendt 1992, 37–38). Without irony, the narrator concludes, "The Tribunal certainly knew how to give meaning to our lives" (38). Written in first-person narrative form, the novel depicts the central figure's subsequent travels all over the North Island, from urban to suburban and rural topographies, articulating a phe- nomenology of landscape in this state-sponsored search for his modern (indigenous) family. While the narrative is inscribed in the chronological, real time of the protagonist, it results in the character's partial recovery of his indigenous genealogy and history, an entirely different understanding of family than he had anticipated. Although Wendt borrows freely and self-consciously from a large repertoire of (post)modern narratives, from the dystopic films *Blade Runner* and *2001: A Space Odyssey* to the novels *Brave New World*, *1984*, and *One Flew over the Cuckoo's Nest*, his text ultimately affirms a localized and corporeal definition of place in the wake of globalized, postmodern, and corporate hegemonies. Like David Harvey's work, Wendt suggests that "cosmopolitanism bereft of geographical specificity remains abstracted and alienated reason, liable, when it comes to earth, to produce all manner of unintended and sometimes explosively evil consequences" (Harvey 2000, 557). The protagonist's most meaningful relationship is established with the native and urban "True Ones," resistant indigenous characters who are the only ones capable of living outside the panopticon of the corporate state and who function as its suppressed foundation. *Black Rainbow* has cleverly incorporated many of the ideologies utilized in the poststructuralist call for a politics of culture modeled on a simulacrum that denies authentic origins, and it seems to be a direct engagement with the scholarship of Fredric Jameson, Jean-François Lyotard, and Jean Baudrillard.[6] As the novel demonstrates, these deconstructive critical methodologies destabilize cultural origins and thus are not easily reconciled with indigenous epistemologies of genealogical continuity.

This chapter can be read as a response to James Clifford's call to press the limits of terms such as Anthony Appiah's "rooted cosmopolitans," and to engage critically with a kind of "indigenous cosmopolitanism" that does not polarize routes and roots and which does not simply rehearse the linear model of colonial modernity (Clifford 2001, 470, 476–477).[7] I have adopted a tidalectic methodology that foregrounds a type of globalized indigeneity that cannot be reduced to overdetermined structures (where agency cannot exist) and which also problematizes ahistorical simulacra that destabilize native genealogy. In its recuperation of the term "native," this work builds upon the scholarship of Teresia Teaiwa (2001b) in recognizing its roots in the constitution of the western anthropological imagination as well as a viable, shifting, and self-reflexive position of ontological, epistemological, and political subjectivity. Wendt's novel presents a *mediated* genealogical

202

origin in that the protagonist recovers his indigenous heritage, positioning the (historical) body as a site of resistance, while calling attention to its social and narrative construction. His implementation of a destabilized genealogical "essence" calls into question what has been called the novel's postmodernism. While the novel offers a surface of postmodern aesthetics, its foundation derives from a historical politics in which knowledge of the Maori context of Aotearoa/New Zealand is vital. This is why *Black Rainbow* emphasizes the indigenous subject's struggle with postmodern intertextuality in a quest to seek what the protagonist calls the "blank spaces" where native agency may be inscribed.

Globalizing Deconstruction: A Selective Genealogy of the Pacific Islands Debate

Globalization certainly is not restricted to the material movements of peoples and commodities, but also includes what Edward Said (1983) and James Clifford (1992) refer to as "travelling theories"; in this case deconstructive methodologies have traveled from Euro-American metropoles to the Pacific Islands and adapted for various purposes.[8] The debates in Hawai'i between Roger Keesing, Jocelyn Linnekin, and Haunani-Kay Trask suggest that this was the first terrain of significant—and contentious—impact. A remarkably similar debate later surfaced in Aotearoa/New Zealand after the publication of Allan Hanson's article, "The Making of the Maori" (1989) over the extent to which native identities are socially constructed. In the early 1980s, in the midst of intense indigenous activism, anthropologist Jocelyn Linnekin published a number of essays that positioned Kanaka Maoli cultural revival as socially constructed. Like other scholarship focused on invented traditions,[9] Linnekin argued with Richard Handler that "to refer to the past, to take account of or interpret it, implies that one is located in the present, that one is distanced . . . the relationship of prior to present is symbolically mediated, not naturally given" (Handler and Linnekin 1984, 287). The layering of a symbolic relationship to the past over the *naturalizing* genealogical ties that constitute indigenous identities spurred deep controversy in Hawai'i. The "invention of tradition" debate was taken to a disturbing extreme by the U.S. government in 1985 during hearings about the appropriation of the island of Kaho'olawe, which had been terribly damaged by U.S. military operations. Citing Linnekin's work on how Kanaka Maoli "constructed" the sacredness of Kaho'olawe, the Navy report concluded that indigenous claims were simple "fakery" (Trask 1991, 166). After the suspicious deaths of two activists occupying the island, the bombing "exercises" were discontinued in 1990, although the United States still maintains over 100 military installations in the state and counting.[10] While Linnekin responded with a critique of the Navy's use of her scholarship (1991, 175), it is clear that the U.S. military-industrial complex was astute enough to implement vulgar deconstructive methodologies for its own hegemonic ends. I have cited this example because as critics, we need to think carefully about the material, social, and political consequences of destabilizing originary narratives of history. Following the work of Barbara Johnson and others, my point is to suggest that further investigations are needed to address the uneven "consequences of theory" (1991). Here deconstruction functions as a strand in the complex fabric of globalization; its localization in Hawai'i has had a profound impact on the Kanaka Maoli sovereignty movement.

While scholarship in the Pacific has been marked by serious contention over "how natives think," anthropologist Roger Keesing took the social constructivist argument to an alarming extreme.[11] In "Creating the past," Keesing disavowed indigenous agency by contending that Pacific Island "assertions of identity based on idealizations of the ancestral past draw heavily on anthropological concepts—particularly ideas about 'culture'—as they have entered Western popular thought." These idealizations, Keesing argued, were "derivatives of Western critiques of modern technology and progress" (1989, 23). In this vulgar deconstruction, the polarized divide between Pacific cultural nationalists and anthropologists becomes most visible. Keesing concluded that native "rhetoric is itself squarely shaped by anthropology's concepts and categories" (24). While not the lone voice in this train of thought,[12] Keesing's genealogy did not leave any strategies for indigenous activists to challenge Euro-American occupation beyond a binary reactionism. When Haunani-Kay Trask responded scathingly (1991), Keesing defined her argument as "a great leap backward . . . a quarter century out of date" (1991, 168). In Keesing's terms, indigenous peoples struggle to keep up with the "progressive" scholarship of the academic, whose path-breaking ideology predetermines future counter-discourse. According to this line of argument, indigenous resistance is unthinkable without its western intellectual genealogy. Rather than following the vein of deconstructive methodologies by destabilizing ontological and interpretive certainty, Keesing evacuated indigenous epistemologies and enclosed them within a European genealogical framework. Unable to break itself from a Manichean bind of power and counter-resistance, the native subject, in Keesing's argument, is forever locked in a (false) aporia. This impetus to break free of western epistemologies of resistance has profoundly influenced Wendt's vision of the entanglement between indigenous subjects and the state apparatus that enforces "liberation" from personal, cultural, and national history. In *Black Rainbow*, the protagonist's struggle is analogous to the debate described above: to secure a strategy for indigenous sovereignty that is neither predetermined by western epistemology nor a facile reaction against it.

Native Historicism and the State

The issues I have summarized above are by no means isolated to Hawai'i. In 1989 U.S. ethnographer Allan Hanson argued a similar reappraisal of Maori historiography, including the legend of the Great Fleet of the first Polynesian arrivants to Aotearoa/New Zealand (1989). Although he was not the first scholar to suggest the process of Maori cultural invention, his work caused considerable debate precisely because of the political and economic reconfigurations instituted by the New Zealand state in this era.[13] According to Jonathan Lamb, Hanson's work was not well received because "it was politically as well as culturally insensitive to cast doubt on the authenticity of tribal memories at the very time the perceived accuracy of these memories was crucial" to treaty claims (Lamb 1990, 667).[14]

A series of meetings were held at the University of Auckland over the implications of Hanson's article, where Wendt held a chair and during the period he was writing *Black Rainbow*. The globalization of the New Zealand market, the social construction debate, and the institution of government agencies to process treaty claims all seem to have informed Wendt's futuristic vision of a dehistoricized society that *absorbs* native history. Significantly, his protagonist is a bank clerk who becomes entwined in a Kafkaesque superstructure of a global surveillance state called the Tribunal. It is only towards the end of the narrative that we learn his name, Eric Mailei Foster: "another character out of fiction rooted in Franz Kafka's faceless nightmares" (Wendt 1992, 229). Strikingly reminiscent of the Waitangi Tribunal hearings process, *Black Rainbow* is framed by the protagonist's "confessions" of his personal history so that "the self-sacrificing Tribunal" will "assume the guilt and responsibility" for discrimination against natives and others. After these histories have been "confessed," the Tribunal requires its citizens to live "wholly in the present, the eternal instant" (28), literally absorbing and thus homogenizing personal and cultural inequity. The emphasis on the "ever-moving present" (148), adopted from Huxley's *Brave New World*, resonates with the social constructivist stance discussed earlier and suggests a rather disturbing telos for the state's involvement in treaty reparations. As Mason Durie has pointed out, many fear that once Maori claims are settled, the treaty will be relegated to the remote past, becoming an archaic historical document rather than a founding—and guiding—tenet of the nation (1998, 213).

In the above cases, access to and interpretation of history have been denied to those who have the most at stake in its compensation. In the suggestively titled chapter, "No History/Herstory," Wendt's narrator observes about himself and his wife, "I have no history. She has no herstory. Our children's history began with us but that's all—there is no time before that. History is a curse, the Tribunal has ruled. We must be free of it to be" (1992, 21). The Tribunal's philosophy sounds suspiciously like Keesing's "aspir[ation] to liberate us from pasts, both those of our ancestors and those of [colonial or other] domination" (1989, 25). Yet far from sanctioning this erasure of history, Wendt's narrator knows there "must be an easier way of defeating evil, stopping the rewriting of history" (1992, 65). As the novel reveals, the Tribunal's objective is more accurately defined as the *rescription* rather than "liberation" of history.

It is not a coincidence that *Black Rainbow*'s Tribunal consists of a chairperson and two members, which reflects the Waitangi Tribunal constituency as established by the 1975 Treaty Act.[15] While the Waitangi Tribunal appoints its members in three-year terms, Wendt's three-member Tribunal changes every week; his protagonist "imaged the Tribunal [as] an indefinite line of threes, much like a hive, functioning to the same purpose, pattern, design" (24). His invocation of the hive is a reference to the Wellington "Beehive," a building that houses the Executive Wing of Parliament, where all legislative acts regarding the treaty are established and where settlements are signed. Interestingly, the Tribunal that awards the protagonist with his "final reference" paper, which interpellates him as an "ideal citizen" who "survived" the "prescribed Process of Dehistoricizing" (33), is represented by important writers and historians of the Pacific. While one of the first Waitangi Tribunal members was M. P. K. Sorrenson, whose most famous work includes a debunking of the colonialist myth of the Great Fleet of Maori settlers, in Wendt's text this figure is replaced by Bernard Smith, author of *European Vision and the South Pacific* (1959), an early deconstruction of colonialist Orientalism that predated Edward Said's work by almost twenty years. As such, the Pacific roots of the social construction debate may be traced to Smith, whose work was directed at European rather than indigenous cultural mythologies.[16]

Questions of public and state historiography were at the forefront of national consciousness in the time period Wendt was writing *Black Rain-*

bow. A year before its publication, the Waitangi Tribunal had released a three-volume report on the Ngai Tahu tribal claims, unprecedented in terms of local historical scope. Tribunal historians began to publish queries about the tightening relationship between academic research and the state. In "History and historians before the Waitangi Tribunal," Tribunal member Alan Ward suggested that for some, the extension of the Tribunal's jurisdiction to claims dating back to the 1840 treaty meant "that it opened to judicial scrutiny most of New Zealand's colonial history in a community ill-prepared to handle the possible consequences" (Ward 1990, 150). Raising the question as to what it means to align academic historians with "one of the most important arenas of state authority, a tribunal of the Department of Justice" (151), Ward called for reflection about the epistemologies at work in the Tribunal's narrative consolidation of the testimony of lawyers, historians, activists, claimants, elders, and state officials. As Ward and Giselle Byrnes have pointed out, changes in government policy towards the treaty in the 1980s resulted in an unprecedented demand for national historians to service Maori claimants, the Tribunal, and the Crown. Historiography became a lucrative business and an expanded domain of the state. In a nation that was detaching itself from the British "motherland" and had only recently introduced local history into school curricula, Tribunal reports became common texts in New Zealand history courses.[17] These vital issues about the uses and abuses of historiography in the service of the state are analogous to *Black Rainbow*'s broader questions about the politics of history.

If we can reduce the treaty proceedings to one of bicultural substitution—the transfer of Maori collective memories to the settler state in exchange for resources, capital, and the recognition of rangatiratanga (sovereignty), Wendt's novel suggests that the linear trajectory of global capitalism, increasingly entangled with the New Zealand state, will appropriate and transfigure memories of colonization. In *Black Rainbow*, oral testimonies are "replaced with histories that please us" (Wendt 1992, 65), signifying an institutionalization of contemporary desire grafted over the legacy of historical misdeeds. While the Waitangi Tribunal has made a tremendous contribution to the print media distribution of local historiography (and has handled these materials very sensitively), the potential for appropriation in these new global configurations is significant. This helps explain why the protagonist's personal history and quest for his family are reshaped and broadcast "worldwide, as a shining example of how every citizen should play the Game of Life" (181).

Wendt's frequent references to state media, particularly television and newspapers, become more meaningful when we place them in some historical context. In 1989 the Labour government deregulated the media, causing the then Minister of Broadcasting to boast of "the most open communications market in the world" (Kelsey 1995, 112). Within two years, over 90 percent of metropolitan newspapers were controlled by two transnational corporations (including Rupert Murdoch), Radio New Zealand went bankrupt, and all television media became either privatized and/or owned by U.S. and Canadian conglomerates. Local prime-time programming for television immediately fell to 12 percent. (Kelsey 1995, 112–113). As with the deregulation of state-owned lands and fisheries, Maori were deeply concerned that there were no safeguards to maintain cultural programming, particularly the Maori language, which is protected under the treaty.[18] The rapid consolidation of New Zealand telecommunications into transnational corporate hands had a profound impact in terms of delocalizing the national imaginary, a shift that Wendt has repeatedly commented upon in his essays and has integrated into the novel. Our narrator, a prolific consumer of beer, international food, flash cars, expensive clothing, and Hollywood sitcoms, is deeply entangled in American technology's "mobilization of desire and fantasy," but is as yet unclear about its "politics of distraction" and homogenization of historical time and space (Harvey 1989, 61).[19] By the time he is able to critically "re-read" the Tribunal's metanarrative, he is already quite literally absorbed into state-televised media, broadcast "worldwide" as a hero, a product of transnational exchange and desire.[20]

In *Black Rainbow*'s surveillance state, the power to determine what is "pleasing" and to whom is monopolized by the faceless powers of the Tribunal. Movements labeled under the guise of destabilizing history are revealed to be a concealment of the hegemony that seeks to erase the unequal repercussions of colonization. This is demonstrated by the Tribunal's repeated substitution of the term "history" with "guilt," which ultimately produces an assimilated and homogenous state subject. Since citizens must "confess" to the Tribunal their presumed historical complicity with some unstated misdeed, the Tribunal is unable to fully enact "dehistoricization," which it defines as the effort "to be free of our past, our guilt" (Wendt 1992, 33).[21]

A critique of the conceptual inability to abandon history is made in the novel's many allusions to the protagonist's increasingly "savage" behavior. In the process of his quest, the narrator is faced with a number of violent struggles, nearly all of which result in his opponent's death ("deconstruction") or serious injury. He admits, "I'd panicked at the way I'd become someone else, a savage" (77), which is confirmed with numerous other references of his reversion to "savagery" (98, 11, 184). The currency of this term is notable for two reasons. First, the Tribunal system of the "ever-moving present" (106) cannot be maintained without a dialectical engagement with the past. Like the anthropological arguments to empty the signification of history, such "liberation" is a temporal impossibility in a capitalist telos. Since the Tribunal has banished mortality, hunger, violence, and even metaphysics, the state is founded on the movement of capitalist "progress" beyond the "savagery" of history. Despite its assurance otherwise, the state's *teleology* is profoundly entangled with its assumed binary opposite: native *genealogy*. Because history has left a palpable residue, the supposedly timeless state cannot entirely suppress indigenous historical difference. This capitalogic model of history cannot be fully enforced because linear, "progressive" time presupposes a "savage" past from which it must advance. Although the narrator is racially unmarked for most of the novel, his constant dismissal by salesmen and service employees suggests a tangible residue of racism that constitutes the market sector of the state's "ever-moving present." Since nearly everyone interpellates him as "brown" (193), he is continually monitored for native "reversion." Thus, both national and individual histories become entangled despite the Tribunal's prescription that its citizens live in the "eternal instant" (28).[22] Of course it is his simultaneous "progress" in this teleological quest, coupled with his increasingly violent "degeneration," that makes the worldwide broadcast of his life so popular. As my discussion explains below, the narrator needs to discredit the free-floating, history-as-simulacra lauded by the Tribunal in order to find the "essence" and origins of his family. In *Black Rainbow*, the recovery of a native family (in its broadest symbolic definition) can only be achieved by negating postmodern atemporality.

While the narrator initially believes history is a "curse" (21) he gradually learns through his association with the True Ones that the Tribunal is "reordinarizing" its citizens into placid "otherworlders" whose livelihood is dependent on the Tribunal's master structure. While the events of the novel take place in Aotearoa/New Zealand, Wendt emphasizes that this surveillance structure is constituted by an alliance between local, state, and transglobal capitalism. For instance, the Puzzle Palace that the protagonist must "re-read" (147) in order to secure his family is a U.S. creation, proliferated globally by the Council of Capitalist Presidents (82). As Paul Sharrad points out (2003, 209), Wendt adopted the term from James Bamford's exposé of the U.S. National Security Agency, *The Puzzle Palace*

(209). In an essay Wendt explains his "chilling fear" about "the largest, most efficient and sophisticated information-gathering storehouses in the world" (1987, 86). *Black Rainbow* makes the connections between the hegemonies of state, military, and global capitalism explicit. The narrator must theoretically challenge (reread) this structure in order to exist beyond its totalizing parameters.

The protagonist's struggle to maintain difference in the face of capitalist homogenization is central to the novel; the ironically named "*other-worlders*" embrace everything except social or cultural difference. While many have pointed out the ways in which the postmodern city is constituted by heterogeneous and intersecting social geographies, Wendt's Tribunal has cordoned off specific urban Zones, which, while providing socially forbidden pleasures, are ultimately "guided scientifically" (1992, 82). Those that push the literal boundaries of these Zones (which include theaters for literary fetishes and romancing the "South Seas") are sent off to "reordinarization" centers. Offering a sanitized and monitored space for the limited circulation of desire, these Zones contain and control difference through state mediation, reconfiguring Foucault's spatial "heterotopias" (1986) into temporal "homotopias." Otherworlder difference is absorbed and homogenized by the Tribunal's metastructure in ways similar to Keesing's move to assimilate native agency within the boundaries of western epistemology. Reading Wendt's Pacific metropolis alongside Appadurai's well-known discussion of the overlapping mediascapes, technoscapes, finanscapes, and ideoscapes of the postmodern city (1996), we might conclude that the late capitalist homogenization of these four elements has placed the *ethnoscape* under constant erasure.

The Nuclear Pacific: Master Narratives and Local Resistance

Wendt's protagonist consistently struggles to establish autonomy and difference amidst literary, capitalist, and state metanarratives. After his successful completion of the "process of Dehistoricizing" (1992, 33), he must relocate and reconstitute his immediate family. Its state-orchestrated disappearance foregrounds the Tribunal's need to assert itself as a nonbiological familial replacement in the modality of many national imagined communities. Consequently the narrator is continually reminded of the "usual truth" that "THE TRIBUNAL IS YOUR FAMILY" (35). Given the importance of establishing tribal and genealogical affiliations for the treaty claims process, Wendt's suggestion that the state appropriates ethnic kinship relations in order to replace them with homogenous institutional networks under the guise of "forgiveness" is not accidental. In perhaps the most devastating critique of the treaty reparations process, one of Wendt's characters composes this jingle: *"Repentant fool is the rule ... forgiveness is what sells consumer civilization / to pagans, socialists and other non-capitalists"* (170 author's emphasis).

Due to the "confession" of his familial history, the narrator remains unaware of his indigenous heritage for a good portion of the novel. His acquisition of native genealogy is primarily fostered through female characters, rendering a division between the paternal actions of the state and the feminized roots of indigenous culture.[23] This echoes the gendered binary embedded in critiques of the "molestation" of local, feminized cultures by the masculinized processes of globalization that I explored in the introduction. Since the narrator "discovers" his/tory through the Tribunal president's computer files, his access to indigeneity is mediated by the technologies of surveillance. Like current attempts to historicize a pre-European past, access to tradition is negotiated through the archives of missionaries, literate settlers, and the colonial state. This causes an interpretive aporia in the text, in which genealogy and history are accessible—to readers and the protagonist—only through the archives of the Tribunal computer. As Sharrad notes, the "hero succeeds in his rebellion according to the rules of what the book questions: both he and the Tribunal ultimately rely on *factual* accuracy, even though their collective games are all fabular/discursive constructs" (2003, 213).

In *Black Rainbow*, the protagonist's quest and its narration through print and visual technologies seem overdetermined by the genres of twentieth-century science fiction, social realism, dystopia, and the detective novel. Because the Tribunal has self-consciously integrated various fictions into the protagonist's quest, Wendt highlights the entanglement between literary and institutional narratives of the nation. For instance, the Tribunal requires that the protagonist read a Janet Frame novel (*Faces in the Water*, 1961) before embarking on his familial quest, and this alters the protagonist's view of the New Zealand landscape and implicates the novel in the nation-building tradition. Wendt continually plays with intertextuality, seeking a space for native agency amidst master narratives. For instance, Sister Honey and Nurse Ratched, characters from Frame's (1961) and Ken Kesey's (1962) novels respectively, capture the protagonist and complain they are trapped in their authors' narrative frames. Since they are Tribunal agents, they highlight the way in which the state can appropriate critiques of hegemonic institutions for its own homogenizing ends, in remarkably similar ways to the absorption of Waitangi Tribunal historiographies. When they inject him with "Erectol," a drug that induces sexual desire without orgasmic relief, Wendt invokes the Japanese Floating World (ukiyo) of the Tokugawa period, a timeless and sensual artistic space that transcends the banalities of mortality and earthly things. Wendt's Floating World is also devoid of sociopolitical history, and he situates this moment of meta-intertextuality in the transitory space of a hotel room. While these elements are similar to the traditional ukiyo, Wendt suggests sexual and individual desires are ultimately unattainable. This intertextual maneuver creates a *circumscribed* original narrative by hybridizing the sensual ukiyo and bleak dystopia. It is in this way that the transfer from ukiyo to dystopia offers the character a new narrative intervention for his/tory, but in this case without sexual or textual "relief."

While the novel integrates a wide variety of global fictions, the character's quest for his family is also a recovery of the narrative histories of local space. The literary cartography of Aotearoa/New Zealand is explored through direct encounters with canonical realist narratives; the protagonist engages with characters derived from the works of Maori and Pakeha novelists such as Keri Hulme, Witi Ihimaera, and Maurice Gee. Near the conclusion, the Tribunal computer recommends that the protagonist read *Black Rainbow*. The novel is dedicated to and draws its title from another intertextual artist, Hone Papita Raukura (Ralph) Hotere, whose work with New Zealand literary figures and social activists aligns multiple artistic genres with social protest and gestures to the localization of global resistance. Hotere's "Dawn/Water Poem" and "Black Rainbow" lithographs (1986) protest French nuclear testing at Moruroa Atoll and are continual touchstones in the protagonist's quest. While Sharrad points out that Wendt's art anticipates both the commodification of masculine desire ("Erectol" as a proto-Viagra), as well as popular "reality" programs (2003, 210), equally prescient is the novel's inscription of local forms of resistance to the nuclearization of the Pacific, which are uncannily predictive of events to come. Hotere's "Black Rainbow" series, featuring a doomsday clock that haunts Wendt's narrator, protests French nuclear testing, including 41 atmospheric and 137 underground nuclear explosions in the Tuamotu Archipelago between 1966 and 1974. In that time period alone, the total nuclear yield was fifteen megatons, equivalent to one U.S. detonation over Bikini Atoll, and over a thousand times more destructive than the bombs dropped on Nagasaki and Hiroshima.

Wendt's invocation of the nuclearization of the Pacific is not only an obvious refutation of colonial narratives that position the "South Seas" outside of the trajectories of modernity, but also gestures to the ways in which European imperialism has transformed spatial relations through the mobilization of eschatological technologies. After Algerian independence forced France to cease their nuclear testing there in 1962, the French militarized the Tahitian economy, imported thousands of army personnel, and established an artificial "economy of transfer" (devastating dependency) in exchange for unregulated military access to Moruroa, Fangataufa, and Faaʻa Atolls (Firth and Von Strokirch 1997, 339).[24] The commencement of French nuclear testing, perhaps one of the most disturbing manifestations of neocolonial globalization, was simultaneous with local and regional protest. In 1966, in direct opposition to France's official denial of any detrimental environmental effect, New Zealand monitoring stations began reporting high levels of nuclear fallout all over the southern hemisphere (Firth and Von Strokirch 1997, 343). By the 1970s, antinuclear protests were transpacific and international phenomena. Aotearoa/New Zealand and Australia brought France to the U. N. International Court of Justice, but this did nothing to stop the tests, nor did France's later signing of the Partial Test Ban Treaty prevent them from continuing atmospheric tests ten years after all the other nuclear powers had desisted (344–345). A number of test-site accidents in the 1970s and 1980s in the Tuamotu Archipelago, including fatal radiation exposure of employees, a suboceanic landslide that caused a tidal wave, and a storm that dislodged and spread plutonium and barrels of radioactive waste into the open sea, catalyzed another series of protests by Maʻohi activists in Tahiti and throughout the region. While indigenous mobilization was certainly perceived as a threat to France (M. King 1986, 20), the protests were unheeded by incoming President Mitterand, who resumed the tests after a brief hiatus in 1984 (Firth and Von Strokirch 1997, 347; Dibblin 1988, 204).

France's blatant disregard for international regulations resulted in a tightening of regional and global alliances, and it is in this immediate context that we may position Hotere's lithograph and Wendt's novel. On Hiroshima Day in 1985 all but three nations of the South Pacific Forum signed the Treaty of Rarotonga, which ratified the Pacific region as a nuclear-free zone.[25] Both Hotere and Wendt memorialize the 1985 French bombing in Auckland harbor of the Greenpeace ship *Rainbow Warrior*, which had been preparing for a protest voyage to the nuclear test site at Moruroa. The ship sank and one crewmember was killed. The *Rainbow Warrior* had just returned from relocating the islanders of Rongelap, who had been suffering severe health problems and mortality rates since the United States dropped the seventeen-megaton bomb "Bravo" on the neighboring Bikini Atoll.

Rongelap was in the direct line of Bravo's fallout, but Congress did almost nothing to assist in relocation, even while U.S. reports were warning the islanders not to ingest local food thirty years after the detonation (Dibblin 1988, 4; M. King 1986, 6–7). An international outcry over the bombing of the *Rainbow Warrior* led to the discovery and arrest of French secret service agents in New Zealand and the reluctant establishment by the French government of a brief internal inquiry. To international incredulity, they determined that France was not responsible. President Mitterand resisted pressure to meet with and apologize to Greenpeace and in fact threatened Moruroa protestors with arrest. Months later, a government leak substantiated Mitterrand's involvement, and the United Nations forced France to apologize and financially compensate Aotearoa/New Zealand for the damage.[26]

I have summarized these important events because they have been eclipsed in the "ever-moving present" of late capitalist globalization, a point that Wendt encodes through a complex chain of intertextual references that include colonial master narratives as well as trajectories of regional and global resistance. U.S. nuclear testing at Bikini Atoll and the consolidation of new forms of indigenous, transpacific, and global activism thus function as an integral history to local artistic production and dissemination. "Black Rainbow," Hotere's lithograph, memorializes violent neocolonialism in both Moruroa and Aotearoa/New Zealand, reflecting an indigenous and global tidalectic of ideological and material exchange. The very transparency of nuclear practices in the Pacific and the bombing of the *Rainbow Warrior* challenge assumptions that late capitalist hegemonies are somehow exceedingly slippery, ephemeral, and hard to pinpoint. While critics seem to dismiss "the nuclear era" as outdated Cold War rhetoric, few of the recent studies on globalization or postcolonialism even mention the contested events that have transpired in the Pacific region over the past four decades. Hotere's work, referred to repeatedly by Wendt's protagonist as "the lithograph," offers an alternative to Benjamin's dystopic vision of art and mechanical production (1992). The reproduction and dissemination of Hotere's counter-memory suggest the ways in which artifacts of an uneven and contested series of historical practices find their way to Wendt's futuristic landscape and facilitate new generations of resistance. Read in a future intertextual trajectory, the rainbow of Wendt's title anticipates his important anthology, a "rainbow of poetry and prose" from the Pacific Islands, entitled *Nuanua* (1995a). As such, one may read dual globalizations in the "Black Rainbow" of nuclear eschatology as well as the transpacific and global resistance movements that contribute to a new generation of Pacific literatures.

The same year *Black Rainbow* came into print, France declared a moratorium on nuclear testing in the Pacific after twenty-six years of destruction. But the doomsday clock that both Hotere and Wendt invoke was to resume three years later, when President Chirac resumed nuclear testing in blatant violation of the Nuclear Non-Proliferation and Euratom Treaties. Despite intense worldwide protest, including riots in Tahiti and a U.N. General Assembly vote to cease the tests immediately, France conducted six of its eight anticipated nuclear "experiments" over the course of a year. On the ten-year anniversary of the sinking of its namesake, the second *Rainbow Warrior* voyaged to Moruroa to resume the protest. In an insidious adaptation of the poststructuralist simulacrum, France defended these additional tests on the grounds that they were necessary to model computer simulations, which in turn were needed for the eradication of future testing. The language of nuclear "testing," which erases the material and physical reality of tremendous human, political, and ecological destruction, allows the French government to ideologically segregate a total of 179 nuclear explosions in the Tuamotu Archipelago from the real.[27] Once isolated from actual material affects (compounded by the fact that the French government prohibits studies of the sites), a seemingly harmless chain of replications is unleashed, where the computer simulation of a "test" is articulated simply as the copy of a copy, which prevents the copy-to-be, future testing. The originary and eschatological ends of the spectrum, explosive "testing" and outright nuclear war, are suspended by a series of presumably harmless repetitions exacted upon a series of tropical islands that, as my introduction explained, had already been dehistoricized in the eighteenth-century colonization of the "South Seas." This mystification of nuclearization has been so successful that most critics writing about globalization in the 1990s seemed unaware that nuclear destruction has constituted the past and present and is not simply a threat for the future. Even expansive studies such as Michael Hardt and Antonio Negri's *Empire* (2000) relegate nuclearization to one paragraph. While they determine that "from no other standpoint is the passage from modernity to postmodernity and from modern sovereignty to Empire more evident than it is from the standpoint of the bomb" (2000, 345), they define this in linear terms as the "*capacity* for destruction" (346, my emphasis), an eschatological narrative of militarization rather than its continuing perpetuation. Thus Wendt's novel can be seen as a historical engagement with the dystopian militarization of a region as an important counter-narrative to the utopian myth of isolated and ahistorical islands.

Mapping Native Urbanization

The nuclearization of the Pacific catalyzed a global resistance movement that is often mistakenly categorized in reactive terms. Graham Hingangaroa Smith points out that "we Indigenous peoples should be concerned with accentuating preemptive and proactive actions rather than being sidetracked into being overtly concerned with reactive responses" (2000, 210). Warning about the "politics of distraction" that constitute postmodern shifts in Aotearoa/New Zealand and elide questions of accountability, Smith vocalizes widespread concerns as to how to best mobilize and protect indigenous interests in the face of multiple national and global transformations. Similarly, Wendt's protagonist struggles against a system that precludes native agency as facile resistance to state and global hegemonies. It is for this reason that the "Determinism vs Free Will" question arises continually in the novel. Within the metastructures of state homogenization and nationalist literary canons, the central character attempts to "reread" such institutions in a way that will allow an alter/native epistemology. In Keesing's terms, the protagonist can only achieve agency as a reaction to state hegemony, in which case native historicism replicates "outdated" anthropology. Yet if the indigenous subject "modernizes," then native history can only be dissolved into a simulacrum without cultural origins. If the protagonist denies his origins, he cannot retrieve his indigenous genealogy (the family), which is the point of the quest. His uneasy relationship to ideological genealogies is visible when he writes, "Determinism vs Free Will. It appears that the Tribunal/President have prearranged all that is and will be, even the Game of Life, to outlaw crime/poverty/war/violence/all the negative emotions/etc. *Who 'determined' the Tribunal/President?*" (1992, 149, my emphasis).

If the structure of *Black Rainbow*'s society is predetermined, who is responsible for its genealogy? The central issue here is one of political and personal origins. Like the narrator's eventual recovery of his indigeneity, this disclosure is simultaneous with his "re-reading" of his relationship to the state. In Wendt's vision, structuralism begs the question of origins, whereas poststructuralism brackets off the referents of history, which are vital to the reconstruction of indigeneity. Wendt mediates between these polarizations by attributing a composite parentage to his protagonist. He discovers that the Tribunal President is his (nonbiological) father and recovers the memory of his biological mother, a resistant indigenous woman who was eventually seduced by the Tribunal's "ever-moving present" and died in a state hospital. Significantly his (white) father is associated with the immediate, hegemonic present, while his (native) mother is relegated to historic memory, reiterating the operative gendered dualisms of most scholarship seeking to parse out global/local distinctions. (Wendt's own characters accuse him of "sexism" by the end of the novel.) As a product of both state institutions as well as a resistant indigenous underground, Wendt locates narrative possibility in the "meta-physical" body of his character, and stitches together the division between (abstract) history and (corporeal) memory. He comes to realize:

> Though the Tribunal has banned history, we are what we remember, the precious rope stretching across the abyss of all that we have forgotten. . . . And the history, the fabulous storehouse of memories, of our love, opened and gave reason and meaning to my quest across the abyss, a quest which had turned me into a heretic defying the Tribunal and all I'd been raised to believe in. (1992, 178)

Personal and cultural memory become the objective of the quest, encompassed within the broader narrative of family. This is not to say Wendt discredits the allure of free-floating simulacra, because his narrator, like his mother before him, is quite literally seduced by the "continuous present." For a good part of the novel, Wendt's character seems derived from Lyotard's summation of postmodern eclecticism: "one listens to reggae, watches a western, eats McDonald's food for lunch and local cuisine for dinner, wears Paris perfume in Tokyo and 'retro' clothes in Hong Kong; knowledge is a matter for TV games. . . . But this realism of the 'anything goes' is in fact that of money" (1996, 76). As the protagonist becomes increasingly seduced by the monetary and symbolic capital provided by the Tribunal, and caught up in the progressive logocentric telos of the detective genre, he becomes more dependent upon the constant reminders from the True Ones about the need to recover his "aiga," the Samoan word for family.

The novel's construction of a mediated indigenous essence is exceedingly complex, based as it is on an originary genealogy that is also constituted by a phenomenology of urban landscapes and global resistance. This marks an important break with the naturalizing metaphors of native space-time continuity that I explored in the previous chapter. In contrast, *Black Rainbow*'s oxymoronic title and dystopian landscape dismantle the indigenous epistemologies that are generally symbolized by botanical images, rendering a schism in the metaphysical conflation of people with place. Wendt locates the modern indigenous community in the "young Polynesian" street kids who cannot be "reordinarized" and are released back into the Tribunal metropolis. Their "'refusal to be like . . . law-abiding citizens'" is attributed by some characters to "their blood" (1992, 27). Here, indigenous bodies are placed in a historical trajectory of ancestral resistance to state hegemony (their blood), even while their presence symbolizes the suppressed "heart of the city" (28). Although these characters are dispossessed from the traditional and naturalizing markers of indigenous identity (native genealogies, languages, and continuous land occupation), Wendt suggests that precontact epistemologies might be excavated. For instance, while digging in his urban garden, the narrator "remembered the Polynesian word for earth and blood was the same: *eleele*" (35), solidifying indigenous ties to the land within the urban structure of the state. As the narrator is not "marked" at this point by native ancestry, this recollection represents a genealogical residue indicative of the continuity of indigenous cultural tradition. The protagonist asserts that the street kids could be his children, and this familial bond is strengthened over the course of the novel. This presents an important alternative not only to the enforced familiality of the Tribunal, but the nuclear family he has been "programmed" to create. It is in this way that native genealogy and the family, at once corporeal and performative, are differentiated from facile, ethnic-based ancestry.

The street kids, known as the True Ones, also claim mixed ancestry, highlighting the contingency of indigeneity as well as its regional and global histories. Although they resist the assimilating Tribunal, their dissidence is not overdetermined by its structure, as Keesing might argue. While their continuity with Polynesian cultural tradition is fragmented due to the suppression of their histories, occasionally they invoke familial practices of tangi (mourning), oral storytelling, and the remnants of their native languages. The True Ones have partial access to their genealogies and recite their personal histories, despite the Tribunal's prohibition. It is in this way that the Tribunal state is revealed as a palimpsest over native presence, which has literally been sent "underground." Importantly, the True Ones are not merely symbols of an ancestral (and rural) past, but a self-conscious foundation of the urban state. As one of them points out, "'A city is layers of maps and geographies, layers of them, centuries of it. We were the first, our ancestors, no matter what lies the Tribunal says. So our maps are at the bottom of the bloody heap'" (134).

Importantly, *Black Rainbow* foregrounds the processes of migration and settlement that constitute modernity, adding a historical dimension to theories that privilege postmodern urban space. Wendt positions indigenous presence as the foundation of the metropole, rather than coding this presence as profoundly unnatural. While scholars of urban cartographies such as Edward Soja and David Harvey have contributed much to our understanding of the fractures and fissions of postmodern space, few if any of these authors concede the deep indigenous historical presence that has been "bulldozed" under subsequent urban migrations and constructions. By focusing on mid- to late-twentieth-century shifts in the constitution of the postmodern city and locating the process of globalization only in recent decades, these theorists have not elucidated a temporal trajectory that might bring indigenous subjects in a productive and continuous dialogue with (post)modernity.

In contrast, Wendt challenges the shallow temporality of these models by rendering indigenous presence in Aotearoa/New Zealand's largest city, Auckland (Tamaki), and by highlighting native continuity to the present time. Entitled "On Maungakiekie," the chapter describes the protagonist's morning walks with his wife to this important urban landmark, an ancient volcano that bears the markings of multiple layerings of settlement. Originally one of the geologically formative progenitors of Aotearoa, the volcano came to be inhabited by diverse Maori iwi (tribes); its strategic location between multiple waterways meant that it became a densely concentrated and pan-tribal metropolis well before the arrival of Europeans. In the nineteenth century, Sir John Logan Campbell purchased the land for farming and then gifted the property and paddocks to the newly emergent nation. In his will he bequeathed an obelisk memorial, dedicated to those whom he and his colleagues presumed would soon be extinct: the "Great Maori Race." In a scene that likens discourses of fatal impact with Hotere's doomsday clock, this phallic and imperialist monument is deemed "awful" by the protagonist's wife (11). She establishes indigenous spatial continuity by observing, "The Pakeha have changed even the landscape but *they're* still here" (12, author's emphasis). Later she performs a ceremony at Maungakiekie by circling the memorial with the Hotere lithograph, "reinvesting everything with mana" (power), and singing in "an ancient language" to "those who had been there before" (18). This remains one of the few and recurrent memories that the protagonist retains of his wife once she has disappeared. Later, when he locates his family, genealogy, and the Hotere lithograph, he returns to Maungakiekie and explains:

> Many of us are compelled, instinctively, to return to spiritual sites
> that are encompassed in the stories of our lives, sites that our creator
> beings turned themselves into or invested with mana. For me Maunga-
> kiekie was one because it was there that my wife, with her courage and

sight, had started our rebellion against the Tribunal. She'd summoned the agaga [soul] of our ancient Dead with the Hotere icon to hold back the doomsday clock; she'd linked us again to the earth and to our Dead. (242)

Because "earth" is synonymous with "blood," Wendt constructs a layered genealogy that resonates with the rhizomorphic settlement articulated in the novels of both Mitchell and Hulme, discussed in the previous chapter. Wendt literally engages whakapapa's definition "to layer" by drawing attention to the ways in which Maungakiekie and other areas of the city are both constituted and constitutive of the social production of space. With Hulme and Mitchell, he shares Wilson Harris's impetus to "visualize links between technology and living landscapes in continuously new ways that [take] nothing for granted in an increasingly violent and materialistic world" (Harris 1999, 43). Yet these "new ways" are deeply linked to the precontact historiographies and metaphysical genealogies of the originary and surviving people. Invoking the ancient trickster Maui, the protagonist determines he will not try to "trap Ra," the sun deity, as the legend has it, but rather wait for Ra "to invest [him] with its essence, turn [his] flesh and history into sinews of the light that bound everything with its unbreakable genealogy. All creatures, all things, all elements" (Wendt 1992, 242). This genealogy functions as a vital counter-narrative to the fragmentation of the postmodern city, which erases history. As such, the novel offers up the term "history" as a synonym rather than an antonym to indigeneity.

In an essay, Wendt comments on the suppressed histories of Aotearoa / New Zealand:

> Our maps give voice to the tragic silence of the Mountain. To the wounds in the agaga of Aotearoa, wounds that won't heal despite fundamentalist Rogernomics, the Capitalist Knights of the Business Roundtable . . . exhortation[s] that we are all Kiwis and there are no "pure-bloods" left; despite the refusal, even by some bewigged academics, historians and writers, to admit that enormous injustices have been committed against the Tangata Maori. (1995b, 37)

It is because of his concern with shifting cartographies that Wendt does not isolate the Maungakiekie scenes as more "authentic" indigenous spaces than, say, built environments. While his wife may have originated the novel's chain of resistance, it is the young characters (rather than guiding elders) who reflect an energizing and dynamic indigenous present as well as establish narrative continuity with the precontact past. For instance, some of the names of the True Ones are drawn from the birds that accompanied the demigod Maui when he attempted to win immortality for humanity by passing through the vagina of the goddess Hine Nui te Po. In the legend, when Piwakawaka (fantail) giggled, the goddess awoke and crushed Maui to his death between her legs. In Wendt's revision, which aligns Maui with other canonical male voyagers such as Odysseus, his companions facilitate the object of his mission rather than hinder it.[28] The conflation of the Greek and Polynesian myths in Wendt's novel emphasizes an ancient, cross-cultural history of transgression against superstructures, and an intertextuality of local and global resistance.

These urbanized native characters are crucial to the protagonist's search; their position "outside" the system offers the epistemological tools for the recovery of his history. Once the protagonist befriends the street kids and is exposed to their criticism of the state, he is able to "re-read" the palace in a way that enables him to locate his family. The Puzzle Palace, where his family is hidden, cannot be "read" by the narrator; it poses only the "harmless repetitions" (1992, 138) of the simulacrum. Thus he determines that he is "*reading* it wrongly" (139). He struggles with the hermeneutic circle, remembering his wife's words, "We see what we believe" (138). This viewpoint is immediately countered by Fantail/Piwakawaka, who is named after Maui's "cheeky bird" (142). After helping the protagonist survey the building, she argues, "'Don't throw that profound view of what is real and what ain't. You know how many metres I walked in those corridors? That's what was real for me. I felt the tiredness, I saw and smelled the walls, the offices, those awful people'" (138). The True Ones are the first to suggest that the Tribunal has "'fucked [him] up good ... left [him] brown on the outside and filled [him] with white, otherworlder bullshit'" (123). This is confirmed by the narrator's failure to refer to his missing family throughout much of the text. The narrator becomes too caught up in the "profound view" and the theoretical components of his mission, but the True Ones repeatedly remind him that his aiga remains the object of his search. The protagonist's inability to act in any way except against the system rather than *for* the retrieval of his family is ultimately corrected.

The True Ones physically aid the protagonist and reorient him towards indigenous traditions, while their location in the literal underground of the city provides a new inscription of urban indigeneity. The whare, or home, is a "safehouse" (157) underneath the city stocked primarily with Maori literature and an intertextual reference to Wendt's novel

Ola. Wendt indigenizes the underground trope of Ralph Ellison's work. He writes, "There was a centuries-old genealogy, in literature and film, of persecuted groups and minorities going underground to survive. Underground, they organized resistance to the powers above ground" (156–157). After entering the safehouse, a space of storytelling and resistance, the protagonist is informed about the history of "otherworlder oppression and arrogance," which nearly "erased, physically and culturally," (157–158) the "Tangata Maori." Here the novel literally descends into the depths of history, where Wendt self-consciously implicates his novel as a "familiar text about all the other texts about invasion, oppression, racism and totalitarian reordinarination" (158).

While the underground-resistance plot may be familiar, Wendt adds an important twist to the construction of nativism. The True Ones are sometimes referred to as "Tangata Maori," literally, the "common people," and at other times called "Tangata Moni." While "moni" is the word for truth in Samoan, it is also the Maori transliteration of money, or economic value. Although it seems paradoxical to inscribe the urban indigenous poor as "the money people," Wendt seems to be invoking not only the ways in which native subjects are falsely interpellated by the subjugations of transnational capital, but he is also gesturing to how the treaty claims process has instituted a legal exchange of history for capital, while simultaneously demarcating spatially "authentic" versus "inauthentic" discourses of indigeneity. The year *Black Rainbow* was published, the Treaty of Waitangi (Fisheries Claims) Settlement Act was signed between Maori and the Crown, following a long process of hearings over what came to be known as the multimillion dollar "Sealord deal," a transfer of state fisheries into corporate hands with the agreement that one-third of the assets would be set aside for Maori. While the act specifically designated all Maori as treaty partners, a series of government rulings allotted financial compensation only to Maori affiliated with iwi, despite the fact that nearly 50 percent of Auckland Maori were unable to establish tribal affiliations through whakapapa (Durie 1998, 95). According to some scholars, "'Iwi' became the master narrative for constructing the identities and citizenship of Maori in the present. The urban Maori social movement thus turned to challenging that narrative" (Meredith 2000, 9). Subsequently, the 1990s were categorized as a litigious decade of "fighting over fish," as multiple high court rulings and appeals furthered the political and economic divide between "urban Maori" and "iwi Maori," in a way that suggests a "reification of certain neo-traditional Maori organizational forms" (Barcham

2000, 138).[29] Wendt's True Ones anticipate Maori urban dispossession; he suggests indigenous peoples must incorporate other epistemologies into local whakapapa to articulate the layering of a multiethnic subjectivity.

This historical context has factored significantly into Wendt's vision of the indigenous urban subject, which draws upon transpacific rather than specifically Maori genealogies. Rather than rooting native resistance in terms of one nation's first people, Wendt broadens this into a profoundly globalized series of material and cultural relations. While this minimizes the differences and tensions between Maori and the large body of Pacific Island migrants who have reshaped the contours of Auckland since the 1950s, it also inscribes a future of transpacific sites of resistance. As a rebellious subculture, the Tangata Moni came about when they "merged with [their] sisters and brothers from the Islands who were also being reordinarinised, and became the Tangata Moni, the True People. A tough breed, the toughest" (1992, 158). The relationship here between Maori, Pacific Islanders, and "many pakeha / palagi [whites], who saw the injustice in reordinarination" (158) and joined them, presents a global indigeneity based on a politics of resistance and does not promote a rigid authentication of culture. This is in keeping with Wendt's definition of an Oceanic sensibility that recognizes that "no culture is ever static and can be preserved like a stuffed gorilla in a museum" (1993, 12), while conceding that "too fervent or paranoid an identification with one's culture . . . can lead to racial intolerance" (13). Wendt's True Ones provide an antidote to a reductive vision of New Zealand biculturalism through a genealogy that draws, on the one hand, from the complex cultural traditions of the Pacific, and is forged, on the other, through dynamic and shifting social practice. This is underlined by Wendt's use of the Samoan term for family to promote a broader, pan-Pacific and global indigeneity that is politically located in the urban soil of Aotearoa.

Wendt's vision of genealogical contingency is confirmed when his protagonist discovers his previous name, Patimaori Jones. "Pati" is not only Wendt's Samoan name, but translates as "patched" in Maori. Thus his full name is a combination of layered Pacific languages, identities, English nomenclature, and "blaxploitation" films of the United States.[30] During his interview with his father, the Tribunal president, Patimaori relearns his mother's name, Patricia Manaia Graceous, an obvious reference to Patricia Grace, whose novel *Potiki* bears similar thematic concerns to *Black Rainbow*. In an article, Wendt states that one of *Potiki*'s characters "is [his] grandmother" (1995b, 20). In his novel, he derives his character from this celebrated Maori author, positioning Grace as his protagonist's biological mother and remapping a native genealogy for the literature of Aotearoa/New Zealand. His use of literary and familial genealogies rescript the cartographies of Pakeha nationalism and literary canons.

The protagonist learns through the Tribunal's computer files that as a teenage rebel with Maui-like charm, Patimaori was taken in by the Tribunal president who determined that "the magic of the printed word will tame him, convert him to civilization, make him thirst for our cargo, like primitives in the past" (Wendt 1992, 226). While Supremo/Patimaori Jones has been tremendously successful as a Hunter for the Tribunal, he has "reverted" to his previous "uncivilized" ways and has been reordinarized into the bank clerk whose identity begins the novel. Importantly, while Patimaori was taught English, Eric Foster was instilled with a love of twentieth-century literature in order to prevent further "reversions" to his murderous ways. In this way the language and narrative production of the state are obvious agents for state-sanctified behavior, a point I return to below in my discussion of narrative form and the nationalist project.

Patimaori murders his Tribunal Father, the playfully named Joseph Starr Linn, an action predetermined by this state-orchestrated quest. Afterwards, the narrator recovers the space of native agency by determining that his future "lay in the *blanks*" of the computer files and struggles to recover his suppressed memories of his mother. He finds solace in "the work of Tangata Maori writers, [his] ancestors, finding in them the identity and past [he had] been denied." Here Wendt interjects a quote from Maori activist Donna Awatere:

> Who I am and my relationship to everyone else depends on my whakapapa, on my lineage, on those from whom I am descended. One needs one's ancestors therefore to define one's present. Relationships with one's tipuna are thus intimate and causal. It is easy to feel the humiliation, anger and sense of loss which our tipuna felt. And to take up the kaupapa they had. (244)[31]

In the "ever moving present" of the Tribunal State, a sinuous and corporeal relationship between past, present, and future is not obtainable.

In the previous chapter I explored the historical importance of the courtroom to Aotearoa/New Zealand and how it institutionalizes opposing epistemologies between Pakeha and Maori. Similarly, *Black Rainbow*'s concluding chapters circulate around the question of indigenous identity as it is performed for a state judicial process. After trial by a jury who accuse him of "inverse racism" for reclaiming Tangata Maori status, the narrator is declared guilty. In a scene reminiscent of current cultural politics over the Treaty of Waitangi claims, a white jury member (a parody of C. K. Stead)[32] argues "our ancestors were not responsible for the Tangata Maori's demise. We brought them the Light of Science and Reincarnation and Eternal Life." The protagonist retorts that this "rhetoric catered to the rabble's prejudice and ignorance of our true history which the Tribunal has banned. For to know our past was to know our 'utopia' was a lie, an evil" (255). Because the discourse of history is banned, further discussion is silenced in the courtroom. But the symbolic residue created by the Tribunal's Enlightenment temporality creates a fissure in the pedagogical nation-space of the courtroom that cannot be unified. The narrator cannot remain within the Tribunal State in his current form as a Tangata Maori, cognizant of his genealogy and history. Maori heritage is incompatible with the capitalist nation-state, which causes the death of the protagonist and, by extension, the possibility for Maori historiography. While the protagonist has the option of being reincarnated into any other subjectivity than his self-conscious indigenous self, he chooses permanent death, but the novel ends without a definitive outcome. Wendt has resisted the linear trajectory of the text; he refuses closure by supplying a number of possible conclusions in his final chapter, which, like *the bone people*'s prologue, is entitled "Endings / Beginnings." Drawing upon an indigenous spiral historiography, the form of Wendt's novel evades the teleology of the global capitalist state.

After citing a number of possible endings, the last words of the text declare, "Readers are free to improvise whatever other endings / beginnings they prefer" (267). This is not to be read as an abandonment of native agency, for this is found in the story itself, and the possibilities of both narrative and interpretation that "lay in the *blanks*" between narratives. While the protagonist realizes that the "Game of Life is stacked . . . [he] did have a choice in the ways of fulfilling [his] quest and [his] dying / living. We are, in the final instance, allegories that are read the way the reader chooses. Or, put another way, we are allegories that invent and read themselves" (265). Here Wendt carefully maneuvers out of a trap where identity either functions in an ahistorical simulacrum or is structurally overdetermined. He concludes this passage with a reminder about language and narrative: "The act of recording this story in words has determined the story it has turned out to be" (265). It is this concern with metanarratives that I will now examine in my concluding comments on the "third world" novel.

"Third World" Postmodernization

Because of *Black Rainbow*'s complex engagement with metanarratives, it has been categorized as postmodern.[33] Certainly it has the playful intertextuality of this form, but I would like to emphasize the distinction between surface aesthetics and the political impetus to inscribe a mediated native essence amidst the irruptions of global postmodernity. If postmodern narratives destabilize ontologies and endlessly defer meaning, they necessarily undermine the protagonist's claim to indigenous ancestry or whakapapa. *Black Rainbow* suggests that originary difference is incompatible with the telos of the global capitalist state.

225

Appiah highlights the problematics of applying the term "postmodern" to writers of the postcolonial era. "The role that Africa, like the rest of the third world, plays for Euro-American postmodernism . . . must be distinguished from the role postmodernism might play in the third world" (1992, 157). In his examination of Yambo Ouologuem's novel *Bound to Violence* (1968), Appiah finds that the novel delegitimizes "the form of realism [and] the content of nationalism . . . it identifies the realist novel as part of the tactic of nationalist legitimation and so it is *postrealist*" (1992, 150). Clearly the postrealist project has some resonance with Wendt's objectives in *Black Rainbow*, seen in his critique of the Tribunal's use of national literature to suppress native resistance and "reversion." The realist novel in Aotearoa/New Zealand has a particular relationship to white-settler nation-building. As the first Samoan writer to rescript native literary and national identity in Aotearoa/New Zealand, Wendt cannot afford to uphold the realist novel if he is simultaneously to situate native agency outside the boundaries of the homogenizing nation-state. Appiah's interpretation of Ouologuem's novel is suggestive:

> Because this is a novel that seeks to delegitimate not only the form of realism but the content of nationalism, it will . . . seem to us misleadingly to be postmodern. *Mis*leadingly, because what we have here is not postmodern*ism* but postmodernization; not an aesthetics but a politics, in the most literal sense of the word. After colonialism, the modernizers said, comes rationality; that is the possibility the novel rules out. (1992, 152)

The temporal trajectory that Appiah outlines is relevant to New Zealand nationalism, for no tangata whenua would agree that colonialism and native subjugation could be defined as "rationality" and progress. In his depiction of the Tribunal and its suppression of history, Wendt has to delegitimize the metastructure of the state, which is complicit with the realist, nation-building novel. It is for this reason that *Black Rainbow*'s genre is most strongly aligned with the dystopic novel and ultimately posits a critical postmodern*ization* of nationalism, rather than upholding the aesthetics of postmodernism. Wilson Harris, an outspoken critic of the realist novel, explains, "Realism is authoritarian in the sense that it has to stick to one frame. It cannot bring other texts into play" (1992, 26). Writers invested in recovering suppressed histories may be limited by the realist genre due to its replication of capitalist teleology. While Wendt's earlier novels employed a loose social realism, it is surely significant that his first novel to be set exclusively in Aotearoa/New Zealand has departed from this form. As Harris explains, "Progressive realism erases the past. It consumes the present and it may very well abort the future with its linear bias" (72). Wendt's narrative palimpsest recovers native cultural continuities through a complex postmodernization that is juxtaposed against the homogenizing teleology of the Tribunal's utopia. Unlike the nation-building novels discussed in the previous chapter, Wendt's dystopia retains little hope for the nationalization process; by looking to the future, he positions global resistance as the "underground" root of globalization itself.

Coda: Postmodern Flows and Cultural Unmoorings

Through his movements across the shifting cartographies of the authoritarian state, Wendt's narrator determines that "everything was floating, in flux," and that he "was of that floating" (1992, 190). The city is often described tidalectically, in aquatic terms, "like a black-furred sea," (135), or a "sea of dark shadow" (12) where "traffic surged by like metallic sea creatures driven by the waves of wind" (141).[34] He is haunted by dreams of drowning and of swimming without movement, which are only alleviated when he is able to enact the metaphysical condensation of *eleele* (earth) and blood (35). In this way he anticipates the teleologies of landfall that I explore in more detail in the following chapter. As the narrator learns to reconstruct both his indigenous self and his urban extended family, his dreams of drowning are replaced by the dreams of singing whales, as well as "whales [that] bled under a sun that didn't move across the sky" (152). This is, to quote Hone Tuwhare's antinuclear poem, "no ordinary sun."[35]

One might position Wendt's aquatic imagery alongside the vast body of scholarship on the process of late capitalist globalization, a "liquid modernity" (Bauman 2000) that consistently adopts watery metaphors to explain the process of migratory "flows," "oceanic" transformations, economic "surges" and "tides," as well as the "floods" of new immigrants. With the destabilization of terrestrial and nationalist imaginaries, the presumed boundlessness of the earth's oceans seems to provide a limitless vocabulary with which to conceptualize such radical transformations. Yet, as this book has argued, oceanic cartographies are no less derivative of culturally specific histories than the recent trajectories of globalization. While we may position nuclear detonations in the Tuamotu Archipelago as neocolonial or hegemonic products of globalization, this is not simply a case of unstable routes but rather of specific historical roots. By locating what some theorists refer to as "early modern globalizations" (Held et al. 1999, 413), we may trace a continuum from eighteenth-century European colonization of the Pacific and its romantic discourse of idyllic islands to its more contemporary and technological forms of globalization that rely upon analogous interpellations of island primitivism in order to reconfigure Moruroa and Bikini atolls into nuclear laboratories. This chapter has argued that it is equally important to trace out the multiple and conflicting currents of globalization in order to ensure that surface flows are not confused with less visible but no less powerful historical undertows. To this end, Wendt's novel suggests a circulation between the subterranean "underground" of resistance and the subaquatic, transnational space of shifting currents and flows. Hence, to borrow from Kamau Brathwaite, we find that regional "unity is submarine" (1974, 64). The recurrent image of whales suggests other currents of globalization, such as the transpacific indigeneity of "water ties" evident in Witi Ihimaera's *The Whale Rider* (1987), a novel that offers a broad and profoundly historical genealogy of Pacific peoples while also illuminating the ways in which all creatures that constitute the Pacific whakapapa are impacted by nuclear pollution.[36]

In his assessment of Pacific Island literature in the watery "wake" of globalization, Subramani points out that "the rising tide of corporate capitalism will not lift all boats . . . the only boats that will be lifted will be those of the owners and managers of the process; the rest of us will be on the beach facing the riding tide" (2001, 8). Presuming that "in Oceania, problems of globalism are only half-articulated," Subramani determines "there are no counter narratives" and calls for a radical "countervision" to emerge out of Pacific literary production (9). I have positioned *Black Rainbow* as a direct engagement with national and global master narratives, one perhaps overlooked by those who might substitute the novel's surface aesthetics for its localizing politics. Certainly Wendt's characters are set culturally adrift amidst the "ever-moving present" of the late capitalist state, but they maintain their indigenous roots in these globalizing routes. To be set culturally adrift amidst dehistoricized postmodern flows neither precludes a phenomenology of the environment, nor does it prevent the reconstitution of precapitalist genealogies. By drawing on the Pacific navigation system of etak, these depthless flows are given new historical meanings. As I have mentioned, in etak's maritime methodology, a series of intersecting swells at sea are defined as a reflecting "root" (Lewis 1994, 198), a historical consequence of unseen territories submerged over the horizon. Recognizing these historic "roots" helps determine locality amidst global flows and to chart a course that brings into visibility a regional and global articulation of a "unity" that is "submarine."

Landfall

Carib and Arawak Sedimentation

Amerindians play an important symbolic role in the West
Indian search for identity. The very absence of Indians is a
source of regret to Creoles, who find it hard to feel at home
in lands lacking visible remains of an ancient past. Cultural
nationalism throughout the Caribbean today promotes the
search for Arawak and Carib remains. Finding them will not
meet the need for roots; however, for living West Indians have
little real connection with Amerindian culture or descent.
—David Lowenthal, *West Indian Societies*

Nationalism fosters a reflexive consciousness of tradition.
  —Jocelyn Linnekin, "Defining Tradition"

I conclude this book by examining the ways in which the indigenous
Caribbean is employed in anglophone island literature to validate the
process of landfall or cultural sovereignty in the wake of transnational
globalization. This chapter marks an important shift in Caribbean literature because the region is often characterized in terms of diaspora, despite
the fact that there has been a remarkable increase in the production of
fictional texts that nativize Caribbean landscapes. The recent shift from
diaspora to indigenous narratives can be likened to the conceptual system
of "moving islands" where a "multiple reference orientation" (Lewis 1994,
148) brings home, self, and destination into dynamic relation. Implement-
ing etak allows us to chart the different registers of indigenous discourse
in island literatures and to examine Caribbean navigations towards cultural
landfall. In this chapter I explore how indigenous presence is literally excavated as a trope of terrestrial Caribbean history, particularly in Michelle
Cliff's *No Telephone to Heaven* (1987) and Merle Collins's *The Colour of
Forgetting* (1995). I read these novels as validating a tidalectic engagement
of roots and routes, upholding cultural creolization and offering a poetic

corrective to conservative and materialist approaches to Caribbean historiography. Because they imagine histories of culture through local space, the landscape, mobilized by Carib and Arawak characters, functions "not as an object to be seen or a text to be read, but as a process by which social and subjective identities are formed" (W. J. T. Mitchell 1994, 1). The concern with local landscape is of historical importance because, as Glissant explains, the long history of violence in the Caribbean plantation system has prevented "nature and culture" from forming "a dialectical whole that informs a people's consciousness" (1989, 63). As Michelle Cliff asks, "When our landscape is so tampered with, how do we locate ourselves?" (1991, 37). Consequently, an entanglement between history and culture becomes possible through what Glissant calls "the language of landscape" (Glissant 1989, 145). As I will explain, these novels construct indigenous landscapes, or native space, in order to point in two directions in time: the "deep" Caribbean history of the past and the imperative to imaginatively incorporate this history in the forging of a sovereign, creolized future.

Although the Caribbean has a vastly different indigenous history from Oceania, one sees a remarkably similar shift to native historiography, particularly in the anglophone islands. While there is a long and continuing tradition of indigeneity in the continental Caribbean nations of Guyana, Surinam, and Belize, the resurgence of native *islander* representation is remarkable because the majority of indigenous island peoples were forcibly enslaved, relocated, and in many cases, decimated by the introduction of diseases to which they had no immunity. As a result, native presence was nearly eradicated, a genocide of astounding proportions that in some islands occurred within fifty years of European arrival. Nevertheless, we must resist the myth of "fatal impact," which rehearses this violence discursively, by emphasizing the continuity of material and cultural presence of indigenous contributions to Caribbean and Atlantic modernity.[1] While the first 300 years of European presence in the Caribbean were marked by indigenous resistance to the appropriation of resources and land, by the eighteenth century the decimation of native cultures resulted in a critical scholarly turn to the entanglement of European, African, and, more recently, Asian creolization. The British were relative latecomers to the Caribbean, arriving after the erasure and forced migration of most of the indigenous island population by other Europeans. Thus British narratives have often used French and Spanish exploits for their own nationalistic ends as exemplary of the Catholic "barbarism" of their European counterparts in a way that diffracts British entanglement with the native Caribbean, especially St. Vincent.[2] For this reason this chapter will focus on indigenous islander representations in the anglophone Caribbean in order to highlight how native peoples and symbols have been (re)imagined as key tropes of historiography. This marks a break from the previous chapters that examined indigenous literary production. The longer process of creolization in the island Caribbean necessitates a different lens to foreground the tidalectic process by which the routes of diaspora are rooted in Caribbean soil. In contradistinction to the works discussed in the first section of this book, which construct a chronotope of diasporic bodies at sea, these nativizing texts function as an alter/native historiography to reroot the ancestral bodies at the bottom of the Atlantic into the Caribbean landscape.

I have organized this chapter into three general paradigms of narrative indigenization of the anglophone Caribbean. The first section addresses the complex and ambiguous role of the Carib/Arawak figure in a process that Glissant refers to as "Indianization," an ideologeme that displaces African heritage by focusing on a selective alterity of the past. The word "cannibal" is etymologically derived from the interpellation of the native Caribbean; thus the second section focuses on the trope of indigenous cannibalism, interpreted here as a fear of the consumption of otherness and a means of erecting boundaries between communities. Turning to *No Telephone to Heaven*, I argue that the protagonist of Cliff's novel utilizes a discourse of ethnic displacement in which her whiteness is consumed by native ancestry. I draw parallels between two forms of symbolic anthropophagy, *boundary cannibalism* and *creolizing cannibalism*, to argue that the protagonist Clare displaces her visible whiteness by supplanting European history with indigenous antecedents in order to legitimize the people / land relationship in Jamaica, thus facilitating native nationalism as a counternarrative to U.S. corporate imperialism. I conclude that Clare's complex genealogies are never integrated due to Jamaican social segregation, thus her heritage is experienced as bifurcated, or stratified, until her death, when she merges with the passive landscape to ruinate. The final section of this chapter expands the discussion on indigenous genealogies by examining Glissant's critique of filial narratives, the narrow ethnic genealogies that he views as epistemological precursors to colonial invasion. Glissant calls for a Caribbean cultural creolization based on the eradication of filiation, which is fictionally represented in *The Colour of Forgetting*'s concern with creole blood. In this novel there is no hierarchy of ethnic genealogies, and the character who is the most obvious metaphor of the indigenous past, Carib, "may or may not have been a descendant by blood" (Collins 1995, 4). All of the works examined in this chapter respond to Glissant's call to mend the split between nature and culture that derives from the history of the Caribbean plantocracy. While colonial settlers "cannot afford the Romantic luxury of bathing in the past, in deep history, because the past is the domain of the Other, and history is the history of dispossession" (Bunn 1994, 143), these novels reveal that in the Caribbean this "history of dispossession" is exactly what needs excavation.

The three layers, or native strata, I have outlined are by no means representative of all native Caribbean ideologemes, but they do provide a general template for recent literary and theoretical entanglements with indigenous historiography. As I have explained, diaspora theory has gained such currency that the majority of writers who are not inscribing "ex-isle" from the Caribbean are often overlooked. This is exacerbated by certain formations of American ethnic studies, which often incorporate Caribbean writers living in the United States into a national canon and tend to neglect those whose literatures can best be described as primarily concerned with indigenizing the Caribbean landscape. While most North American and British scholarship turns to postnational narratives, many of the texts I examine in this chapter and throughout this book have not been examined in ways that would engage with their inscriptions of a creole cultural nationalism. For the imaginative return to indigenous history and heritage reflects a concern with national and regional origins, an inquiry into the human sediment of the past. As is the case in Oceania and elsewhere, the texts examined here draw upon an assumption that prior historical occupation of land (made corporeally present through ancestry or living memory) legitimizes present social formations. While each do so in different ways, they are all strongly informed by an effort to naturalize the present Caribbean population's relationship to the turbulent past, an effort constituted in part by continuing outmigration from the region. Ultimately, "[w]hen one rediscovers one's landscape, desire for the other country ceases to be a form of alienation" (Glissant 1989, 234).

I also position these novels as direct engagements with Wilson Harris's critique of both the realist narrative and reductive materialist historicism of the Caribbean. In *History, Fable and Myth in the Caribbean and Guianas,* Harris draws attention to the ways in which colonial and Marxist historiographers have been limited by a materialist frame that is unable to draw upon "unpredictable intuitive resources" (1995b, 17) that would liberate subjects and spaces from relations of property. According to Harris, West Indian historians have replicated plantocracy ideologies by categorizing land and slaves in terms of economic relations.[3] Drawing upon Harris, Brathwaite has made the same critique, warning that "the plantation model . . . is in itself a product of the plantation and runs the hazard of becoming as much tool as tomb of the system that it seeks to understand and transform" (1975, 4). Harris calls for an imaginative and figurative engagement with the pre-Colombian history of the region, a genre of writing that breaks the prison of materialist realism. He contends that "a philosophy of history may lie buried in the arts of the imagination" (Harris 1995b, 18).

While Brathwaite and Harris's critiques of Caribbean historicism were first published in the 1970s and do not characterize all regional histories, the gap between realist and poetic historicism remains, as Paget Henry's *Caliban's Reason* explores in great detail. By engaging with regional philosophies of history, Henry concludes that "a poeticist engagement would raise our consciousness about the operations of liminal dynamics and categories in historicist thinking. This has the potential to expand our awareness of epistemic formations, to open dialogues with excluded positions, and hence to change our epistemological outlook" (2000, 257). What Henry characterizes as "a search for origins, or an attempt to create a myth of origins," (249) is a central concern in the novels discussed here, particularly in terms of pre-Colombian presence. Both texts dismantle the chronological narrative structure of the novel, presenting what Glissant has called "a tortured chronology of time" that epitomizes the literature of the Americas (1989, 144).[4] Cliff and Collins, trained as a historian and political scientist respectively, have turned to fictional forms in order to bring the "arts of the imagination" in a closer dialogue with "folk" traditions, landscape histories and materialist critique. Thus I read their texts as actively engaging with Harris's critique of realist narratives, revealing how reductive relations of property prevent the post-independence "folk" from obtaining access to native land and, by extension, cultural sovereignty.

This poeticist engagement with the histories of the landscape reflects a departure from the realist coming-of-age narrative that has characterized so much of Caribbean literature in English. The previous chapter examined what Anthony Appiah calls the "postrealist" novel, a product of the critique of the form of realism and the content of postcolonial nationalism (1992, 157). What Appiah observes in the African novel is particularly relevant to the novels of Cliff and Collins, whose works represent the disappointments of postcolonial nationalism and as a result are consciously experimenting with alternative knowledges and forms. And while Caribbean discourse is associated with an almost utopian model of creolization that emerged from the dystopian context of the plantocracy, these works suggest that Afro-centric models of Caribbean nationalism have posed ongoing challenges to the idealized model of heterogeneity. Generally speaking, I suspect that the recent turn to excavate an indigenous history in the anglophone island context derives from a desire on the one hand to metaphysically "root" African diaspora history as the originary layer for nationalist culture and, on the other hand, a simultaneous drive to problematize the conflation of black cultural nationalism with indigeneity itself. Consequently, current tensions between creole populations (read: indigenous) and East Indian descendants in the region may be deflected historically onto a safer, more distant past with other "Indians" who are not perceived to challenge the discourse of ethnic nationalism.

Excavating the Carib/bean: Indianization

Although the terms "Arawak" and "Carib" are rooted in European mis-recognition of the Caribbean, they continue to be relevant for indigenous communities in the region.[5] The term "cannibal" was derived from Colum-bus's interpretation of the Arawak's description of their island neighbors; to this day, this problematic division between "warlike Caribs" versus "peace-ful Arawaks" perseveres in the popular imagination and functions at some level in the literature I engage here. Anthropologists have demonstrated that the arbitrary divisions drawn between these two groups are similar to the rigid lines drawn between Melanesian, Polynesian, and Micronesian peoples in the Pacific. In both cases Europeans grafted stable ethnic car-tographies onto island populations that were highly mobile and who used the ocean as "an aquatic highway" (Watters 1997, 88). This reminds us of the ways in which islanders have become discursively constructed by colo-nists in terms synonymous with isolation. Since most native islanders were exported or exchanged as laborers by Europeans, it becomes additionally difficult to pinpoint an originary island homeland for many of these early Caribbean peoples. As Peter Hulme has shown, the European desire to then categorize distinct Black, White, and Red Carib populations reveals the intrinsic complexity of the region's early colonial history (1986).[6] This creolization of native cultural formations is representative of the ways in which the history of the Caribbean is as much a tradition of land settlement as it is of migration and diaspora. Here I am concerned with charting the ways in which indigenous islanders travel as discursive figures, haunting landscapes throughout the Caribbean as traces, remnants, and autonomous subjects.

The past few years have witnessed an unprecedented excavation of indigenous Caribbean history, which is in stark contrast to the popular "fatal impact" narrative that native peoples were exterminated by Europeans. While scholars of the Caribbean typically recognize the indigenous populations of continental Caribbean nations, and at times the Caribs of Dominica, as a whole one could say that the native peoples of the Antilles were literally erased from historical record until very recently. In the past decade, a number of important anglophone collections in history, cultural studies, and anthropology have reflected this regeneration—or excavation—of the native Caribbean islander. Although scholars such as Douglas Taylor, Irving Rouse, and others had been publishing works in this field for decades, it was not until the publication of Peter Hulme's *Colonial Encounters: Europe and the Native Caribbean* (1986) that multidisciplinary scholarship on the indigenous Caribbean gained visibility.[7] The countless scholarly texts produced on the topic in the past decade indicate a remarkable trend in mining the sediment of Caribbean alterity. In the novels I discuss here, the native islander is inscribed as a trope of Caribbean history who is brought into complex relation with African, Asian, and European settlers. Thus it is not an accident that after an era of black nationalism there has been a deepening of Caribbean ethnic historiography where indigeneity, the presumed origin of the region, has gained tremendous currency.

Not surprisingly, this indigenous excavation has traveled between disciplines, appearing increasingly in anglophone Caribbean novelists who have turned to native island history. Like the increase in scholarship on cannibalism, the renewed interest in the native Caribbean has much to do with the ways in which national fictions engage global capitalism. This imaginary excavation of indigenous historiography represents a significant change since the early 1980s when Wilson Harris lamented that "there are collections of Amerindian artifacts throughout the West Indies but ... [these] legacies are regarded as basically irrelevant to, or lacking significance for, the late twentieth-century Caribbean" (1983, 124).[8]

Not all forms of indigenous historiography are radical revisions of colonial narratives. In fact, there is a shallow process of excavation that has been traditionally used for conservative ends, which Glissant refers to as "Indianization." A critique of the discourse of Indianization, or the temporal and spatial binary opposition of "victor and vanquished" can be seen in the work of Antiguan writer Jamaica Kincaid. She has employed Carib presence most obviously in *The Autobiography of My Mother* (1996), but Caribbean indigeneity also formed a small but important part in *Lucy* (1990). The protagonist migrates from the Caribbean to the United States to work as an au pair, and she uncovers in her employer Mariah a marked contiguity between white liberal and colonial discourse. When Mariah explains that her American Indian "blood" means that she is "good at catching fish and hunting birds and roasting corn" (1990, 39), Lucy responds:

> To look at her, there was nothing remotely like an Indian about her. Why claim a thing like that? I myself had Indian blood in me. My grandmother is a Carib Indian. That makes me one-quarter Carib. But I don't go around saying that I have some Indian blood in me. The Carib Indians were good sailors, but I don't like to be on the sea; I only like to look at it. To me my grandmother is my grandmother, not an Indian. My grandmother is alive; the Indians she came from are all dead. If someone could get away with it, I am sure they would put my grandmother in a museum, as an example of something now extinct in nature, one of a handful still alive. In fact, one of the museums to which Mariah had taken me devoted a whole section to people, all dead, who were more or less related to my grandmother. (40)

Lucy concludes that Mariah "says it as if she were announcing her possession of a trophy" (40) and wonders, "How do you get to be the sort of victor who can claim to be the vanquished also?" (41)[9] As Derek Walcott has asserted, "Choosing to play Indian instead of cowboy . . . is the hallucination of imperial romance" (1998, 58). Lucy's critique is multilayered; Mariah's privileged racial and social position allows her to objectify her familial and national past, as well as to essentialize Indian cultural practices, which are reduced to hunting and gathering. Consequently, the static, corn-roasting Indian who is frozen into the past displaces the "one-quarter Carib" present subject who works for this white American family, mystifying the continuous relationship between European and U.S. hegemony. Mariah's Indianization highlights the ways in which a focus on rigid temporal and spatial forms of historical diversity ultimately erase the native present or presence. This is aptly foregrounded in Wilson Harris's novel *Jonestown* (1996), an imaginative return to the 1978 cult suicide where Jonah (Jim) Jones, a white liberal from the United States, generates a more literal indigenous destruction. He informs the native Guyanese narrator, "'The heathen are a stick with which to beat my cursed society. Use the heathen savage as a clarion call when you wish to upbraid your civilization. Pretend to be black or red or yellow. Say you understand . . . Eskimos, South Sea islanders, whatever'" (1996, 118–119). The narrator responds, "He spoke to me, his close associate, as if I were not there. I was no savage! I was invisible in my Dream-book" (119). Through Mariah and Jonah, we can define Indianization as a facile appropriation of indigenous genealogy and selected cultural traditions in a way that relegates native subjects to the remote past, suppressing the present nexus of social and political power. As Harris observes, "A purely formal appropriation of the material of the past reduces the past to a passive creature to be manipulated as an ornament of fashion or protest or experimentation" (1998, 31). Indianization's danger—when entangled with "charismatic" white liberals like Jim Jones—cannot be overlooked. In Jonestown's "indescribable horror," the narrator reports that "not all drank Coca-Cola laced with cyanide. Some were shot like cattle. Men, women and children" (Harris 1996, 3).

Indianization is not only a hallmark of reductive multiculturalism in the Americas, but has appeared throughout the Caribbean and is inextricably linked to narratives of the nation. The difference between a white or black settler population's relation to nativism is often measured by who stands to gain by "silencing the past." Michel-Rolph Trouillot reminds us that "the production of traces is always also the creation of silences" (1995, 29). Lucy exposes Mariah's Indianization and brings forth the unequal social foundations upon which Mariah builds her white liberal nativism. Mariah's appropriation of particular historical facts of "blood" displaces her understanding of the relationships between her selective genealogy, her present race/class privilege, and her Caribbean au pair. In such linear and mystifying historiographies, "the focus on the Past often diverts us from the present injustices for which previous generations only set the foundations" (Trouillot 1995, 150).

Indianization not only positions historical alterity as an "ornament of fashion," but also deflects attention from other ethnic histories and genealogies. In *Caribbean Discourse*, Glissant warns of native "pseudohistory" utilized by the elite, who used Indianization as a displacement of African origins and slavery. Since "the Carib Indians on the Francophone islands are all dead, and the Indians of French Guiana pose no threat to the existence of the system . . . Indianization thus has advantages: it glosses over the problem of Martinican origins, it appeals to one's sensitivity, it offers a pseudohistory and the illusion of cultural (pre-Colombian) hinterland, all of which is rendered harmless in advance . . . because the Caribs have already been exterminated (1989, 210).[10] Although Caribbean Indianization is more complexly layered in terms of ethnicity than the U.S. context I've discussed above, it employs the same segregation of time and space. According to historian David Lowenthal, native Caribbean peoples have been seen as "backward and ignorant savages" (1972, 184), relegated to poor agricultural regions and yet some have claimed Amerindian ancestry to supplant African heritage (185).[11] This selective genealogy is visible in parts of the Spanish-speaking Caribbean, especially the Dominican Republic, as national discourse celebrates Taíno figures such as Enriquillo and Anacoana over the perceived Africanism of Haiti.[12] Throughout the Americas, a gesture to indigenous presence in the past, abstractly imagined through the narrative of familial ancestry or spatial history (the "native" landscape), is a vital component in the forging of the national present and future.

Yet in the Caribbean, the ethnic histories of indigenous, African, Asian, and European peoples have been layered in ways that leave a residue of social stratification in the imagined historical landscape. As Lowenthal explains, "Creole hostility toward Amerindians has additional roots. Large scale African slavery was instituted in part to 'save' the Indians..., Europeans ruthlessly enslaved Africans and romanticized Indians as noble savages. The stereotype that Indians preferred death to loss of liberty reinforced the distinction" (1972, 184). The debate of how to best narrate indigenous presence in the anglophone Caribbean islands is symptomatic of these tensions in regional historiography. There is a long and rich discourse in the Caribbean that, generally speaking, variously posits native Caribbean peoples either as complicit with European plantocracy (assisting Europeans in capturing maroons), or as idealized and romantic antecedents. One can trace this ambiguity in the work of V. S. Naipaul, who initially depicted Amerindians as living embodiments of the violence of colonial history in *The Middle Passage* (1962). He writes, "Everyone knows that Amerindians hunted down runaway slaves; it was something I had heard again and again...and whenever one sees Amerindians, it is a chilling memory" (1962, 99).[13] Like Mariah, Naipaul positions native subjects in such a colonial frame that the objectifying discourse about the Amerindian past becomes the only possible template to read the indigenous present or presence. In an earlier chapter I discussed Naipaul's pessimism with regard to West Indian historiography and his reliance upon colonial historians such as James Anthony Froude.[14] I return to his critique because scholars have missed the fact that indigenous Caribbean presence is a constitutive part of Naipaul's historiography. Seven years after this travelogue was published, he prefaced *The Loss of El Dorado: A History* by invoking the indigenous peoples of Trinidad, whose tribal name marks the landscape and town in which Naipaul was born and raised. Although with his typical irony he *writes* that their disappearance "is unimportant; it is part of nobody's story," (1962, 12), it is only by discovering their presence in the historical archives that this writer, who previously declared the "futility" of West Indian history, can gain a sense of "wonder" (11) at the narrative history of the Caribbean region and embark on a historiography that blends a novelist's sensibilities with the European textual record of conquest and resistance.

In a figurative way, *The Loss of El Dorado*, while it reduces native presence to a past that is buried under colonial narrative, suggests a historical alliance between African and Amerindian peoples through the shared experience of conquest. By contrasting this text to *The Middle Passage*, I read these two works as exemplary of the two poles of Indianization discourse—first, a condemnation of native participation in colonization that reduces the Amerindian present/presence to the past, followed by an acknowledgment of shared history, which again utilizes European colonial discourse as the only parameter in which to view Amerindian past and present. In other words, Naipaul upholds the materialist model that Harris, Brathwaite, and Henry sought to dismantle. He avoids the romantic noble savage in his partial recuperation of the indigenous subject, but the alliances that some anthropologists are now accrediting to African and indigenous Caribbean populations suggests that native romanticization has, in some cases, come full circle. Rather than idealizing native Caribbean peoples as noble savages who are configured as whitewashed antecedents in opposition to ancestral African history, some scholarship silences native Caribbean complicity with the European colonial project in an effort to unify a complex cultural history.[15]

Jay Haviser had documented this new version of Indianization in Bonaire, where he observes an "enhanced appreciation of Amerindians as symbols for collective representation" (1995, 139).[16] But this appreciation functions in inverse proportion to a deeper understanding of native history. "The gap between a strengthening of identification with Amerindians coupled with a declining knowledge of Amerindians on the part of the younger generation, is an excellent example of the trend towards romanticizing such identification to the point that it becomes a purely symbolic identification with the Amerindian legacy" (151). While the participants interviewed in this study did not communicate a desire to distance themselves from African heritage, many of the foods, traditions, and burial places they identified as native Caribbean were in fact African (152). This is not to suggest that conflation of various inheritances is necessarily a cause for alarm, but to highlight the ways in which particular silences reappear in the recovery of the Caribbean past and the spiral historiography that repeatedly returns to the same lost object.

Haviser observes a "shift between the older generation, who identify Amerindianess as a personal inheritance, and the younger generation, who identify Amerindianess as a symbolic representation" (152). This "personal inheritance" I interpret as a genealogical and corporeal relationship to the past as articulated in the previous chapters. In that discussion I examined the tensions between "meta-physical" genealogies (whakapapa) and scholars who argue that "the relationship of prior to present is symbolically mediated, not naturally given" (Handler and Linnekin 1984, 287). I explained that an assertion of a "symbolic" relationship to the past over the *naturalizing* genealogical ties that define native identities creates an epistemological gap that cannot be reconciled. Michelle Cliff uses a similar strategy in that her protagonist's indigenous and African genealogies validate her otherwise constructed white body in Jamaica, but the layers of her heritage remain stratified. The younger Bonairian generation's relationship to native history, described by Haviser as symbolic, has relevance to Collins's novel in that native historiography is deliberately destabilized from corporeal claims of blood and filiation.

From Cannibalism to Ruinate: *No Telephone to Heaven*

While at one point scholars felt that "Arawak remains . . . are hardly sufficient for an original cultural reorientation and definition" (W. I. Carr quoted in Lowenthal 1972, 186),[17] the works I discuss in this chapter are invested in recuperating indigeneity for creole cultural nationalism. The discourse of nativism in the Caribbean is inextricably tied to nation-building and the attempt to naturalize a people's relationship with the land. "In the arena of political discourse and nation building, where indigenous people are central symbols, Caribbean cultures carry an indigenous legacy" (S. Wilson 1997, 213), but this legacy can often obscure the process of Caribbean creolization or signal stratification in which one cultural layer obscures the remains of another.

Like Kincaid's *Lucy*, native inheritance facilitates an identificatory turning point in Michelle Cliff's *No Telephone to Heaven*. In this novel Clare Savage reverses the trajectory of Atlantic crossings by migrating from Jamaica to the United States and then to England, aligning herself with dominant cultural identities (passing) until she sees the statue of Pocahontas in Gravesend, England. Shortly afterwards, she leaves the art institute in which she is studying, travels across Europe with her African-American lover Bobby, and when he disappears, she returns to independent Jamaica to become involved in a movement to redistribute the resources of the land. While it is not only the recognition of Pocahontas that causes Clare to question her displacement in the "Old World," the Amerindian trope does cause an important turning in the novel that has not been previously addressed.

Pocahontas is not from what we refer to today as the Caribbean, but if we utilize Peter Hulme's definition of this region as outlined in *Colonial Encounters*, Pocahontas becomes an important symbol of the early European discursive creation of the Americas. Hulme's map of the early colonial region extends from eastern Brazil to the early settlements of Virginia. "Textually this region incorporates at its northern boundary John Smith's 'rescue' by Pocahontas (near Jamestown) and at its southern boundary Robinson Crusoe's plantation" (P. Hulme 1986, 4). In this way Cliff and Hulme extend the geopolitical boundaries of the Caribbean and Clare, the "light savage," comes to see herself as a product of a complex history that is the story of the creolization of the Americas.

The Pocahontas scene significantly takes place in a graveyard, one of the spatiohistorical motifs of the novel, which reiterates Cliff's concern with the long history of Caribbean diaspora and its terms of settlement. The scene echoes an earlier moment when her mother Kitty, in exile in Brooklyn, visits the grave of the "faithful servant" Marcus, who was "frozen to death crossing the water during the perilous winter of 1702." Like her daughter many years later, Kitty "feared she would join him" (1987, 63). Kitty returns to what she refers to as "her touchstone of a grave" (77) until she leaves this country of exile for her homeland. The concern with burial in unsanctified ground remains a theme throughout the novel and is seen in other characters, such as Christopher's attempt to rebury his grandmother, Paul's inability to locate his servant Mavis's homeland after her murder, and Kitty's later burial away from the family plot. The division between the placement of the navel string and the displacement of the deceased is never reconciled until Clare's death at the end of the novel.

The Savage women's concern with ex-isle and burial outside their homeland is made apparent in Clare's mirror experience of her mother's visit to the Brooklyn cemetery. The family's connection to African roots is expanded to Amerindian when, many years later, Clare visits the statue of Pocahontas, a "gift from the Colonial Dames of America," which she initially describes as, "Bronze. Female. Single figure. Single feather rising from the braids. Moccasined feet stepping forward, as if to walk off the pedestal on which she was kept. A personification of the New World, dedicated to some poor soul who perished in pursuit of it" (1987, 135). Clare's Eurocentric training leads her to "suspect allegory" in any representation of a female figure; therefore, unlike her mother, she does not immediately recognize its colonial and personal significance. Then she realizes, "It was not that at all. No; this was intended to signify one individual and mark her resting place" (1987, 136). This scene reflects her earlier identification with the heroine of *Jane Eyre* until she realizes that the fictional form, like the allegorical, "tricked her," and she comes to see herself as Jean Rhys's Bertha, interpreted as "Jamaican. Caliban. Carib. Captive" (116). Like Harris's work, Cliff consciously dismantles the realist novel and engages with Harris's call for a radical examination of Amerindian origins and legacies that cull "the arts of the imagination."

Once Clare is able to free herself from the structures of European narrative form and genre, she recognizes Pocahontas as a historical precursor and begins to draw more significant connections between their two lives. Clare "found two stained-glass windows, one showing her baptism, full-grown, wild, kneeling at the font. Found she had been tamed, renamed Rebecca. Found she had died on a ship leaving the rivermouth and the country, but close enough for England to claim her body . . . in her twentieth year" (136). For the twenty-year-old Clare, Pocahontas's exile in England and her subsequent burial in this colonial motherland is a narrative that too closely parallels and perhaps foreshadows her own life. The Pocahontas scene represents an important turning point when Clare conflates herself with this Amerindian exile. "Something was wrong. She had no sense of the woman under the weights of all these monuments. She thought of her, her youth, her color, her strangeness, her unbearable loneliness. Where was she now?" (137). The novel's narrator has already described Clare as "a light-skinned woman, daughter of landowners, native-born, slaves, émigrés, Carib, Ashanti, English" (5), but until this point Clare has made no attempt to publicly proclaim any Amerindian heritage. She is so stricken with exteriority that it is only by seeing herself reflected externally that she begins to comprehend the relationship between her mixed heritage and her exile in England.

Clare abruptly leaves Gravesend for London and in the next scene identifies herself as a native Caribbean and African subject. When Clare complains to her Anglo-English friend about racist comments made about Africans, Liz assures her the "'words weren't directed at you'" (139). In response, Clare personalizes her own ancestry by asserting that she is "by blood" of African descent. In Clare's two attempts to establish a corporeal link to native and African ancestry, her white friend undermines the relationship; Liz insists Clare's "blood has thinned." For the first time in the novel, Clare claims Amerindian heritage and informs Liz, "'Some of my ancestors were Caribs . . . cannibals'" to "shock" her audience. Once again,

Liz undermines the significance of corporeality by replying, "'That's ancestors. Some of mine wore skins and worshiped fire'" (139). The dismissive
European response to the discourse of corporeal ancestry, as I explained in
a previous chapter, highlights an important epistemological gap between
some western and indigenous discourses. Liz and Mariah employ a selective genealogical narrative, "thinning" out the corporeal claims of the colonial past on the bodies of European and indigenous present/presence. As
an ideological mirror to Mariah's discourse of blood, this European dis-
membering of the past mystifies the relationship between ancestry, colonial history, and the unequal social formations of the present.

The "shock" factor in this scene, which echoes the embracing of anthropophagy by Brazilian modernists, exists only because Clare is determined
to make a corporeal relationship to ethnic otherness. Rather than abstract-
ing a distant relationship to the Caribs, or questioning whether their practice of cannibalism was in fact a construction on the part of Europeans to
justify native slavery, or even claiming "peaceful Arawak" heritage, Clare
embraces one of the most taboo images of western modernity and establishes a history of blood to her present body. This does not position Clare
as corporeally linked to *natural* savages, but to their opposite. As Peter
Hulme explains, "Human beings who eat other human beings have always
been placed on the very borders of humanity. They are not regarded as
*in*human because if they were animals their behavior would be natural and
could not cause the outrage and fear that 'cannibalism' has always provoked"
(1986, 14). By strategically positioning herself as an unnatural other, Clare
distinguishes herself from the Anglo-English community. Building upon
the work of William Arens, Hulme defines cannibalism as "the image of
ferocious consumption of human flesh frequently used to mark the boundary between one community and its others" (1986, 86). Hulme refers to
the Arawaks, who informed Columbus that their island neighbors were
cannibals, and the way in which Europeans appropriated this information, quickly redrawing the cartography of the Caribbean along arbitrary
boundaries between "peaceful Arawaks" and "Caribbee Islands." But when
this form of boundary cannibalism is used in relation to Clare's identity, it
becomes obvious that she is strategically using a "ferocious" genealogy to
"mark the boundary" between herself and the colonial English motherland
into which she has been incorporated. This is particularly important for
a character like Clare, who, benefiting from her light skin, has not questioned the racial boundaries erected between her European and African/
Amerindian ancestry.

Wilson Harris, perhaps the Caribbean's biggest proponent of symbolic, creolizing cannibalism, has continually returned to this theme of consuming the other throughout his work. In his essay "Judgement and dream," he explains that the Caribs "consumed a morsel of the flesh of their enemy and they thought thereby they would understand the[ir] secrets" (1999a, 22). Rather than reacting with the abhorrence so common to most responses to cannibalism, Harris envisions consuming the other as a productive practice, a "deeply moral compulsion to contend with innermost bias in humanity and to consume some portion of that inner rage, inner fire, associated with cruel prejudice" (23). When Harris's theory is aligned with Clare's effort to reclaim presumed savagery, it highlights how Clare ingests the Carib and African other by claiming their blood in her body, yet, by extension, this validates her English identity as the consuming subject. In other words, her invocation of cannibalism creates a corporeal boundary between herself and the Anglo-English. Unlike boundary cannibalism, creolizing cannibalism refers to consumption of the other, or consumption of African and Carib heritage and alterity. This leaves Clare's Anglo-English heritage in an irreconcilable ethnic space, an aporia where she is visibly the white creole who symbolically consumes the other, while simultaneously being the other who erects a boundary against the Anglo-English.

This conflict between racial identities arises later in the novel and highlights the bifurcated strata of Clare's ethnicity. Soon after her reclamation of African and Amerindian identity, Clare returns to Jamaica when her friend Harriet writes, "Jamaica needs her children" (Cliff 1987, 140). There she participates in a resistance movement to reclaim her homeland from U.S. corporate and elite nationalist rule. The discourse of filiation, so apparent in the discussion with Liz above, becomes substituted by the discourse of landscape, place, and nation. While Clare's alignment with Amerindian identity catalyzes her decision to return home, her cultural allegiances shift in Jamaica; the roots that she prioritizes become Afro-Jamaican, seen in her reclamation of her grandmother's land. Similar to Kincaid's Lucy, Cliff's protagonist excavates Amerindian heritage as a signpost to achieving a multiethnic Caribbean identity that layers African ancestry and cultural systems over the native Caribbean. To draw from the epistemologies of etak, we may say that her navigation between these two island nations employs a "multiple reference orientation" (Lewis 1994, 148), but one that is not continuous between segments. In England, Clare utilizes the western navigational "self-centre system" where a complex network of relations is calculated with the (consuming) self as a somewhat rigidly defined locus. The "home-centre reference system," which Clare uses in Jamaica, is a cognitive method that prioritizes the geographic points of land and seascape to gain physical and cultural bearings. In etak, both conceptual systems are used for successful navigation and landfall, but Clare's inability to bring both self and home into complex relation creates a bifurcated subject, existing in a limbo tension between Carib, Arawak, European, and African heritage.

By juxtaposing particular scenes in the novel, Clare's displacement of Amerindian heritage is rendered visible. The first scene of significance takes place during an economic crisis in the nation where many Jamaicans are displaced from land and resources. In a chapter called "The Great Beast," Harriet describes to Clare her horror over her discovery that what she has just eaten with "her people" was an iguana. She recognizes that "this ancient monster faced her, was in her." When Harriet realizes it was stolen from the zoo, she exclaims to Clare, "'What does it mean when we people have to break into a zoo to steal lizard for nyam? When we people nyam monster? . . . better never come. We locked past that. We locked in time, sister. We in fockin' lockstep. We ancestor nyam lizard too . . . . Despair too close sometime. Everyt'ing mus' change, sister'" (1987, 188). Harriet's reference to "ancestors" is ambiguous, but since the precolonial Caribbean would not be necessarily associated with "despair," we must assume that she refers to African ancestry and the poverty and dispossession that have resurfaced despite Jamaican independence. If one pursues this reading, then there is a break in the narrative between an African past and Amerindian. The word iguana itself is Arawakan, and the Arawaks were voluntary hunters and consumers of iguanas; this creature has functioned as an important trope of Amerindian presence in Caribbean literature, especially in the poetry of Derek Walcott.[18] While it is significant that these iguanas are in the zoo (in a museum like Lucy's ancestors), Harriet's horror over the consumption, the eating of this "monster" that "was in her," can be read alongside Harris's creolizing cannibalism as a rejection of the other, a revulsion regarding particular Amerindian practices. While one could argue that Clare is unaware of this Arawak practice, it would be unlikely since she has "studied the conch knife excavated at the Arawak site in White Marl . . . the shards of hand-thrown pots . . . the petroglyphs hidden in the bush" (193).

By turning to Cliff's description of rural Jamaica (which never fails to portray the triptych: Arawak, landscape, and iguana), we can better understand the problems posed by Amerindian presence. In a scene immediately preceding Harriet's despair, Clare returns to her grandmother's land, which is described as "the chaos of the green—reaching across space, time too it seemed. When only Arawaks and iguanas and birds and crocodiles and snakes dwelt here. Before landfall. Before hardship" (172). Certainly one has to question how the Arawak got to Jamaica if not by landfall, but the passage makes clear a rather idealistic Arawak/land essentialism that is central to the novel's structure. Clare then has a "rebaptism" in the water and is symbolically returned to the land (172). These particular scenes are significant because they reveal the fact that the text has slipped from positioning Clare as the conflated Carib/cannibal in England to becoming Arawak/native when she is in Jamaica. Arawak nativism is depicted as acceptable when it is associated with the passive land, but repulsed from the nation when experienced as a dietary practice. What is noticeably absent from this indigenous dyad is Carib *cannibalism*, which leaves its trace in the horror and revulsion exemplified by impoverished Jamaicans ingesting iguana "monsters." Harriet seems to suggest that national poverty has caused Jamaicans to revert, first to "nyam . . . dog . . . cat . . . rat . . . mongoose . . . [and then] monster," and the unspoken and final reversion to the ancestry she invokes can only be the consumption of *each other*. This, I believe, is what causes Harriet to vomit "onto her fastidious, angry self" (188), and is symbolically fulfilled, as I will explain, by the betrayal of the revolutionaries.

Cliff is utilizing two differently inflected discourses of cannibalism in the novel, which are determined by national space and race. The first is Hulme's definition of boundary cannibalism, underlined by Clare's disassociation from Liz while in England. The second is Harris's creolizing cannibalism, where the visibly white Clare must consume the indigenous other in order to digest her bias. But creolizing cannibalism can only be enacted when Clare is in England, as a means of ingesting her own genealogical others. When she returns home, she recodes herself as black and therefore cannibalism—a metaphor of consuming the African or indigenous other—becomes abhorrent. One could argue that if Clare practiced creolizing cannibalism in Jamaica it would be inscribed as the consumption of whiteness, which is exactly the ethnicity she attempts to subsume. In Harriet's view, creolizing cannibalism represents an evolutionary regression, made apparent when one of the revolutionaries' own, like quashees of the past, betrays their objectives and causes their deaths. Ultimately, the narrative reveals that *active* and *present* indigenous practices, such as cannibalism, are repulsed from the nation-space because they contribute to the deaths of those who attempt to redistribute national resources. If, as Zita Nunes argues, all acts of cannibalism produce a residue, then the ultimate indigestible remnant of Jamaican history in this novel is the quashee, or betrayer.

The prophecy of cannibalism is suggested when immediately after Harriet's rejection of the "monster" in her body, she tells Clare "it time" to meet the revolutionaries. The revolutionary community is later shown to contain within itself a quashee who consumes his or her own. In an effort to distance herself from the abhorrent genealogy invoked by Arawaks consuming iguanas, Clare is interviewed and responds in contradicting ways of her allegiance. When she is asked, "To whom do you owe your allegiance?" Clare answers, "I have African, English, Carib in me" (189) in a way that echoes the displaced speaker of Walcott's poem "The Schooner *Flight:*" "I have Dutch, nigger, and English in me/and either I'm nobody or I'm a nation" (1986, 346). For Clare, genealogy does not answer the question of her solidarity, and while she substitutes "Carib" for Walcott's "Dutch," she has never associated her Carib heritage with the Jamaican land; in fact her refusal to recognize active indigenous cannibalism in her native land leads to her destruction. The discourse of ancestry here is destabilized; although the unnamed African interviewer is likened to the "color of (Clare's) grandmother," she reminds Clare not to substitute the markers of race for political allegiance. This invokes Clare's earlier discussion with Liz, who also dismantles the discourse of genealogy. Yet if Clare cannot claim her identity through her ethnically layered genealogy, where can her allegiance be located?

The novel's answer to this question is found immediately after Clare's recitation of her heritage. She admits that she ultimately "owes [her] allegiance to the place [her] grandmother made," and the interviewer responds, "Place again?" (189). The feminization of place has been commented upon by Cliff herself in her essay "Caliban's daughter." She writes, "For me, the land is redolent of my grandmother and mother. The same could be said of Clare Savage, who seeks out the landscape of her grandmother's farm as she would seek out her grandmother, mother. There is nothing left at that point but the land, and it is infused with the spirit and passion of these two women" (1991, 46). The relationship Clare has to her own homeland is an ambiguous one, which is not reconciled by female lineage or by the novel's conflation of woman and land. During her interview with the resistance movement, Clare had slipped from explaining that "the history that [she] brings to [her] students" is "the history of their . . . our homeland," underlining her continuing displacement. Clare is working through a "new sort of history," which demands an awareness that "it involves" her (1987, 193). But her attempt to work through a Jamaican historiography that transcends the material and economic models discussed earlier leads to a conflict between the manifestation of colonial hegemony in the present and the always inaccessible indigenous past. Her inability to come to terms with the deep history of the socionatural landscape of Jamaica, while it becomes her ultimate allegiance, is exactly what prevents her from reconciling her complex ancestry during her lifetime. The discussion of cannibalism and genealogy above suggests that there are unequal social formations that prevent her from drawing upon her various ethnicities. Unable to integrate a "multiple reference orientation" between home and self, she becomes a stratified and stranded subject.

In her quest for native heritage, Clare's rejection of the specter of Carib/cannibalism prevents her access to Arawak/land and causes her demise. After a quashee betrays the revolutionaries, Clare is killed in the "bitterbush" (208). Jamaican history is rendered as a tautology, which suggests that this attempt to reoccupy the land, to reclaim an indigenous tradition "before landfall . . . before hardship" can only be met with death. As the narrator comments, "So lickle movement in this place. From this place. Then only back and forth, back and forth, over and again—for centuries" (16). To extend the cannibalism metaphor, it is the refusal to internalize the monster, to recognize the historic cannibalizing of one's own that prevents the success of the revolutionaries. For the ingestion of the other to be successful, one must first acknowledge the power and presence of the enemy within. Thus while the text seems to draw upon Amerindian heritage, it is the refusal to acknowledge the practice of cannibalism, symbolically excavated from historical quashees, that thwarts the reclamation of the land for present, living Jamaicans.

At the moment of her death, Clare "remembered the language. Then it was gone" (208). The last page of the novel is filled with the calls of birds. In an essay Cliff remarks, "Her death occurs at the moment she relinquishes human language, when the cries of birds are no longer translated by her into signifiers of human history, her own and her people's, but become pure sound, the same music heard by the Arawak and Carib" (1991, 46). Cliff returns us to her novel's concern with history, burial, and native landscape. Clare's "mother's landscape" (1987, 173) is a space of "unquiet ground" due to "the anger of spirits, who did not rest, who had not been sung to their new home" (174). In their despair, the slaves who occupied this ground had eaten dirt (174), a literal ingestion of the native landscape that causes death. This "unquiet ground" suggests that the land holds the national history of betrayal, bloodshed, and displacement. The troubled spirits of the past anticipate the modern quashee, whose betrayal leads Clare to a full recovery of the native Caribbean, but achieved only in death. The landscape of Clare's indigenous epiphany is significantly populated, present with ghostly Arawak and Carib, who are brought together for the first time and located in the imaginary nation-space of Jamaica. To summarize my argument, in Clare's genealogical history, the Arawak and Carib worlds are always at odds with each other, and sedimented nativism, or the integration of the two indigenous histories, can be obtained only beyond Clare's life and language. The fact that the Carib are not associated with the Jamaican land until after Clare's death (and textually, after the novel in Cliff's essay) suggests that the novel's passive Arawak/land is haunted by the specter of the active Carib/cannibals. This is particularly striking when we consider that, historically speaking, the Carib never did settle in Jamaica.

Cliff's return to the indigenous Caribbean at the moment of Clare's death suggests that the strata of this landscape are founded upon multiple Amerindian legacies, the historical space of Jamaica "before landfall," yet contradictorily populated by humans. If "many modern [Caribbean] people view themselves as rightful heirs to the land by virtue of their indigenous ancestry rather than because of their relationship to conquering ancestors" (S.Wilson 1997, 212), then Cliff's novel utilizes this genealogical prerogative as a foundation of an unrealizable national belonging. As the novel continually struggles against the *active* native Caribbean (iguana-eating Arawak and cannibal Caribs), it indicates that Clare still desires a *passive* indigenous landscape. Cliff provides us with a critique of Indianization by revealing how landscape histories maintain an active relationship to the present that, if ignored, results in deadly consequences for human subjects.

In *No Telephone to Heaven*, there is a split between the way the landscape incorporates various histories and the way these histories are carried by human bodies. At the level of human social formations, Clare's ethnicity is layered—like stratum but without sedimentation of her cultural heritage. In another context, David Bunn, building upon Freud, has referred to this as anaclisis, "or the 'propping' of one landscape paradigm upon another" (1994, 144). While Bunn sees this as indicative of colonial historiography (in that colonial discourse cannot recognize previous inhabitants of the land without challenging their own narratives of *terra nullius*), it has relevance to Clare's negotiation of her identity in that she cannot afford to integrate the various ethnicities within the black and white polarizations of her society. The divisions between African, European, and indigenous genealogies are predicted in the early pages of the novel where the narrator recites Clare's complex ethnic heritage and positions her on a truck called *No Telephone to Heaven*, a vehicle or vessel of intended sovereignty where Clare sits "alongside people who easily could have hated her" (Cliff

1987, 5). It is because of this racial polarization that indigeneity becomes the third space beyond the always-competing black and white. This third space is unattainable within the binary system in which Clare exists, and results in anaclisis since there are no present Carib or Arawak to challenge her occupation of indigenous historical / imaginary space.

In the novel, her grandmother's rural land is perhaps the only space that allows the coexistence of multiple histories, demonstrated in the interplanting of African and Amerindian crops. "They found, in the process of clearing the land, things that had been planted long before—before even the grandmother—which had managed to survive the density of the wild forest. Cassava. Afu. Fufu. Plantain" (1987, 11).[19] Clare remains a figure of ethnic stratification, of anaclisis, and the only true sedimentation occurs in the earth, where the farm has been left to "ruinate." As Cliff explains, this is the process by which human settlement may "lapse back into 'bush'" (1) and it is the same and *only* process by which Clare, in returning her lifeless body back to the consuming earth, will merge with the botanical "signifiers of human history" (1987, 173).[20]

From Landscape Filiation to the "Complicity of Relation": *The Colour of Forgetting*

> Indigenous peoples are . . . symbols of resistance to external
> domination . . . they were the first to fight against colonial-
> ism and the first to fall victim to it. Thus the indigenous
> peoples are one of the most powerful symbols of defiance
> against colonial oppression.
> —S. Wilson, "The Legacy of the Indigenous People of
> the Caribbean"

In describing the conglomeration of Jamaican revolutionaries aboard the truck called *No Telephone to Heaven*, the narrator of Cliff's novel anticipates the tautology of violence and raises a question that is never answered by her protagonist, "Fighting among themselves—as usual. How did they come to this?" (1987, 19). Like the vessel of sovereignty ironically imagined as *Sure Salvation* in Chapter One, this vehicle is torn by racial and social hierarchies that prevent its successful navigation into the future. While Cliff explores the anaclisis of Clare's genealogy in order to excavate its historical precursors, Merle Collins's *The Colour of Forgetting* seems to be posing the same question but turns more to the land than genealogy for its answers. While both novels undermine linear narrative time, revealing how the present formations of these different Caribbean societies are occupied by spirits of the past, Cliff adopts a temporal trajectory that brings Clare back in time to Arawak and Carib, while Collins begins with native history and concludes somewhat more hopefully with the nation's future generation of children. Both texts trace multiple generations of Caribbean families, rely on Amerindian images for their excavation of the past, and are punctuated by violent struggles against repressive governmental and corporate regimes. While one can summarize both novels as primarily concerned with investigating the political and social practices that displace Caribbean people from their own land and the ways in which these practices can be resisted, the texts differ in their inscription of what constitutes "native blood" and national belonging. While Cliff inscribes a passive landscape that is contradictorily at odds with its human population, Collins depicts a more active dialectic between the community and the land so that the "signifiers of human history" are part of the very landscape.

The Colour of Forgetting represents a significant break from Collins's earlier coming-of-age novel, *Angel* (1987), not only in its narrative form and subject, but by its focus on the competing blood ties that contribute to the creolization of the fictionalized Paz Island community and the ways in which Carib history haunts the violent events of the community's present. The character Carib, who frames the novel, enters the text, reciting her mantra, "Blood in the north, blood to come in the south, and the blue crying red in between" (1995, 3). Carib repeats this message, at my counting, over forty times and her tautological message has a different referent each time it is declared. On the first page she invites the reader to "'look at them. Running and jumping. Jumping and screaming. You hear the voices coming up from the bush? Forgotten and consoled. Forgotten and drowned. And the blue crying red in between'" (1995, 3). Carib, we are told, is speaking from Leapers' Hill, where "the Amerindian people . . . escaped their French pursuers by jumping off the cliff into the sea. Since then, legend had it, the sea in that part of the island was particularly angry sometimes, churned up with remembering" (4).[21] Invoking tidalectics, and foreshadowing the novel's conclusion, the violent practices of the land slip into the water rendering, to draw again from Derek Walcott, "the sea (as) history" (1986, 364). Although the tidalectics between land and sea are of crucial significance, Collins builds upon the transoceanic imaginary to explore the layering process of land settlement and cultural sovereignty. Like Walcott's poem which asks "where are your monuments, your battles, your martyrs?" (364) Collins's work investigates the often-conflicting ways that a community memorializes its heritage. While Carib physically represents the role of the community's memory, there is a lack of adequate monuments to Paz Island's ancient past. "A people who had given the island such a proud memory had on the spot no monument to their bravery but the voice of the woman called Carib" (1995, 4). The importance of monumentalizing the history of the land is a major concern in the novel and can be seen through the reliance on material stone markers, plaques, toponyms, oral and written tradition, and the traces on the land itself that signify the history of human and nonhuman settlement. Like Derek Walcott and others, Collins broadens the signifiers of history in an effort to deconstruct Froude and Naipaul's assertion that the West Indies is bereft of historical consequence. As I will explain, one of the novel's main objectives is to weave together poeticist, materialist, and landscape histories. Thus this island's historiography is exceedingly complex and cannot be defined by one particular type of narrative. Since Carib is perhaps the most central and present character in the novel, a corporeal symbol of the nation's past and future, she facilitates the island's memory as her female ancestors did before her. "She, and her mother before her, and, it was rumoured, her mother before her had been given the name Carib because of the regular pilgrimage to this hill, named Leapers' Hill in memory of the brave Amerindians. The Caribs were thus not quite forgotten, having as their shrine an entire hill, verdant with undergrowth" (4). While the land may mark the spots of historical significance, too often the people need verbal cues. Carib's voice, in "its endless effort to kick-start their memory" (5), plays this role. Collins points out that the community often neglects their dialectic with the land; therefore Carib is always positioned at important sites of the island's history, at monuments and in the cemetery at Leapers' Hill.

Heterotopia and the "Language of Landscape"

While Collins refers to the island as Paz, the real Leapers' Hill is located in Grenada, Collins's home and the space that informs the conflicted topos of the novel. Like many islands in the Caribbean (and Oceania), Grenada has a layered history of settlement, rendered visible by its complex toponymy: Camerhogne (Carib), Concepción (from Columbus), Mayo (from Alonso de Hojeda, a companion of Amerigo Vespucci), Granada (from the Spanish), La Granade (French), and after the Treaty of Paris, the English changed it to its current name, Grenada (Brizan 1984, xvii). Each name invokes a particular formation of time-space and cultural settlement, which often reflects anaclisis rather than sedimentation. As I explained in the introduction, the interpellation of tropical islands has reflected a European mystification of the colonial process, layering utopian names over the dystopian brutality of the plantation complex. The complex layering of this island's history is made apparent in Collins's narrative by conflating time and space, and by drawing attention to the naming practices of the multiple cultures that called this island home.

Calling attention to the mystification of colonial violence, Collins attributes the name Paz to an ironic Spanish Catholic reference to the slave markets of the island's early history, a derivative of "*pax tecum*. Peace be with you. Pax. With a slap. Take that" (1995, 17). The Carib name for the land, Camerhogne, is described in contrast "like a howl. Like music" (19). Other names of the island's towns, cities, and topography include Content, Mon Repos, Soliel, Nigger Yard, Worker's Row, Colony Hospital, Paradise, Paradise River, Après Toute, and Perd Temps. The conglomeration of English, Latin, Spanish, French, Creole, and Carib names all reflect the often-contradictory social histories that are represented in this small island, and many of them signify a space beyond or lost to time. This can be likened to what Michel Foucault refers to as heterotopia—a space that reveals the fallacy of colonial *terra nullius*. To Foucault, *utopia* is characterized as "a space that is other, another real space, as perfect, as meticulous, as well arranged as ours is messy, ill constructed and jumbled" (1986, 27). Foucault "wonders if certain colonies have not functioned somewhat in this matter" (27), and certainly this is evident in names such as Paradise, Paradise River, and Mon Repos. The practice of *heterotopology*, a hallmark of Collins's novel, juxtaposes "in a single real space several spaces, several sites that are in themselves incompatible" (Foucault 1986, 25). Collins contrasts the illusion of isolated utopian space ("Paradise River" and "Après Toute") against the "jumbled" material world that was created in the Caribbean plantation systems ("Nigger Yard" and "Worker's Row"). The novel's emphasis on heterotopia does not, however, privilege human settlement over landscape history. Collins is cognizant of Wilson Harris's critique of the ways in which modernity, a radical break from tradition that took place in the Caribbean well before it traveled back to Europe, has created a "hollowing of space" (Harris 1999, 63) characterized by the subjugation of the nonhuman world to linear narratives of progress. It is for this reason, I suggest, that Collins foregrounds the land's response to its layered history of settlement. *The Colour of Forgetting* can be read as a response to Harris's call to enact a "density of perception that gives reality to interwoven primordial and man-made worlds" (ibid., 62).

The novel's excavation of Paz Island's heterotopology necessarily complicates historical space, highlighting the ways in which colonial history and the plantation system prevent a "natural" layering of human sediment over time. The presence of the character Carib, a "meta-physical" manifestation of the island's pre-Colombian past in the present, highlights the island's *perd temps*, also conjured in the title of the novel. This implies Glissant's description of the "tortured sense of time" in the literature of the Americas, derived from "the haunting nature of the past" (1989, 144). Throughout the novel the community encounters various spirits that indicate that "the haunting nature of the past" is central to any understanding of the space of the present. The "spirit of a tree, homeless and roaming" (Collins 1995, 159) repeatedly appears, and in the ruins of the old sugar mill, "African people still walking around" (95). The village settlement is a space where "the mountain whispered its magic to itself. And Ajakbe's mother wailed in the wind" (58). Ajakbe, the young daughter of the spirit woman lajabless, appears to one villager and is nearly adopted until lajabless's spirit voice calls from the cocoa fields (65). The nation's plantation history (cocoa, sugar cane, and nutmeg) literally haunts the present space of this mountain community, where the spirits represent the land's response to history. The novel unites what Glissant has called "transferred space" and "suffered time" so that "memory" is "stamped on the spatial reality" (1989, 144). As a narrative technique, the haunting of the past is a device that deconstructs linear chronology. This is evident when the character Mamag invokes spiral time by explaining, "'Everything that happening today... it happen before .... Yesterday is today, is tomorrow, is the day after.... Is long, long time Carib telling us what is to happen'" (Collins 1995, 85, 86). Collins's novel does not confront linear time by inscribing a tautology (like *No Telephone to Heaven*), but adopts a spiral narrative form that creates a dialogue between the haunting nature of the past and the promising capacity for change which is attributed to the future.

What Glissant refers to as "the language of landscape" (1989, 145) is most apparent in the novel's description of the various settlements on the island's mountain. Collins constructs a layered toponymy, a colonial heterotopology that condenses time and space. The Scots first called it "Arthur's Seat . . . like some place they knew at home, and it became theirs. But not for long, and never, really" (1995, 19) since the Africans quickly renamed it Attaseat, "claiming the magic" (20). Collins draws attention to the cultural differences between "the language of landscape" and perceptions of land possession. Terrestrial belonging is inflected differently when "the Scots adventurers, coming long after the paths had been cleared of Amerindian footprints," find the mountain "sinister." The Scots sugarcane planters are contextualized as part of a series of arrivals to the mountain who have no relationship with this landscape or the Carib, "since by the time they came, the Caribs were gone, the French had left and the Scots knew no other name"(19). In contrast, Africans are depicted as having a dialectical engagement with the land since they are "not afraid of the brambles and the frog croaks and the monkeys swinging far above and all the strange animal sounds. . . . Perhaps the Africans just knew better how to talk with the spirit of this land that people said the Caribs, who had another name too, used to call Camerhogne" (19). The Africans' cre-olization of European toponyms and their ability to speak the language of the land is coded as naturalizing sediment in opposition to the displaced Scots. The novel indicates that certain settlements are stratified, whereas African arrivants have experiential and cultural access to Carib sediment. Unlike Cliff's novel, there is not a hierarchy of arrival or transparent access through genealogy. Instead, each people's relationship to the land is deter-mined by their cultural familiarity through the landscape of their previous homeland and their experiential dialectic in transplanted space.

The Colour of Forgetting engages a spatial imagination that is not simply reducible to material production; this is evident in the description of the various settlements on the island's mountain. The mountain topos is an important site of maroonage and thus not determined by the plantocracy system that informs so much of the region's historiography. Collins repeat-edly demonstrates that the mountain land is not deemed valuable by the Scots, the other European planters, or the contemporary elite of Paz Island because its coolness does not allow the successful cultivation of sugarcane. However, the mountain is not entirely unmarked by the plantocracy sys-tem for, as mentioned, it is haunted by slave ghosts, and the present com-munity is exploited by the nutmeg plantocracy before and after indepen-dence. However, the mountain does allow a considerably less-determined space for the community to develop a more naturalized relationship to the land, through subsistence farming and generations of *relatively* uninter-rupted settlement. The mountain topos also allows certain members of the village to purchase and inherit land affordably, unlike the tourist beaches referenced throughout the novel.

The use of rural space as a trope for the naturalized and therefore metonymically indigenous aspects of Caribbean heritage is evident in many Caribbean novels.[22] As discussed in the first chapter, these novels often erect a duality between the folk aesthetic of the rural community and the more repressive colonial inheritance of urban space. The importance of land settlement, the imaginative occupation of a region's landscape, is central because European plantocracies often determined this relationship. With the exception of Glissant, few have theorized the significance of this dialectic between people and the land. Glissant explains that the plantocracy's compression of land/labor prevented "Caribbean people [from relating] a mythological chronology of this land to their knowledge of this country, and so nature and culture have not formed a dialectical whole that informs a people's consciousness" (1989, 63). The Caribbean "landscape is its own monument: its meaning can only be traced on the underside. It is all history" (11). In Caribbean narratives, "[t]he individual, the community, the land are inextricable in the process of creating history" (105).[23] In moving away from the models of materialist realism, Collins offers a model of landscape history that pushes the boundaries of what the local government and plantocracy of her novel deem, in the words of one character, "uneconomic" (1995, 163).

The Colour of Forgetting inscribes the dialect between nature and culture in a number of natural metaphors that are significant tropes in the novel. The human history of the land is often mirrored by flora and fauna, such as the competition between crapaud and monkey, or between the immortelle and cocoa tree, but Collins does not reduce the land to simple mimesis of the human population. Situated in the chapter "Ti-Moun and Cosmos," the rivalry between trees is contrasted to the brothers whose lives are explored in the chapter. Unlike the immortelle and cocoa's battle for sunlight, "Ti-Moun and Cosmos were planted apart. Not wanting each other's sunlight, they grew apart, each wondering at the other's branching" (1995, 32). In this passage, the people and land are not essentialized in idealistic ecological relation; the flora and fauna that surround the human population are also settlers, highlighting the ways in which landscape renders the complex material processes of transplantation and settlement. For example, breadfruit, imported to the Caribbean from Tahiti by William Bligh, is related to the brothers and the rivalry against other trees. There is probably no other region in the world that has been more radically altered in terms of flora and fauna than the Caribbean. Collins brings together native flora of the Caribbean landscape (like cocoa)[24] and imported, colonial crops such as breadfruit and nutmeg (a product of the "Spice Islands" of Indonesia) to naturalize both indigenous and imported transplants in ways remarkably similar to Mitchell's *Amokura*. Transplanted peoples and flora become sedimented in the landscape; routes become rooted in complex rather than static and sedentary relation. This is significantly different from Cliff's topography, where Arawak are situated "before landfall," and the historical fact that plants like cassava were indigenous imports is overlooked.

Through its naturalizing depiction of the relation between transplanted and indigenous human beings and flora, *The Colour of Forgetting*
employs Wilson Harris's call for writers to "deepen out perception of the
fauna and flora of a landscape of time which indicates the kind of room or
space or material vision of time in which whole societies conscripted themselves" (1995b, 48). Like Glissant, Harris suggests that "the mysterious
fauna and flora of legend, in which philosophies of time gestate, may offer
continuity from the remote past into the future" (1995b, 49). The continuity inscribed between the present and past is an attempt to undermine
colonial balkanization and to examine the ways in which multiple human
and nonhuman elements have contributed to the fashioning of Paz Island's
heterotopia. Thus the novel engages a phenomenology of landscape that is
both poetic and deeply informed by material history.

The temporal continuity offered through the land, however, is not
inscribed without conflict. For example, Carib functions in the novel as a
corporeal reminder of the history embedded in the land because certain
members of the community have neglected the dialectic. In other words,
the landscape of *The Colour of Forgetting*, although obviously mediated by
the author, is an active *participant* in its own historical process. The major
difference between the two novels is that while Cliff represents the land as
unrecuperable to contemporary Jamaicans, Collins concentrates upon the
exchange between the landscape and its residents. Thus Collins's landscape
is dynamic and even consuming and cannibalistic—the very activity that
Cliff's protagonist cannot accept. For example, the rocks associated with
the Carib Leapers' Hill "had eaten" (Collins 1995, 197) a young boy, and
a subaquatic volcano, erroneously presumed inactive, claims the life of an
infant. When the community begins to argue over "land confusion" (44),
the nonhuman world erupts in the text. In the chapter "The Land," the
government is overthrown by socialists, but this gets far less textual space
than the nonhuman response: tree spirits confront the villagers, balls of
fire are seen in the sky, noises are heard from the old, slave-run sugar mill,
and "in the night not only the spirits but the cats took over" and haunt the
villagers (59). Later the island is threatened by a hurricane, an Arawakan
word that entered the English language around the same time as cannibal
(P. Hulme 1986, 100) and which has figured prominently as a metonym
for native history in Caribbean literature. In *The Colour of Forgetting* the
African and indigenous past is separated from passive land essentialism,
where indigenous history is positioned as a moment in a series of human
arrivals.

A second but no less important difference between the two novels is the complex and shifting dialectic between land and genealogy. While Cliff utilizes genealogy to validate Clare's occupation of her homeland, Collins reveals the ways in which some discourses of blood or kinship often *prevent* these naturalizing ties. This is exemplified in two events in the novel where blood is shed over the acquisition of land. In the first scene, the dispute is over the suppression of particular aspects of cultural genealogy, whereas in the second, the conflict arises on a national level over the difference between workers of the land and those who view it as a passive object. Of course, those with experiential knowledge are located in a social class without adequate representation, even though their own "blood" or kin are the dispossessors. While fauna and flora "may offer a continuity from the remote past into the future," Collins's novel suggests that blood inheritance does not necessarily follow the same trajectory. In fact, the cannibalism associated with the blood-sucking loupgarou of folk memory functions as an ancestral presence that *symbolizes rather than anticipates* the conflict between humans over the nonhuman world.

The Discourse of Blood and the "Complicity of Relation"

The first apparent battle over land occurs in the novel's recent past, where the Malheureuse family have their claims to land inheritance challenged by a returning member of the family. Thus domestic stability is coded positively in contradistinction to the disrupting practice of recent transitory migrants. Oldman Malheureuse wills his land to his five adult children; it is divided up equally between them and then passed on to their children. When Oldman's grandson Dolphus returns from Cuba, he insists that the land was left for "legitimate" children only and since "law is law" (1995, 49), most of the family is disinherited. Because many of the grandchildren were born before their parents' marriage, this causes their disenfranchisement from the only land of their family memory. Ti-Moun, whose love and labor on the land are inscribed as central to his being, is legally forced off his plot. The eviction paper that signifies European law is unfathomable in Ti-Moun's epistemology because "the land was what [he] knew. His house on the land was what he know. There was nothing else" (51). When he refuses to leave, he is brutally beaten and never fully recovers. The family land is split up, and many members migrate overseas or to the city to earn an alternative living.

The community reflects back on Carib's warning and realize, "'Grow up here hearing Carib talk about land confusion and about blood to come. Never thought [we] would see it in this Attaseat here'" (59). But as Mamag explains, "I know how land confusion is no respecter of blood. Family does kill family in this business, all for the good of the land and for the family name" (44). To Mamag, there is no inherent ontological relationship between blood kinship and solidarity. She warns her (grand)niece, "'You is you own and you only person in this world. Not friend, not family. . . . Don't trust a soul, child. . . . And always tell anybody close to you . . . what is the colour of blood, how it flow and who it is that cut the skin to see it flow'" (70). Rather than upholding genealogy as the unifying metaphor of national belonging, Collins draws instead upon the discourse of place. When the local community builds a new home for Ti-Moun and his family, Mamag explains to Willive, it was "'*stranger* that put their hand and head together, that help . . . your father to make a living. He own blood make him eat the very bread that the devil knead'" (71, author's emphasis). In contrast to Cliff's novel, genealogy does not solidify the dialectic with the land, but may hinder it.

The discourse of blood in this novel is complex because there are no privileged genealogies. No claims to Amerindian ancestry are made, and the African ancestor from whom the Malheureuse family descends, inherited both name and "blood" from his European master. As her narrator observes, "Mixture in the blood of the story. Not simple" (17). The novel often repeats the primordial example of bloodshed, when the African slave John Bull was beaten to death in the Paz City market by the French carpenter, Malheureuse. Years later Jim-Bull Malheureuse, the son of a slave woman and her master, is born. "And if Boss-Man Malheureuse could walk tall with the story of the ancestor in his soul, who says that Jim-Bull, that get the blood not from the asking, don't have the right?" (20)

Since this is a family with a complex ancestry of both "victor and vanquished," the novel reveals that it is not the "mixture of blood," but the *denial* of this genealogy that causes the conflict. In other words, the characters who adopt Eurocentric legal and filial narratives are faulted for neglecting the social valences of place. Thus Collins's novel is working against the dominant material historiographies that privilege linear plantation narratives and the discourse of possession or property over folk epistemologies that are far more complicated in terms of temporality, heterotopology, and belonging. This becomes apparent when Mamag argues with her brother Son-Son, who has facilitated the family's loss of land by claiming that certain members are illegitimate. "'You that so fraid of bastard blood,' she ask her brother, 'how you managing to walk around every day with Malheureuse own in you veins? . . . Is like you feel white blood bastard more respectable than straight black blood bastard? If you is prince then you is pauper, too'" (50). Since the family has inherited "bastard blood" from European and African heritage, Mamag points out the hypocrisy of substituting one cultural legacy for the other, a critique that has been leveled at dominant forms of Caribbean historiography. Mamag eventually disassociates herself from the claims of kin and announces, "'All who want to say them is family must come and confront me to talk. I have no loupgarou family. Not one ounce of blood-sucking family I have'" (76).

The loupgarou, also signified by the ball of fire mentioned earlier, represents an engagement with what in Cliff's novel functions as the quashee. The loupgarou serves as an otherworldly reminder of the ways in which the imaged structures of kinship at the familial, national, and colonial levels continue to benefit economically from the blood of rural folk. This is a different inflection of cannibalism that is more analogous to vampirism than Wilson Harris's creolizing "morsel of flesh." Entangled with material manifestations of the national body, the loupgarou functions as a metaphor of economic relations of capital that mystify boundaries through the reification of labor. So while Mamag connects the loupgarou to the process of kin cannibalizing each other, her grandniece Willive ties this directly to the nutmeg plantation system before and after independence. Willive will not let her son Thunder shell nutmeg because, as she explains, "'Watch the colour. You see it? That is how it living. By sucking me blood. Is a blasted loupgarou, you hear me? It sucking my blood. I don't want it to take yours'" (100). She invokes a Marxist critique of the capitalist appetite that "only slightly quenches the vampire thirst for the living blood of labor" (Bartolovich 1998, 212). In this case, post-independence nutmeg production continues to consume the folk of Paz Island, where there is little experiential difference between primitive colonial accumulation and the new socialist government that aligns its industries with a neoimperialist global market. The *blood-sucking* loupgarou substitutes the discourse of *cannibalizing* capital because this economic system must reach its natural limits through the total consumption of both land and labor. Yet Collins does not simplistically project capitalist consumption outside of the island's natural and cultural boundaries. Marx's observation, in Jerry Phillips's gloss, that "capitalism will produce revolution (effectively cannibalise its own body) because the human being is condemned by his or her nature to struggle for (utopic) freedom" (Phillips 1998, 185) is prescient to the novel's conclusion.[25]

The loupgarou and Carib's tautological warning of "blood to come" are recognized only by Mamag, who insists "we should listen to Carib" when the rest of the community deems her "mad" (1995, 10). Consequently, the prophecy of blood and the historical "mixture of blood" are woven together in the novel in ways that elude most of the characters. The text brings these together through Mamag's great-grand nephew Thunder, a Shango-like figure who represents the new generation and who is deeply involved in the family's second major struggle over land and kinship. Thunder's father Ned, who has married into the Malheureuse family, is prompted by Carib and Mamag to narrate a similar story to that of John Bull regarding ancestry and bloodshed, which is positioned as central to Thunder's understanding of familial and national history. Ned's (East) Indian ancestors were brought to Paz as indentured servants, further complicating the family's genealogy and gesturing to the broader ethnic constituency of the Caribbean. Ned, however, was named after his African slave ancestor, who was also beaten to death like John Bull in the market center of Paz's "sister-island Eden" (165). Both murders were carried out with impunity, documented on paper as death by "fits"; significantly, they take place within each island's urban economic center, an ideological and narrative "heart of darkness" that defines people as property. The notable difference in this family's history is that the plantation driver murders the slave victim. Invoking Cliff's specter of the quashee, Ned explains, "'Is like we working against weself from time'" (140). All characters in the novel have inherited the blood and history of the "victor and vanquished," or in Collins's terms, "murderer and victim" (94). In some cases family members literally have "Malheureuse" blood. Collins's concern with recording these histories, without suppressing one ancestry for another, is reiterated when Thunder's father urges him "'to write Ned's name in the ground . . . say all the things that Ned couldn't say. Have to write thing down, since writing is the fashion these days'" (141). Here the discourses of inheritance and monumentalization are brought together, rendering the new form of historiography that is expected from the next generation.

I dwell here on the novel's construction of genealogy because it inscribes the process of nativizing the Caribbean which Glissant relates to land settlement and origins:

> Concerning the Antilles, for example, there is a lot of discussion concerning the legitimacy of land "possession." According to the mysterious laws of rootedness (of filiation) the only "possessors" of the Archipelago would be the Caribs or their predecessors, who have been exterminated. The restrictive force of the sacred always tends to seek out the first occupants of a territory (those closest to an original "creation.") So, in the Caribbean, would this be Caribs and Arawaks

> or other older and, consequently, more legitimate and "determin-
> ing" populations? The massacre of the Indians, uprooting the sacred,
> has already invalidated this futile search . . . . But the consequences
> of European expansion [are] precisely what forms the basis for a new
> relationship with the land: not the absolute ontological possession
> regarded as sacred, but the complicity of relation. (1997, 147)

Although he has greatly exaggerated the decimation of the Caribs, I agree with Glissant's interpretation of the imaginative tendency to seek out primordial occupants, "those closest to an original 'creation.'" However, I would argue that this search is certainly not perceived as futile, given the trend I have outlined to imaginatively populate the islands with indigenous presence. It is apparent that "the complicity of relation" is at work in Collins's novel, where the people who are the most rooted in the traditions of the land are those who have cultivated and maintained this long relationship. In contrast, Clare attempts to stake her claim through genealogy, the "force of the sacred." Denying the presence of active indigeneity, represented by the cannibalizing quashee, results in Clare's literal death.

In contrast, the conclusion of Collins's novel suggests that "those who have endured the land's constraint . . . have also begun to foster these new connections with it, in which the sacred intolerance of the root, with its sectarian exclusiveness, has no longer any share" (Glissant 1997, 147). I have already discussed the ways in which the "mixture of blood" indicates a recognition of this "new relationship," and the fact that Carib, "who may or may not have been a descendant by blood," destabilizes the discourse of filiation. I would like to conclude this chapter by turning to the final land conflict, the prophecy of blood depicted in *The Colour of Forgetting* as an example of the violence that erupts when "the complicity of relation" is not recognized by the emergent material historiography of the socialist state.

Thunder's parents are employed by the two exploitative, postnational industries of Paz Island: Willive shells nutmeg and Ned is a bellhop at a tourist hotel. Reading the land as both past and future, they engage in this labor so that Thunder can obtain an overseas education and eventually purchase a small piece of land on Attaseat Mountain. When Thunder obtains a white-collar job with the Ministry of Tourism, he enters a different social class and accordingly forgets the "language of landscape," substituting this with the relations of property and ethnic ancestry formulated by the growing Afrocentric socialist movement. Ned had already warned him against this "colour of forgetting," imploring Thunder not to forget "all of us people around here . . . that know red mud" (1995, 142). Thunder's

English education contributes to a cognitive split between the epistemologies of his living and ancestral kin and the utopian objectives of the new socialist government.

Like all the scenes of conflict in the novel, the issue derives from discordant definitions of land possession. The government, with Thunder's support, initiates a movement to create cooperative landowning of larger lots, forbidding private ownership of those that are less than five acres. Smaller lots are deemed "uneconomic," and this causes a schism between the younger, school-educated generation and their laboring parents. As Ned and Willive had been saving for years to acquire their own piece of land, they feel betrayed by their son for his involvement in the party. The issue centers around social class and the complicity of relation, evident when Ned exclaims, "'What they know about land? If they never had land and get chance to have an acre, they would know about uneconomic'" (163). Willive reprimands Thunder, "'You who know what land confusion do in your family, I don't see how you could be talking this nonsense'" (166).

The discourse of blood that was so apparent in the earlier conflict over familial land is still present in that Thunder is their blood relation, but it becomes subsumed by the conflict over the complicity of relation to the land. This is shared by other families; what initially began as a Malheureuse family dispute expands to the national level. As Carib had predicted many years before, "'a nation divided against itself . . . cannot stand'" (10). The conflict erupts in the market square of Paz City, where the community is torn apart by arguments, stone throwing, and bullets. Although this is the space of the island's early slave markets, there are no monuments to the trade in human lives. Only the colonial and neocolonial are marked in national memory, symbolized by a plaque for the soldiers of Britain's wars and a monument to the "Great Country" (the United States) that intervened in the island's affairs. The present acts of violence and communal division take place in the very space that is dismembered from its local past, yet at the same time is haunted by an epistemology that reduces people and land to economic terms. The local and global implications of reductive materialist epistemologies are summarized in Willive's letter to the Government Land Commission, "If you think two acres here in Content village uneconomic, then you have somebody in another bigger country thinking the whole of Paz that all-you ruling uneconomic because it so small . . . so you do away with me and my land and they do away with you" (164).

Here we come full circle to Epeli Hau'ofa's argument, rehearsed in the introduction to this book: European colonial cartographies that emphasize island isolation and smallness perpetuate a sense of cultural and material "belittlement" among island nations. Like Hau'ofa, Collins seems to argue that an unquestioning complicity with transnational capitalism undertaken by island governments suppresses local folk epistemologies in favor of consuming globalization. In attempting to develop Paz for the global capitalist market, the ruling party has missed the connections between the economic tyranny of the slave state and the ways in which the socialist state, caught in the same prison of history, translates local space into a national commodity. Wilson Harris reminds us that "in consolidating national or local political and economic self-interest," history "becomes the servant of a material vision of time" (quoted in Brathwaite 1975, 4).

After the eruption of violence, the novel seems to conclude on an overall positive note: Willive and Ned retire on their land; Thunder learns that his young daughter is already calling for the monumentalization of the nation's past; and Carib feels the bloodshed is "not happening again" (1995, 212). Yet to read *The Colour of Forgetting* tidalectically allows us to see how the novel poses a challenge to the sovereignty of the new generation. The narrative concludes with the colors of the Caribbean Sea, which have changed from blue, "the colour of forgetting" (185), to "grey-green" (214), which would seem to indicate the end to this cycle of historical amnesia and bloodshed. But the tumultuous presence of Kick-'em-Ginny, a subaquatic volcano significantly located between the utopian spaces of Paz and Eden, suggests that the conflict over blood, the presence of familial loupgarou, and the problem of how to maintain the complicity of relation with the land is not resolved. The new generation has a more tenuous relationship to the land due to the migratory pull of an overseas education, which prevents their establishing a meaningful relationship with the rural space of their grandparents. This highlights the novel's epistemological bind: if rural spaces are the site of "authentic" human and nonhuman history, what becomes of the national telos in the wake of increasing urbanization and outmigration from the region? How does one maintain local roots to resist the undertow of global routes?

It is because of this spatial bind that Thunder slips back into a discourse of genealogy, signifying an ambiguous future for the new generation. Because he is unable to link the past of his family to the present/future of his country, he projects this continuity through his daughter Nehanda, named after the Zimbabwean revolutionary. While Nehanda seems to embody the spirit of African resistance to colonialism, she never appears directly in the novel, and she is never associated with a particular place.

Thunder had previously taken no responsibility for his daughter, going to England for his education while Nehanda's mother raised her at home. After the eruption in the marketplace, his mother prompts him to recognize his responsibility, and he comes to the realization that while he was "worrying about the past . . . Nehanda, she in front" (210). He decides that her "generation . . . will write the names that we ignore all this time" (201). Thunder's recognition would seem to deconstruct the responsibility associated with women to physically and imaginatively reproduce the nation's past and future, but Thunder traces his legacy of responsibility from Carib (and her female antecedents) to Nehanda, bypassing his own (male) accountability. Thunder's formal education and his distance from ancestral land causes him to construct a gendered duality through the narrative of ethnic blood. It is by calling upon the discourse of corporeal reproduction—a call to take responsibility for the nation's children—that Thunder uneasily situates his nation's more promising future.

The novel suggests that the transition between the corporeal presence of the indigenous past (Carib) to the Africanized future (Nehanda) is not continuous. The question of remembering indigenous presence on the land seems to be answered when the nation creates a stone monument. Carib, the last generation of women prophets, has not had children, so it seems the island will be released from its tautological history. If "this woman Carib was like another country. A new country" (22), as one character describes her, then she has outlived her purpose. Carib's role to "kick-start their memory" (5) is supplanted by the submarine volcano called "Kick-em-Ginny" that suggests that it is more than regional unity that is submarine. "Kick-em-Ginny," a reminder of the geological origins of islands and the way that they are continually expanding, erupts at the end of the novel and causes the death of young child. It seems that once the community assumes that the landscape is passive and extinct, they must be reminded of their contract with the region's spatial history. Significantly, the novel concludes with the depiction of both local and tourist characters on a small boat, spatially severed from the land and caught between Paz and Eden. While they are terrified by the submarine eruption, they are somewhat reassured by Carib's now questionable prophesy of a less violent future. Although the new generation may hold promise, one infant has died and it remains unclear how, besides a stone monument, the community will remember their history. Finally, even though the community is depicted as breaking the tautology of history, if one reads the text against the grain, it becomes clear that Amerindian presence is not a part of the nation's future.

If one excavates the indigenous metaphors embedded in the text, Amerindian presence literally becomes flattened by the community's material progress. I turn to one of the recurring motifs of the novel, crapaud (frog) and monkey, fauna of Paz Island that are usually paired together. The former continually exclaims from the drain, "'Wait a while,'" while the latter insists from the tree top, "'Things cool'" (18, 21, 39). At times their voices compete or blend together so that one adopts the other's message. Sometimes crapaud hears "dogs and horses and footsteps hunting men who had run from plantations" (21), and at other points both are silent (53). The monkey/crapaud dyad reiterates Harris's prediction that the fauna of landscape "may offer a continuity from the remote past into the future."

If one turns to the scholarship on mythological images of the indigenous Caribbean, monkey and crapaud signify a deeper history than consciously intended by the author, suggesting the ways in which landscape histories inform cultural production.[26] Henri Petitjean Roget explains that native Caribbean "art is based on the recurrent association of the fruit-eating bat and the tree frog. Both themes are not only the most commonly depicted but are also associated according to an immutable order... all over the Caribbean, for nearly 1,500 years, from the Salaloids to the Tainos, and under multiple variations—artwork always represents these two beings together in this manner" (1997, 103). Certainly the bat/frog image has some relationship to the inscription of monkey and crapaud in *The Colour of Forgetting*, especially as these images are found on petroglyphs and pottery throughout the Caribbean, including Grenada. Roget asserts that the "frogs belong to a lower level, that of moisture. They symbolize femininity... in the primeval world as depicted in the myths, women were frogs and men were bats" (105). The gendered division of these figures may also be analogous to the novel's feminization of indigenous heritage, evident in Carib's lineage of women prophets. Roget concludes that the frog represents "Atabeira, the 'primeval mother of humankind'" who "is always depicted above the fruit-eating bat that itself is no other than 'the hero who brings mankind the cultural goods'" (108). If we pursue this connection between the dyads of monkey/crapaud and bat/frog, then the novel inscribes much more than the loss of Carib's lineage.

In one of the concluding chapters of the novel, Carib, like Shakespeare's Caliban, physically walks around the island, recounting its history to an imagined audience and speaking with the various spirits of the land. She notices the markers of development, such as electricity, but recognizes this to be a symbol of global capitalism, since "is other people far away with switch, saying when is light, when is darkness" (Collins 1995, 184).

During her interior monologue, she passes a busy street and warns, "Keep out of the road. Crapaud, stay in the drain." But crapaud's message, "Wait a while," is literally wiped out in the island's movement towards progress. As Carib explains, crapaud believes the "car light will stop if it just hold up the two front feet to say wait a while. And you see crapaud as a result? Dead in the road" (180). Like the mule killed on the new road of progress in the conclusion of Sam Selvon's *A Brighter Sun*, Collins's narrative discloses that "natural" sacrifices are a component of the nation's trajectory towards modernization. This is also evident in Thunder's inability to integrate the legacy of his ancestral land with his current social position. If we read crapaud as a metaphor for the native Caribbean, then the presence of island indigeneity is exterminated in the quest towards economic development. In this novel, the new generation has not constructed an alter/native complicity of relation to the land, flora, or fauna. In the face of globalized material progress, Amerindian presence becomes flattened sediment, receding to the alterity of the past.

Coda: Carib and Cannibal Remnants

Despite centuries of colonial entanglement, Europeans always arrived belatedly to the scene of indigenous cannibalism. The bones that littered the floors of huts or caves, campfires or coastal shores, perceived as evidence of anthropophagy, suggest an inaccessible history of cannibalism, a "pastness" of indigenous practices that could never be integrated into the present except through the textual production of contact narratives. The "pastness" of cannibalism has thus functioned as a metonymy for the "pastness" of the symbolic Caribbean native, depicted as the ultimately unrecoverable subject who can only be accessed through corporeal or narrative "remnants" (P. Hulme 2000). But one of the more productive narrative remnants in recent times has been the poetic excavation of the region's history, and thus these novels can be likened to the Carib bone-flute that Wilson Harris locates as "a confessional organ involved in, yet subtly repudiating, the evil bias of conquest that afflicted humanity" (1999, 106). If we recuperate Hulme's cartography of the Caribbean, including Brazil, then the trace of indigenous remnants in the literary production of the Americas is broadened across space and time. Haroldo de Campos has suggested that the symbolic cannibalism once lauded by the Brazilian modernists, exemplary of a creolization process that privileges local time and space, has relevance today. He predicts that "writing will increasingly mean rewriting, digesting, masticating" (quoted in Bellei 1998, 100). Cliff and Collins are clearly involved in narratively "digesting" the remnants of Caribbean historiography where, like the Brazilian modernists, what was previously deemed "irrational" or "matriarchal" by the masculinist colonial process is now repositioned as a poetic counter to Eurocentric materialist history.[27] While the modernists were involved in the project of cultural nation-building in the wake of European colonialism and plantocracy, the novelists discussed here are examining the forcible routes of transnational capitalism, particularly the ways in which the United States "reaches" towards its southern neighbors with a consuming appetite for both land and labor. To return to one of the epigraphs for this chapter, it is far more than nationalism that "fosters a reflexive consciousness of tradition." Thus both Michelle Cliff and Merle Collins raise the difficult question as to which historical and narrative "remnant" can be recuperated in the continuing spatiotemporal tension between the local and global, roots and routes, and between linear materialism and the "arts of the imagination." Wilson Harris's suggestion that creolizing cannibalism, a deeply *transformative* practice for the consumer, opens possibilities for the ways in which even global capitalism, when faced with its own supplementary remnant, must heed the destabilizing song of its "confessional organ."

Epilogue

"Nothing on the land and nothing under the water ever stay steady, too long, you know. Everything moving up and down and sideways, according as to how life and death always going. So hold on tight, and watch yourself, Anancy!"
— Andrew Salkey, *Anancy, Traveller*

I would like to conclude this book with a few comments on how the geo-poetics of routes and roots remap the dynamic relations of space in ways that help us deepen our concepts of time and its ruptures. In the story "Middle Passage Anancy" from which this epigraph is drawn, the trickster spider becomes a witness to the "Dance of the souls of the dead slaves," a "spectacle of memory and history exploding out of the waves and all over the bubbling Atlantic" (1992, 13). The spectacle causes a "roots change" (14) in Anancy's character, a recognition of how this "dread scene," a performance of the violence of the past, reflects a spiral of sacrifice and regeneration that incorporates the present, disrupting the linear concept of time. As one of the souls tells him, "The triangle trade don't stop. It still happening in different shape and form. It dress up and walking and talking in another style" (12). Throughout this book I have emphasized the ways in which social and political formulations of the present inspire the recuperation of certain aspects of the past and, in some cases, displace contemporary violence. Diaspora and globalization rely on a discourse of fluidity and flows, a gendered grammar of the oceanic that I have connected to the recent territorialism of the Law of the Sea. Moreover, the forces of globalization have also produced a larger traffic in slaves than the middle passage; the history of the trade thus becomes the antecedent, metonymy, and in some instances, the historical substitute for contemporary violence. To Glissant, this submarine history *"sowed in the depths the seeds of an invisible presence"* (1989, 67, author's emphasis), a presence that can be read dually as the legacy of bones at the bottom of the sea that Walcott has so eloquently memorialized (1986, 1990), as well as an ongoing presence / present, in which iron chains, bones, and blood become the symbols and symptoms of continuing violence and dispossession.

Elsewhere I have argued that this tidalectic between routes and roots, the past and the present, is exemplified in Edwidge Danticat's short story, "Children of the Sea" (1996), a work that compresses space-time so that contemporary Haitian refugees find themselves incorporated into the history of the middle passage.[1] Fleeing from the *tonton macoutes*, two unnamed lovers write to each other after forced separation; the epistolary form echoes the orality of call and response and the tidalectic between land and sea. The male character escapes in a small boat headed for Miami while the woman retreats to the "blood-drenched earth" of her family home (Danticat 1996, 27). The woman writes from the roots of a banyan tree, a symbolic space of the ancestors, while her lover responds from his sinking boat, navigating the routes of transoceanic history. Here the sea is not inscribed as a void, *aqua nullius* to be imprinted with the expectations of the migrant, but has its own history into which the subject is incorporated. The author observes, "There are special spots in the sea where lost Africans who jumped off the slave ships still rest, that those who have died at sea have been chosen to make that journey in order to be reunited with their long-lost relations" (168). The Haitian refugees are rendered as "children of the sea" because, as Glissant has explained, its "abyss is a tautology" (1997, 6), an oceanic cycle of diaspora and violence, understood tidalectically as the end product of the nationalist practices of the "blood-drenched earth" that renders the sea as the perpetual circulation of blood.

Danticat's "children of the sea" use an old sheet for a sail, spotted with semen and blood (1996, 3), two of the bodily fluids I have shown are vital to understanding the grammar of the transoceanic imaginary. Their sinking boat, a failed vehicle of sovereignty, draws upon the metaphysical conflation of the circuits of blood, sperm, and water as these fluids are channeled through transoceanic vessels. This concept of the vessel of blood, or the sea as blood, has been articulated in the deep history of biology, evident in Borgese's explanation that when our primordial ancestors left the sea, "they carried with them blood that is like seawater" (1975, 36). The metaphysical exchange between these fluids may be depicted as the product of transoceanic diaspora, as when Eric Roach determines that his ancestral migration from Africa to the Caribbean renders him an "amphibious" subject, incorporating "the sea tides in [his] blood" (1992, 96). The metaphor may also be understood genetically, apparent in Dening's description of the originary settlers and vehicles of Oceania as founding blood vessels.

In their "minds and bodies" reside the "cultural DNA of two millennia through all the Pacific" (2004, 9).

The metaphysical relationship between the flow of the oceans and the circulation of the seas may also be rendered as its opposite: while the human body may be thought to circulate the blood of the seas, the sea may also be imagined as a conduit for human blood. The latter is a far more threatening prospect because it encodes the dissolution of the human into the hydraulics of planetary circulation. For example, in writing of the tremendous ethnic and gendered violence of the seventeenth-century Caribbean, Carmen Boullosa's narrator remarks, "It was blood and not water that kept Tortuga afloat in the middle of the sea" (1991, 69). Although inscribed in far more ominous terms than the Africans who wait for Danticat's narrator at the bottom of the sea, in Boullosa's bloody Caribbean, the "waters of the sea have a sudden need for flesh" (162). In fact, it is this sacrificial consumption of the human that leads Robert Sullivan to imagine the ancient star paths traced by Pacific navigators as a type of territorialism, for "what belongs to water belongs to blood" (1999, 3). Yet if humans can claim the seas as ethnic inheritance, configuring the transoceanic imaginary as genealogical origin, then the future of this cycle means that the ocean consumes all humans, as our current global warming crisis makes all too clear. In Sullivan's collection, the personified ocean speaker observes the transoceanic voyagers who cross its surface and admits, "some of these I have taken / into the waters of my being" (103). As our creator, consumer, and our future, the sea is also "part human" (103).

It is this latent violence in the human-sea relationship that produces these compelling metaphors, visible in the works discussed in this book and in Lingikoni Vaka'uta's painting on the cover, *No'o 'Anga* (Tied shark). Significantly, the painting depicts the sea as history, crowded with navigators, bird guides, double-hulled voyaging canoes, and supernatural figures, both male and female. According to the artist, the title derives from a Tongan fishing ritual in which the village observes a strict taboo while the men voyage to deep waters to attract sharks with their rattles, conch blasts, and chants. In tidalectic fashion, any loss of human life at sea is attributed to the people of the land. The largest shark to appear, understood as the goddess Hina, is garlanded with flowers, while the other sharks are caught with ropes. They will not be injured in the water but hauled onto the vessel and killed with wooden clubs.[2] Thus the creature that is probably the greatest threat to the people of the sea is at once honored and sacrificed, signifying an oceanic cycle of tribute and violence, submersion into the depths and a bloody emergence for its submarine creatures. This cycle is reiterated in the curvilinear patterns in which the human and shark complete a circle on the right side of the painting and where the divers and voyagers mirror the forms of fish and sharks on the left. Most of all, it is seen in the humanized form of Hina herself, who grimaces as she offers her fellow creatures for tribute and sacrifice. Her indirect gaze beyond the frame implicates us in this exchange, as viewers.

I began this epilogue with Anancy, sitting on a rock in the Atlantic, witnessing a ritual performance to memorialize the violence of the sea as history and the sea as blood. After witnessing torture, dismemberment, and revenge in the ghost ships of the passage, Anancy is tipped from the rock, loses his balance, and is submerged in the water. A soul of the dead slaves informs him that nothing, including land, is constant. As she states in the epigraph, the rock is literally a moving island, a reminder that "nothing on the land and nothing under the water ever stay steady" (1992, 15). This represents a geopoetics and a geopolitics, a recognition of a tidalectic relationship between land and sea, roots and routes, and the continuity of violence and its resistance. Anancy's submersion in the transoceanic imaginary is a crucial reminder of the witness's participation in and responsibility to that memory and history—as well as ours.

Notes ～～～～～～～～～～～～～～～～～～～～～～～

Introduction

1. To paraphrase Glissant, the "west" is less of a place than an unfinished project (1989, 2). My use of broad terms like European, Caribbean, and Pacific are necessary to outline my argument but should not be taken to displace the real complexity of peoples associated with these geographic regions.

2. See also Walcott's sense that "there is a strength that is drawn from island peoples in that reality of scale in which they inhabit. There is a sense both of infinity and acceptance of the possibility of infinity" (1996, 159).

3. I have adapted this term from Connery (1996) who writes of an "oceanic feeling" that helped to constitute the "regional imaginary" of the Pacific Rim. Connery's work has helpfully outlined Euro-American apprehensions of the ocean; my work diverges in its focus on how island writers imagine the tidalectic histories of their seascapes. The transoceanic imaginary is a growing field of inquiry; see especially Klein and Mackenthun's collection (2004) and Baucom (2005).

4. For excellent discussions of England's bounded nationalism, see the works of Beer (1989) and Cohen (1998). See also Edmond and Smith's important collection (2003) on European inscriptions of islands, which came to my attention as this book was going to press.

5. I borrow the term from Cohen, who explains, "Great Britain was far too large and complex to lend credence to its existence as a simple eye-land. Indeed the colonial enterprise owes much of its utopian drive to the quest for an ideal surrogate island state, an Illyria, whose small-scale physical geography would furnish a natural symbol of sovereignty" and control (1998, 19).

6. On Darwin, see Beer (1983). For Rousseau's Caribbean sources, see P. Hulme and Whitehead (1992) and Bongie (1998). See Grove for his Indian Ocean and Pacific Island inspirations (1995).

7. See Bitterli (1989) and Grove (1995) on the island refreshment motif and Sheller on colonial and tourist consumption (2003).

8. See O'Gorman (1961); Washburn (1962); Flint (1992); and Zamora (1993). Washburn points out that landfall was anticipated; Spanish documents repeatedly mention the objective to acquire "tierra firme" and "yslas." "Tierra firme" was not the antonym to island but its synonym (1962, 11).

9. Imaginary islands such as Antillia and the Antipodes virtually disappeared from maps for centuries until Renaissance cartography. For romantic constructions of Tahiti, see B. Smith (1985). William Eisler discusses the search for the Antipodes (1995).

10. Later eighteenth-century voyages into the Pacific would transport Terra Australis farther westward with the explorers. "The persistence of this myth is astonishing since it received no support by any voyagers" for over 300 years of transpacific crossings (Bitterli 1989, 157). Terra Australis was a "bipolar" discursive configuration of barren, brutal savagery or bountiful and receptive islanders (Eisler 1995, 2). This bipolar vision was then transferred onto the Pacific, segregating "soft primitives" of Tahiti and Tonga, from the "hard primitives" of Aotearoa, Papua New Guinea, and Australia; see B. Smith (1985).

11. See Hassan (1980).

12. Peter Hulme explains that Carib and Arawak "mark an *internal* division within European perception of the native Caribbean . . . the radical dualism of the European response to the native Caribbean—fierce cannibal and noble savage—has such obvious continuities with the classical Mediterranean paradigm that it is tempting to see the whole intricate web of colonial discourse as weaving itself in its own separate space entirely unaffected by any observation of or exchange with native Caribbean cultures" (1986, 46, 47).

13. See James, "From Toussaint L'Ouverture to Fidel Castro" (in 1993) and Mintz (1985).

14. Quoted on the frontispiece of Dibblin (1988). I discuss these events in Chapter Four.

15. http://www.scuba-safaris.com/pages/destination/marshall_islands/index.html

16. Vanuatu details gleaned from Lal and Fortune (2000).

17. For instance, the deity of the sea throughout Oceania is usually the creator of humankind. Tangaroa (Ta'aroa, Kanaloa) links the creation of the world with the personification of the sea and appears in the poetry of Albert Wendt, and Robert Sullivan. Similarly, Caribbean deities such as the Arawak Atabey and Orehu, goddesses of the waters, were coupled with African deities such as the Yoruba orisha Oshun (of rivers and the sea), Agwè (the Dahomeyan vodun of fishing), and Yemanja (of the ocean). They have featured prominently in the poetry of Walcott, Brathwaite, and Nichols.

18. I very much regret that I do not have the space to include a chapter about Indian diaspora to both island regions as there are ample connections between the middle passage and crossing *kala pani*. I have been working on this topic for some time in a forthcoming essay, titled "Crossing *Kala pani:* Remapping Transoceanic Diaspora."

19. See Dayan's excellent critique of Gilroy, which succinctly calls attention to the problematics of reducing the slave ship to a "vessel of transit and means to knowledge" (1996, 7).

20. Compare Brathwaite with Wordsworth's *Prelude* IX: "That which the heavens displayed, the liquid deep/ Repeated; but with unity sublime!" (1952–1959, 606–608).

21. Anglophone Caribbean and Pacific history has been marked by various imperial efforts to consolidate the region. Froude exposes the material objectives of the British imperial project in creating a federation of the Leeward Islands in the late nineteenth century and encouraging "English and American capitalists [to] bring their money and their enterprise" (1969, 163). See Mintz (1966) and Moya Pons (1979) on regional identities, which I explore further in DeLoughrey (2000).

22. Froude relies on the discourse of genealogy ("Norse blood") and continually draws upon ethnic inheritance, while Benítez-Rojo focuses on Caribbean cultural syncretism to destabilize racial essence.

23. See Van Dyke, Zaelke, and Hewison, eds. (1993), Borgese (1998), and the U. N. website http://www.un.org/Depts/los/index.htm.

24. This is the irreverent shadow title of my book, amusingly coined by Chris Harbrant.

25. See Ives (1995, 108–109).

26. For an analysis of the fungibility of gendered fluids, see Laqueur (1990) and Grosz (1994). On the gendering of the global/local, see Freeman (2001). This is discussed in Chapter Two.

27. See Rediker (1987), who questions the association of the ship with the world. My analysis here grew out of two previous articles, DeLoughrey (1998a and 1998b), which examined patriarchal narratives of black diaspora and the sea as history in Caribbean literature.

28. See Clifford (1997, 2000, and 2001) for his thoughtful engagement of both diaspora and indigenous studies, which have been important influences throughout this book. For a development of the model of routes and roots in relation to a sea of islands, see Jolly 2001a.

Chapter 1: Middle Passages

1. See also Brathwaite where he describes "a tidal dialectic" (1983, 42).

2. "Cognitive mapping in the broadest sense comes to require the coordination of existential data (the empirical position of the subject) with unlived, abstract conceptions of the geographic totality" (Jameson 1991, 52).

3. Examined in DeLoughrey (1998b).

4. Although he does not discuss the middle passage, Beckles (1997) traces an intellectual genealogy of modernity in the plantation context, beginning with C. L. R. James and Eric Williams. See also Rohlehr, who argues that "the World Wars caused a sense of displacement which Blacks had already known because the Middle Passage was their first World War. Europe experienced a sense of displacement, dislocation and diaspora through which Blacks had already lived" (1992,

113). My discussion of modernity draws from the work of Hall et al. (1996), Hall, Held, and McGrew (1992), and Giddens (1990). Baucom's important work (2005) on this topic was published when this book was in press.

5. To my knowledge, Sundquist (1993) was the first to position the slave ship as chronotope. Gilroy (1993) expands this, and Dayan (1996) provides a vital critique of its reduction to metaphor.

6. Linebaugh and Rediker (2000) adopt the term "hydrarchy" from the seventeenth-century writings of Richard Brathwaite.

7. See Duban (1983), who traces a relationship between whaling and early American expansionism, and Connery (1995). Springer asserts that Mahan's work (1890) was used to justify American expansion (1995, 13–14). See Philbrick (1961) on how literary production contributed to U.S. maritime imperialism.

8. Maritime imperialism contributed to a rise in eighteenth-century nautical dictionaries; here I invoke the title of one of the earliest British maritime dictionaries, Smith's *A sea grammar* (1627). See Rediker (1987) for a discussion of seamen's speech communities.

9. See, for instance, Soja (1989) on the subordination of space to time.

10. Ruskin once argued: "Since the first dominion of men was asserted over the ocean, three thrones, of mark beyond others, have been set upon its sands: the thrones of Tyre, Venice, and England" (quoted in Peck 2001, 197).

11. The astrolabe, an Islamic instrument of reckoning east for prayer and for astronomical calculation, like the compass, the hourglass, cross-staff, and algorisms (the means of calculating with nine figures and zero), were adopted by western Europe through Mediterranean and African trade routes. On the astrolabe, see Crosby (1997). On the compass, perhaps originating from China, see Braudel (1972–1973). On algorisms, adopted through Arab and Hindu exchange, and the cross-staff (the Arab kamal), see Waters (1967, 197, 199, 210).

12. See Waters (1967, 205, 219).

13. This remains a persistent legacy; after conceding Drake's role in the slave trade, the online *Encyclopaedia Britannica* describes him in these patriotic terms: "More than any other of England's bold privateers, he had helped to set England on the way to becoming the mistress of the seas."

14. See the introduction for more on how the Treaty of Tordesillas catalyzed European debates about ocean space as property.

15. See Bakhtin (1981) on how in early Greek novels these chronotopes prioritize time over space.

16. Like most nineteenth-century novels, Marryat's oeuvre invokes slavery as a metaphor for submission to romance or as a sailor's critique of European hydrarchy.

17. See Connery (1996).

18. Laura Brown dates this shift to the seventeenth century (2001). See also Edwards (1994).

19. In the late eighteenth century, copper hulls increased ships' speed and their ability to outrun naval blockades. See Mannix (1962) and Hugh Thomas (1997) for details on the increased number of enslaved Africans shipped to the Americas (especially Brazil and Cuba) by agents of nations that had criminalized the trade.

20. This information and the preceding quote were taken from www.middlepassage.org, a URL that is no longer extant.

21. One exception is Thornton (1992), who discusses the complex river networks utilized in the European-African trade.

22. There seems to be some confusion about the spatial connotations of the term. The second edition of the online *Oxford English Dictionary* defines the middle passage as: "The middle portion (i.e., the part consisting of sea travel) of the journey of a slave carried from Africa to America"; and this is drawn from Lloyd's *Navy & slave trade* (1949). The *OED* suggests that African slaves had three segments to their journeys. This is quite different from Lloyd's definition of the triangular itineraries of the ship.

23. For example, French historians writing of the "commerce triangulaire" use the English term.

24. The *OED* dates it to Clarkson (1788).

25. Turner's painting, based on deaths on the slave ship *Zong*, has been discussed by Gilroy as an example of the erasure of the middle passage (1993, 14); while he suggests Ruskin's emphasis on maritime naturalism suppresses the drowning of slaves, the Ruskin quote used here sublimates slavery by conflating the threatening waves with frenzied masses. The painting has also inspired David Dabydeen's poem "Turner," which focuses on "the submerged head of the African in the foreground" that "had been drowned in Turner's . . . sea for centuries" (1994, ix). See also Baucom's recent work (2005).

26. The concept of "crossing the river" has been fused with other histories and spaces. For instance, the Christian teleology of salvation (the river Jordan) has been mapped upon the Mississippi. There are ample African-derived folk tales of figures like High John the Conqueror and others who have recrossed the Atlantic, either by walking, flying, or travel in the afterlife.

27. Alfred Wegener's theory of continental drift (1912) was scorned until Fred Vine and Drummond Matthews introduced the "spreading ridge" function of the midocean. See Prager (2000, 145–147).

28. I refer here to Linebaugh, Gilroy, Rediker, and Bolster. Although it has been overlooked, Joseph Harris's *Global dimensions of the African diaspora* (proceedings of a 1979 conference) had already outlined a complex circumnavigation of the Atlantic world by black (masculine) subjects (1982).

29. Here I've been influenced by Wilson Harris's incisive analysis of the Froude/Thomas debate of West Indian historiography (1995b).

30. Glissant was influenced by these debates and adopted the capitalized distinction in *Caribbean discourse* (1989, 64). Another likely influence includes Foucault (1970).

31. See Baugh (1977), first presented at Carifesta 1976. See Rohlehr (1970) and Wilson-Tagoe (1998) on Caribbean cultural historiography.

32. Glissant explains "the 1976 Caribbean Festival was organized in Jamaica around Caribbean heroes: this time, Toussaint Louverture, José Martí, Juarez, Bolivar, Marcus Garvey. A popular gathering at this time consecrated in a spectacular and massive way what had been until then nothing but a dream of intellectuals. In this way, Carifesta conveyed to a collective consciousness the impulses of a few" (1989, 67).

33. Walcott warned about the currency of historical narratives of trauma, the commodification by black nationalists who "charge tickets/for another free ride on the middle passage" (1986, 269), those "sea-parasites on the ancestral sea-wrack/ whose god is history" (1986, 270). Paradoxically, these figures have much to share with Naipaul's colonial and materialist vision in *The middle passage;* although the culturally and racially divisive practices of the Caribbean plantation system could be destabilized by claims to collective transoceanic origins, the commodification of a nongenerative and victimizing historiography of the ocean upholds the same divisive colonial paradigm. Although gesturing to transoceanic itineraries, Walcott suggests, might open a broader and more fluid conceptualization of creolization and New World origins, the Euclidean grid of the plantocracy has not necessarily released its grip.

34. Lamming is an important exception, especially his novels *The emigrants* (1954) and *Natives of my person* (1972). I have explored his masculine mode of diaspora in DeLoughrey (1998a).

35. See Lamming (1984, 45–46); Wilson Harris "Tradition and the West Indian novel," first published in 1964 (1999); Wynter "Reflections on W. I. Writing and Criticism" (1969, 35–39); and Birbalsingh (1988).

36. Lamming has since modified his critique of Hearne's work, but forty years later still asserts that a working relationship with the soil of the Caribbean authenticates regional belonging for all resident diasporan populations. For his later evaluation of Hearne, see his interview with Dance (1992).

37. This tension between nature and culture is explored in DeLoughrey, Gosson, and Handley (2005). See Chapter Five for more on Wilson Harris's critiques of the social realist novel.

38. C. L. R. James's *Minty Alley* (1935) had been one of the first anglophone texts to consciously destabilize the anthropological relationship between the middle-class writer and the "folk." For a nuanced reading of the relationship between the London-based West Indian writer and the "folk," see Brathwaite (1970b). See also Rohlehr's theory of a "folk-urban continuum"(1992). On the appropriation of peasant/folk nationalism, see Griffith (1996) and Edmondson (1999).

39. On Hearne's geographical influences, see his interview with Binder (1984, 102), and Hudson (1992).

40. See Binder (1984, 111).

41. The process of recording these words in the ship's log catalyzes the captain's childhood memory of acquiring literacy, highlighting de Certeau's assertion that in modernity: "Learning to write has been the very definition of entering into a capitalist and conquering society" (1984, 136). Like a blank page, *aqua nullius* is mapped and managed, made a text and place, through the will of a European subject (de Certeau 1984, 134).

42. Hogarth's artwork has also drawn the attention of David Dabydeen (1987). The character Reynolds is also drawn from the visual arts, a point Peter Hulme kindly brought to my attention.

43. See Márquez (1983), an insightful essay that uses this quote to explore Hearne's ambivalence to any history of class unity.

44. I'm especially grateful to Dominick LaCapra for helping me work through this point.

45. The ship is well known as a state and religious vessel. The fictional slave ship of Charles Johnson's *Middle passage* (a text clearly in a dialogue with Hearne's) is called the *Republic*.

46. On limbo, see Murphy (1994, 166–171) and Desmangles (1992, 154–155).

47. Building upon Elaine Scarry's theories of the (de)construction of the tortured subject, Spillers makes a compelling argument for the necessity of the "domestic," defined as "a common origin of cultural fictions that are grounded in the specificity of proper names," such as the "patronymic" to engender subjects (1987, 72).

48. On Conrad, see Hunter (1983, 35–40).

49. In *Folk culture of the slaves in Jamaica*, Brathwaite argues "that it is in the nature of the folk culture of the ex-African slave, still persisting today in the life of the contemporary 'folk,' that we can discern that the 'middle passage' was not, as is popularly assumed, a traumatic, destructive experience, separating the blacks from Africa, disconnecting their sense of history and tradition, but a pathway or channel between this tradition and what is being evolved, on new soil, in the Caribbean" (1970a, 7).

50. Hearne may have been influenced by Césaire and Walcott's plays about the "Black Jacobins" and the will to power. See Edmondson (1999) for an examination of the failed-revolution motif in Caribbean literature.

51. See Bender (1988, 7–17), who also links Mahan's work to a Darwinist theory of sea power. See also Springer (1995, 25–30) for its importance to U.S. fiction, and Hunter (1983) for its influence on Conrad.

52. See Hearne's essay "What the Barbadian means to me " (1972).

53. "Not only has the journey from the Old World to the new varied with each century and each method of transport but needs to be re-activated in the imagination as a limbo perspective when one dwells on the Middle Passage: a limbo gateway between Africa and the Caribbean" (Wilson Harris 1999, 157).

Chapter 2: Vessels of the Pacific

1. To avoid privileging indigenous over diasporan narratives and vice versa, I have chosen not to capitalize the term "native." At times this term is used interchangeably with "indigenous." This interchangeability does not mean that the terms are static; the use varies greatly according to place, history, and political agenda. Where applicable, I try to use specific terms such as "Kanaka Maoli," which I use synonymously with "Hawaiian." Like the word "native," the terms "Hawaiian" and "Tahitian" refer to indigenous peoples rather than later settlers. Notes on terminology are outlined in more detail in the preface. The work of Noenoe Silva (2004) and discussions with J. Kehaulani Kauanui have been of great help as I clarify my own position on these vexed issues of terminology.

2. See for instance Jolly (2001a and 2001b); Sharrad (1998); the special issue of *The Contemporary Pacific* (13:1), (Subramani 2001 and its responses); and *The Contemporary Pacific* (13:2) edited by Diaz and Kauanui (2001).

3. Of those articles in *A new Oceania* (1993), see especially Naidu, Griffen, Borer, and Veitayaki.

4. The term "diaspora" is not universally acceptable in indigenous circles and is perceived by some as an American conceptual import, but it has been used to explore many Pacific contexts. See Clifford (2000); Subramani (2001); T. Teaiwa (2005).

5. Although recent Cook Island and Maori writers have helped popularize an indigenous mapping as the Ocean of Kiwa, this was not the shared term for all Polynesians. According to Best, Kiwa was the ocean guardian with his wife Hine Moana (formerly Parawhenuamea), (1924, 152–153). These women figures associated with the ocean have been largely erased. Kiwa was the navigator of the *Takitimu* canoe, but thought by Tregear to be distinct from the ocean deity (1889, 111). Kiva means "blue space" in Cook Islands Maori. On the ocean as a "vast plaza," and "supreme marae" (Marae nui atea), see T. Henry (1928, 143). For the many women associated with the sea and canoes, see Pukui's glossary of Hawaiian deities (Pukui and Elbert 1971).

6. See Spate (1979).

7. Sorrenson traces the tradition of comparing Polynesian seafarers to the Vikings (1979, 50).

8. There are many excellent sources on the construction of the Pacific as a region. Those helpful to my research include B. Smith (1985); Sharrad (1990); Wendt (1993); Wilson and Dirlik (1995b); Connery (1995 and 1996). Spate (1979) and Dirlik (1993) favor the European construction hypothesis. Wesley-Smith (1995) outlines a trajectory of how the field developed as an institutional discipline. Kaunanui (2004) provides a concise argument for decoupling Asia and the Pacific.

9. The term "Third World" was developed by the French economist Alfred Sauvy in the 1950s, who likened colonized regions to the "Third Estate," the commoners of the French Revolution. See the introduction to Hadjor (1992) for a

genealogy of the concept. The same year that Wallerstein published his influential work, Shuswap Chief George Manuel popularized the term "Fourth World" (1974).

10. He explains: "The idea of national culture was a manufacture of the bourgeois West all along. . . . The age of transnational corporatism alters the idea once again. National culture is increasingly irrelevant; multiculturalism holds the day now as a tradable commodity" (1995, 69).

11. Interestingly, its early formulation did not segregate Rim from Basin. See A. P. Elkin's *Pacific Science Association* for the complex, interdisciplinary academic ties forged between Russia, Japan, Australia, China, France, New Zealand, Canada, and the United States to further their strategic interests in the Pacific, including the international trustees of the Hands-Around-the-Pacific-Movement, established in 1911, later renamed the Pan-Pacific Union (1961, 14). According to I. C. Campbell, the 1940 Colonial Development and Welfare Act expanded British research in its colonies; the 1947 South Pacific Commission, headed by the new colonial powers in the Pacific, called for the research and dissemination of "every imaginable subject from anthropology to zoology . . . and even a literature board" (1992, 187). Australia followed with a military school for studies in its territories, Papua and New Guinea, in the 1940s; and Auckland University opened anthropology as a discipline "expecting . . . improved administration" of Maori, Samoan, and Cook Island peoples (Campbell 1992, 188).

12. I draw on their astute connections between island isolation and the U.S. military establishment of the discipline, as well as their critique of Goodenough, to which I have added my own observations about the nuclear semantics of his writing. The PSB was primarily concerned with Micronesia, but as Goodenough's comments suggest, they were rapidly adapted to Oceania.

13. See the website of the oversight group, the South Pacific Regional Environment Programme (SPREP) http://www.sprep.org.ws/topic/pollution.htm

14. See the U.S. Atomic Energy Commission report on Bikini (1954).

15. For more on the laboratory concept, see Kirch (1986) and Wesley-Smith (1995).

16. My point here is not to suggest that the militarization of the Pacific has gone unnoticed, especially as Wilson and Dirlik have addressed this in their collection (1995b). Rather, my point is that once U.S. scholars begin to speak in terms of Rim-Basin relations, sustained analyses of the "Pacific theater" of war, the nuclearization of the Island region, and the links between the military and academic production are noticeably absent. Once "Rim-speak" took on a late capitalist Asian-United States trajectory in the 1990s, questions about the nuclearization of the region seemed to vanish, even while France continued its detonations in Moruroa until 1996. For more on these events, see Chapter Four. See also Teaiwa (2000).

17. On the utopian Pacific, see Connery (1996); Dirlik (1993); Wilson (2000).

18. The term derives from Charles De Brosses (1756), who meant the Pacific Islands in general; nearly a hundred years later Dumont d'Urville popularized the

terms "Melanesia" (dark islands) and "Micronesia" (small islands) to signify separate language-culture groups. See discussion later in the chapter and N. Thomas (1997, 133–155).

19. See Howe (2003) for a regional overview, especially 45–47 on Aryan sources, and the introductory chapter to Sorrenson (1979). See McClintock (1995) on colonial patriarchy and its structure of a "White Family of Man." On the development of the Aryan family, see Trautmann (1997).

20. Taylor and Wetherall (1995) contend that immigration narratives weaken indigenous claims and cite New Zealand historian Michael King's suggestion that "in the beginning we were all immigrants to these islands, our ancestors boat people who arrived by waka, ship and aeroplane" (cited in Taylor and Wetherall 1995, 76); Belich (1996) uses the same trope of migratory origins to open his book.

21. See Finney (1994) for a genealogy of voyaging theories.

22. See Feinberg's collection (1995) (especially Lepowsky), Lewis (1994), and Chappell (1997).

23. This is not to suggest that the migration traditions were discarded or that Islanders were less active travelers—since European presence Islanders have been captured, recruited, or have volunteered to serve as navigators, translators, travelers, whalers, missionaries, laborers, and soldiers on European and American ships. See Chappell (1997).

24. See Cheesman and Foster (1975, 95). Mormons have utilized Heyerdahl's white genealogy of the Pacific to justify and expand the missionary process there (Cheesman and Foster 1975, 106, 110).

25. South Sea fiction was largely written by U.S. military servicemen, including bestselling authors James Hall, Charles Nordhoff, and Robert Dean Frisbie. This is explored in DeLoughrey (2002).

26. See Pardo (1975, 19); S. Brown et al. (1977, 63); Anand (1993, 78–79).

27. In 1937 Eric de Bisschop sailed from Taiwan to Hawai'i and then to France on a modern double-hulled vaka. In 1956, the same year of Sharp's study, de Bisschop sailed the raft *Tahiti-Nui* against the prevailing currents with a crew of Tahitians to Chile in order to disprove Heyerdahl's theory. Both voyages have largely been forgotten. See Bader, McCurdy, and Chapple (1996, especially 96, 102); Howe (2003, 111–113).

28. For more on this era, see R. Crocombe (1992).

29. For more on these events, see Walker (1990).

30. See Walker (1990); Nelson (1991); Irwin (1992), to name only a few.

31. See Golson (1972); Terrell, Hunt, and Gosden (1997, 161).

32. See Foucault (1980, 146–148). He suggests that the discourse of aristocratic blood was replaced by *"an analytics of sexuality"* (148) and downplays the role of race (149). See Stoler (1995). My thanks to Radhika Mohanram for her guidance on this.

33. Here I extrapolate from L. Brown's argument. Schama points out that Plato had likened bodies of water to blood circulation and explores this as a "fluvial

myth" adopted by later European "hydraulic societies" (1995, 258). His encyclope-
dic scholarship focuses on the river but has nothing to say about the ways in which
the ocean was a vital space of imperial imagination and practice. L. Brown argues
persuasively that "the prominence of the sea and of shipping in English life is a
distinctive development of the seventeenth and especially the eighteenth centuries"
and traces this through an expansive reading of this era's literary texts (2001, 57).

283

34. See also Mohanram (2003).

35. See also Allen (2002).

36. For a summary of regional initiatives see Lal and Fortune (2000, 326–
331).

37. For more on the history of colonized Hawaiʻi, see Kameʻeleihiwa (1992)
and Silva (2004). For a chronology of political activism, see Dudley and Agard
(1993, 107–115).

38. See McGregor (2002), Morales (1984), and Wood (1999). The struggle
over the sovereignty of Kahoʻolawe made it one of the places most documented
by the military; see U.S. Department of the Navy (1983) and Keene (1985). As I
explain in Chapter Four, Keene is cited by Trask as an abuse of the "cultural construction" debate.

39. See also John Dominis Holt whose *On being Hawaiian* (1974) features a
voyaging canoe on the cover and also addresses broader questions of voyaging and
regionalism. My thanks to Chad Allen for bringing this to my attention.

40. Interestingly, the term for this visit in Hawaiian is "huakaʻi," which may
have a similar etymological connection to "diaspora" in its derivation from "kaʻi,"
to lead, and "hua," meaning egg, ovum, and seed (Pukui and Elbert 1971).

41. See Taylor and Wetherall (1995).

42. The insistence on a remote island for nuclear testing is questioned by the
fact that the French considered Clipperton Island as a test site, but its location was
deemed too distant for their ships. French nuclearization of the Pacific is discussed
in more detail in Chapter Four.

43. For instance, in Maori, the keel is the "puna," or backbone, while the
"puhi" is the waka's decorative ornament or topknot. The waka's carved figurehead,
"parata," is a term also used to describe sculpted ancestral figures that adorn Maori
meetinghouses, communal historiographic structures with analogous semantics as
the vessel of the people. On the puhi and parata, see Haddon and Hornell (1975,
211). Haddon and Hornell do not explore the corporeal language of the vaka and
thus any errors in translation are my own. My thanks also to the Oceanic Anthropology Discussion Group (ASAO) for their help in sustaining this point.

44. See Vanessa Griffen (1993) and Jolly's important critique of the ways in
which scholars have adopted the "peoples of the sea" metaphor for Pacific identities to the exclusion of mountain-based communities in Papua New Guinea and
elsewhere (2001a). The vaka is a common symbol for a chief in Rotuma and other
areas of the Pacific (Howard 1995, 136). In the Marshall Islands, the hull of the
vaka is coded in masculine terms, while the smaller, stabilizing outrigger is femi-

nized, semantically invoking the community's conjugal relations that are vital to the performance of the canoe and social integrity as a whole (Carucci 1995, 20). While the canoe has functioned as a metaphorical body, in other cases the body has become literally inscribed as a voyaging canoe. Carucci demonstrates Marshallese tattoo designs suggest that "the body, fully fashioned, is the vessel islanders used to face the voyage of life" (1995, 17).

45. Diaz (2003). He draws from Emwalu's comments at a symposium on Micronesian seafaring in Guam in November 1994.

46. The Polynesian Federation was promoted by white advisors to the king, such as Walter Murray Gibson. See Kuykendall (1967, 340–371), Daws (1980, 152–158), and Silva (2004) for more on the "Merrie Monarch." Interestingly, the *Kaimiloa*'s namesake was sailed from Hawai'i to France in 1937–1939 by Eric de Bisschop to demonstrate the viability of the double-hulled sailing vessel. His voyage was largely ignored by followers of Heyerdahl and Sharp, although he inspired transoceanic sailing in Hawai'i. See note 27.

47. On Henry, see R. Crocombe (1976); on the festival, see the Polynesian Voyaging website http://pvs.kcc.hawaii.edu/rapanui/perpetuation.html. One of the Tahitian canoes recreated the ancient voyage of Tangi'ia, a founder of Rarotonga.

48. On the impact of African literature on the Pacific, see Sharrad (2001).

49. See M. Crocombe, *Third Mana Annual of Creative Writing* (1977); she was inspired by the Beiers when she was living in Papua New Guinea and generated similar initiatives when she and her husband Ron relocated to USP. See also Wendt's introduction to *Lali* (1980), Subramani's groundbreaking work (1992), Simms (1986), and Sharrad (1993b); on SPACLALS, see Tiffin (1978).

50. On the Frisbies, see Sharrad (1994) and DeLoughrey (2002). Cook Island published writing dates back to the nineteenth century with native missionary texts. Although it is a regional "first," *Makutu* has generally been overlooked with the exception of Subramani 1992 (14–17), and Sharrad (1998).

51. Given how anthropologists have emphasized men's fear of a feminized bewitchment at sea (and flying witches), Eri may be reassigning the danger to a western military appropriation and suppression of the kula ring. Compare Malinowski (1922, 241–244), and Campbell (2002), discussed below.

52. Witi Ihimaera has characterized this era as a moment when New Zealand was reconfiguring its relation to its own indigenous peoples, the "Pacific within," and the broader regional economic and political relations of the Islands and the Rim (1991).

53. See R. Crocombe (1976), which anticipates many of these divisions, Narokobi (1982), and the responses to Hau'ofa (1993b).

54. The most helpful sources on the coup include the work in Brij Lal's special issue of *The Contemporary Pacific* 2 (Spring 1990).

55. I explored the nation as a ship in the previous chapter.

56. The only source to comment on the novel is Sharrad (1998).

57. In terms that Davis has adopted almost word for word, Buck followed

the Aryan model of S. Percy Smith to argue that while "in Indonesia, the sea salt entered into their blood and changed them from landsmen to seamen" (1938, 26).

58. Sharp imagined a homosocial ship in his accidental-drift theories. This notion of masculine diaspora is visible in C. F. Goldie's unfortunate representation of starving, storm-tossed Polynesians in "The arrival of the Maori in New Zealand" in 1898, parodied in Sullivan (1999, 14–15).

59. Other historic women travelers had their gender changed when transcribed by western anthropologists. I have consulted all of Davis's original sources: women figures are especially visible in Best (1924 and 1975), T. Henry (1928), Pukui and Elbert (1971), S. P. Smith (1898–1899), Te Ariki-Tara-Are (1919–1920). For a recovery of women in Maori oral traditions, see Yates-Smith (1998). My thanks to Alice Te Punga Somerville for this last reference. Nei Nim'anoa is a Gilbertese navigator employed in T. Teiawa's poetry collection of the same name. See Hina-the-canoe-pilot in T. Henry (1928), the chant of Kahikilaulani, a woman who voyaged to Hawai'i (Kawaharada 1995, 8), and Silva's recuperation of women voyagers in Hawai'i (2004, 19). As much as Herb Kane argues that voyages were for adventure or to "satisfy curiosity about the girls from another island" (1997, 12), these oral traditions suggest many women traveled between Tahiti and Hawai'i in pursuit of men, siblings, and family members.

60. The complexity of gendered space is addressed in S. Campbell (2002). See her discussion of Trobriand land versus sea space (154–160), and how these axes are gendered vertically and horizontally (177–190). See also Pomponio (1990).

61. Beckwith argues that in *The Kumulipo*, the canoe is gendered masculine (and phallic). "The canoe is, like the plant stalk, a symbol in riddling speech of the male procreative organ. The epithet 'long' ... emphasizes ... the long continuance of the stock down the ages from the first divine procreator" (1970, 182). S. Campbell likens the canoe to the penis in Vakuta (2002, 160).

62. Writing of the Trobriands, Malinowski's *Argonauts* records the canoe as a flying woman in a skirt (1922, 138). S. Campbell confirms the canoe can be seen as a flying witch in Vakuta (2002, 147).

63. In Davis (1992b, 257–262). Interestingly, Iro's son discovers the murder and then wears his deceased mother's pelvic bones around his shoulders in mourning; this is a reminder of the procreative and sexual body that generates the genealogies of masculine voyaging culture. Davis may have created this part of the story. For his sources, see Te Ariki-Tare-Are (1919–1920). See T. Henry's version in (1928, 537–552).

64. On the role of women and weaving the sails, see the forthcoming collection by Kauanui and Sinavaiana (2006).

65. On the cultural partitioning of the region, see Kirch (2000), B. Smith (1985), N. Thomas (1989), Howe (2003), and the special issue of the *Journal of Pacific History* 38, no. 2, September 2003. My thanks to members of the Oceanic Anthropology list, especially Ben Finney, for their guidance about this partition.

66. I have compared Davis's version carefully to his sources and can find no

indication that Tutapu was identified as Melanesian. Davis's sources include Buck (1938, 119–121) and Te Ariki-Tara-Are (1919–1920). In fact, the latter's "History and Traditions" part VII (1919) includes women and children in the voyages and suggests that Tangi'ia's family is Melanesian (see 185–187). See note 83.

67. See S. P. Smith (1898–1899), Part III, especially his ethnocentric comments against Fijians (4–23). This is the single most influential source on Davis's novel. Smith's prejudices are also replicated in another of Davis's sources, Henry and Tuiteleleapaga (1980).

68. Even his missionary source, Thomas Williams, explains that Tongans adopted the canoe and sail from the Fijians (1860). Williams also reports many women sailors (85). On how the drua was imported to Tonga, see Routledge (1985, 17, 48–49).

69. See T. Henry (1928, 125). Davis derived this Fijian story from the popular accounts of the sailor Cannibal Jack (John Jackson). On Jackson's influence, see Obeyesekere (1998); Jackson's story was uncritically reiterated in Davis's source, Clunie (1977, 64–65, 84).

70. Like the number eight, the he'e/fe'e is prominent in Samoan and Hawaiian cosmologies. Its likening to a pet in Maori tradition is thought to signify a star path for landfall. See Buck (1938, 74–75). Kawaharada writes that the main god of navigation is Ta'aroa (Kanaloa), god of fishing and the sea, represented by the octopus (1995, xiv). See his account of he'e legends (1999, 7, 12). S. Campbell connects the octopus and canoe (2002, 115).

71. See Nunn (2003).

72. See Finney's account of the significance of the Hokule'a's visits there in "The Sin at Awarua" (2003).

73. See also Sorrenson (1986, 1.77)

74. In fact, Te Rangi Hiroa thought that the Marquesas might be the Hawaiki for Hawaiians.

75. See Buck's comments about his ancestral links to Rarotonga (1938, 104–107). He interviewed Davis's ancestors during his fieldwork in the Cook Islands (see Davis 1992a, 70).

76. See his correspondence with Ngata in Sorrenson (1986, 1.186–188).

77. Through his second wife, Davis is related to the Pa Ariki line, descended from Tangi'ia, of the Takitumu canoe. See Buck (1938, 121) and R. Crocombe (1964, 9–11).

78. See the discussion in Sorrenson (1979), Orbell (1991), Kirch and Green (2001), and Taumoefolau (1996).

79. Sorrenson explains that "the idea of a Great Fleet was essentially the construct of European collectors and editors of Maori traditions, not of Maoris themselves" (1979, 84). While nineteenth-century historians credited between four to fourteen great canoes with arriving at the shores of Aotearoa from a mythical homeland called Hawaiki, Sorrenson argues the myth has been adopted by Maori sovereignty groups and activists because "it enables them to establish a right of

occupation in New Zealand, long before the coming of the Pakeha. Just as their real stake in the land has diminished, so their claim to a cultural historical identity has become more important" (1979, 84).

80. I explore *Ola* and *The whale rider* in an unpublished article (1999).

81. Compare this to "Havai'i, the mother of lands, rests serene in the centre of Polynesia and will live on forever though we, her sons, may pass into oblivion" (Buck 1938, 150).

Chapter 3: Dead Reckoning

1. See Gilroy (1993 and 1997) and Malkki (1997).

2. The spiral, as Albert Wendt observes, is an intrinsic component of both narrative and space. Pacific "maps and fictions are all in the spiral which encompasses the stories of us, in the ever-moving present, in the Va, the Space-Between-All-Things which defines us and makes us part of the Unity-that-is-All" (1995b, 15).

3. See DeLoughrey (1999).

4. "Uri" is the Maori term most similar to western notions of vertical descent. See Metge (1967, 127–128) on written technology and whakapapa books.

5. See Metge (1967, 127) and Makereti (1986, 37).

6. See Kawharu (1975), Simmons (1990, 84), and Metge (1967, 132).

7. In addition to the works of Metge (1967 and 1995), O'Regan (1987), and Royal (1999), some of the most helpful articulations of this complex system in Aotearoa have included Johns (1983), Kawharu (1975), Salmond (1991), Scheffler (1964), Schwimmer (1990), Simmons (1990), and Takino (1999). For the Hawaiian context, see Kauanui (1998) and Valeri (1990).

8. Metge argues that written technology has fixed whakapapa, whereas oral production maintains a process of historiography that is fluid and interpretive in form (1967, 129).

9. Ihimaera's first volume in this series explains that Maori descent alone, rather than written or cultural content, was the criteria by which authors were included in the volume (Ihimaera et al. 1992, 14).

10. In *Potiki*, Grace writes, "There was no past or future . . . all time is a now-time, centred in the being. It was a new realisation that the centred being in this now-time simply reaches out in any direction towards outer circles, these outer circles being named 'past' and 'future' only for our convenience. The being reaches out to grasp these adornments that become part of the self. So the 'now' is a giving and a receiving between the inner and outer reaches, but the enormous difficulty is to achieve refinement in reciprocity, because the wheel, the spiral, is balanced so exquisitely" (1986, 39).

11. Mitchell's *Amokura* (1978) was not included in the first anthology of Maori literature in English, *Into the world of light* (1982), and received only a brief mention in the *Oxford companion to New Zealand literature*. Ihimaera and Long subsequently included an extract from *Amokura* in the first volume of *Te Ao Mārama*

(1992). They claim Patricia Grace as the first Maori woman novelist in their first anthology (1982), but do not mention that Mitchell published her novel the same year.

12. See Allen (2002). For many readers it will not be a surprise that whakapapa are often contested and do not strictly follow the rules of blood descent. My suggestion is that anthropological studies of Maori and Polynesian cultures have tended to overemphasize the cognatic structure of such systems in a way that subsumes the performative, contextual, and dynamic aspects of genealogical reckoning.

13. See Patricia Burns (1980). Following Mitchell, I have also drawn upon William Carkeek (1966), Te Rauparaha (1980), and William Travers (1872).

14. This narrative technique has ample precedence in other regions of the Pacific. For example, of the Samoan context, Wendt has written, "Our elders' stories were our earliest maps and fictions; they were a view of the dimensions, geography, values, morality and aspirations of the world and way of life we were born into. It was a world in which everything was of one process: the web that was the individual person was inseparable from the web of aiga[family]/village/tribe, which were inseparable from the web of atua [gods] and the elements and the universe. And in that process everything was endowed with sacredness or mana" (1995b, 21).

15. For example, the term "Ngati," which prefaces many tribal names in Aotearoa, translates as "descendant of." Metge explains that increasingly, the prefix "Ngati" reflects a location (a city name) rather than an ancestor (1967, 134).

16. According to Moore and Edgar's *Flora of New Zealand* (1961), the flax is characterized as a rhizome, but the various nurseries I consulted in Aotearoa/New Zealand question this taxonomy. The plant can be propagated by both root graft and cuttings. For more on the cultural importance of flax to Maori women, see Te Awekotuku (1993), Puketapu-Hetet (1989), and Menzies (1996). My thanks to Briar Wood and Maureen Lander for their assistance with this question.

17. This is epitomized in the proverb "Groups join, [to get] a shared descent line" (Metge 1995, 210).

18. See Scheffler (1964) and Metge (1967 and 1995, 62–64).

19. Te Akau, Te Rauparaha's most senior-ranking wife, claims descent from Te Arawa of the Lake Taupo region. Since Mere's father was the son of Te Akau's first marriage to the chief of Ngati Raukawa (from whom Te Rauparaha inherited the greenstone mere), our narrator is not a "blood" relation to Te Rauparaha. Te Rauparaha inherited some of his mana or power from Ngati Raukawa through the consent of the dying chief and his subsequent marriage to this chief's wife, Te Akau.

20. On waka (voyaging canoe) historiographies, see Chapter Two.

21. See Evans (1997) and Alpers (1964).

22. According to the documents generously supplied to me by Margareta Gee of the National Library of New Zealand, Mitchell had access to information about

her narrator's parents but chose not to include it in the novel with the exception of this testimony in the land court.

23. This is why O'Regan asserts that it is critical "to assess for what purpose it was assembled" (1992, 25).

24. I've discussed this at length in my article on *Potiki* (1999); see also Metge, who explains, "the meetinghouse is not only named after an important ancestor: it is symbolically his or her body. Its ridgepole *(tahuhu)* is his backbone, a carved representation of his face *(koruru)* covers the junction of the two barge boards *(maihi)* which are his arms, the front window *(mataaho)* is his eye, and the visitor steps through the door into his *poho* (chest), enclosed by the rafters *(heke)* which are his ribs" (1967, 230). See Te Awekotuku (1993) and Mita (2000) on discursive production symbolized through the marae, and Allen (2002) on the wharenui and contemporary literature.

25. On the relationship between Tane and Maori literature, see Whaitiri and Ihimaera (1997).

26. Royal explains, "All traditional whakapapa leads back to Ranginui and Papatuanuku: they represent the physical venue within which the phenomenal world exists" (1999, 82). Trask contends that the Hawaiian relationship to land "is more than reciprocal. It is familial. The land is our mother and we are her children. This is the lesson of our genealogy" (1993, 80). See also Kauanui (1998) on the ways in which genealogy and the discourse of "blood" are utilized in Hawai'i.

27. In a few places in the text, Mitchell concedes that the Muaupoko (Ngai Tara) people, of the Kurahaupo waka, are tangata whenua of the region. Yet her narrator complains about Maori and Pakeha "lies" in court and suggests that Te Rauparaha should have completed his violent conquest of the tangata whenua to prevent claims against Ngati Raukawa (82–83)

28. See Mohanram (1999, 138–142).

29. On the voyages, see Alpers (1964) and Evans (1997). See K. Teaiwa's article on the scattering of phosphate from Banaba all over Australia and New Zealand, a literal fertilization by the soil of the Pacific Islands (2005).

30. See O'Regan on manawhenua debates between iwi and how whakapapa is packaged for the Tribunal (1992). See also Metge (1995, 131). For the Hawaiian context, see Valeri (1990, 159, 182).

31. See Stead's argument against "affirmative action" in publishing (1989), Wendt's critical commentary (1995b), and Fee's analysis of the debate (1989).

32. Best defines the puku as the repository of ancestral memory, emotion, and desire (1954, 54). See also Salmond (1985, 240).

33. This invokes a broader Pacific epistemology of corporeal polity: Wendt observes, "We are real and connected in the gafa/whakapapa of the bone, le ivi, te iwi, which is the whenua, the placenta, the land, the eleele" (1995b, 17).

34. This does not suggest Hulme is unaware of iwi history. See her piece with Turcotte (1994) in which she discusses her founding ancestor, Tahu-potiki, of Kai Tahu. While she is not specific in her tribal assignation of the canoe awakened by Joe, it is the waka *Takitimu*, navigated to the South Island and, by some accounts, left in the gorge by Tahu-potiki. See Mitira's *Takitimu* for a recounting of these events (1990, 44). Chapter Two discusses the importance of this waka *(Takitumu)* to the Cook Islands.

35. See McLeod (1987), who sees it as a "utopian text," and O'Brien, who critiques the appropriation of Simon's otherness (1990). Bongie engages questions of modernity and creolization (1998).

36. Hulme does not extend her nationalism beyond the bicultural British/Maori binary, but her reliance on a combination of genealogy and familial construction would not preclude other ethnicities from national inclusion.

Chapter 4: Adrift and Unmoored

1. See Krech (1999), who uses this example for different objectives, and Lobo and Peters's collection on urban indigeneity (2001).

2. I suspect this discomfort with the urban indigenous subject has also impacted the reception of a number of Maori writers. The urban-based literature of Apirana Taylor, Bruce Stewart, and even the later novels of Alan Duff have received far less critical attention than their more rural-based narrative counterparts in the works of Patricia Grace and Witi Ihimaera. (Duff's novel *Once were warriors*, and the film that followed, are obvious exceptions.)

3. For more on these tremendous socioeconomic shifts, see Kelsey (1995 and 2000). See Durie (1998) and Walker (1996) on the repercussions for Maori.

4. Since it is an interpretive rather than judicial arm of the government, the Tribunal's recommendations on each case are referred to the Office of Treaty Settlements.

5. See Sorrenson (1990) and Ward (1990) who, following the aegis of post-structuralism, have addressed the difficulties in presenting evidence in a positivist legal forum. See Salmond's response to Ward (1990), which brings up the question of competing epistemologies when genealogy or whakapapa is not recognized as historiography. See also Ward (1996).

6. This is a point taken up in DeLoughrey (1999).

7. Clifford's sources are derived from Appiah (1992 and 1998).

8. Some of this debate has been summarized in Tobin (1995). The Keesing, Linnekin, and Trask articles cited here have been reprinted in Hanlon and White, eds. (2000), which includes a thoughtful rejoinder from Jolly.

9. For its early appearance in anthropology, see Wagner (1981); in history, see Anderson (1991), Hobsbawn and Ranger (1983), and O'Gorman (1961).

10. Kaho'olawe was returned to Hawai'i in 1994. In a bizarre twist, a U.S.

Navy report insisted that the thousands of rubber tires on the island should not be removed as they have "historic" importance because of their use during the Vietnam War. The Protect Kahoʻolawe ʻOhana continues to spearhead the cleanup and revitalization of native flora. See Chapter Two.

11. I refer here to the well-known debates between Sahlins (1995) and Obeyesekere (1992) over Captain Cook's demise in Hawaiʻi.

12. Appiah makes a similar argument when he writes "defiance is determined less by 'indigenous' notions of resistance than by the dictates of the West's own Herderian legacy—its highly elaborated ideologies of national autonomy of language and literature as their cultural substrate" (1992, 59).

13. Sorrenson (1979) and Simmons (1976) critiqued the Great Fleet and Io legends as Pakeha constructions decades before. This is discussed in detail in Chapter Two.

14. While Lamb critiques Hanson for harboring an allegiance to "a notion of a grounding truth" that underlines the invented legends, Hanson's article, unlike Keesing's, at least maintained a theoretical "blank space" in which Maori historiographers could articulate cultural continuities that might be employed in appeals against the Crown.

15. It was expanded to seven members in 1985. See Walker (1990, 254–255), and Sharp (1991).

16. Wendt's work also addresses the historicist revisions of the narrative of Kupe, argued by many nineteenth- and early twentieth-century anthropologists to be the Polynesian "discoverer" of Aotearoa. One chapter details a community's claim to their founding ancestor, "Kupenicus Tane," and includes many of the critiques of this Pakeha myth. Simmons (1976) meticulously addressed the ways in which Sir George Grey and S. Percy Smith had homogenized Maori oral accounts of Kupe by erasing genealogical inconsistencies. The texts in question appear as parodies in Wendt's novel (1992, 201).

17. Just as the government delocalized the economic structure in its pursuit of the assumed benefits of *global* capital, the demand for specifically *local* cultural histories intensified and gained tremendous currency. While Tribunal historians have conceded the conflicts between the deconstruction of originary narratives and the positivism required by the courtroom, they warn that financial and time constraints prevent them from addressing "historical context" in the overriding demand for empirical "content" (Byrnes 2004, 18). The Tribunal is notoriously overburdened and slow to release their reports—some members have died before claims have been processed. Both the real and the fictional Tribunals seem to be "dealing with two distinct types of knowing . . . where power is still weighted in favour of European conventions" (Byrnes 2004, 22). Although the novel is futuristic in form, Wendt explains in an interview, "*Black Rainbow* is not really about the future—it's about *now*, the possibilities of what is happening now" (Sarti and Evans 1998, 209).

18. When this issue was brought to the Waitangi Tribunal, they recommended

the suspension of media sales until radio frequencies could be allocated to Maori (Durie 1998, 68). For three years the relation between the treaty and media assets was debated before the nation's highest courts, which ultimately ruled against Maori claims although they instituted some protective schemes (Durie 1998, 69).

19. Interestingly, Wendt's protagonist refuses to read the national newspaper (which reports only good news), suggesting resistance to Anderson's "imagined community."

20. Walter Benjamin demonstrated how film is appropriated by the totalitarian state, focusing on the aestheticization of politics as a vital tool of German fascism (1992). Similarly, Wendt comments on the possibilities of new technologies, but finds them "frightening when we realize that all that information and those memories can be altered/spliced/re-edited to arrive at any 'truth,' or put to any use by the owners of that information" (1987, 86).

21. While Benjamin suggested that state emphasis on the future diverts working-class attention from present sacrifice (1992, 252), in *Black Rainbow* the state's emphasis on the present suppresses the continuing inequities of the past.

22. The language Wendt uses for late capital temporality is remarkably similar to the "now time" that he, Patricia Grace, and others categorize as spiral time. Yet because spiral time incorporates—and legitimates—the past, present, and future, this must be differentiated from the suspension of historical time enforced by the fictional Tribunal.

23. It is his wife who first tells him "you're brown too" (1992, 193). After his memory of this event and the sight of "Tangata Moni," the narrator begins to notice other Polynesian peoples who were previously "unmarked" in his gaze.

24. The early atmospheric tests in 1966 were immediately followed by the French government's refusal to report statistical mortalities or testing data, a military takeover of the capital's hospital, and insistence that the tests were safe for islanders even while they evacuated European personnel.

25. See Dibblin (1988, 223). The initial signatories of the treaty included Australia, Tuvalu, the Cook Islands, Fiji, Kiribati, Aotearoa/New Zealand, Niue, and Samoa. Many newly independent Pacific Island nations incorporated antinuclear policies in their constitutions. Discarding the "majority tyranny" model of western democracy, these nations integrated localized, consensus-building imaginaries commonly referred to as the Pacific Way. See Chapter Two.

26. This was in exchange for the secret service agents, whom France released from jail two years later. Details of these events have been gleaned from Dibblin (1988), M. King (1986), and Firth and Von Strokirch (1997). This was followed by a trade war waged by France against New Zealand and the U.S. expulsion of New Zealand from The Australia, New Zealand, United States Security Treaty (ANZUS) due to its 1987 legislation to prohibit nuclear ships from its harbors (Dibblin 1988, 225). Under the leadership of Prime Minister David Lange, New Zealand declared its harbors "nuclear-free zones," to the great annoyance of the United States. The events that unfolded in New Zealand in the mid to late 1980s

are enough to suggest that former U.S. Vice President Dan Quayle's threats to have Lange "liquidated" over his antinuclear policy are far less trifling than we might assume. Lange reported this incident only in 2002. See Havely (2002).

27. These justifications were not new. U.S. officials had convinced the Bikinians to abandon their ancestral homes "for the good of mankind and to end all world wars," leaving this deeply Christian community little time to decide whether they were "willing to sacrifice [their] island for the welfare of all men" (Dibblin 1988, 21). See Teaiwa (2000) on the sexualization of the tests.

28. The True One, Aeto, invokes the Greek eagle (Aetos) that ate the liver of Prometheus when he was chained to a mountain in the Caucasus. Like Maui, Prometheus attempted to recover fire and immortality for humanity. Sharrad points out that the Samoan word for eagle is "aeto," derived from a missionary classicism that is embedded in indigenous language (2003, 217).

29. I suspect that these contestations are partially responsible for some scholarship attempting to solidify whakapapa as an indigenous epistemology. In some cases the most visible promulgators of its centrality are the same figures who stand to benefit the most from dismissing urban Maori as inauthentic. These events continue to be deeply contested. See Walker (1990 and 1996); Durie (1998); and *Te Whanau o Waipareira Report* (1998). See Maaka (1994), Ivison, Patton, and Sanders (2000) and Barcham (1998 and 2000). Although urban Maori iwi such as West Auckland's Te Whanau o Waipareira had formed to service and support pan-tribal immigrants after World War II, they have been unable to authenticate their tribal status in the fishery claims due to increasingly litigious and judicial state structures that reify cognatic descent lines. In the wake of these significant fractures, Mason Durie points out the palpable "risk that Maori will be divided into landowning and landless categories, a short step from status and nonstatus. Nor is it helpful to heap blame on the landless themselves for not being more vigilant in keeping the fires burning or to accept that Treaty land settlements are just if they simply confirm the position of those who already have title to land" (1998, 145).

30. My thanks to Ken Arvidson for his help with "Pati" and for his generous feedback on this chapter. The character's previous name (Supremo Jones) and role as a state-sponsored Hunter plays upon the film *Cleopatra Jones*.

31. See note 6.

32. On Stead, see the previous chapter. See Wendt (1995b) for his condemnation of Stead's attempts to relegate Maori to the past by denying the brutality of the colonial process and by insisting that those with "partial" Maori genealogy have no claim to Maoriness.

33. See Ellis (1994), who cogently argues for Wendt's "postmodernism of resistance," and Sharrad's argument that Wendt's postmodernism does not lead to "theoretical quietism" (2003, 216, 220–221).

34. It is tempting to read Wendt's aquatic city in terms of the oceanic sublime that Den Tandt (1998) locates. But *Black Rainbow* is far less concerned with the gothic and uncanny than the indigenous roots of postmodern routes.

35. Tuwhare's antinuclear poem, first published in 1958, has served as the epigraph and rallying point of many antinuclear texts and organizations and has been noted by Arvidson for its innovative weaving between naturalized indigenous metaphors (the tree and sun) and profoundly unnatural colonial practices (nuclear detonations) (1993, 26).

36. As the predominant symbol of Greenpeace, whales also suggest the liberating potential of what Kuehls refers to as the "ecological problematic" (1996, 146), a space of political practices that can take advantage of the transversality of modern states by incorporating technology, particularly visual and print media, to consolidate a global ecological movement.

Chapter 5: Landfall

1. There are notable exceptions to this rule. Dominica has a Carib territory but, as in French Guiana, reserves have caused contention. See Lowenthal (1972, 185). There are more native peoples present in the Caribbean mainland due to relocation and natural barriers to European colonists and missionaries.

2. See P. Hulme and Whitehead (1992, 45–61).

3. Higman has traced a "golden age" constructed by Caribbean historians using these same criteria (1999, 155–161).

4. See also O'Callaghan, who argues that Caribbean women writers educated under the British colonial education system have destabilized realist narrative structure as a response to "master" narratives such as the Victorian novel (1993, 6).

5. As Peter Hulme and others have pointed out, the terms Arawak, Carib, Taino, Ciboney, and Ciguayo Arawak, ethnographic terminology used to differentiate native islanders, are themselves products of European misrecognition and were not in use before 1492. What Hulme calls "Mediterranean discourse," defined as "conjoining the classical and the Biblical" (1986, 35), was grafted onto native Caribbean subjects. Although "'Carib' had been the first ethnic name reported to Europe from the New World" (62), it did not reflect the islanders' self-ascription. Columbus had anticipated the islands of Cathay, so when native islanders of Hispaniola expressed their fear of the neighboring Cariba/Calina or Carib who were thought to consume the flesh of their enemies, Columbus conflated the soldiers of the "Great Khan" (in Spanish, Can) with a group that became known as warlike Caribs. See Hulme and Whitehead (1992). See also Sued Badillo (1995) and Whitehead (1995a).

6. See also Guillermo Wilson (1998).

7. Hulme coedited with Whitehead *Wild majesty: Encounters with Caribs from Columbus to the present day* (1992), an important volume that collects 500 years of European contact narratives. See also Whitehead (1995), S. Wilson (1997), Rouse (1992), Stevens-Arroyo (1988), and Keegan (1992).

8. Ramchand, as early as 1969, pointed out the lack of literary interest in the

anglophone Caribbean's indigenous populations, with the exception of Guyanese writers Harris and Mittelholzer (Ramchand 1969).

9. Kincaid's work generally makes reference to ancestral and cultural inheritance from the Carib peoples of Dominica, but overall Lucy's native inheritance is erased when she concludes, "I had realized the origin of my presence on the island—my ancestral history—was the result of a foul deed" (1990, 135). Her concern with African inheritance, slavery, and colonialism overrides her native inheritance and relegates it to a literary trace, which only appears in *Lucy* as her refusal to objectify her own living relatives.

10. The Caribs, of course, have *not* been exterminated, as those living in St. Vincent and the continental Americas will attest. But Glissant's point is relevant in that it highlights the ways in which formulations of ethnic pasts become passive ornaments of history.

11. See Glissant (1989, 261). Lowenthal reports, "In the French Antilles, highly placed men of colour and whites married to coloured women could buy birth certificates proving Carib ancestry so as to disavow African" (1972, 48).

12. See Manuel de Jesús Galván's nineteenth-century novel, *Enriquillo* (1954) and Sommer (1983) for more on the Indianization of Dominican heritage.

13. Compare this to Peter Martyr's fifteenth-century observation of enslaved Caribs in Spain: "There was no one who saw them who did not shiver with horror, so infernal and repugnant was the aspect nature and their own cruel character had given them" (quoted in P. Hulme 2000, 8).

14. For an insightful examination of this discussion, see Wilson-Tagoe (1998).

15. In contrast to the "chilling memory" suggested by Naipaul's initial response to Amerindian presence, anthropologist S. Wilson asserts, rather idealistically, "Africans and indigenous peoples were united in being tyrannized by Europeans and saw the benefits of collaboration, as the emergence of such groups such as 'Black Caribs' suggests" (1997, 212).

16. One should not assume that Haviser's study of Bonaire represents the entire region; rather it highlights some of the symbolic functions of indigenous representations. My thanks to Peter Hulme on this point. See also Gullick (1995), who focuses on St. Vincent and comes to a similar conclusion.

17. Author cited by Lowenthal (1972, 186).

18. See *Omeros* (1990) in particular. For the linguistic and cultural history of the iguana, see Highfield (1997, 164).

19. Since European vessels facilitated the transplantation of many of these crops, European ancestry remains a silent presence in this sedimentation of the landscape.

20. Clare's stratification rehearses earlier West Indian depictions of the white creole woman. See O'Callaghan (1993, 32–35).

21. For more on this event, see Honeychurch, "The leap at Sauteurs." The leap

also encodes the events of Prime Minister Maurice Bishop's 1983 arrest and assassination, in which frightened Bishop supporters leapt off the cliff at Fort George.

22. See, for instance, Merle Hodge's *Crick crack, monkey* (1970), Jacques Roumain's *Masters of the dew* (1978), and Simone Schwarz-Bart's *The bridge of beyond* (1982).

23. See DeLoughrey, Gosson, and Handley (2005).

24. Cocoa is endemic to the Caribbean but not in Grenada.

25. For two helpful sources on the relationship between transnational capitalism and cannibalism, see Bartolovich (1998) and J. Phillips (1998).

26. Personal discussions with Merle Collins.

27. I've benefited here from discussions with Zita Nunes. On the Brazilian modernists, see Bellei (1998) and Madureira (1998).

Epilogue

1. Explored in DeLoughrey 1998.

2. Discussion with the artist.

References

Allen, Chadwick. 2002. *Blood narrative: Indigenous identity in American Indian and Maori literary and activist texts.* Durham: Duke University Press.

Allott, Philip. 1993. *Mare nostrum:* A new international law of the sea. In *Freedom for the seas in the 21st century: Ocean governance and environmental harmony,* eds. Jon M. Van Dyke, Durwood Zaelke, and Grant Hewison, 49–71. Washington, DC: Island Press.

Alpers, Anthony. 1964. *Maori myths & tribal legends.* Auckland, NZ: Longman Paul Ltd.

Amalu, Sammy. 1976. Sail on, Hokuleʻa, and link our empire. *The Sunday Star-Bulletin and Advertiser,* August 1. A15.

Anand, R. P. 1993. Changing concepts of freedom of the seas: A historical perspective. In *Freedom for the seas in the 21st century: Ocean governance and environmental harmony,* eds. Jon M. Van Dyke, Durwood Zaelke, and Grant Hewison, 72–86. Washington, DC: Island Press.

Anderson, Benedict. 1991. *Imagined communities.* London: Verso.

Appadurai, Arjun. 1988. Putting hierarchy in its place. *Cultural Anthropology* 3:36–49.

———. 1996. *Modernity at large: Cultural dimensions of globalization.* Minneapolis: University of Minnesota Press.

Appiah, Anthony Kwame. 1992. *In my father's house: Africa in the philosophy of culture.* New York: Oxford University Press.

———. 1998. Cosmopolitan patriots. In *Cosmopolitics: Thinking and feeling beyond the nation,* eds. Pheng Cheah and Bruce Robbins, 91–116. Minneapolis: University of Minnesota Press.

Te Ariki-Tara-Are. 1919–1920. History and traditions of Rarotonga. *Journal of the Polynesian Society.* Trans. S. Percy Smith. Part VII (vol. 28: 183–197), Part IX (vol. 29: 11–16), and Part X (vol. 29: 45–65).

Arvidson, Ken. 1993. The emergence of a Polynesian literature. In *Readings in Pacific literature,* ed. Paul Sharrad, 20–38. Wollongong: New Literatures Research Centre.

Awatere, Donna. 1984. *Maori sovereignty.* Auckland, NZ: Broadsheet.

Te Awekotuku, Ngahuia. 1993. *Mana wahine Maori.* Auckland, NZ: New Women's Press.

Bachelard, Gaston. 1983. *Water and dreams: An essay on the imagination of matter.* Trans. Edith R. Farrell. Dallas: Pegasus Foundation.

Bader, Hans-Dieter, Peter McCurdy, and Jefferson Chapple, eds. 1996. *Proceedings of the Waka Moana Symposium 1996.* Auckland: New Zealand National Maritime Museum.

Badillo, Jalil Sued. 1995. The island Caribs: New approaches to the question of ethnicity in the early colonial Caribbean. In *Wolves from the sea,* ed. Neil L. Whitehead, 61–89. Leiden: KITLV Press.

Bakhtin, M. M. 1981. *The dialogic imagination: Four essays.* Trans. Caryl Emerson and Michael Holquist. Austin: University of Texas Press.

Ballantyne, John. 1994. On Defoe. In *Robinson Crusoe by Daniel Defoe,* Norton critical edition, ed. Michael Shinagel, 266–267. New York: W. W. Norton & Co.

Barcham, Manuhuia. 1998. The challenge of urban Maori: Reconciling conceptions of indigeneity and social change. *Asia Pacific Viewpoint* 39, no. 3 (December): 303–314.

———. 2000. (De)constructing the politics of indigeneity. In *Political theory and the rights of indigenous peoples,* eds. Duncan Ivison, Paul Patton, and Will Sanders, 137–151. Cambridge: Cambridge University Press.

Barlow, Cleve. 1991. *Tikanga Whakaaro: Key concepts in Maori culture.* Auckland, NZ: Oxford University Press.

Barthes, Roland. 1972. *Mythologies.* Trans. Annette Lavers. New York: Paladin.

Bartolovich, Crystal. 1998. Consumerism, of the cultural logic of late cannibalism. In *Cannibalism and the colonial world,* eds. Francis Barker, Peter Hulme, and Margaret Iversen, 204–237. Cambridge: Cambridge University Press.

Batchelder, Samuel. 1929. Some sea terms in land speech. *New England Quarterly* 2, no. 4 (October): 625–653.

Baucom, Ian. 2005. *Specters of the Atlantic: Finance capital, slavery, and the philosophy of history.* Durham: Duke University Press.

Baugh, Edward. 1977. The West Indian writer and his quarrel with history. *Tapia* 7, Feb. 25 and 27: 6–11.

Bauman, Zygmunt. 2000. *Liquid modernity.* Cambridge: Polity Press.

Beckles, Hilary. 1977. Capitalism, slavery, and Caribbean modernity. *Callaloo* 20, no. 4: 777–789.

Beckwith, Martha W. 1970. *Hawaiian mythology.* Honolulu: University of Hawai'i Press.

Beer, Gillian. 1983. *Darwin's plots: Evolutionary narrative in Darwin, George Eliot, and nineteenth-century fiction.* London: Routledge and Kegan Paul.

———. 1989. Discourses of the island. In *Literature and science as modes of expression,* ed. Frederick Amrine, 1–27. Boston: Kluwer Academic Press.

Belich, James. 1996. *Making peoples: A history of the New Zealanders from Polynesian settlement to the end of the 19th century.* Honolulu: University of Hawai'i Press.

Bellei, Sérgio Luiz Prado. 1998. Brazilian anthropophagy revisited. In *Cannibal-*

ism and the colonial world, eds. Francis Barker, Peter Hulme, and Margaret Iversen, 87–109. New York: Cambridge University Press.

Bender, Bert. 1988. *Sea-brothers: The tradition of American sea fiction.* Philadelphia: **299** University of Pennsylvania Press.

Benítez-Rojo, Antonio. 1992. *The repeating island.* Trans. James E. Mariniss. Durham: Duke University Press.

Benjamin, Walter. 1992. *Illuminations.* Trans. Harry Zohn. London: Fontana Press.

Best, Elsdon. 1924. *The Maori.* Wellington: H. H. Tombs.

———. 1954. *Spiritual and mental concepts of the Maori.* Wellington: R. E. Owen, Govt. Printer.

———. 1975. *Polynesian voyagers: The Maori as a deep-sea navigator, explorer, and colonizer.* Wellington: A. R. Shearer, Govt. Printer.

Bhabha, Homi K. 1994. *The location of culture.* London: Routledge.

Binder, Wolfgang. 1984. Subtleties of enslavement: An interview with the Jamaican writer John Hearne. *Komparatistische Hefte* 9–10:101–113.

Birbalsingh, Frank. 1988. *Passion and exile: Essays in Caribbean literature.* London: Hansib Publishing.

Bitterli, Urs. 1989. *Cultures in conflict: Encounters between European and non-European cultures, 1492–1800.* Trans. Ritchie Robertson. Cambridge: Polity Press.

Bolster, W. Jeffrey. 1997. *Black jacks: African American seamen in the age of sail.* Cambridge, MA: Harvard University Press.

Bongie, Chris. 1998. *Islands and exiles: The Creole identities of post/colonial literature.* Stanford: Stanford University Press.

Bonnemaison, Joël. 1994. *The tree and the canoe: History and ethnography of Tanna.* Trans. and adapted by Josée Pénot-Demetry. Honolulu: University of Hawai'i Press.

Borer, Douglas. 1993. Truth or dare? In *A new Oceania: Rediscovering our sea of islands*, eds. Eric Waddell, Vijay Naidu, and Epeli Hau'ofa, 84–87. School of Social and Economic Development, University of the South Pacific. Suva, FJ: Beake House.

Borgese, Elisabeth Mann. 1975. *The drama of the oceans.* New York: Harry N. Abrams, Inc.

———. 1993. The process of creating an international ocean regime to protect the ocean's resources. In *Freedom for the seas in the 21st century: Ocean governance and environmental harmony*, eds. Jon M. Van Dyke, Durwood Zaelke, and Grant Hewison, 23–37. Washington, DC: Island Press.

———. 1998. *The oceanic circle: Governing the seas as a global resource.* New York: United Nations University Press.

Boullosa, Carmen. 1997. *They're cows, we're pigs.* Trans. Leland H. Chambers. New York : Grove Press.

Brathwaite, Edward Kamau. 1970a. *Folk culture of the slaves in Jamaica.* London: New Beacon Books.

———. 1973. *The arrivants: A new world trilogy.* Oxford: Oxford University Press.

———. 1974. *Contradictory omens: Cultural diversity and integration in the Caribbean.* Mona, Jamaica: Savacou Publications.

———. 1975. Caribbean man in space and time. *Savacou* 11/12 (September): 1–11.

———.1976. Caribbean man in space and time. In *Carifesta forum: An anthology of twenty Caribbean voices,* ed. John Hearne, 199–208. Kingston, Jamaica: Carifesta 76.

———. 1982. Gods of the middle passage. *Caribbean Review* 9, no. 4: 18–19, 42–44.

———. 1983. Caribbean culture: Two paradigms. In *Missile and capsule,* ed. Jurgen Martini, 9–54. Bremen: Universität Bremen.

———. 1999. *ConVERSations with Nathaniel Mackey.* Staten Island, NY: We Press.

Braudel, Fernand. 1972–1973. *The Mediterranean and the Mediterranean world in the age of Philip II.* Trans. Siân Reynolds. New York: Harper and Row.

Brizan, George I. 1984. *Grenada: Island of conflict: From Amerindians to people's revolution, 1498–1979.* London: Zed Books.

Brown, J. Macmillan. 1907. *Maori and Polynesian, their origin, history, and culture.* London: Hutchinson.

Brown, Laura. 2001. *Fables of modernity: Literature and culture in the English eighteenth century.* Ithaca: Cornell University Press.

Brown, Seyom, Nina W. Cornell, Larry L. Fabian, and Edith Brown Weiss. 1977. *Regimes for the ocean, outer space, and weather.* Washington, DC: The Brookings Institution.

Browne, Janet. 1992. British biogeography before Darwin. *Revue d'histoire des sciences* 45, no. 4: 453–475.

Buck, Peter (Te Rangi Hiroa). 1938. *Vikings of the sunrise.* New York: A. Stokes.

Bunge, Frederica M., and Melinda W. Cooke, eds. 1984. *Oceania, a regional study.* Washington, DC: Government Printing Office.

Bunn, David. 1994. "Our wattled cot": Mercantile and domestic space in Thomas Pringle's African landscapes. In *Landscape and power,* ed. W. J. T. Mitchell, 127–174. Chicago: University of Chicago Press.

Burns, Patricia. 1980. *Te Rauparaha: A new perspective.* Wellington, NZ: A. H. and A.W. Reed, Ltd.

Byrnes, Giselle. 2004. *The Waitangi Tribunal and New Zealand history.* New York; Oxford University Press.

Campbell, I. C. 1992. *A history of the Pacific Islands.* Christchurch, NZ: Canterbury University Press.

Campbell, Shirley. 2002. *The art of Kula.* Oxford: Berg.

Carew, Jan. 1984. The Caribbean writer and exile. *Komparatistische Hefte* 9–10: 23–40.

Carkeek, W. 1966. *The Kapati Coast: Maori history and place names.* Wellington, NZ: A. H. and A. W. Reed.

Carpenter, Kevin. 1984. *Desert isles and pirate islands*. Frankfurt: P. Lang.

Carucci, Laurence M. 1995. Symbolic imagery of Enewetak sailing canoes. In *Seafaring in the contemporary Pacific Islands*, ed. Richard Feinberg, 16–33. DeKalb: Northern Illinois University Press.

Césaire, Aimé. 1969. *Return to my native land*. Trans. John Berger and Anna Bostock. London: Penguin.

Chappell, David A. 1997. *Double ghosts: Oceanian voyagers on EuroAmerican ships*. Armonk, NY: M. E. Sharpe.

Chatterjee, Partha. 1989. The nationalist resolution of the women's question. In *Recasting women: Essays in colonial history*, eds. Kumkum Sangari and Sudesh Vaid, 233–253. New Delhi: Kali for Women Press.

Cheesman, Paul R., and Millie Foster Cheesman. 1975. *Early America and the Polynesians*. Provo, UT: Promised Land Publications.

Clarkson, Thomas. 1788. *An essay on the impolicy of the African slave trade*. London: J. Phillips.

Cliff, Michelle. 1987. *No Telephone to Heaven*. New York: Random House.

———. 1991. Caliban's daughter: *The tempest* and the teapot. *Frontiers* 12, no. 2: 36–51.

Clifford, James. 1988. *The predicament of culture: Twentieth-century ethnography, literature and art*. Cambridge, MA: Harvard University Press.

———. 1992. Traveling cultures. In *Cultural studies*, eds. Lawrence Grossberg, Cary Nelson, and Paula Treichler, 96–116. New York: Routledge.

———. 1997. *Routes: Travel and translation in the late 20th century*. Cambridge, MA: Harvard University Press.

———. 2000. Valuing the Pacific: An interview with James Clifford. In *Remembrance of Pacific pasts*, ed. Robert Borofsky, 92–99. Honolulu: University of Hawai'i Press.

———. 2001. Indigenous articulations. *The Contemporary Pacific* 13, no. 2 (Fall): 468–490.

Clunie, Fergus. 1977. *Fiji weapons and warfare*. Suva, FJ: Fiji Museum.

Cohen, Phil. 1998. Who needs an island? *New Formations* 33: 11–37.

Collins, Merle. 1987. *Angel*. London: The Women's Press.

———. 1995. *The colour of forgetting*. London: Virago Women's Press.

Columbus, Christopher. 1992. The letter of Columbus (1493). In *Wild majesty: Encounters with Caribs from Columbus to the present day*, eds. Peter Hulme and Neil L. Whitehead, 9–16. Oxford: Clarendon Press.

Connery, Christopher. 1995. Pacific Rim discourse: The U. S. global imaginary in the late Cold War years. In *Asia / Pacific as space of cultural production*, eds. Rob Wilson and Arif Dirlik, 30–56. Durham: Duke University Press.

———. 1996. The oceanic feeling and the regional imaginary. In *Global / local: Cultural production and the transnational imaginary*, ed. Rob Wilson and Wimal Dissanayake, 284–311. Durham: Duke University Press.

Corbin, Alain. 1986. *The foul and the fragrant: Odor and the French social imagination*. Cambridge, MA: Harvard University Press.

————. 1994. *The lure of the sea: The discovery of the seaside in the Western world 1750–1840*. Trans. Jocelyn Phelps. Cambridge: Polity Press.

Cousteau, Jacques. 1976. The perils and potentials of a watery planet. In *Oceans: Our continuing frontier*, eds. H. William Menard and Jane L. Scheiber, 13–17. Del Mar, CA: Publishers Inc.

Crocombe, Marjorie. 1974. Ed. and Introduction. *Mana annual*. Suva, FJ: SPCAS. np.

————. 1977. Ed. and Introduction. *Third Mana annual of creative writing*. Suva, FJ: SPCAS.

Crocombe, Ron. 1964. *Land tenure in the Cook Islands*. New York: Oxford University Press.

————. 1976. *The Pacific Way: An emerging identity*. Suva, FJ: Lotu Pasifika Production.

————. 1992. *Pacific neighbours: New Zealand's relations with other Pacific Islands*. Canterbury, NZ: Centre for Pacific Studies.

Crosby, Alfred W. 1986. *Ecological imperialism: The biological expansion of Europe, 900–1900*. Cambridge: Cambridge University Press.

————. 1997. *The measure of reality: Quantification and Western society, 1250–1600*. New York: Cambridge University Press.

Curtin, Philip D. 1968. Epidemiology and the slave trade. *Political Science Quarterly* 83, no. 2 (June): 190–216.

Dabydeen, David. 1987. *Hogarth's blacks: Images of blacks in eighteenth-century art*. Athens: University of Georgia Press.

————. 1994. *Turner: New & selected poems*. London: Cape Poetry.

D'Aguiar, Fred. 1997. *Feeding the ghosts*. Hopewell, NJ: The Ecco Press.

Dance, Daryl Cumber. 1992. Conversation with George Lamming. In *New World Adams: Conversations with contemporary West Indian writers*, 133–144. London: Peepal Tree Press.

Danticat, Edwidge. 1996. *Krik?Krak!* London: Abacus.

Darwin, Charles. 1928. *The origin of species*. New York: Dutton.

Davies, Carole Boyce. 1992. *Black women, writing and identity: Migrations of the subject*. New York: Routledge.

Davis, Pa Tuterangi Ariki Tom. 1992a. New directions for Pacific history. In *Pacific history: Papers from the 8th Pacific History Association Conference*, ed. Donald Rubinstein, 69–72. Guam: University of Guam Press.

————. 1992b. *Vaka: Saga of a Polynesian canoe*. Auckland, NZ; Suva, FJ: Institute of Pacific Studies and Polynesian Press.

————, and Lydia Davis. 1960. *Makutu*. London: Michael Joseph.

Daws, Gavan. 1968. *Shoal of time: A history of the Hawaiian Islands*. New York: Macmillan.

————. 1980. *A dream of islands: Voyages of self-discovery in the South Seas*. New York: W. W. Norton & Co.

Day, A. Grove. 1987. *Mad about islands*. Honolulu: Mutual Publishing.

Dayan, Joan. 1996. Paul Gilroy's slaves, ships and routes: The middle passage as metaphor. *Research in African Literatures* 27, no. 2 (Summer): 7–14.

De Certeau, Michel. 1984. *The practice of everyday life.* Trans. Steven Rendall. Berkeley: University of California Press.

Deleuze, Gilles, and Felix Guattari. 1977. *Anti-Oedipus: Capitalism and schizophrenia.* Trans. Robert Hurley, Mark Seem, and Helen R. Lane. New York: Viking Press.

———. 1987. *A thousand plateaus: Capitalism and schizophrenia.* Trans. Brian Massumi. Minneapolis: University of Minnesota Press.

DeLoughrey, Elizabeth. 1998a. Gendering the voyage: Trespassing the (black) Atlantic and Caribbean. In *Thamyris: Caribbean women's writing/imagining Caribbean space* 5, no. 2: 205–231.

———. 1998b. Tidalectics: Charting Caribbean "peoples of the sea." *SPAN* 47 (October): 18–38.

———. 1999. The spiral temporalities of Patricia Grace's *Potiki. Ariel* 30, no. 1 (January): 59–83.

———. 2000. Some pitfalls of Caribbean regionalism: Colonial roots and migratory routes. *Journal of Caribbean Literatures* 3, no. 1 (Fall): 51–71.

———. 2002. White fathers, brown daughters: The Frisbie family romance and the American Pacific. In *Literature and racial ambiguity*, eds. Teresa Hubel and Neil Brooks, 157–186. Amsterdam: Rodopi Press.

———, Renée Gosson, and George Handley, eds. 2005. *Caribbean literature and the environment: Between nature and culture.* Charlottesville: University Press of Virginia.

Den Tandt, Christophe. 1998. *The urban sublime in American literary naturalism.* Urbana: University of Illinois Press.

Dening, Greg. 1980. *Islands and beaches: Discourse on a silent land, Marquesas, 1774–1880.* Honolulu: University of Hawai'i Press.

———. 2004. *Beach crossings: Voyaging across times, cultures, and self.* Philadelphia: University of Pennsylvania Press.

Desmangles, Leslie. 1992. *Faces of the Gods: Vodou and Roman Catholicism in Haiti.* Chapel Hill: University of North Carolina Press.

Diaz, Vicente M. 1996. Moving islands: Toward an indigenous tectonics of island historiography. Paper presented at Contested Grounds, Center for Pacific Island Studies Conference (December). Honolulu: University of Hawai'i.

———. 2000. Sacred vessels: Carolinian navigation as critique and aesthetic. Screening and lecture, American Indian Studies and American Studies Departments, University of Minnesota.

———. 2003. Sahyan Tasi Fache Mwaan: Intervoyage(r)s between the central Carolines and the Marianas: A multimedia presentation. July 7, 2003. National Endowment for the Humanities Summer Institute. Honolulu, Hawai'i.

———, and J. Kehaulani Kauanui. 2001. Native Pacific cultural studies on the edge. *The Contemporary Pacific* 13, no. 2 (Fall): 315–342.

303

Dibblin, Jane. 1988. *Day of two suns: US nuclear testing and the Pacific Islands.* London: Virago Press.

304   Diedrich, Maria, Henry Louis Gates, Jr., and Carl Pedersen, eds. 1999. *Black imagination and the middle passage.* New York: Oxford University Press.

Dirlik, Arif, ed. 1993. *What is in a rim? Critical perspectives on the Pacific region idea.* Boulder, CO: Westview Press.

Douglas, Mary. 1966. *Purity and danger: An analysis of the concepts of pollution and taboo.* New York: Praeger.

Duban, James. 1983. *Melville's major fiction.* DeKalb: Northern Illinois University Press.

Dudley, Michael K., and Keoni Kealoha Agard. 1993. *A call for Hawaiian sovereignty.* Reprint edition. Honolulu: Na Kane O Ka Malo Press.

Durie, Mason. 1998. *Te Mana, Te Kawanatanga: The politics of Maori self-determination.* Oxford: Oxford University Press.

d'Urville, Jules-Sébastien-César Dumont. 2003. On the islands of the great ocean. Trans. Isabel Ollivier, Antoine de Biran, and Geoffrey Clark. *The Journal of Pacific History* 38, no. 2: 163–174.

Earle, Sylvia. 1995. *Sea change: A message of the oceans.* New York: Fawcett.

Edmond, Rod, and Vanessa Smith, eds. 2003. *Islands in history and representation.* London: Routledge.

Edmondson, Belinda. 1999. *Making men: Gender, literary authority, and women's writing in Caribbean narrative.* Durham, NC: Duke University Press.

Edwards, Philip. 1994. *The story of the voyage: Sea narratives in eighteenth-century England.* New York: Cambridge University Press.

Eisler, William. 1995. *The furthest shore: Images of Terra Australis from the Middle Ages to Captain Cook.* Cambridge: Cambridge University Press.

Elkin, A. P. 1961. *Pacific Science Association, its history and role in international cooperation.* Honolulu: Bishop Museum Press.

Ellis, Juniper. 1994. A postmodernism of resistance: Albert Wendt's *Black Rainbow.* *Ariel* 25, no. 4: 101–114.

Eri, Vincent. 1970. *The crocodile.* Victoria: Penguin Books Australia.

Espinet, Ramabai. 2003. *The Swinging Bridge.* Toronto: Harper Canada.

Evans, Jeff. 1997. *Nga Waka o Nehera: The first voyaging canoes.* Auckland, NZ: A. H. and A. W. Reed.

Fabian, Johannes. 1983. *Time and the Other: How anthropology makes its object.* New York: Columbia University Press.

Fee, Margery. 1989. Why C. K. Stead didn't like Keri Hulme's *the bone people:* Who can write as other? *Australian and New Zealand Studies in Canada* 1 (Spring): 11–32.

Feinberg, Richard, ed. 1995. *Seafaring in the contemporary Pacific Islands.* DeKalb: Northern Illinois University Press.

Figiel, Sia. 1996. *The girl in the moon circle.* Suva, FJ: Mana Publications.

Figueroa, John J. 1972. John Hearne, West Indian writer. *Revista / Review Intera-mericana* 2, no.1 (Spring): np.

Finney, Ben. 1979. *Hokule'a: The way to Tahiti*. New York: Dodd, Mead.

———. 1994. *Voyage of rediscovery: A cultural odyssey through Polynesia*. Berkeley: University of California Press.

———. 2003. *Sailing in the wake of the ancestors: Reviving Polynesian voyaging*. Honolulu: Bishop Museum Press.

Firth, Stewart, and Karin Von Strokirch. 1997. A nuclear Pacific. In *The Cambridge history of the Pacific Islanders*, eds. Donald Denoon et al., 324–358. Cambridge: Cambridge University Press.

Flint, Valerie. 1992. *The imaginative landscape of Christopher Columbus*. Princeton: Princeton University Press.

Foucault, Michel. 1970. *The order of things: An archeology of the human societies*. New York: Vintage Books.

———. 1972. Preface. In *Anti-Oedipus: Capitalism and schizophrenia*, eds. Gilles Deleuze and Félix Guattari. Trans. Robert Hurley, Mark Seem, and Helen R. Lane, xi-xiv. Minneapolis: University of Minnesota Press.

———. 1977. Two lectures. In *Power/Knowledge*, 78–108. New York: Pantheon.

———. 1980. *History of sexuality*. Vol. 1. Trans. Robert Hurley. New York: Pantheon Books.

———. 1986. Of other spaces. *Diacritics* 16: 22–27.

Frame, Janet. 1961. *Faces in the water*. Christchurch, NZ: Pegasus Press.

Freeman, Carla. 2001. Is local:global as feminine:masculine?: Rethinking the gender of globalization. *Signs* 26, no. 4: 1007–1037.

Freud, Sigmund. 1961. *Civilization and its discontents*. Trans. James Strachey. New York: W. W. Norton.

Frisbie, Florence Johnny. 1948. *Miss Ulysses from Puka-Puka*. New York: Macmillan.

———. 1959. *The Frisbies of the South Seas*. Garden City, NY: Doubleday.

Froude, James Anthony. 1886. *Oceana: Or, England and her colonies*. London: Longmans, Green.

———. 1969. *The English in the West Indies: Or, the bow of Ulysses*. New York: Negro University Press.

Galván, Manuel de Jesús. 1954. *Enriquillo*. Trans. Robert Graves. Bloomington: Indiana University Press.

Gates, Henry Louis. 1988. *The signifying monkey: A theory of Afro-American literary criticism*. New York: Oxford University Press.

Gegeo, David Welchman. 2001a. Cultural rupture and indigeneity: The challenge of (re)visioning place in the Pacific. *The Contemporary Pacific* 13, no. 2 (Fall): 491–507.

———. 2001b. (Re)visioning knowledge transformation in the Pacific: A response to Subramani's "The Oceanic Imaginary." *The Contemporary Pacific* 13, no. 1 (Spring): 178–183.

305

Gerbi, Antonello. 1985. *Nature in the New World.* Trans. Jeremy Moyle. Pittsburgh: University of Pittsburgh Press.

Giddens, Anthony. 1990. *The consequences of modernity.* Stanford: Stanford University Press.

Gikandi, Simon. 2001. Globalization and the claims of postcoloniality. *The South Atlantic Quarterly* 100, no. 3 (Summer): 627–658.

Gilroy, Paul. 1993. *The black Atlantic: Modernity and modern consciousness.* Cambridge, MA: Harvard University Press.

———. 1997. Diaspora and the detours of identity. In *Identity and difference,* ed. Kathryn Woodward, 299–346. Milton Keynes: Open University Press.

———. 2000. *Against race: Imagining political culture beyond the color line.* Cambridge, MA: Harvard University Press.

Glissant, Édouard. 1989. *Caribbean discourse: Selected essays.* Trans. Michael Dash. Charlottesville: Caraf Books/University of Virginia.

———. 1997. *Poetics of Relation.* Trans. Betsy Wing. Ann Arbor: University of Michigan Press.

Golson, Jack, ed. 1972. *Polynesian navigation; a symposium on Andrew Sharp's theory of accidental voyages.* Wellington, NZ: A. H. and A. W. Reed.

Goodenough, Ward. 1957. Oceania and the problem of controls in the study of cultural and human evolution. *Journal of the Polynesian Society* 66:146–155.

Gordon, Mary. 1991. *Good boys and dead girls and other essays.* New York: Viking.

Gorman, M. L. 1979. *Island ecology.* London: Chapman Hall.

Grace, Patricia. 1978. *Mutuwhenua: The moon sleeps.* Auckland, NZ: Penguin Books, Ltd.

———. 1986. *Potiki.* London: The Women's Press, Ltd.

Griffen, Vanessa. 1993. Putting our minds to alternatives. In *A new Oceania: Rediscovering our sea of islands,* eds. Eric Waddell, Vijay Naidu, and Epeli Hau'ofa, 56–67. Suva, FJ: Beake House.

Griffith, Glyne A. 1996. *Deconstruction, imperialism and the West Indian novel.* Kingston, Jamaica: University of the West Indies Press.

Grosz, Elizabeth. 1994. *Volatile bodies: Toward a corporeal feminism.* St. Leonards, NSW: Allen and Unwin.

Grove, Richard H. 1995. *Green imperialism: Colonial expansion, tropical island Edens and the origins of environmentalism, 1600–1860.* Cambridge: Cambridge University Press.

Guest, Harriet. 1996. Looking at women: Forster's observations in the South Pacific. In *Observations made during a voyage round the world,* by Johann Reinhold Forster, eds. Nicholas Thomas, Harriet Guest, and Michael Dettelbach, xli–liv. Honolulu: University of Hawai'i Press.

Guillermo Wilson, Carlos. 1998. The Caribbean: Marvellous cradle and painful cornucopia. In *Caribbean creolization: Reflections on the dynamics of language, literature and identity,* eds. Kathleen Balutansky and Marie-Agnès Sourieau, 36–43. Gainesville: University Press of Florida.

Gullick, Charles J. M. R. C. 1995. Communicating Caribness. In *Wolves from the sea*, ed. Neil L. Whitehead, 154–162. Leiden: KITLV Press.

Haddon, Alfred C., and James Hornell. 1975. *Canoes of Oceania*. Honolulu: Bishop Museum Press. 307

Hadjor, Kofi Buenor. 1992. *Dictionary of Third World terms*. New York: I. B. Tauris.

Hall, Stuart, David Held, and Tony McGrew. 1992. *Modernity and its futures*. Cambridge: Polity Press in association with the Open University.

—— et al. 1996. *Modernity: An introduction to modern societies*. Cambridge: Blackwell Publishers.

Handler, Joshua. 1993. Denuclearizing and demilitarizing the seas. In *Freedom for the seas in the 21st century: Ocean governance and environmental harmony*, eds. Jon M. Van Dyke, Zaelke Durwood, and Grant Hewison, 420–434. Washington, DC: Island Press.

Handler, Richard, and Jocelyn Linnekin. 1984. Tradition: Genuine or spurious. *Journal of American Folklore* 97, no. 385: 273–290.

Hanlon, David, and Geoffrey M. White, eds. 2000. *Voyaging through the contemporary Pacific*. Lanham, MD: Rowman and Littlefield.

Hanson, Allan. 1989. The making of the Maori: Culture invention and its logic. *American Anthropologist* 91, no. 4: 890–902.

Hardt, Michael, and Antonio Negri. 2000. *Empire*. Cambridge, MA: Harvard University Press.

Harrington, James. 1992. *The commonwealth of Oceana and a system of politics*. ed. J. G. A. Pocock. Cambridge: Cambridge University Press.

Harris, Joseph E. 1982. *Global dimensions of the African diaspora*. Washington, DC: Howard University Press.

Harris, Wilson. 1967. *Tradition, the writer and society*. London: New Beacon Publications.

——. 1983. *The womb of space: The cross-cultural imagination*. Westport: Greenwood Press.

——. 1992. *The radical imagination: Lectures and talks*, eds. Alan Riach and Mark Williams. Liège: Université de Liège.

——. 1995a. The composition of reality: A talk with Wilson Harris. By Vera M. Kutzinski. *Callaloo* 18, no. 1: 15–32.

——. 1995b. *History, fable and myth in the Caribbean and Guianas*. Wellesley: Calaloux.

——. 1996. *Jonestown*. London: Faber and Faber.

——. 1998. Creoleness: The crossroads of a civilization? In *Caribbean creolization: Reflections on the dynamics of language, literature and identity*, eds. Kathleen M. Balutansky and Marie-Agnès Sourieau, 23–35. Gainesville: University Press of Florida.

——. 1999. *Selected essays of Wilson Harris: The unfinished genesis of an imagination*, ed. Andrew Bundy. New York: Routledge.

Harvey, David. 1989. *The condition of postmodernity*. London: Basil Blackwell Ltd.

——. 2000. Cosmopolitanism and the banality of geographical evils. *Public Culture* 12, no. 2: 529–564

308   Hassan, Nawal Muhammad. 1980. *Hayy Bin Yaqzan and Robinson Crusoe.* Baghdad, Iraq: Al-Rashid House.

Haugen, Keith. 1976. Hokuleʻa return voyage doubtful. *Honolulu Star-Bulletin,* June 10. A2.

Hauʻofa, Epeli. 1993a. A beginning. In *A new Oceania: Rediscovering our sea of islands,* eds. Eric Waddell, Vijay Naidu, and Epeli Hauʻofa, 126–139. Suva, FJ: Beake House.

——. 1993b. Our sea of islands. In *A new Oceania: Rediscovering our sea of islands,* eds. Eric Waddell, Vijay Naidu, and Epeli Hauʻofa, 2–16. Suva, FJ: Beake House.

——. 1997. The ocean in us. In *Dreadlocks in Oceania,* vol. 1, 124–148.

——. 2000. Pasts to remember. In *Remembrance of Pacific pasts,* ed. Robert Borofsky, 453–471. Honolulu: University of Hawaiʻi Press.

Havely, Joe. 2002. Former New Zealand chief claims Quayle threatened him. *CNN,* March 28. http://archives.cnn.com/2002/WORLD/asiapcf/auspac/03/28/nz.lange/

Havister, Jay B. 1995. Towards romanticized Amerindian identities among Caribbean peoples. In *Wolves from the sea,* ed. Neil L. Whitehead, 139–153. Leiden: KITLV Press.

Headrick, Daniel R. 1988. *The tentacles of progress: Technology transfer in the age of imperialism, 1850–1940.* New York: Oxford University Press.

Hearne, John. 1956. *Stranger at the gate.* London: Faber.

——. 1960. At the Stelling. In *West Indian stories,* ed. Andrew Salkey, 51–68. London: Faber.

——. 1962. *Land of the living.* London: Faber.

——. 1972. What the Barbadian means to me. In *Caribbean essays: An anthology,* ed. Andrew Salkey, 17–22. London: Evans Brothers Ltd.

——. 1976. Introduction. In *Carifesta forum: An anthology of twenty Caribbean voices,* ed. John Hearne, vii–xi. Kingston, Jamaica: Carifesta 76.

——. 1981. *The Sure Salvation.* London: Faber and Faber.

——. 1984. Interview by K. T. Sunitha. *Literary Half-Yearly* 25, no. 2 (July): 112–120.

——. 1992. Interview by Daryl Cumber Dance. In *New World Adams: Conversations with contemporary West Indian writers,* 99–107. Leeds: Peepal Tree Press.

Held, David, et al. 1999. *Global transformations: Politics, economics and culture.* Stanford: Stanford University Press.

Helmreich, Stefan. 1992. Kinship, nation and Paul Gilroy's concept of diaspora. *Diaspora* 2, no. 2: 243–249.

Henry, Brother Fred, and Nikolao I. Tuiteleleapaga. 1980. *Samoa: An early history.* Pago Pago: American Samoa Dept. of Education.

Henry, Paget. 2000. *Caliban's reason: Introducing Afro-Caribbean philosophy.* New York: Routledge.

Henry, Teuira. 1928. *Ancient Tahiti.* Honolulu: Bishop Museum Press. **309**

Herskovits, Melville J. 1938. *Dahomey: An ancient West African kingdom,* vols. 1, 2. New York: J. J. Augustin.

Heyerdahl. Thor. 1950. *Kon-Tiki: Across the Pacific by raft.* Trans. F. H. Lyon. Chicago: Rand McNally.

Highfield, Arnold R. 1997. Some observations on the Taino language. In *The indigenous people of the Caribbean,* ed. Samuel Wilson, 154–169. Gainesville: University Press of Florida.

Higman, Barry. 1999. *Writing West Indian histories.* London: Macmillan Education.

Hobsbawn, Eric, and Terence Ranger, eds. 1983. *The invention of tradition.* Cambridge: Cambridge University Press.

Hodge, Merle. 1970. *Crick, crack monkey.* London: Heinemann.

Holt, John Dominis. 1974. *On being Hawaiian.* Honolulu: Topgallant Publishing Co.

Honeychurch, Lennox. The leap at Sauteurs: The lost cosmology of indigenous Grenada. http://www.uwichill.edu.bb/bnccde/grenada/conference/papers/LH.html

Honolulu Advertiser. 1976. Valiant Hokule'a. June 4. A12.

Honolulu Star-Bulletin. 1976. Hokule'a fight wasn't racist, Kane declares. June 18. C-7.

Howard, Alan. 1995. Rotuman seafaring in historical perspective. In *Seafaring in the contemporary Pacific Islands,* ed. Richard Feinberg, 112–143. DeKalb: Northern Illinois University Press.

Howe, K. R. 2003. *The quest for origins.* Honolulu: University of Hawai'i Press.

Hudson, Brian J. 1992. The landscapes of Cayuna: Jamaica through the senses of John Hearne. *Caribbean Geography* 3, no. 3: 175–186.

Hulme, Keri. 1983. *the bone people.* London: Picador/Pan Books, Ltd.

———, and Gerry Turcotte. 1994. Reconsidering *the bone people. Australian and New Zealand studies in Canada* 12: http://www.arts.uwo.ca/~andrewf/anzsc/anzsc12/hulme12.htm

Hulme, Peter. 1981. Hurricanes in the Caribees: The constitution of the discourse of English colonialism. In *1642: Literature and power in the seventeenth century,* eds. Francis Barker et al., 55–83. Proceedings of the Essex Conference on the Sociology of Literature. Essex: University of Essex.

———. 1986. *Colonial encounters: Europe and the Native Caribbean.* London: Methuen.

———, and Neil L. Whitehead, eds. 1992. *Wild majesty: Encounters with Caribs from Columbus to the present day.* Oxford: Clarendon Press.

———. 2000. *Remnants of conquest: The island Caribs and their visitors, 1877–1998.* London: Oxford University Press.

Hunter, Allan. 1983. *Joseph Conrad and the ethics of Darwinism*. London: Croom Helm.

310

Hutcheon, Linda. 1988. *A poetics of postmodernism: History, theory, fiction*. New York: Routledge.

Hyam, Ronald. 1993. *Britain's imperial century, 1815–1914: A study of empire and expansion*. Lanham, MD: Barnes and Noble.

Ihimaera, Witi. 1986. *The matriarch*. Auckland, NZ: Heinemann.

———. 1987. *The whale rider*. Auckland, NZ: A. H. and A. W. Reed Publishing.

———. 1991. The long dark tea-time of the South: New Zealand's search for a Pacific identity. In *The South Pacific: Problems, issues and prospects*, ed. Ramesh Thakur, 133–144. New York: St. Martin's Press.

———, and D. S. Long, eds. 1982. *Into the world of light: An anthology of Maori writing*. Auckland, NZ: Heinemann.

———, et al. 1992. Kaupapa. *Te Ao Mārama: Contemporary Maori writing*. Vol. 1, ed. Witi Ihimaera. Auckland, NZ: A. H. and A. W. Reed.

Illich, Ivan. 1987. *H₂O and the waters of forgetfulness: Reflections on the historicity of "stuff."* Berkeley: Heyday Books.

Irwin, Geoffrey. 1992. *The prehistoric exploration and colonisation of the Pacific*. Cambridge: Cambridge University Press.

Ives, Kim. 1995. The unmaking of a President. In *Haiti: Dangerous crossroads*, ed. North American Congress on Latin America, 105–112. Boston, MA: South End Press.

Ivison, Duncan, Paul Patton, and Will Sanders, eds. 2000. *Political theory and the rights of indigenous peoples*. Cambridge: Cambridge University Press.

Jackson, Moana. 1993a. Indigenous law and the sea. In *Freedom for the seas in the 21st century: Ocean governance and environmental harmony*, eds. Jon M. Van Dyke, Durwood Zaelke, and Grant Hewison, 41–48. Washington, DC: Island Press.

———. 1993b. Nga Kupu Timatanga (There is a story that needs to be told). In *Freedom for the seas in the 21st century: Ocean governance and environmental harmony*, eds. Jon M. Van Dyke, Durwood Zaelke, and Grant Hewison, xiii–xvi. Washington, DC: Island Press.

James, C. L. R. 1963. *The black Jacobins: Toussaint L'Ouverture and the San Domingo revolution*. New York: Vintage Books.

———. 1978. *Mariners, renegades & castaways: The story of Herman Melville and the world we live in*. Hanover, NH: University Press of New England.

———. 1993. *The C. L. R. James Reader*, ed. Anna Grimshaw. Oxford: Blackwell.

Jameson, Fredric. 1991. *Postmodernism or, the cultural logic of late capitalism*. Durham: Duke University Press.

Jeans, Peter D. 2004. *Ship to shore: A dictionary of everyday words and phrases derived from the sea*. New York: McGraw Hill.

Johns, Atihana Moana. 1983. Nga Whakapapa Maori—Maori genealogy. *Under the Southern Cross: Papers to be presented at the Third Australasian Congress on Gene-*

alogy and Heraldry, 7–9 July, 1998, 137–143. Hamilton: New Zealand Society of Genealogists.

Johnson, Barbara. 1991. Introduction: Truth or consequences. In *Consequences of theory*, eds. Jonathan Arac and Barbara Johnson, vii–xii. Baltimore: Johns Hopkins University Press.

Johnson, Charles Richard. 1990. *Middle passage*. New York: Atheneum.

Jolly, Margaret. 1997. From Point Venus to Bali Ha'i: Eroticism and exoticism in representations of the Pacific. In *Sites of desire, economies of pleasure: Sexualities in Asia and the Pacific*, eds. L. Manderson and M. Jolly, 99–102. Chicago: University of Chicago Press.

———. 2001a. Imagining Oceania: Indigenous and foreign representations of a sea of islands. In *Framing the Pacific in the 21st century: Co-existence and friction*, eds. Daizaburo Yui and Yasua Endo, 29–48. Tokyo: Center for Pacific and American Studies, University of Tokyo.

———. 2001b. On the edge? Deserts, oceans, islands. *The Contemporary Pacific* 13, no. 2 (Fall): 417–466.

Jussawalla, Feroza, and Reed Way Desenbrock. 1992. *Interviews with writers of the post-colonial world*. Jackson: University Press of Mississippi.

Kame'eleihiwa, Lilikala. 1992. *Native land and foreign desires*. Honolulu: Bishop Museum Press.

Kanahele, George. 1982. *Hawaiian renaissance*. Honolulu, HI: Project Waiaha.

Kane, Herb Kawainui. 1997. *Ancient Hawai'i*. Captain Cook, HI: The Kawainui Press.

Kauanui, J. Kehaulani. 1998. Off-island Hawaiians "making" ourselves at "home": A (gendered) contradiction in terms? *Women's Studies International Forum* 21, no. 6: 681–693.

———. 2002. The politics of blood and sovereignty in *Rice v. Cayetano*. *PoLAR* 25, no. 1: 110–128.

———. 2004. Asian American studies and the "Pacific question." In *Asian American studies after critical mass*, ed. Kent Ono. Malden, MA: Blackwell Press.

———, and Caroline Sinavaiana, eds. 2006. Women writing Oceania. Special issue, *Pacific Studies* 29, no. 1 (March).

Kawaharada, Dennis, ed. 1995. *Voyaging chiefs of Hawai'i*. Honolulu: Kalamaku Press.

———. 1999. *Storied landscapes: Hawaiian literature and place*. Honolulu: Kalamaku Press.

Kawharu, I. Hugh. 1975. *Orakei: A Ngati Whatua community*. Wellington: New Zealand Council for Educational Research.

Keegan, William. 1992. *The people who discovered Columbus: The prehistory of the Bahamas*. Gainesville: University Press of Florida.

Keene, Dennis. 1985. *Kaho'olawe Island, Hawaiian ethnic significance overview*. Honolulu: Prepared for the U.S. Department of the Navy, Pacific Division, Naval Facilities Engineering Command, Pearl Harbor, Hawai'i.

Keesing, Roger. 1989. Creating the past: Custom and identity in the contemporary Pacific. *The Contemporary Pacific* 1 (Spring / Fall): 19–42.

———. 1990. Reply to Trask. *The Contemporary Pacific* 2: 168–171.

Kelsey, Jane. 1995. *The New Zealand experiment: A world model for structural adjustment?* Auckland, NZ: Auckland University Press.

———. 2000. *Reclaiming the future: New Zealand and the global economy.* Toronto: University of Toronto Press.

Kemp, Peter, ed. 1976. *The Oxford companion to ships and the sea.* Oxford: Oxford University Press.

Kesey, Ken. 1962. *One flew over the cuckoo's nest.* New York: Viking Press.

Kincaid, Jamaica. 1990. *Lucy.* London: Picador.

———. 1996. *Autobiography of my mother.* New York: Farrar, Straus and Giroux.

King, Ernest J. 1945. *Third Report to the Secretary of the Navy.* Issue 3 (December). http://www.ibiblio.org/hyperwar/USN/USNatWar/USN-King-3.html#VII

King, Michael. 1986. *Death of the "Rainbow Warrior".* Auckland, NZ: Penguin Books.

Kirch, Patrick V. 1986. Introduction: the archeology of island societies. In *Island societies: Archeological approaches to evolution and transformation,* ed. P. Kirch, 1–5. Cambridge: Cambridge University Press.

———. 2000. *On the road of the winds: An archaeological history of the Pacific Islands before European contact.* Berkeley: University of California Press.

———, and Roger C. Green. 2001. *Hawaiki, ancestral Polynesia: An essay in historical anthropology.* Cambridge: Cambridge University Press.

Klein, Bernhard, and Gesa Mackenthun, eds. 2004. *Sea changes: Historicizing the ocean.* New York: Routledge.

Krech, Shepard. 1999. *The ecological Indian: Myth and history.* New York: W. W. Norton and Company.

Kristeva, Julia. 1982. *Powers of horror: An essay on abjection.* Trans. Leon S. Roudiez. New York: Columbia University Press.

Kuehls, Thom. 1996. *Beyond sovereign territory: The space of ecopolitics.* Minneapolis: University of Minnesota Press.

Kuykendall, Ralph S. 1967. *The Hawaiian kingdom.* Vol. 3. Honolulu: University of Hawai'i.

Kyselka, Will. 1987. *An ocean in mind.* Honolulu: University of Hawai'i Press.

Lal, Brij V. 1990. Introduction to "As the dust settles: Impact and implications of the Fiji coups." *The Contemporary Pacific* 2: 1–10.

———, and Kate Fortune, eds. 2000. *The Pacific Islands: An encyclopedia.* Honolulu: University of Hawai'i Press.

Lamb, Jonathan. 1990. The New Zealand sublime. *Meanjin* 49:663–675.

Lamming, George. 1954. *The emigrants.* Ann Arbor: University of Michigan Press.

———. 1974. *Natives of my person.* London: Picador.

———. 1984. *The pleasure of exile*. London: Allison and Busby.

Land, Isaac. 2001. Customs of the sea: Flogging, empire, and the "true British seaman" 1770 to 1870. *Interventions* 3, no. 2: 169–185.

Laqueur, Thomas. 1990. *Making sex: Body and gender from the Greeks to Freud*. Cambridge, MA: Harvard University Press.

Leed, Eric J. 1991. *The mind of the traveler: From Gilgamesh to global tourism*. New York: Basic Books.

Lefebvre, Henri. 1991. *The production of space*. Trans. Donald Nicholson-Smith. Oxford: Blackwell.

Lepowsky, Maria. 1995. Voyaging and cultural identity in the Louisiade archipelago of Papua New Guinea. In *Seafaring in the contemporary Pacific Islands*, ed. Richard Feinberg, 34–54. DeKalb: Northern Illinois University Press.

Lewis, David. 1994. *We, the navigators: The art of landfinding in the Pacific*. Second edition. Honolulu: University of Hawai'i Press.

Linebaugh, Peter, and Marcus Rediker. 2000. *The many-headed hydra: Sailors, slaves, commoners, and the hidden history of the revolutionary Atlantic*. Boston: Beacon Press.

Linnekin, Jocelyn. 1983. Defining tradition. *American Ethnologist* 10:241–252.

———. 1991. Text bites and the r-word: the politics of representing scholarship. *The Contemporary Pacific* 2:172–177.

Lobo, Susan, and Kurt Peters, eds. 2001. *American Indians and the urban experience*. Walnut Creek, CA: Altimira Press.

Lowenthal, David. 1972. *West Indian societies*. London: Oxford University Press.

Loxley, Diana. 1990. *Problematic shores: The literature of islands*. New York: St. Martin's Press.

Lyotard, Jean François. 1996. Answering the question: What is postmodernism? In *Modernism/postmodernism*, ed. Peter Brooker, 139–150. London: Longman.

Maaka, Roger. 1994. The new tribe: conflicts and continuities in the social organisation of urban Maori. *The Contemporary Pacific* 6, no. 2: 311–336.

Madureira, Luís. 1998. Lapses in taste: "Cannibal-tropicalist" cinema and the Brazilian aesthetic of underdevelopment. In *Cannibalism and the colonial world*, eds. Francis Barker, Peter Hulme, and Margaret Iversen, 110–125. New York: Cambridge University Press.

Mahan, Alfred Thayer. 1957. *The influence of sea power upon history, 1660–1783*. New York: Hill and Wang.

Makereti (Maggie Papakura). 1986. *The old-time Maori*. Auckland, NZ: New Women's Press.

Malifa, Sano. 1975. *Looking down at waves*. Suva, FJ: Institute of Pacific Studies.

Malinowski, Bronislaw. 1922. *Argonauts of the western Pacific*. New York: E. P. Dutton and Co.

Malkki, Liisa. 1997. National geographic: The rooting of peoples and the territorialization of national identity among scholars and refugees. In *Culture, power, place: Explorations in critical anthropology*, eds. Akhil Gupta and James Ferguson, 52–74. Durham, NC: Duke University Press.

314　Malo, David. 1903. *Hawaiian antiquities (Moʻolelo Hawaii)*. Honolulu, Hawaiian Gazette Co.

Mannix, Daniel Pratt. 1962. *Black cargoes: A history of the Atlantic slave trade, 1518–1865*. New York: Viking Press.

Manuel, George. 1974. *The Fourth World: An Indian reality*. Don Mills, ON: Collier-Macmillan Canada.

Márquez, Roberto. 1983. The stoic and the Sisyphean: John Hearne and the angel of history. *Anales del Caribe* 3: 240–277.

Maury, Matthew Fountaine. 1857. *The physical geography of the sea*. New York: Harper and Brothers.

McClintock, Anne. 1995. *Imperial leather: Race, gender, and sexuality in the colonial conquest*. New York: Routledge.

McGregor, Davianna Pomaikaʻi. 2002. Kahoʻolawe: Rebirth of the sacred. *Amerasia Journal* 28, no. 3: 68–84.

McLeod, Aorewa. 1987. Private lives and public fictions. In *Public and Private Worlds: Women in Contemporary New Zealand*, ed. Shelagh Cox, 67–81. Wellington: Allen and Unwin/Port Nicholson Press.

Mead, Margaret. 1957. Introduction to Polynesia as a laboratory for the development of models in the study of cultural evolution. *The Journal of the Polynesian Society* 66:145.

Melville, Herman. 1990. *Benito Cereno*. New York: Dover Publications.

Menzies, Trixie Te Arama, ed. 1996. *He Wai: A song. First Nation's women's writing. Waiata Koa Collection*. Auckland, NZ: Waiata Koa.

Merchant, Carolyn. 1983. *The death of nature: Women, ecology, and the scientific revolution*. San Francisco: Harper and Row.

Meredith, Paul. 2000. Urban Maori as "new citizens": The quest for recognition and resources. Paper presented to the Revisioning Citizenship in New Zealand Conference, University at Waikato, Feb. 22–24.

Merleau-Ponty, M. 1962. *Phenomenology of perception*. Trans. Colin Smith. London: Routledge.

Metge, Joan. 1967. *The Maoris of New Zealand*. London: Routledge and Kegan Paul.

———. 1990. Te Rito O Te Harakeke: Conceptions of the Whaanau. *Journal of the Polynesian Society* 99, no. 1 (March): 55–92.

———. 1995. *New growth from old*. Wellington, NZ: Victoria University Press.

Meyer, Manulani Aluli. 2001. Our own liberation: Reflections on Hawaiian epistemology. *The Contemporary Pacific* 13, no. 1 (Spring): 124–148.

Mintz, Sidney. 1985. *Sweetness and power: The place of sugar in modern history*. New York: Viking Penguin.

Mita, Merata. 2000. Storytelling: A process of decolonisation. *Te Pua:* 7–18.

Mitchell, June. 1978. *Amokura*. Auckland, NZ: Longman Paul.

Mitchell, W. J. T., ed. 1994. *Landscape and Power*. Chicago: University of Chicago Press.

Mitira, Tiaki Hikawera. 1990. *Takitimu*. Auckland, NZ: South Pacific Books.　　**315**

Miyoshi, Masao. 1995. Sites of resistance in the global economy. *Boundary 2*, 22, no. 2: 61–81.

Mohanram, Radhika. 1999. *Black body: Women, colonialism and space*. Sydney: Allen and Unwin.

———. 2003. White waters: Race and oceans down under. *Journal of Colonialism and Colonial History* 4, no. 3 (Winter): 1–69.

Moore, L. B, and E. Edgar. 1961. *Flora of New Zealand*. Vol. II. Wellington, R. E. Owen.

Morales, Rodney, ed. 1984. *Hoʻi Hoʻi Hou: A tribute to George Helm & Kimo Mitchell*. Honolulu: Bamboo Ridge Press.

Montesquieu, Charles de. 1748. *The spirit of laws*. Trans. Thomas Nugent, 1752. http://www.constitution.org/cm/sol.htm

Moya Pons, Frank. 1979. Is there a Caribbean consciousness? *Americas* 31, no. 8: 33–36.

Murphy, Joseph M. 1994. *Working the spirit: Ceremonies of the African diaspora*. Boston: Beacon Press.

Naidu, Vijay. 1993. Whose sea of islands? In *A new Oceania: Rediscovering our sea of islands*, eds. Eric Waddell, Vijay Naidu, and Epeli Hauʻofa, 49–55. Suva, FJ: Beake House.

Naipaul, V. S. 1962. *The middle passage*. New York: Vintage Books.

———. 1969. *The loss of El Dorado: A history*. New York: Vintage Books.

Nairn, Tom. 1977. *The break-up of Britain: Crisis and neo-nationalism*. Atlantic Highlands, NJ: Humanities Press.

Narokobi, Bernard. 1982. *The Melanesian Way*. Suva, FJ: Institute of Pacific Studies.

National Academy of Sciences. 1989. *Our seabed frontier: Challenges and choices*. Commission on Engineering and Technical Systems. Washington, DC: National Academies Press.

Nelson, Anne. 1991. *Nga waka Maori: Maori canoes*. Auckland, NZ: Macmillan.

Nichols, Grace. 1983. *I is a long memoried woman*. London: Karnak House.

Nunn, Patrick D. 1994. *Oceanic islands*. Oxford: Blackwell.

———. 2003. Fished up or thrown down: The geography of Pacific Island origin myths. *Annals of the Association of American Geographers* 93, no. 2: 350–364.

Obeyesekere, Gananath. 1992. *The apotheosis of Captain Cook: European mythmaking in the Pacific*. Princeton: Princeton University Press.

———. 1998. Cannibal feasts in nineteenth-century Fiji: Seamen's yarns and the ethnographic imagination. In *Cannibalism and the colonial world*, eds. Francis Barker, Peter Hulme, and Margaret Iversen, 63–86. Cambridge: Cambridge University Press.

O'Brien, Susie. 1990. Raising silent voices: The role of the silent child in "An imaginary life" and "the bone people." *SPAN* 30 (April): 79–91.

O'Callaghan, Evelyn. 1993. *Woman version: Theoretical approaches to West Indian fiction by women.* New York: St. Martin's Press.

O'Gorman, Edmundo. 1961. *The invention of America: An inquiry into the historical nature of the New World and the meaning of its history.* Bloomington: Indiana University Press.

Orbell, Margaret. 1991. *Hawaiki: A new approach to Maori tradition.* Christchurch, NZ: Canterbury University Press.

O'Regan, Tipene. 1987. Te Kupenga o nga Tupuna: The net of ancestry. In *From the beginning: The archeology of the Maori,* ed. John Wilson, 21–26. Auckland, NZ: Penguin.

——. 1992. Old myths and new politics: Some contemporary uses of traditional history. *The New Zealand Journal of History* 26, no. 1 (April): 5–27.

——. 1993. Who owns the past? Change in Maori perceptions of the past. In *Te Ao Marama 2: Regaining Aotearoa,* ed. Witi Ihimaera, 337–340. Auckland, NZ: Reed.

O'Rourke, Dennis. 1986. *Half life: A parable for the nuclear age.* Videorecording. Los Angeles: Direct Cinema, Ltd.

Ortner, Sherry. 1974. Is female to male as nature is to culture? In *Woman, culture, and society,* eds. Michelle Zimbalist Rosaldo and Louise Lamphere, 67–87. Stanford: Stanford University Press.

Ouologuem, Yambo. 1968. *Bound to violence.* Trans. by Ralph Mannheim. London: Heinemann Educational Books.

Pardo, Arvid. 1975. *Common heritage: Selected papers on oceans and world order 1967–1974,* ed. Elisabeth Mann Borgese. Malta: Malta University Press.

Peck, John. 2001. *Maritime fiction: Sailors and the sea in British and American novels, 1719–1917.* New York: Palgrave.

Pelton, Robert D. 1980. *The trickster in West Africa: A study of mythic irony and sacred delight.* Berkeley: University of California Press.

Pendergrast, Mick. 1987. *Te Aho Tapu: The sacred thread.* Honolulu: University of Hawai'i Press.

Peter, Joakim. 2000. Chuukese travellers and the idea of horizon. *Asia Pacific viewpoint* 41, no. 3 (December): 253–267.

Philbrick, Thomas. 1961. *James Fenimore Cooper and the development of American sea fiction.* Cambridge, MA: Harvard University Press.

Phillips, Jerry. 1998. Cannibalism qua capitalism: The metaphorics of accumulation in Marx, Conrad, Shakespeare and Marlowe. In *Cannibalism and the colonial world,* eds. Francis Barker, Peter Hulme, and Margaret Iversen, 183–203. Cambridge: Cambridge University Press.

Pomponio, Alice. 1990. *Seagulls don't fly in the bush: Cultural identity and development in Melanesia.* Honolulu: University of Hawai'i Press.

Prager, Ellen. 2000. *The oceans.* New York: McGraw-Hill.

Pratt, Mary Louise. 1992. *Imperial eyes: Travel writing and transculturation.* New York: Routledge.

Puketapu-Hetet, Erenora. 1989. *Maori weaving.* Auckland, NZ: Pitman.

Pukui, Mary Kawena, and Samuel H. Elbert. 1971. *Hawaiian dictionary.* Honolulu: University of Hawai'i Press.

Raban, Jonathan. 1992. *The Oxford book of the sea.* New York: Oxford University Press.

Ramchand, Kenneth. 1969. Aborigines: Their role in West Indian literature. *Jamaica Journal* 3, no. 4 (December): 51–54.

Ratuva, Sitiveni. 1993. David vs Goliath. In *A new Oceania: Rediscovering our sea of islands*, eds. Eric Waddell, Vijay Naidu, and Epeli Hau'ofa, 94–97. Suva, FJ: Beake House.

Te Rauparaha, Tamihana. 1980. *The life and times of Te Rauparaha*, ed. Peter Butler. Waiura, New Zealand: Alister Taylor.

Rediker, Marcus. 1987. *Between the Devil and the deep blue sea: Merchant seamen, pirates, and the Anglo-American maritime world, 1700–1750.* Cambridge: Cambridge University Press.

Rhys, Jean. 1966. *Wide Sargasso Sea.* London: Deutsch.

Rika-Heke, Powhiri. 1996. Margin or centre? Let me tell you! In the land of my ancestors I am the centre. In *English postcoloniality: Literature from around the world*, eds. Radhika Mohanram and Gita Rajan, 147–163. Westport: Greenwood.

Roach, Eric Merton. 1992. *Flowering rock: Collected poems 1938–1974.* London: Peepal Tree Press.

Roberts, Walter Adolphe. 1940. *The Caribbean: Story of our sea of destiny.* New York: Negro University Press.

Robie, David. 1999. *Blood on their banner: Nationalist struggles in the South Pacific.* Leichhardt: Pluto Press Australia.

Roget, Henri Petitjean. 1997. Notes on ancient Caribbean art and mythology. In *The indigenous people of the Caribbean*, ed. Samuel Wilson, 101–108. Tallahassee: University Press of Florida.

Rohlehr, Gordon. 1970. The historian as poet. *The Literary Half-Yearly* 11: 171–178.

———. 1992. *The shape of that hurt and other essays.* Port-of-Spain: Longman Trinidad Ltd.

Roumain, Jacques. 1978. *Masters of the dew.* Trans. Langston Hughes and Mercer Cook. London: Heinemann.

Rouse, Irving. 1992. *The Taínos: Rise and decline of the people who greeted Columbus.* New Haven: Yale University Press.

Routledge, David. 1985. *Matanitu: The struggle for power in early Fiji.* Suva, FJ: University of the South Pacific.

Royal, Te Ahukaramu Charles. 1999. Nga Kawa e hangaia ai he Matauranga Maori: Whakapapa as a research methodology. In *Proceedings of Te Oru Rangahau Maori Research and Development Conference*, 78–87. Palmerston North, NZ: Massey University.

317

Ruskin, John. 1903. Of water, as painted by Turner. In *The works of John Ruskin*, eds. E. T. Cook and Alexander Wedderburn, vol. III, 537–572. London: George Allen.

Sahlins, Marshall. 1985. *Islands of history*. Chicago: University of Chicago Press.

———. 1995. *How "natives" think: About Captain Cook, for example*. Chicago: University of Chicago Press.

Salkey, Andrew. 1992. *Anancy, traveller*. London: Bogle L'Ouverture Press.

Salmond, Anne. 1985. Maori epistemologies. In *Reason and morality*, ed. Joanna Overing, 240–263. London: Tavistock.

———. 1990. Commentary. *New Zealand Journal of History* 24, no. 2: 164–167.

———. 1991. Tipuna—ancestors: Aspects of Maori cognative descent. In *Man and a half: Essays in Pacific anthropology and ethnobiology in honour of Ralph Bulmer*, ed. Andrew Pawley, 343–356. Auckland, NZ: The Polynesian Society.

Said, Edward. 1983. Travelling theory. In *The world, the text and the critic*, 241–242. Cambridge, MA: Harvard University Press.

Sarti, Antonella, and Christopher Bennet Evans. 1998. Interview with Albert Wendt. In *Spiritcarvers: Interviews with eighteen writers from New Zealand*, 207–212. Amsterdam: Rodopi.

Schama, Simon. 1995. *Landscape and memory*. New York: A. A. Knopf.

Scheffler, H. W. 1964. Descent concepts and groups: The Maori case. *Journal of the Polynesian Society* 73, no. 2 (June): 126–133.

Schwart-Bart, Simone. 1982. *The bridge of beyond*. London: Heinemann.

Schwimmer, Eric. 1990. The Maori Hapu: A generative model. *Journal of the Polynesian Society* 99, no. 3 (September): 297–317.

Scott, Dick. 1991. *Years of the Pooh-Bah: A Cook Islands history*. Auckland, NZ: Hodder and Stoughton.

Scott, George Ryley. 1939. *The story of baths and bathing*. London: T. W. Laurie Ltd.

Sharp, Andrew. 1956. *Ancient voyagers in the Pacific*. Wellington, NZ: The Polynesian Society.

Sharp, Andrew. 1991. *Justice and the Maori: Maori claims in New Zealand political argument in the 1980s*. Auckland, NZ: Oxford University Press.

Sharrad, Paul. 1990. Imagining the Pacific. *Meanjin* 49, no. 4 (Summer): 597–606.

———. 1993a. Countering encounter: Black voyaging after Columbus in Australia and the Caribbean. *Kunapipi* 15, no. 3: 58–72.

———, ed. 1993b. *Readings in Pacific literature*. Wollongong, NSW: New Literatures Research Centre.

———. 1994. Making beginnings: Johnny Frisbie and Pacific literature. *New Literary History* 25:121–136.

———. 1998. Pathways in the sea: A pelagic post-colonialism? In *Literary archipelagoes*, ed. Jean-Pierre Durix, 95–108. Presses Universitaires de Dijon.

———. 2001. Out of Africa: Literary globalization in the winds of change. *South Atlantic Quarterly* 100, no. 3 (June): 717–728.

———. 2003. *Albert Wendt and Pacific literature: Circling the void.* Manchester: Manchester University Press.

Sheller, Mimi. 2003. *Consuming the Caribbean: From Arawaks to zombies.* New York: Routledge.

319

Silva, Noenoe K. 2004. *Aloha betrayed: Native nationalism and resistance in Hawai'i.* Durham: Duke University Press.

Simmons, D. R. 1976. *The great New Zealand myth: A study of the discovery and origin traditions of Maori.* Wellington, NZ: Reed.

———. 1990. Whakapapa: The heritage of the Māori ancestors. In *1990 genealogical convention: New Zealand Society of Genealogists,* 83–89. Waiuku, NZ: W. J. Deed Printing.

Simms, Norman. 1986. *Silence and invisibility: A study of the literatures of the Pacific, Australia and New Zealand.* Washington, DC: Three Continents Press.

Sinavaiana-Gabbard, Caroline. 2001. *Alchemies of distance.* Kane'ohe, HI: Tinfish Press.

Sinclair, Keith. 2000. *A history of New Zealand,* Revised edition. Auckland: Penguin Books.

Smith, Bernard. 1985. *European vision and the South Pacific.* New Haven: Yale University Press.

Smith, Graham Hingangaroa. 2000. Protecting and respecting indigenous knowledge. In *Reclaiming indigenous voice and vision,* ed. Marie Battiste, 209–224. Vancouver: University of British Columbia Press.

Smith, John. 1627. *A sea grammar.* London: Printed by John Hauiland.

Smith, Linda Tuhiwai. 1999. *Decolonizing methodologies: Research and indigenous peoples.* New York: St. Martin's Press.

Smith, S. Percy. 1898–1899. Hawaiki: The whence of the Maori. *Journal of the Polynesian Society* 7:137–177; 8:1–48.

Sobel, Dava. 1995. *Longitude: The true story of a lone genius who solved the greatest scientific problem of his time.* New York: Walker.

Soja, Edward W. 1989. *Postmodern geographies: The reassertion of space in critical social theory.* New York: Verso.

Sommer, Doris. 1983. *One master for another: Populism as patriarchal rhetoric in Dominican novels.* Lanham: University Press of America.

Sorrenson, M. P. K. 1979. *Maori origins and migrations: The genesis of some Pakeha myths and legends.* Auckland, NZ: Auckland University Press.

———, ed. 1986. *Na To Hoa Aroha: From your dear friend: The correspondence between Sir Apirana Ngata and Sir Peter Buck 1925–50.* 3 vols. Auckland, NZ: Auckland University Press.

———. 1990. Giving better effect to the treaty. *New Zealand Journal of History* 24, no. 2: 135–149.

Spate, O. H. K. 1979. *The Spanish Lake.* Minneapolis: University of Minnesota Press.

Spillers, Hortense. 1987. Mama's baby, papa's maybe: An American grammar book. *Diacritics* 17 (Summer): 65–80.

Spivak, Gayatri Chakravorty. 1985. The Rani of Sirmur. In *Europe and its others*, vol. 1, eds. Francis Barker, Peter Hulme, Margeret Iverson, and Diana Loxley, 128 Sharp, Andrew–151. Proceedings of the Essex Conference on the Sociology of Literature, July 1984. Colchester: University of Essex Press.

———.1990. *The Post-Colonial critic: Interviews, strategies, dialogues,* ed. Sarah Harasym. New York: Routledge.

Springer, Haskell. 1995. *America and the sea: A literary history.* Athens: University of Georgia Press.

Stead, C. K. 1989. *Answering to the language: Essays on modern writers.* Auckland, NZ: Auckland University Press.

Stepan, Nancy. 1982. *The idea of race in science: Great Britain 1800–1960.* Hamden: Archon Books.

Stevens-Arroyo, Antonio. 1988. *Cave of the Jagua: The mythological world of the Taínos.* Albuquerque: University of New Mexico Press.

Stewart-Harawira, Margaret. 1993. Maori, who owns the definition? The politics of cultural identity. *Te Pua* 2, no. 1/2: 27–34.

Stoler, Ann Laura. 1995. *Race and the education of desire: Foucault's history of sexuality and the colonial order of things.* Durham: Duke University Press.

Subramani. 1988. Gone bush: A novella. In *The Fantasy Eaters,* 77–136. Washington, DC: Three Continents Press.

———. 1992. *South Pacific literature: From myth to fabulation.* Revised edition. Suva, FJ: Institute for Pacific Studies.

———. 2001. The oceanic imaginary. *The Contemporary Pacific* 13, no. 1: 149–162.

Sullivan, Robert. 1999. *Star waka.* Auckland: Auckland University Press.

———. 2005. *voice carried my family.* Auckland: Auckland University Press.

Sunday Advertiser, The. 1976. Hokule'a and our Pacific. August 1. B2.

Sundquist, Eric J. 1993. *To wake the nations: Race in the making of American literature.* Cambridge, MA: Harvard University Press.

Takino, Ngaronoa Mereana. 1999. Academics and the politics of representation. In *Proceedings of Te Oru Rangahau Maori Research and Development Conference,* 286–290. Palmerston North: Massey University

Taumoefolau. 1996. From *Sau 'Ariki to Hawaiki. *Journal of the Polynesian Society* 105: 385–410.

Taylor, Stephanie, and Margaret Wetherall. 1995. Doing national construction work. *Sites: A Journal for South Pacific Cultural Studies* 30: 69–84.

Teaero, Teweiariki. 2004. *Waa in storms.* Suva, FJ: Institute of Pacific Studies, University of the South Pacific.

Teaiwa, Katerina Martina. 2005. Our sea of phosphate: The diaspora of Ocean Island. In *Indigenous diasporas and dislocations,* eds. Graham Harvey and Charles D. Thompson, 169-191. London: Ashgate.

Teaiwa, Teresia Kieuea. 1995. *Searching for Nei Nim'anoa.* Suva, FJ: Mana Publications.

———. 1999. Reading Paul Gauguin's *Noa Noa* with Epeli Hau'ofa's *Kisses in the Nederends:* Militourism, feminism, and the "Polynesian" body. In *Inside out: Literature, cultural politics and identity in the New Pacific,* eds. Vilsoni Hereniko and Rob Wilson, 249–264. Lanham, MD: Rowman and Littlefield.

———. 2000. bikinis and other s/pacific n/oceans. In *Voyaging through the contemporary Pacific,* eds. D. Hanlon and G. White, 91–112. Lanham, MD: Rowman and Littlefield.

———. 2001. Militarism, tourism, and the Native: Articulations in Oceania. PhD diss., University of California at Santa Cruz.

———. 2005. Native Thoughts: A Pacific studies take on cultural studies and diaspora. In *Indigenous diasporas and dislocations,* eds. Graham Harvey and Charles D. Thompson, 15-35. London: Ashgate.

———. 2006. On Analogies: Rethinking the Pacific in a global context. *The Contemporary Pacific* 18, no. 1: 71-87.

Terrell, John Edward, Terry L. Hunt, and Chris Gosden. 1997. The dimensions of social life in the Pacific: Human diversity and the myth of the primitive isolate. *Current Anthropology* 38, no. 2 (April): 155–195.

Thomas, Hugh. 1997. *The slave trade: The story of the Atlantic slave trade, 1440–1870.* New York: Simon and Schuster.

Thomas, Nicholas. 1989. The Force of ethnology: Origins and significance of the Melanesia/Polynesia division. *Current Anthropology* 30: 27–34.

———. 1997. *In Oceania: Visions, artefacts, histories.* Durham, NC: Duke University Press.

Thompson, Robert Farris. 1983. *Flash of the spirit: African and Afro-American art and philosophy.* New York: Random House.

Thornton, John. 1992. *Africa and Africans in the making of the Atlantic world, 1400–1680.* New York: Cambridge University Press.

Tiffin, Chris, ed. 1978. *South Pacific images.* Brisbane: South Pacific Association for Commonwealth Literature and Language Studies.

Tilley, Christopher. 1994. *A phenomenology of landscape: Places, paths, and monuments.* London: Berg Publishers.

Tobin, Jeffrey. 1995. Cultural construction and Native nationalism: A report on the Hawaiian front. In *Asia/Pacific as space of cultural production,* eds. Rob Wilson and Arif Dirlik, 147–169. Durham, NC: Duke University Press.

Trask, Haunani-Kay. 1991. Natives and anthropologists. *Contemporary Pacific* 2: 159–167.

———. 1993. *From a Native daughter: Colonialism and sovereignty in Hawai'i.* Monroe, ME: Common Courage Press.

———. 1999. *Light in the crevice never seen.* Honolulu: Calyx Books.

Trautmann, Thomas R. 1997. *Aryans and British India.* Berkeley: University of California Press.

Travers, W. T. L. 1872. *Some chapters in the life and times of Te Rauparaha.* Wellington, NZ: James Hughes.

Tregear, Edward. 1889. Kiwa, the navigator. *Journal of the Polynesian Society* 7, no. 26: 111–112.

Trouillot, Michel-Rolph. 1995. *Silencing the past: Power and the production of history.* Boston: Beacon Press.

U. N. Division for Ocean Affairs and the Law of the Sea. *Oceans and Law of the Sea.* http://www.un.org/Depts/los/index.htm

U.S. Atomic Energy Commission. 1954. *Report on the Conference on long term studies of Marshall Islands.* July 12–13. http://worf.eh.doe.gov/ihp/chron/A30.PDF

U. S. Department of the Navy. 1983. *Kahoʻolawe cultural study. Part I: Historical documentation.* Honolulu: Environmental Impact Study Corp.

Valeri, Valerio. 1990. Constitutive history: Genealogy and narrative in the legitimization of Hawaiian kingship. In *Culture through time: Anthropological approaches*, ed. Emiko Ohnuki-Tierney, 154–192. Stanford: Stanford University Press.

Van Dyke, Jon M. 1993a. International governance and stewardship of the high seas. In *Freedom for the seas in the 21st century: Ocean governance and environmental harmony*, eds. Jon M. Van Dyke, Durwood Zaelke, and Grant Hewison, 13–22. Washington, DC: Island Press.

———. 1993b. Protected marine areas and low-lying atolls. In *Freedom for the seas in the 21st century: Ocean governance and environmental harmony*, eds. Jon M. Van Dyke, Durwood Zaelke, and Grant Hewison, 214–228. Washington, DC: Island Press.

———, Durwood Zaelke, and Grant Hewison, eds. 1993c. *Freedom for the seas in the 21st century: Ocean governance and environmental harmony.* Washington, DC: Island Press.

Vega, Ana Lydia. 1989. Cloud cover Caribbean. In *Her true-true name*, eds. Pamela Mordecai and Betty Wilson, 106–111. Portsmouth: Heinemann.

Veitayaki, Joeli. 1993. Balancing the book: How the other half lives. In *A new Oceania: Rediscovering our sea of islands*, eds. Eric Waddell, Vijay Naidu, and Epeli Hauʻofa, 116–121. Suva, FJ: Beake House.

Waddell, Eric, Vijay Naidu, and Epeli Hauʻofa, eds. 1993. *A new Oceania: Rediscovering our sea of islands.* Suva, FJ: Beake House.

Wagner, Roy. 1981. *The invention of culture.* Chicago: University of Chicago Press.

Walcott, Derek. 1986. *Collected poems: 1948–84.* New York: Farrar, Straus and Giroux.

———. 1990. *Omeros.* New York: Farrar, Straus and Giroux.

———. 1996. *Conversations with Derek Walcott*, ed. William Baer. Jackson: University Press of Mississippi.

———. 1998. *What the twilight says.* New York: Farrar, Straus and Giroux.

Walker, Ranginui. 1990. *Ka Whawhai Tonu Matou: Struggle without end.* Auckland, NZ: Penguin.

———. 1996. *Nga pepa a Ranginui: The Walker papers.* Auckland, NZ: Penguin.

Wallace, Alfred Russell. 1975. *Island life.* 1880. New York: AMS Press.

Wallerstein, Immanuel. 1974. *The modern world system: Capitalist agriculture and the origins of the European world economy in the sixteenth century.* New York: Academic Press.

Ward, Alan. 1990. History and historians before the Waitangi Tribunal. *New Zealand Journal of History* 24, no. 2: 150–167.

———. 1996. Historical method and Waitangi Tribunal claims. In *The certainty of doubt: Tributes to Peter Munz,* eds. Miles Fairburn and W. H. Oliver, 140–156. Wellington. NZ: Victoria University Press.

Washburn, Wilcomb. 1962. The meaning of "discovery" in the fifteenth and sixteenth centuries. *The American Historical Review* 68, no. 1: 1–21.

Waters, D. W. 1967. Science and the techniques of navigation in the Renaissance. In *Art, science, and history in the Renaissance,* ed. Charles S. Singleton, 189–237. Baltimore: Johns Hopkins Press.

Watters, David R. 1997. Maritime trade in the prehistoric eastern Caribbean. In *The indigenous people of the Caribbean,* ed. Samuel M. Wilson, 88–99. Gainesville: University Press of Florida.

Wendt, Albert. 1973. *Sons for the return home.* Auckland, NZ: Longman Paul.

———. 1977. *Pouliuli.* Auckland, NZ: Longman Paul.

———. 1979. *Leaves of the banyan tree.* Auckland, NZ: Longman Paul.

———, ed. 1980. *Lali: A Pacific anthology.* Auckland, NZ: Longman Paul.

———. 1987. Novelists and historians and the art of remembering. In *Class and culture in the South Pacific,* ed. Anthony Hooper, 78–92. Auckland, NZ: Auckland University Press.

———. 1991. *Ola.* Auckland, NZ: Penguin.

———. 1992. *Black Rainbow.* Honolulu: University of Hawai'i Press.

———. 1993. Towards a new Oceania. In *Readings in Pacific literature,* ed. Paul Sharrad, 9–19. Wollongong, NSW: New Literatures Research Centre.

———, ed. 1995a. *Nuanua.* Honolulu: University of Hawai'i Press.

———. 1995b. Pacific maps and fiction(s): A personal journey. In *Asian and Pacific inscriptions,* ed. Suvendrini Perera, 13–43. Bundoora, Australia: Meridian.

Wescott, Joan. 1962. The sculpture and myths of Eshu-Elegba, the Yoruba trickster. *Africa* 32, no. 4 (October): 336–353.

Wesley-Smith, Terence. 1995. Rethinking Pacific Islands Studies. *Pacific Studies* 18, no. 2: 115–138.

Whaitiri, Reina, and Witi Ihimaera. 1997. The forest of Tane: Maori literature today. *Manoa* 9, no. 1: 76–85.

Te Whanau o Waipareira Report. 1998. Wellington, NZ: Waitangi Tribunal; GP Publications.

Whitehead, Neil L. 1995a. Ethnic plurality and cultural continuity in the Native Caribbean. In *Wolves from the sea,* ed. Neil L. Whitehead, 91–111. Leiden: KITLV Press.

————, ed. 1995b. *Wolves from the sea.* Leiden: KITLV Press.

Williams, Denis. 1969. *Image and idea in the arts of Guyana.* Edgar Mittelholzer Memorial Lecture. Georgetown, Guyana: Ministry of Information.

Williams, Eric. 1944. *Capitalism & slavery.* New York: Capricorn Books.

Williams, Herbert. 1957. *A dictionary of the Maori language.* Sixth edition. Wellington, NZ: Owen.

Williams, Raymond. 1989. *The politics of modernism.* London: Verso.

Williams, Thomas, B. 1860. *Fiji and the Fijians.* New York: D. Appleton and Company.

Wilson, Rob. 2000. *Reimagining the American Pacific.* Durham: Duke University Press.

————, and Arif Dirlik. 1995a. Introduction: Asia/Pacific as space of cultural production. In *Asia/Pacific as space of cultural production,* eds. Rob Wilson and Arif Dirlik, 1–14. Durham: Duke University Press.

————, and Arif Dirlik, eds. 1995b. *Asia/Pacific as space of cultural production.* Durham: Duke University Press.

Wilson, Samuel. 1997. The legacy of the indigenous people of the Caribbean. In *The indigenous people of the Caribbean,* ed. Samuel Wilson, 206–213. Gainesville: University Press of Florida.

Wilson-Tagoe, Nana. 1998. *Historical thought and literary representation in West Indian literature.* Gainesville: University Press of Florida.

Wolff, Janet. 1992. On the road again: Metaphors of travel in cultural criticism. *Cultural Studies* 7, no. 2: 224–239.

Wood, Houston. 1999. *Displacing natives: The rhetorical production of Hawai'i.* Lanham, MD: Rowman and Littlefield.

Wordsworth, William. 1952–1959. *The poetical works of William Wordsworth,* eds. Ernest de Selincourt and Helen Darbishire, vol 5. Oxford: Clarendon Press.

Wynter, Sylvia. 1968 and 1969. Reflections on W. I. writing and criticism. Parts I and II. *Jamaica Journal* 2, no. 4 (December): 22–31; and 3, no. 1 (March): 27–42.

Yates-Smith, Aroha G. R. 1998. Hine, E Hine! Rediscovering the feminine in Maori spirituality. PhD diss., University of Waikato.

Zamora, Margarita. 1993. *Reading Columbus.* Berkeley: University of California Press.

Index ∼∼∼∼∼∼∼∼∼∼∼∼∼∼∼∼∼∼∼∼∼∼

333

About the Author

ELIZABETH M. DELOUGHREY has been educated in England, Aotearoa/New Zealand, and the United States and is an associate professor in the English Department at Cornell University. She has published articles in Caribbean, Pacific Island, and postcolonial studies and is coeditor of *Caribbean Literature and the Environment: Between Nature and Culture* (2005). She is currently working on a book about ecological imperialism in the island tropics.

Production Notes for DeLoughrey / Routes and Roots:
Navigating Caribbean and Pacific Island Literatures

Cover and interior designed by University of Hawai'i Press
production staff with Janson text and Post Antiqua display

Composition by Josie Herr

Printing and binding by The Maple-Vail Book
Manufacturing Group

Printed on 60 lb. Glatfelter Offset, B18, 420 ppi